The Nature of All Being

The Nature of All Being

A Study of Wittgenstein's Modal Atomism

RAYMOND BRADLEY

New York   Oxford
OXFORD UNIVERSITY PRESS
1992

Oxford University Press

Oxford   New York   Toronto
Delhi   Bombay   Calcutta   Madras   Karachi
Petaling Jaya   Singapore   Hong Kong   Tokyo
Nairobi   Dar es Salaam   Cape Town
Melbourne   Auckland

and associated companies in
Berlin   Ibadan

Published by Oxford University Press, Inc.
200 Madison Avenue, New York, NY 10016

Oxford is a registered trademark of Oxford University Press

Library of Congress Cataloging-in-Publication Data
Bradley, Raymond.
The nature of all being : a study of Wittgenstein's
modal atomism/Raymond Bradley.
p. cm.   Includes bibliographical references and index.
ISBN 0-19-507111-5
1. Wittgenstein, Ludwig, 1889–1951.
2. Modality (Logic)-History—20th century.   I. Title.
B3376.W564B69   1992   192—dc20   91-17448

1 3 5 7 9 8 6 4 2

Printed in the United States of America
on acid-free paper

My whole task consists in giving
the nature of the proposition.
In giving the nature of all being.
(And here being does not stand for existence. . . .)

Wittgenstein, NOTEBOOKS 1914–1916
(22 January 1915)

Contents

4. Propositions and the Mirror of the World

5. Worlds in Perspective

Note on References
and Stylistic Conventions

Throughout this book I frequently refer to passages in Wittgenstein's *Notebooks 1914–1916*, ed. G. H. von Wright and G. E. M. Anscombe, trans. G. E. M. Anscombe, (Oxford: Basil Blackwell, 1961). I follow Max Black's system for doing so as outlined in his *A Companion to Wittgenstein's Tractatus* (Ithaca, N. Y.: Cornell University Press, 1964). Thus "*NB* 10(3)" indicates the third paragraph on page 10, where each indented line is counted as starting a new paragraph and the continuation of a paragraph from a previous page is counted as the first paragraph on the page. (Note that the page numbering in the original Blackwell edition of 1961 is different from that in the Harper Torchbook paperback edition of 1969.)

References to passages in Wittgenstein's *Tractatus Logico-Philosophicus,* trans. D. F. Pears and B. F. McGuinness, with an introduction by Bertrand Russell (London: Routledge and Kegan Paul, 1961), are also made in accordance with Black's conventions. Thus "5.525(2)" indicates the second paragraph of section 5.525.

So far as other works are concerned, for those cases in which a work has been reprinted, in whole or in part, in a book that is more conveniently accessible than the original source, page references are to the reprinted source, not the original.

As to style, I have sometimes found it necessary or expedient to employ stylistic conventions different from those promoted by the widely emulated University of Chicago's *Manual of Style*.

First, I have followed the common, though not universal, philosophical convention of mentioning (as opposed to using) linguistic and logical expressions by putting them in quotation marks (rather than the University of Chicago's recommended italics). Quoted expressions can be nested, as in the following:

"'This sentence is false' is meaningless" is false.

Italicized expressions cannot be so nested.

Second, I have followed the British style of putting commas and periods *outside* quotation marks, except for cases in which these punctuation marks occur within the quoted expression. This enables me to write sentences such as the following:

The next formulae requiring our attention are: "(x) (Fx . Gx)", "(∃x) (Fx)", and "(∃x) (Fx . Gx)".

Were I, in such a case, to have followed the usual American convention of putting the commas and final period *inside* the quotation marks, I would have generated names of three ill-formed formulae.

Third, I have adopted the somewhat idiosyncratic (though not unprecedented) convention of putting the names of properties and relations (as distinct from the predicates and relational expressions which express them) in italics. This enables me to make my meaning more perspicuous. For instance, it enables me to draw out the consequences of Stalnaker's theory that other possible worlds are abstract properties (*ways things might have been*) that exist in the actual world (which, he claims, is the instantiation of the property *the way things are*), by writing sentences such as:

> Other possible worlds exist in the instantiation of *the way things are*.

Were I to have used quotation marks around the last four words of this sentence, I would have been taken to be talking about something with which neither I nor Stalnaker are here concerned: the English *expression* "the way things are". And were I to have written those words without italics, absurdity would then have resulted: the way things are, Stalnaker correctly insists, is to be identified not with the property *the way things are* but with the instantiation of that property. I suppose I could have followed a few other authors by writing those words as the hyphenated sequence "the-way-things-are". But my own stylistic preference is to join Stalnaker in putting them in italics.

Finally, by sometimes using contractions such as "I've" instead of such more formal idioms as "I have", I have tried to make the the task of reading this book a little less daunting than it might otherwise be. Wittgenstein and Russell occasionally wrote informal English; and some younger philosophical authors have recently followed suit. I've long thought that a good thing.

Introduction

How does one justify another book on Wittgenstein? That's one question I need to answer. Another is, Why are there so many already? Since answering the latter will help me with the former, I'll start with it.

The reason that so many competing accounts already exist lies in the character of Wittgenstein's published writings. With only a couple of exceptions—a brief book review (in *The Cambridge Review*, 1912–13), and "Some Remarks on Logical Form" (in the *Aristotelian Society Supplementary Volume* 9, 1929)—most of them invite comparison with utterances of the Oracle at Delphi. His sentences have been described as "epigrammatic", "aphoristic", "cryptic", "oracular", and even "Delphic" in style. Notoriously, his claims are seldom elaborated by example and even more rarely backed by anything recognizable as argument, evidence, or elucidation. So it is little wonder that different visitors to the shrine tend to hear what they want to hear and go away with different, often contrary, interpretations. Nor must it be supposed that this is just because we are now at some distance from the author and his times. Even those closest to him when he was first forming and expressing his ideas—philosophers as great as Frege, Russell, Moore, and Ramsey—were more often convinced that Wittgenstein had said something important than they were that they knew what it was. As with them, then, so with us, now. Hence the number and diversity of interpretations that keep appearing.

What my own book contributes to the ever-growing corpus of works on the early Wittgenstein is reflected in its title, *The Nature of all Being: A Study of Wittgenstein's Modal Atomism*. I believe its publication to be justified by the fact that, more than any other expositor known to me, I bring into sharp focus the crucial role which modal notions—the notions of necessity, contingency, possibility, impossibility, and so on—play in Wittgenstein's early thinking.

Frege and Russell (though not Moore or Ramsey) had blind spots about these notions. Frege simply ignored them; Russell, throughout his life, deliberately repudiated them. It was somewhat unfortunate, therefore, that Russell took it upon himself in a series of lectures delivered in 1918, four years before the English publication of Wittgenstein's *Tractatus Logico-Philosophicus*, to tell the philosophical community about the new atomism—"logical atomism" he called it—that he and Wittgenstein had been developing before the First World War. For Russell's atomism was epistemological and extensionalist in emphasis, and his insensitivity to the metaphysical and modal dimensions of Wittgenstein's atomism helped set the pattern for decades of incomprehension and misunderstanding. Frege, for his part, had almost nothing to say about what Wittgenstein was up to. Moore, in his paper "External and Internal Relations" (1919), said that Russell was wrong to ignore the essentially modal character of logic but later seemed to ignore the fact that, by way of contrast, Wittgenstein had emphasized it. And although Ramsey, in his perceptive "Review of *Tractatus*" (1923), briefly mentioned the role of modalities in Wittgenstein's scheme of things, his insight was soon overlooked.

Lack of understanding came from other directions as well. Even one of the founders of modal logic, the American C. I. Lewis, completely failed to understand Wittgenstein's position. In a letter (dated 2 January 1923) to the then-editor of the *Journal of Philosophy*, he wrote, "Have you looked at Wittgenstein's new book yet? I am much discouraged by Russell's foolishness in writing the Introduction to such nonsense. I fear it will be looked upon as what symbolic logic leads to; if so, it will be the death of the subject." In one of the supreme ironies of the history of ideas, Lewis failed to discern, in Wittgenstein's "nonsense", the semantical underpinnings that would one day win philosophical respectability for his own investigations of formal systems for modal notions. The first step towards this respectability was a result of Carnap's *Meaning and Necessity,* published in 1945, in which many key ideas, Carnap acknowledged, were to be found in Wittgenstein's *Tractatus* and, more remotely still, in Leibniz's work. The final step was taken in the early 1960s, as a result of the development of so-called "possible worlds semantics" for modal logics by the likes of Kripke and Hintikka, authors who would acknowledge their indebtedness to Carnap and Leibniz but seem to have overlooked the intermediate ancestry, in Wittgenstein, of many of the ideas to which they give prominence. Before that, it was "open season" for philosophers like Quine, and others of Russell's persuasion, to take shots at modal notions in general and modal logics in particular (especially "essentialistic" quantified modal logic). Far from being the "death of the subject", Wittgenstein's book contained elements that would eventually breathe new life into symbolic logic and the philosophy of logic alike.

Be the historical record what it may, the fact is that the contributions made to modal theorizing by the early Wittgenstein have long been ignored. The fact that modal elements are to be found in Wittgenstein's early thinking has only recently been recognized by a handful of his expositors: Stenius, Stegmuller, and von Wright, most notably. And even they, I believe, have not carried the investigation of modalities in Wittgenstein's atomism as far as it can and ought to go. This is why I try in this book to investigate in a comprehensive, detailed, and systematic way, what I earlier referred to as "modal dimensions of Wittgenstein's atomism".

Some of the more important of my findings can be summarized as follows.

One dimension has to do with the role of modal concepts in his *metaphysics*. Now it is widely agreed that his metaphysics is *atomistic*, that is, that he thinks that everything there is or could possibly be can be constructed out of simple objects that have simple properties and stand in simple relations to one another. But his atomism is also *modal* in the following respects:

(1) Every simple object has what Wittgenstein calls a "form" (2.0141) or "logical form" (2.0233) such that this form is "internal" to its possessor in the sense that

it is "unthinkable [logically impossible] that its object should not possess it" (4.123). The formal properties of his simple objects are (as we nowadays say) "de re necessary" or "essential" to their possessors.

(2) According to whether simple objects have the same or different logical forms (2.0233), they belong to the same or different "logical kinds" (*NB* 70(9-10)).

(3) The internal properties, and corresponding logical kinds, of simple objects make it logically possible for them to combine in certain determinate ways to produce those complexes that he calls "*possible* states of affairs" (2.0124), but also make it logically impossible for them to combine to produce "impossible" situations (5.525).

(4) Any possible combination of possible states of affairs, whether actual or otherwise, comprises an "imagined" (2.022) or "possible" (*NB* 83(2)) world.

(5) Of the states of affairs that are possible only some actually exist, and the totality of these comprises the "real" (actual) world (2.04).

A second modal dimension of Wittgenstein's atomism has to do with his account of *language*. It too is atomistic, in so far as he holds that all significant linguistic structures can be constructed from the simple elements which he calls "names". And it too is modal, insofar as he holds that names can be combined significantly only to the extent that their syntactical behaviors mirror the internal natures of the objects they stand for. Thus, corresponding roughly to (1) through (5) we have:

(1)* The simple component parts of propositions, names, not only stand for simple objects (3.203) but also "stand for the most various forms [of those objects]" (*NB* 23 (1) and 59(10)).

(2)* Each name thereby "signalizes" the logical kind to which the objects belong (*NB* 70(9)).

(3)* The forms, and corresponding logical kinds, of the names make it possible for them to be combined in certain determinate ways to produce significant propositions or "propositions with sense" (5.525), picturing possible states of affairs, but also make it logically impossible for them to combine in certain other ways insofar as the arrangement of names "must, of course, be possible as between the things that the names are representatives of" (*NB* 26(11)). In short, the forms of the component parts of a proposition determine what he calls "the rules of logical syntax" for the construction of significant propositions.

(4)* Any self-consistent totality of significant propositions, whether true or false, describes one of the possible worlds that "God could create" (3.031 and 5.123).

(5)* Of the significant propositions that picture possible states of affairs, only some are actually true, and by the totality of these the actual world is "completely described" (4.26).

A third dimension of Wittgenstein's atomism has to do with his account of the domain of *logic*. When he says, "Logic deals with every possibility and all possibilities are its facts" (2.0121(3)), he really does mean *all* possibilities (and, for that matter, all impossibilities, all necessities, and so on), not just the de dicto ones (ones in which, for instance, necessity is attributed to a whole "dictum" or proposition) but the de re ones as well (ones in which it is held, for instance, that objects possess certain of their properties necessarily, internally, or essentially). Indeed, the context makes it clear that the possibilities he is talking about here are *primarily* the de re ones having to do with the possibilities and impossibilities of combination of simple objects—those combinations which are made possible or impossible (as the case may be) by the de re necessary formal properties of the objects. To be sure, what he calls "the propositions of logic" include truth-functional tautologies, those propositions which are "true for all the truth-possibilities of the elementary propositions" (4.46), that is, which are true "for all possible situations" (4.462). But, as 2.0121 makes clear, they also include necessary truths about the de re possibilities of combination of objects. And in neither case are the truths of logic to be explained merely in terms of our arbitrary determination to use words in certain ways. Wittgenstein does not subscribe to a conventionalist or linguistic theory of necessary truth. Rather, for him, the truths of logic are a reflection of ontology. In the *Notebooks* he writes, "Thus a language which *can* express everything *mirrors* certain properties of the world by these properties which it must have; and logical so-called propositions shew *in a systematic way* those properties" (*NB* 107(6)). And in the *Tractatus* he tells us, "The fact that the propositions of logic are tautologies *shows* the formal—logical—properties of language and the world" (6.12). But, of course, the formal—logical—properties of the world, as we have already seen, are functions of the formal—logical—properties of objects (their de re necessary ones). Hence, the propositions of logic, like the rules of logical syntax for the construction of any significant language, are grounded in the de re modal properties of simple objects.

What I have said so far is very sketchy, and consists in little more than a stringing together of certain of Wittgenstein's still-unexplicated aphorisms. So I'll try to say a little more about some of the points touched on in a moment, before dealing with them in more detail in the chapters that follow. Still, what I've said already should give some foretaste of what is to come and should help make clear the character of the interpretation I advance.

Many fine books, and thousands of articles, have been written about Wittgenstein's *Tractatus Logico-Philosophicus*. Yet among them all little has been said about the themes just spelled out. What other books and articles have left largely unsaid about these matters I have treated at length. Conversely, much that they have said about other matters, they have said so well that I have seldom thought it in need of repetition. So there is little overlap, as I see it, between my treatment and theirs. I have little to say, for instance, about Wittgenstein's views on ethics or aesthetics, on religion or the mystical, or on the ways in which his early philosophical doctrines agree with or differ from his later ones in the *The Blue and Brown Books*, the *Philosophical Investigations*, and other works. I have even less to say about the more technical features of his discussions of logic and mathematics. And I have nothing whatever to say about the social and cultural roots of his views. Hence, any reader who wants to understand these matters would do well to supplement the reading of this book with the reading of others, for instance, those by Anscombe, Black, Favrholt, Fogelin, Goddard and Judge, Griffin, Hacker, the Hintikkas, Janik and Toulmin, Kenny, Malcolm, McGuinness, Pears, Pitcher, Stenius, and von Wright. Often I agree with what these other scholars have said. But where I do not, I have, for the most part, let the disagreement go unremarked, believing that the merits of my account can better be seen from its overall explanatory power than from any point-by-point refutation of rival accounts.

Nevertheless, there is an occasional touch of polemic to be found in this book. Sometimes, when a scholar of Wittgenstein seems to me to have gone systematically wrong on matters of crucial importance, I have tried to show this to be the case. For the most part, however, my most pointed criticisms are reserved for certain contemporary philosophers whose views about possible worlds, essentialism, and related matters seem to pit them against Wittgenstein. For instance, I take issue with Adams, Armstrong, Carnap, Hintikka, Lewis, Rescher, and Stalnaker over their views on such matters as the nature of possibility, the status of the actual world, the status and constitution of nonactual worlds, the status of nonactual objects, what it means to say that a property is essential to an object, the need to distinguish propositions from the worlds in which they are true or false, and so on. By comparing and contrasting Wittgenstein's views with theirs, I have tried to show that he deserves to be regarded as the twentieth century precursor of many of the metaphysical, linguistic, and logical doctrines that they think important. And by arguing, at least in some cases, that Wittgenstein's views are more defensible than theirs, I have sought to show that his doctrines are still worthy of attention. I have also drawn attention to a number of respects in which Wittgenstein's views are so clearly in accord with the views of contemporary theorists, such as Kripke, that we may, with charity, see them as sketchy anticipations of the latter.

All this, however, calls for a radical reinterpretation of Wittgenstein's early work. In order to make the case for my interpretation, I have drawn more heavily than do most commentators on his pre-*Tractatus* writings: the *Notebooks 1914–1916* and the appendices included therein, namely, *Notes on Logic*, *Moore Notes*, and *Letters*. It is here, I believe, that the precedents for Wittgenstein's Tractarian pronouncements are most often to be found. I do not discount the findings of those who claim to find interpretative keys in the writings of Russell, Frege, Hertz, Husserl, Mauthner, Schopenhauer, Kant, or others. There is much, I concede, to be derived from all these comparisons. Yet I cannot but wonder at the tendency of many to pass over Wittgenstein's own earlier writings in virtual silence. In order to redress the balance somewhat I therefore turn repeatedly to these earlier works, so as to determine, where possible, the thoughts and arguments that lie behind the Tractarian aphorisms. The results are salutary for each of the three main fields of my concern: Wittgenstein's theories of metaphysics, language, and logic.

Let's start with his ontology. In the *Tractatus*, Wittgenstein talks about various kinds of *possibilia* : possible states of affairs, possible situations, imaginary worlds, and worlds that a god might create. He says nothing about possible objects (things) as such. Nor does the text give any explicit warrant for supposing that he thinks of the aforementioned *possibilia* in anything like Leibnizian terms. Yet, in the *Notebooks* Wittgenstein explicitly invokes Leibniz's expression "possible worlds" (*NB* 83 (2)) and extends the list of *possibilia* to include "all possible things" (*NB* 99 (1)). The *Notebooks*, then, repeatedly makes it clear that Wittgenstein is not a so-called "modal actualist". He does not believe that only actual objects can exist in other possible worlds. Rather, he takes the view that other possible worlds may be populated by objects drawn from the set of all *possible* things, some being stocked with fewer of these objects than exist in the actual world, some with more. This runs counter to the standard interpretation of his Tractarian position. And it raises once more an issue about which contemporary possible-worlds theorists are in dispute. Attention to these and other hitherto neglected passages helps to throw light on much that is otherwise opaque in the *Tractatus*: on what he means when he says that all possible worlds have a form in common; on his reasons for rejecting certain of Russell's claims about logic and mathematics; and so on.

Attention to the *Notebooks* also throws light on Wittgenstein's metaphysical atomism. In the *Tractatus*, Wittgenstein holds that all imagined worlds, all possible situations, and all possible states of affairs are generated by combinations, or sets of combinations, of objects. Now, notoriously, in the *Tractatus*, objects are said to be simple. But in what sense of "simple"? Many think that he means "propertyless". Yet, when we turn to the *Notebooks*, where Wittgenstein wrestles with the question at great length, we find that there is no warrant for this conclusion. We find, rather, that the term "simple" has what (in the *Tractatus*) he calls "shifting uses"—shifting between what I call metaphysical, semantical, and epistemic uses—in none of which does "being simple" imply "being propertyless". Far from being property-less, it turns out that the simple atoms of his ontology have both accidental ("external") and essential ("internal") properties. Moreover, it turns out that it is precisely because of their essential properties that these simple atoms are able to combine with one another so as to "produce" all the other items in his ontology: material properties, possible states of affairs, possible situations, facts, and even possible worlds. Some of this can be garnered from the *Tractatus* itself. There, in 4.123, he defines an essential property as one that an object possesses in all the worlds in which the object exists. And he explicitly, in 2.01231, ascribes such properties to simple objects as well as nonsimple ones. But the import of these claims is seldom well understood. Attention to the *Notebooks* helps clear away certain of the interpretational barriers to seeing him as an atomist whose atomism is very different from that of Russell. Whereas Russell's is extensionalistic, having no room for modal notions—especially the *de re* (essentialistic) ones—Wittgenstein's atomism is robustly modal and essentialistic.

Nowhere does attention to the *Notebooks* yield more dividends than when it comes to understanding his theory of the way in which language is able to "picture" states of affairs in this and other possible worlds. The outlines of the theory are given in the *Tractatus*. But it is the *Notebooks* that best reveals how the theory is supposed to work. Names go proxy for—are akin to Kripkean rigid designators of—objects, simple and nonsimple alike. In propositions these names are connected experimentally so as to represent possible states of affairs, situations, or worlds. But—and here is the point that is made more emphatically by the *Notebooks* than by the *Tractatus*—"the connection of the propositional components must be possible for the represented things" (*NB* 26 (13)). In other words, the syntactical rules for the possible combination of names in propositions are determined by the internal natures, that is, by the essential properties, of the objects represented. Here, as in many other passages, the *Notebooks* make it clear that, for Wittgenstein, the rules of logical syntax for propositions are quite unlike the arbitrary conventions for assigning meaning (reference) to their constituent names. These rules are forced on us, as it were, by the "essence of the world" (3.3421).

Standard interpretations of the *Tractatus* see it as committed to a wholly extensionalist—more particularly, truth-functional—account of logic. Russell, in his lectures on logical atomism, tried to effect an extensionalist reduction of the de dicto, propositional, modal notions of necessity, impossibility, and possibility to the notions of being always true, never true, and sometimes true, respectively. Wittgenstein's atomist ploy is different, but, according to standard accounts, still an extentionalist one. He tries to reduce these modal notions, respectively, to the truth-functional notions of tautologousness, contradiction, and absence of contradiction. Or so it is said. But does Wittgenstein really turn his back on the Leibnizian construal of these modal notions that his metaphysics suggests? I think not. Joining forces with von Wright, I argue that Wittgenstein's theory of propositional significance commits him to the modal logic known as S5, and, going beyond von Wright, that he subscribes to an extension of that system, S5A (an extension of S5 which treats "actually" as a rigid designator of the actual world). In any case, does Wittgenstein really think that all necessary propositions are molecular truth-functions of their elementary constituents? There can be no doubt that he thought all truth-functional tautologies are, or express, necessary truths. But did he also think the converse? I think not and agree with Ramsey when he wrote, "not all necessary truths can be supposed, or are by Mr Wittgenstein supposed, to be tautologies. There are also the internal properties of which it is unthinkable that their objects do not possess them." Many passages in both the *Tractatus* and the *Notebooks* testify to Wittgenstein's recognition of non-truth-functional necessary truths. The *Notebooks* is replete with examples of statements, such as "a = a" (*NB* 24(6)) and "Language consists of sentences (propositions)" (*NB* 52(4)), which—though he does in fact call them "tautologies"—are certainly not truth-functional tautologies but rather are "necessary truths" insofar as they are, in a Leibnizian-cum-Wittgensteinian sense, "true in all possible worlds". More importantly, in both works Wittgenstein repeatedly talks about necessity, possibility, and impossibility in terms that resist a truth-functional construal. Being a tautology, a proposition with sense, or a contradiction is a way, he tells us, of expressing the necessity, possibility, or impossibility of a situation (5.525). But the possibility or impossibility of a situation, we have already noted, is a function of the de re necessary (essential, internal) natures of the simple objects which make up the substance of this and all other possible worlds. As already noted, he claims—in a passage whose context makes it clear that he is talking about de re possibilities not just de dicto ones—that "Logic deals with every possibility and all possibilities are its facts." (2.0121(3)). Just as it is not for us to make up the rules of logical syntax for language, so it is not for us to decide what to count as the necessities, the possibilities, or the impossibilities of logic. As he puts it, "Logic is not a body of doctrine, but a mirror-image of the world." (6.13).

I do not want to suggest that the *Notebooks* is the font of all interpretational wisdom. It is not. There are some doctrines in the *Notebooks* that do not survive in the *Tractatus*, and others in the *Tractatus* that are not even hinted at in the *Notebooks*. Chief among the former is the doctrine that both logical constants and whole propositions have what Wittgenstein calls *"Bedeutung"* (translated as "reference" by Anscombe), a view which he repudiates in the *Tractatus* where logical constants are denied any representational function whatever and propositions are said to have *"Sinn"* (that is, sense) but not reference. Yet so far as the doctrines I have been discussing are concerned, the two works are in remarkable accord, differing mainly with respect to the fact that the *Notebooks* typically treats them more expansively than does the *Tractatus*. My point, then, is that our understanding of the latter can be, and all too often is, handicapped by neglect of the former.

There is another way, too, in which our understanding of the *Tractatus* can be, and has been, jeopardized: by a faulty English translation. The prose of C. K. Ogden's original (1922) translation is noble and memorable. Who, having read it, can forget his rendering of Wittgenstein's final Tractarian dictum: "Whereof one cannot speak, thereof one must be silent"? Yet, in my view, Ogden's translation is often seriously misleading. I have chosen here to employ the 1961 translation by D. F. Pears and B. F. McGuinness. Like Ogden, they render *"Tatsachen"* as "facts". Where they diverge from Ogden—in a way that I find philosophically important— is in their rendering of the German expression *"Sachverhaltes"*. They translate it as "states of affairs" whereas Ogden translates it as "atomic facts". The significance of this is that if we were to accept Ogden's translation, then since the very grammar of the English expressions "atomic facts" and "facts" make it appear that the former are a proper subclass of the latter, we should have to conclude that *Sachverhaltes* are a proper subclass of *Tatsachen*. But if that were the case, then since a fact (Tatsache) is "whatever is the case" (2), all *Sachverhaltes* would also have to be the case. And that would entail that all *Sachverhaltes* are members of the totality that, according to Wittgenstein, "is the world." (2.04). It would entail that Wittgenstein's ontology encompasses only what is actual, to the exclusion of what is merely possible. Yet Wittgenstein repeatedly claims that some *Sachverhaltes*, like some *Sachlagen* (situations), only possibly exist. The translation by Pears and McGuinness enables us to see that, for Wittgenstein, the relationship between *Sachverhaltes* and *Tatsachen* goes the other way round. *Tatsachen* are a proper subclass of *Sachverhaltes*. *Tatsachen* are those *Sachverhaltes* that not only possibly but also actually exist. Although neither Pears nor McGuinness seems to have noted the fact, their translation opens the way for the kind of understanding of Wittgenstein's ontology that I am promoting here: one that sees it as encompassing all sorts of possible states of affairs, possible situations, and even possible worlds other than those which actually exist.

What, one wonders, might the history of Tractarian exegesis have been like had the Ogden translation not held the field for so many years? At the very least, the actualist interpretations of Wittgenstein's metaphysics, philosophy of language and logic which that translation promoted might sooner have come under scrutiny. But that is mere speculation. The emergence of a possibilist account, such as I offer here, was probably delayed by other factors as well. Among them the long-standing presumption that Wittgenstein's logical atomism should be construed along the same actualist and extensionalist lines as Russell's; the actualist tenor of Russell's Introduction to the 1922 edition of the *Tractatus* itself; Wittgenstein's own failure to state the grounds for his well-known dissatisfaction with the interpretation that

Russell's Introduction fostered; the logical positivist's conviction that the *Tractatus* was a tract devoted to the repudiation of all metaphysical doctrines, including its own; and the general disfavor with which influential philosophers like Quine tended, until fairly recently, to view all modal talk, especially that of the de re (essentialist) kind. Recent trends in metaphysics, philosophy of language, and philosophy of logic are not so dismissive of possibilia. They are rich in developments of the themes that—as I see it—Wittgenstein's early philosophy heralded.

Many years ago, at a time when I had almost completed a more orthodox book on the early Wittgenstein, I had occasion to attend a lecture of Saul Kripke's and to remark to him afterwards that several of his views reminded me of Wittgenstein's. That was the beginning of a lengthy period of reevaluation during which my earlier interpretation withered and the one proposed in this book blossomed. Over the intervening years, I have benefited both from the opposition of philosophers who thought my account too novel to be plausible and from the encouragement of others who themselves resonated to its suggestions. Among those deserving of special thanks are several of my colleagues, or former colleagues, who read and commented on drafts of the manuscript or discussed with me the issues it raises: David Copp, Steven Davis, Philip Hanson, Raymond Jennings, Ali Kazmi (Akhtar), Norman Swartz, and David Zimmerman. A number of other philosophers, in Canada, Australia, New Zealand, and Austria, heard me read versions of various chapters or parts of chapters and gave me valuable comments and criticism. They are too numerous to mention by name. I do, however, want to pay tribute to the influence of the late Brenda Judge and her co-author, Leonard Goddard. Their monograph, *The Metaphysics of Wittgenstein's Tractatus*, published by the *Australasian Journal of Philosophy*, forced me to develop positions, often opposed to theirs, which are central to my interpretation. I particularly valued the discussions I had with them during my visit Down Under in 1984–85. Much the same role was played by another Australian philosopher, David Armstrong, and his paper "The Nature of Possibility" [1986] during my visit in 1987 (see my reply "Possibility and Combinatorialism" [1988]).

The first of these visits was supported by a sabbatical leave fellowship from the Social Sciences and Humanities Council of Canada (SSHRC). Although it has taken me a long time to get the material in this book into final shape, much of it was written, in draft form, either during my tenure of that fellowship or, a year or so earlier, when SSHRC support allowed me to take a lengthy break from my teaching duties at Simon Fraser University. I am much indebted, and grateful, to both institutions.

The Nature of All Being

1

Logical Atomisms: Modal and Nonmodal

In logic, nothing is accidental: if a thing can occur in states of affairs, the possibility of the state of affairs must be written into the thing itself.

(WITTGENSTEIN, *Tractatus*)

1. Introduction

Ludwig Wittgenstein and Bertrand Russell are commonly referred to as "logical atomists". True, the term was not Wittgenstein's; it was Russell who coined it. But the doctrines that Russell used it to label, those set forth in his 1918 lectures entitled "The Philosophy of Logical Atomism", were ones that he claimed had originated with Wittgenstein. His lectures, he said, were "largely concerned with explaining certain ideas which I learnt from my friend and former pupil Ludwig Wittgenstein." ([1918] p. 117). So it is not surprising that, when Wittgenstein eventually published his own work some three years later in German under the title *Logisch-Philosphische Abhandlung* [1921][1] and subsequently in an English translation by C. K. Ogden, with an introduction by Russell, under the title *Tractatus Logico-Philosophicus* [1922],[2] his ideas came to be thought of as akin to those of his former mentor, Russell (despite the fact that Wittgenstein, for reasons which will become clear, disparaged Russell's Introduction as "superficial and full of misunderstanding").

Just how akin their positions were, and in what respects, has long been a matter for debate. Up until the 1950s, the prevailing view seems to have been that Russell had indeed been successful in explaining, in advance, the oracular pronouncements found in Wittgenstein's *Tractatus*. Most philosophers took it for granted that both Russell and Wittgenstein were talking about the same sorts of atoms, namely, sense-data, and that they conceived of compound propositions as being generated, in accordance with the logical theory of truth-functions, from the elementary sense-datum-statements that report our acquaintance with these atoms. There is in fact some evidence that, in the years immediately following the publication of the *Tractatus*, the years during which Wittgenstein largely withdrew from philosophy, Wittgenstein was occasionally tempted to think of his doctrines in this Russellian way.[3] For that was the period during which he was sought out, and engaged in discussions with, two empiricist-minded philosophers: Frank P. Ramsey of Cambridge (Russell's old stalking-grounds), and Freidrich Waismann of the Vienna Circle (where Mach's empiricism was sprouting into the new philosophy of logical empiricism, or logical positivism, as it is sometimes called). Both Ramsey and Waismann were averse to any metaphysical talk about how the world might be apart from our experience of it and doubtless encouraged Wittgenstein to flesh out the bare bones of his doctrines in much the same way as Russell had a few years earlier. At all events, the presumption that Wittgenstein and Russell were saying essentially the same thing persisted at least until midcentury when it was still powerful enough to dominate the account given by John O. Urmson in his *Philosophical Analysis* [1956].[4]

But does Wittgenstein's *Tractatus* itself, or his still earlier *Notebooks 1914–1916,* sustain such an interpretation?

In 1959, Elizabeth Anscombe broke with tradition by arguing forcefully that it does not. The fact is, she concluded in *An Introduction to Wittgenstein's Tractatus*, "that there is hardly any epistemology in the *Tractatus*: and that Wittgenstein evidently did not think that epistemology had any bearing on his subject-matter." (p. 27). Wittgenstein's atoms, his "simple objects", she points out, make up "the substance of the world" (2.021), not the substance of what we know about the world, and the question as to how we can come to know them is one which Wittgenstein, in his published writings, persistently relegates to psychology. I think Anscombe is absolutely right about this and, in Chapter III, will briefly take issue with the recent attempt by Merrill B. Hintikka and Jaakko Hintikka [1987] to revive the old epistemological construal.

But I also think that Anscombe does not bring out the full extent of the differences between Wittgenstein's and Russell's logical atomisms. Although she emphasizes the fact that Russell's atoms are primarily epistemological whereas Wittgenstein's are metaphysical, she makes nothing of the fact that Russell's atoms are viewed from a world-bound perspective whereas Wittgenstein's are not. Anscombe thinks of Wittgenstein's simple objects merely as actuality-constituting, like Russell's. She regards concatenations of such objects, Wittgenstein's *Sachverhalten*, as factual, hence actual entities, and explicitly ([1959], p. 30, fn. 1) rejects Erik Stenius's view that concatenations of these simple objects need not actually exist but may only possibly do so. Thereby she ignores the God's-eye, Leibnizian, perspective that Wittgenstein conveys in his metaphysics. Concomitantly, perhaps even consequently, she also thinks of Wittgenstein's logical doctrines as actuality-constrained, like Russell's. She makes nothing of the fact that Wittgenstein's simple objects have de re modal properties that determine the range of their combinations in possible states of affairs and thereby determine the de dicto modal properties that propositions have according as they are compatible with all, none, or just some of these possible states of affairs. She thereby largely ignores the modal dimensions of Wittgenstein's metaphysics and logic alike, the dimensions that, according to Wittgenstein, can be shown (but not said) by means of language and logic.

Unlike Anscombe, both Erik Stenius and Georg Henrik von Wright have given intimations of the modal character of Wittgenstein's atomism: Stenius, as early as

1960 in his *Wittgenstein's Tractatus*, by emphasizing the possibilist nature of Wittgenstein's metaphysics; von Wright, in his more recent *Wittgenstein* [1980], by emphasizing the modal nature of Wittgenstein's underlying logic. Yet neither von Wright nor Stenius has explored the implications of these modal aspects of Wittgenstein's atomism in quite the way I do. Moreover, the import of their views seems not yet to have been appreciated by the majority of those who think they understand Wittgenstein's early work. In this chapter, therefore, I try to lay the groundwork for an understanding of Wittgenstein's logical atomism, his "modal atomism" as I call it, by comparing and contrasting it with the atomism to which it was for so long assimilated: the world-bound, nonmodal, epistemological atomism of Russell.

First, let's look at some of the ways in which our two atomists agree.

2. Atomism versus Monism

One way of bringing out the similarities between Wittgenstein and Russell is to compare their views with some of the opposing views of philosophers who had preceded them: the British Idealists.

About the turn of the century, shortly before Wittgenstein and Russell reached their atomist conclusions, the prevailing philosophy in England was that of the Absolute Idealists: thinkers like Bernard Bosanquet, Edward Caird, T. H. Green, and above all, the redoubtable F. H. Bradley. These philosophers were monists. They held that Reality—"the Absolute", as they called it—was one thing, not many. And they were wholists. They held that Reality is a single, undivided, seamless, organic whole, none of whose supposed "constituents" can be understood apart from this whole. True, they acknowledged, we ordinarily *think* of reality as if it were composed of many independent things. But this, they held, is only because the finitude of human understanding compels us to make do with partial vision, as it were. Our finitude compels us, as they put it, to "abstract" from the concrete unity of reality in the judgments we make about it. In thought and judgment we impose distinctions and think we see differences that, from a God's-eye point of view, are ultimately insupportable. They are not there in Reality but belong rather to mere Appearance. Hence, insofar as all our judgments presuppose or assert the existence of many parts of reality independent of the one whole, all our judgments are infected with falsity. They may possess a "degree" of truth. But, because they fall short of encompassing the whole of Reality, they are at best only *partially* true.

By way of contrast, Wittgenstein and Russell claimed that reality contains many things, not just one. The judgments we make about these various parts of reality may, on occasion, be *wholly* true, depending on whether or not these parts have the properties or stand in the relations that we assert of them. Far from its being the case that we can only understand these parts to the extent that we understand the whole of which they are parts, the converse is the case. We can only understand any whole—be it reality, a part of reality, or a judgment about reality—to the extent that we analyze it into its simple constituents and understand how these simple constituents are combined with one another so as to produce that whole.

As Russell [1918] saw it, the British Idealists were led to metaphysical monism by a mistaken logical theory:

> There is . . . a logical theory according to which, if you really understood any one thing, you would understand everything. . . . It is rather the other way round. The acquaintance with the simpler is presupposed in the understanding of the more complex; but the logic that I should wish to combat maintains that in order thoroughly to know any one thing, you must know all its relations and qualities, all the propositions in fact in which that thing is mentioned; and you deduce of course from that that the world is an interdependent whole. It is on a basis of that sort that the logic of monism develops. (p. 204)

The logic of Wittgenstein and Russell was "pluralistic" in the sense that it allowed for the existence of many simple independent things: simple objects, simple names, simple propositions, and the like. Thus, Wittgenstein and Russell were united in their opposition to all forms of monism. Their philosophy was "atomistic" in the sense that simple things of these kinds, respectively, are the elements out of which the world, language, and logic are constructed and are the elements in terms of which these latter three are to be understood. Wittgenstein and Russell were united in their opposition to all those forms of wholism that sought to explain simples in terms of the wholes of which they are parts. Russell wrote:

> The logic which I shall advocate is atomistic, as opposed to the monistic logic of the people who more or less follow Hegel. When I say that my logic is atomistic, I mean that I share the commonsense belief that there are many separate things: I do not regard the apparent multiplicity of the world as consisting merely in phases and unreal divisions of a single indivisible Reality. It results from that, that a considerable part of what one would have to do to justify the sort of philosophy I wish to advocate would consist in justifying the process of analysis. (p. 178)

He continued a little later: "The reason I call my doctrine logical atomism is because the atoms I wish to arrive at as the sort of last residue in analysis are logical atoms and not physical ones." (p. 179). Wittgenstein would have agreed.

3. Fifteen "Common" Theses

Wittgenstein and Russell were united not only in what they opposed, but also—at least on the face of it—in many of the specifics of what they defended. Among the principal theses which both endorsed are the following:

Thesis 1: The world is constituted of the totality of facts (Wittgenstein) or "contains" facts (Russell).

Wittgenstein claims: "The world is the totality of facts, not of things." (1.1). And Russell claims: "the world contains facts which are what they are whatever we may think about them . . ." ([1918], p. 183).

Thesis 2: Facts are complex structures made up out of simple objects (Wittgenstein), or particulars (Russell), combined with, or related to, one another.

Thus Wittgenstein tells us: "What is the case—a fact—is the existence of states of affairs. A state of affairs (a state of things) is a combination of objects." (2 -2.01). And Russell claims: " the world can be analyzed into a number of separate things with relations and so forth . . ." ([1918], p. 189).

Thesis 3: Not only facts, but ordinary objects too, are complexes; they are constituted out of simple objects, or particulars, in structured combination with one another.

Thus, in *NB* 69(9), we find Wittgenstein speaking of the "structure" of a complex object such as Socrates. Likewise, Russell says: "all the ordinary objects of daily life are apparently complex entities . . ." ([1918], p. 190).

Thesis 4: Simple objects, or particulars, are unique entities insofar as each "stands entirely alone" and "subsists" in the same kind of way as do Aristotelian substances; it is their combinations that are shifting and subject to change.

Wittgenstein tells us: "Objects make up the substance of the world" (2.021); "Substance is what subsists independently of what is the case." (2.024); and that "Objects, the unalterable, and the subsistent are one and the same" (2.027). In similar fashion Russell says: "Particulars have this peculiarity, among the sort of objects that you have to take account of in an inventory of the world, that each of them stands alone and is completely self-subsistent. It has that sort of self-subsistence that used to belong to substance . . . . each particular that there is in the world does not depend upon any other particular." ([1918], pp. 202–202).

Thesis 5: It is a purely empirical matter, not one for a logician to decide, as to whether this or that thing in the world is a simple object or particular.

According to Norman Malcolm, Wittgenstein told him: "it was not his business, as a logician, to try to decide whether this thing or that was a simple thing or a complex thing, that being entirely an empirical matter." ([1958], p. 86). And Russell writes: "It remains to be investigated what particulars you can find in the world, if any." ([1918], p.199).

Thesis 6: Likewise, how many simple objects there are in the actual world is a purely accidental or contingent matter not capable of being settled *a priori* on the basis of logical considerations. Indeed, it is entirely possible that there should be universes consisting of n simple objects where n is any number from one to infinity.

Wittgenstein subscribes to this thesis when, in *NB* 11(7), he envisages the possibility that "the world consisted of one thing and of nothing else . . ."; and again, in the *Tractatus* 4.2211, when he talks about the possibility—at the other end of the spectrum, as it were—that the world should consist of infinitely many states of affairs each of which, in turn, "is composed of infinitely many objects." Likewise, Russell claims: "There is no reason why you should not have a universe consisting of one particular and nothing else." ([1918], p. 202); and "We are left to empirical observation to determine whether there are as many as n individuals in the world. Among 'possible' worlds, in the Leibnizian sense, there will be worlds having one, two, three, . . . individuals." ([1919], p. 203). Summing up, Russell says: "a world containing more than 30,000 things and a world containing fewer than 30,000 things are both possible, so that if it happens that there are exactly 30,000 things, that is what one might call an accident and is not a proposition of logic." ([1918], p. 240).

These passages from Russell may come as a surprise to some. How can he speak in this way if, as I claimed in my Introduction, neither his metaphysics nor his logic has room for modalities? I'll address this question in section 6 below. For the present, suffice it to say that when it comes to trying to explain how he sees the essential difference between logical and mathematical propositions, on the one hand, and all other propositions, he finds modal ways of speaking unavoidable.

Thesis 7: The words which stand for simple objects, or particulars, are names.

Wittgenstein: "A name means an object. The object is its meaning." (3.203). Russell: "The only kind of word capable of standing for a particular is a proper name . . ." ([1918], p. 200).

Thesis 8: What pass, in ordinary language, for names of complex objects are in need of analysis. Putative names of complex objects, when we analyze the propositions in which they occur, turn out to be replaceable by descriptions (propositional descriptions for Wittgenstein, definite descriptions for Russell).

Wittgenstein: "A complex can be given only by its description, which will be right or wrong." (3.24(2)). Russell: "The names that we commonly use, like 'Socrates', are really abbreviations for descriptions; not only that, but what they describe are not particulars but complicated systems of classes or series. A name, in the narrow logical sense of a word whose meaning is a particular, can only be applied to a particular with which the speaker is acquainted, because you cannot name anything you are not acquainted with. . . . We are not acquainted with Socrates, and therefore cannot name him. When we use the word 'Socrates', we are really using a description. Our thought may be rendered by some such phrase as, 'The Master of Plato', or 'The philosopher who drank the hemlock', or 'The person whom logicians assert to be mortal', but we certainly do not use the name as a name in the proper sense of the word." ([1918], p. 201).

Thesis 9: Names of simples, standing in appropriately structured relations to one another, feature as constituents of elementary propositions.

Wittgenstein: "What constitutes a propositional sign is that in it its elements (the words) stand in a determinate relation to one another." (3.14). Russell is committed to this by the conjunction of the following passages from [1918]: "Proper names = words for particulars." (p. 200). "Particulars = terms of relations in atomic facts." (p. 199). "[In] atomic propositions, the word expressing a monadic relation or quality is called a 'predicate', and the word expressing a relation of any higher order would generally be a verb . . ." (p. 199).

Thesis 10: In an elementary proposition, the constituents must stand in the same structured relation to each other as do the simple objects in any state of affairs, situation, or fact which they represent; they must share the same structure.

Wittgenstein: "The configuration of objects in a situation corresponds to the configuration of simple signs in the propositional sign." (3.21). Russell: "in a logically correct symbolism there will always be a certain fundamental identity of structure between a fact and the symbol for it . . ." ([1918], p. 197).

Thesis 11: A proposition is understood by anyone who understands its constituents.

Wittgenstein: "[A proposition] is understood by anyone who understands its constituents." (4.024(3)). Russell: "You can understand a proposition when you understand the words out of which it is composed even though you never heard the proposition before." ([1918], p. 193).

Thesis 11 is, in effect, an epistemic corollary of the Compositionality Principle, a principle that Wittgenstein attributes to Frege.

Thesis 12: The truth or falsity of a proposition, whether elementary or not, is a function of whether the world is as the proposition says it to be, i.e., of whether the states of affairs or facts in the world involve objects standing in the structured relations which the proposition asserts.

Wittgenstein: " a proposition is true if we use it to say that things stand in a certain way, and they do . . ." (4.062). Russell: "When I speak of a fact . . . I mean the sort of thing that makes a proposition true or false." ([1918], p. 182).

Thesis 12 is, in effect, a version of the Correspondence Theory of Truth, a theory which sees the world as providing so-called "truth-makers" for propositions.

Thesis 13: Molecular propositions can be formed out of elementary proposi-tions by means of such expressions as "and", "or", and "not", logical constants that are constituents of molecular propositions but are not names of anything.

Wittgenstein: "My fundamental thought is that the 'logical constants' are not representatives; that there can be no representative of the *logic* of facts." (4.0312). Russell: "In a logically perfect language the words in a proposition would corre-spond one by one with the components of the corresponding fact, with the exception of such words as 'or', 'not', 'if', 'then', which have a different function." ([1918], p. 197). "You must not look about the real world for an object which you can call 'or', and say, 'Now, look at this. This is "or".'" ([1918], pp. 209-210).

Thesis 14: All significant propositions, with the possible exception of belief-propositions, are truth-functions of elementary propositions.

Wittgenstein: "A proposition is a truth-function of elementary propositions." (5).[5] Russell: "I call these things truth-functions of propositions, when the truth or falsehood of the molecular proposition depends only on the truth or falsehood of the propositions which enter into it." ([1918], p.210).[6]

Thesis 14 is commonly referred to as the Extensionality Principle.

Thesis 15: The tautologies of logic are true for all truth-possibilities of ele-mentary propositions; and their denials, contradictions, are false for all such truth-possibilities.

Wittgenstein: "Among the possible groups of truth-conditions there are two extreme cases. In one of these cases the proposition is true for all the truth-possibilities of the elementary propositions. We say that the truth-conditions are *tautological*. In the second case the proposition is false for all the truth-possibilities: the truth-conditions are *contradictory*. In the first case we call the proposition a tautology; in the second, a contradiction." (4.46). Russell: "Everything that is a proposition of logic has got to be in some sense or other like a tautology." ([1918], p. 240).

Their joint endorsement of these theses provides sufficient reason to describe both of them as "logical atomists". Yet their agreement about these theses is largely verbal since, in every case, they understood them in very different ways.

4. Metaphysical versus Epistemological Atomism

Russell and Wittgenstein are like two painters who use the same captions for vastly different pictures. Both were atomists, to be sure. But Russell thought of his atoms primarily as epistemological ones (the smallest units of human knowledge), whereas Wittgenstein thought of his more as metaphysical simples (the ultimate entities out of which the world itself is composed). True, Russell saw himself as doing metaphysics as well as epistemology. But his ontological inventory was constructed from a human point of view. Wittgenstein, on the other hand, says almost nothing about epistemological matters and presents his ontology as if from a God's-eye standpoint. Both emphasized the role of logic in explicating how the atoms of their respective ontologies, and the complexes constructed out of them, are related to one another. And both thought of formal logic, of the kind developed in *Principia Mathematica*, as "extensionalist": both, as we have seen, subscribed to Thesis 14, the Extensionality Principle. But whereas Russell thought that the extensionalist language of formal logic exhausted all that could be said about logical matters, Wittgenstein did not. Russell had no room, in his official doctrine, for any modal notions. Wittgenstein, by way of contrast, thought that many logical matters could be explicated only in modal terms. The language of formal logic, for Wittgenstein, is extensionalist in so far as its propositions, tautologies, are constructed in accordance with extensionalist principles. The tautologies of logic *say* nothing: that is, they say nothing about the actual world which would distinguish it from any other possible world. But, according to 5.525(2), they do *show* something: they show that the corresponding situations are "certain" or *necessary*. The contradictions of logic, too, say nothing while showing that the corresponding situations are *impossible*. It is only nonlogical propositions, propositions with sense, that say something. And they, too, show something: they show that the corresponding situations are *possible*. All three kinds of proposition feature in the notation of Wittgenstein's logic; but the modal notions of necessity, possibility, impossibility, and the like, do not. Hence that logic can not *say* anything about modal matters. Nevertheless, these modal notions do feature in his characterization of what the notation of logic *shows*. The notation shows what is necessary, what is possible, and what is impossible in the world.

Many of these disagreements between Wittgenstein and Russell arise out of their different philosophical backgrounds.

Russell stands squarely in the British philosophical tradition and—like so many of his predecessors—is preoccupied with epistemological issues. More than that; like so many of them, Russell is dubious about our ability to talk about the world except to the extent that it is somehow "given to us" in experience. Hobbes, Locke, Berkeley, Hume, and Mill are obvious cases in point. Even the dean of British Idealists, F. H. Bradley, is no exception, since as he himself put it, "for me experience is the same as reality." ([1987], p. 128). It comes as no surprise, then, to find that Russell, for all his professed agnosticism as to which things in the world ought to be counted as the simple particulars which his analysis leads him to postulate, ultimately reaches the conclusion that they are objects of immediate acquaintance. They are "passing particulars of the kind that one is immediately conscious of in sense", or "sense-data when they happen to be given to you."

This gives a decidedly epistemological flavor to Russell's construal of many of the theses which he and Wittgenstein seemingly hold in common. It turns out that, for Russell, all the supposed metaphysical constituents of the universe—physical atoms, ordinary objects, persons, facts, propositions, and the world itself—are what he calls "logical fictions", logical constructions out of sense-data. Reexamine the fifteen common theses—especially (1), (2), (3), (4), (5), (6), (7), (11), and (14)—in this light, and it will be obvious why Russell's atomism is better described as epistemological than logical.

Wittgenstein's atomism, by way of contrast, has a decidedly Continental, and metaphysical, flavor. It owes more to Leibniz and his theory of monads, for instance, than to Hume and his account of sense impressions. Wittgenstein's simple objects, whatever they are, are definitely not sense-data or any other contents of human experience. They are metaphysical simples, the indivisible elements of being (*NB* 62(9)) out of which the world itself, as distinct from our knowledge of it, is constructed. Whereas Russell's particulars are ephemeral, passing, fleeting, momentary things, Wittgenstein's are substantial, permanent, unalterable and unchanging (2.027, 2.0271). Whereas Russell's particulars are objects of immediate acquaintance, Wittgenstein's metaphysical simples can be known only "by description, as it were" (*NB* 50(5)), as things that *must* exist (or subsist) as end-products of analysis. Russell holds that a complex object such as Socrates can be given to us not by acquaintance but only by description: can be known, that is, only as the putative bearer of such definite descriptions as "the Master of Plato", or "the philosopher who drank the hemlock." Wittgenstein holds, to the contrary, that it is complex objects with which we are acquainted, simple ones which we can know only by description. "Even though we have no acquaintance with simple objects," he writes, "we *do* know complex objects by acquaintance, [and] we know by acquaintance that they are complex." (*NB* 50(8)).

Wittgenstein and Russell disagree totally about which objects are known by acquaintance and which are known by description. Russell holds that complex objects such as Socrates are logical constructs out of the sense-data of which alone we have knowledge by acquaintance and hence concludes that these complex objects can be known, if at all, only by description. Wittgenstein, however, insists that it is the other way around, complex objects being the things with which we are acquainted, simple ones those which we can know only by description. This reversal of Russell's doctrine shows that something is wrong with the commonly held view that Wittgenstein subscribed to Russell's Theory of Descriptions and took it as his model for propositional analysis. Russell used his Theory of Descriptions to analyze away ordinary names in terms of descriptions and held that such names are "abbreviations" of these descriptions. But ordinary names, for Wittgenstein, are not abbreviations of descriptions in Russell's sense. He discards Russell's Theory of Descriptions and proposes a different sort of analysis, one which leads ultimately to propositions consisting of concatenations of simple names.

Russell and Wittgenstein disagree, too, about the relation which holds between names and objects. For Russell, naming is inseparable from acquaintance with object named. For Wittgenstein, that bond is broken. According to Russell, we give names to the objects of experience, to the particulars with which we are acquainted.

But since according to Wittgenstein, we never experience his metaphysically simple objects, we can never name them. Hence, although Russell has no difficulty citing two examples of simple names—"this" and "that" paradoxically being his paradigms—Wittgenstein does not, indeed cannot, cite any whatever. Yet Wittgenstein is as confident as Russell that in some sense there "are" metaphysically simple objects and simple names that stand for them. The difference is that whereas Russell thinks of simple names as standing in the naming-relation to their bearers only by virtue of human acts of bestowal performed on objects of acquaintance, Wittgenstein thinks of simple names as standing for metaphysical simples *despite* any inability of ours to be acquainted with them or to perform such acts of bestowal.

The relation of simple name to particular, for Russell, is instituted by means of an actual act of human volition. The relation of simple name to metaphysically simple object, for Wittgenstein, cannot require any such actual assignment. It apparently suffices, for Wittgenstein, that such an assignment might be made, as it were, by an omniscient being for purposes of constructing what Wittgenstein calls "a correct conceptual notation" (5.534). This is what Wittgenstein is getting at when, by way of commenting on the notion that there are possible worlds containing infinitely many objects (a corollary of Thesis 6), he writes: "What the axiom of infinity is intended to say would express itself in language through the existence of infinitely many names with different meanings." (5.535(3)). He is not suggesting here, or elsewhere, that *we* could ever be acquainted with infinitely many objects or bestow different names on each of them. The task of bestowing such names on infinitely many objects would be beyond us. And the fact is, in any case, that we cannot be acquainted with, or bestow names on, any simple objects whatever. Yet despite the fact that "*we* cannot analyze PROPOSITIONS so far as to mention the elements by name" (*NB* 62(9–10)), Wittgenstein still believes that such simple indivisible elements of being must exist. Again, he suggests, in 5.535(3), that we can *conceive* of there being worlds populated by infinitely many objects and *conceive* of each of the infinitely many objects in those worlds being given names. But although such worlds are possible, our own world certainly is not one of them.

5. The Two Standpoints:
God's-Eye and "From the Midst"

What I have just been saying amounts to this: Russell sees the world and language from a human-centered, epistemological point of view; Wittgenstein sees the world and language from a God's-eye, metaphysical point of view. True, Russell sometimes says things—for example, in connection with Thesis 6—which suggest that he is capable of adopting the loftier standpoint. His claim that "there are" possible worlds containing n individuals, where n is any number from one to infinity, is a case in point. But it turns out that for Russell these ways of speaking are strictly illegitimate, whereas for Wittgenstein they are not.

The contrast between their two standpoints is well captured by appropriating Wittgenstein's description of the aesthetic viewpoint: "The usual way of looking at things sees objects as it were from the midst of them, the view *sub specie aeternitatis* from outside." (*NB* 83(7)). Russell, we may say, sees things "from the midst of them". Wittgenstein, however, tries to see things "from outside". Consider what Wittgenstein means by "seeing things *sub specie aeternitatis* ." "The thing seen *sub specie aeternitatis*," he tells us, "is the thing seen together with the whole of logical space." (*NB* 83(11)). The concept of logical space, however, does not figure at all in Russell's account of things. Consequently, Russell neither can nor does see things in this light. But Wittgenstein does: "Each thing modifies the the whole logical world, the whole of logical space, so to speak." (*NB* 83(10)). We see the full significance of things only when we see them, not as "among" other things, but as modifying the whole world and the whole of logical space: "As a thing among things, each thing is equally insignificant; as a world each one is equally significant." (*NB* 83(12)). Russell, by seeing things "among" or "from the midst of" other things, is precluded from giving an account of their significance. Wittgenstein, by trying to see things "together with the whole of logical space", aims at showing their significance.

I think it no exaggeration to say that the aim of seeing simple objects, states of affairs, worlds, and propositions, and so on, "together with the whole of logical space", is Wittgenstein's major aim in both the *Notebooks* and the *Tractatus*. In the Preface to the *Tractatus*, Wittgenstein tells us that his aim is to portray the boundaries of what is thinkable; that is, of what is expressible; that is, of what is possible. But the boundaries of what is possible, it turns out, just are the boundaries of logical space. His aim, in other words, is to portray , by means of the propositions of the *Tractatus* , how all things stand sub specie aeternitatis.

Needless to say, propositions purporting to express how things might be seen from the God's-eye point of view are not of the kind that one finds in natural science. They are distinctively philosophical propositions. And since, for Wittgenstein, only the propositions of natural science are contingent and belong to what he regards as the category of "propositions with sense", it follows that propositions which attempt to show how things stand sub specie aeternitatis, along with other philosophical propositions, do not have sense but are, as he puts it, "nonsensical".

Here is a seeming paradox that has long troubled readers of the *Tractatus*, but, properly understood, is not a paradox at all. In calling philosophical propositions "nonsensical", Wittgenstein is in no way detracting from their significance. Rather, he is trying to give them the significance that is their due. In so describing them, he is putting them on a par with the truths of logic, that is, tautologies, which he also calls "nonsensical" (4.4611). Both the truths of logic and those of philosophy are nonsensical, we may take him to be saying, insofar as they fall outside the bounds of what is contingent, and therefore outside the bounds of what it makes sense to treat as a matter for debate. They are not the sorts of propositions that raise questions which experience might conceivably answer. It is not surprising, therefore, nor is it in the least paradoxical, that he should explicitly describe his own propositions in the *Tractatus* as "nonsensical" (6.54(1)). For he regards their truth as akin to the truth of tautologies in respect of the fact that they too are, as he puts it in his Preface (p. 5), "unassailable and definitive". The propositions of philosophy and the propositions of logic alike, when true, show us how things stand sub specie aeternitatis.

Anyone who understands his propositions, Wittgenstein says, must "transcend them". He must climb the ladder of understanding. And then, Wittgenstein assures us, "he will see the world aright." (6.54(2)).

6. Russell's Reductionist Account of De Dicto Modalities

The claims Russell makes about the de dicto uses of the modal expressions, "necessary", "possible", "impossible" and the like—those uses in which we predicate them of whole "dicta" or propositions—are at least as paradoxical as anything that Wittgenstein says about the nonsensicality of philosophical and logical propositions, if not more so. Russell's official position is that it really makes no sense to attribute these properties to whole propositions. Yet when he tries to explain the essential difference between true logical and mathematical propositions, on the one hand, and other true propositions, he finds himself calling the former "necessary" after all and withholding this description from the nonlogical, nonmathematical, ones. His official position is that there is only one world, the real world. Yet when he tries to explain the nature of the necessity that is distinctive of the former kinds of propositions, he finds himself explaining it, in Leibnizian terms, as truth-in-all-possible-worlds. Logical and mathematical propositions are true in all possible worlds. Other propositions, if true, are true only in "this higgeldy-piggeldy job-lot of a world in which chance has imprisoned us." ([1919], p. 192).

Let's look, first, at Russell's official doctrine regarding the de dicto modal notions. It stems from his actualism: from what he refers to as "the sort of realistic bias that I should put into all study of metaphysics" ([1918], p. 216). In accordance with this bias, he continues: "I should always wish to be engaged in the investigation of some actual fact or set of facts, and it seems to me that that is so in logic just as much as it is in zoology. In logic you are concerned with the form of facts, with getting hold of the different sorts of facts, different logical sorts of facts, that there are in the world."

That he should have this actualist bias is not surprising. He is committed to it by his view that all the things we can sensibly talk about either are, or are a logical construction out of, the simple objects, particulars, with which we are immediately acquainted. Obviously we are not, and cannot be, acquainted with anything that lies, as it were, "outside" the actual world.

The consequences of Russell's actualism, however, are likely to strike most of us as counterintuitive. Whereas most philosophers have supposed that the de dicto modalities, whatever their analysis might turn out to be, are properly to be predicated of *propositions*, Russell thinks this to be a mistake which has led to "much false philosophy". "In all traditional philosophy", he writes, "there comes a heading of 'modality', which discusses necessary, possible and impossible as properties of propositions, whereas in fact they are properties of propositional functions." ([1918], p. 231).

By a "propositional function", Russell means "any expression containing an undetermined constituent, or several undetermined constituents, and becoming a proposition as soon as the undetermined constituents are determined." (p. 230). As examples, he cites "x is a man", "x is mortal", and "x is a unicorn". His official account of the modalities holds, "One may call a propositional function *necessary*, when it is always true; *possible*, when it is sometimes true; *impossible* when it is never true." (p. 231). Expressed in his notation, the now-standard one of quantificational logic, his doctrine yields the following equivalences:

"Fx is necessary"   = "(x) Fx"
"Fx is possible"   = "(∃x) Fx"
"Fx is impossible" = "~(∃x) Fx".

Thus Russell says, for instance, that we can attribute necessity to the propositional function "If x is a man, x is mortal" since this is always true; that we can attribute possibility to the propositional function "x is a man" since this is sometimes true; and that we can attribute impossibility to "x is a unicorn" since this is never true. The actual world, then, and that which is always, sometimes, or never true in it, is the measure of all things, of those that are necessary, possible, and impossible, respectively. His official schemas for the analysis of modal notions reduces them to nonmodal ones.

The inadequacy of Russell's account should be immediately evident to anyone who is not in the grip of actualist preconceptions. It certainly was evident to Aristotle (*Posterior Analytics*, Bk. I, Ch. 4) who made a point of arguing that the assimilation of "necessary" to "true in every instance" is incorrect. There is surely a crucial difference, for instance, between the necessity that Russell attributes to "If x is a man, then x is mortal" (on the grounds of its being true in every instance in the actual world), and the necessity that most of us would attribute to "If x is square, then x is rectalinear" (on the grounds of its being true in every instance in both this and every other conceivable world). By virtue of the alleged necessity belonging to "If x is a man, then x is mortal", Russell wants to say that "x is a man" *implies* "x is mortal". But the implication involved is only Russell's own eviscerated *material* implication. As such, it is totally different from the *logical* implication that holds, for instance, between "x is a square" and "x is rectalinear". Judged by Russell's criteria, we would have to say that "x is chordate" implies "x is renate", on the grounds that the corresponding conditional is "always true" in the actual world. Yet the truth of this conditional, most of us would want to say, is merely "accidental", and not at all a matter of logic.

Even Russell, at times, would agree that there is a distinction between what holds accidentally and what holds as a matter of logic. Yet his official doctrine precludes his distinguishing between material implication (the relation that holds between the antecedent and the consequent of a conditional when it is always true as a matter of accidental fact) and logical implication (the relation that holds between antecedent and consequent when the conditional is always true as a matter of logical necessity). For that matter, it precludes his making other logical distinctions as well; for instance, that between the case in which two propositions merely differ in truth-value and the case in which two propositions are genuinely incompatible. His official doctrine leads him to make the preposterous claim, "When I say 'p is incompatible with q' I simply mean to say that they are not both true. I do not mean any more." ([1918], p. 210). Little wonder that Moore accused him of committing a "logical howler". Moore, and others such as the founders of modern modal logic, Hugh MacColl and C. I. Lewis, saw the need to ground our understanding of the logical notions of implication, incompatibility, compatibility, and the like, in a richer ontology than that provided by Russell's actualism, a Leibnizian ontology of possible worlds.[7] And so, I shall argue, did Wittgenstein.

The counterintuitiveness of Russell's official doctrine emerges just as clearly when we turn to its consequences for our understanding of possibility and impossibility. Obviously enough, being impossible is a sufficient condition of never being true. But is it also a necessary condition? Russell would say that if "x is a man and x runs the mile in under three minutes" is never true, then it is impossible. Yet surely this is a mistake, at least for that sense of "impossible" that is at issue, namely logical impossibility. Although it might be that someone's running a mile in fewer than three minutes is physically impossible, we certainly would not want to say that it is logically impossible. And neither, when he is off-guard, so to speak, would Russell.

The faultiness of Russell's official account of the de dicto modalities emerges once more when we consider what he says in support of thesis 6, the claim that it is entirely possible for there to be universes in which there are n individuals, where n is any number from one to infinity. He writes:

> The proposition that there are exactly 30,000 things in the world . . . is not a proposition of logic but an empirical proposition (true or false), because a world containing more than 30,000 things and a world containing fewer than 30,000 things are both possible, so that if it happens that there are exactly 30,000 things, that is what one might call an accident and is not a proposition of logic. ([1918], p. 240)

What can it mean, on his official doctrine, to say that worlds containing more than 30,000 things and worlds containing fewer than 30,000 things "are both possible"? It can only mean that both the propositional function "x is a world and x contains more than 30,000 things" and the propositional function "x is a world and x contains fewer than 30,000 things" are sometimes true. But truth, Russell claims, is something that is conferred on a proposition (and by extension, on a propositional function) by the facts. And facts, by Thesis 1, are what the *actual* world is made up of. So, according to his official theory, he must mean that both these propositional functions are sometimes true in the actual world. But that is certainly false. The propositional function "x is a world and x contains fewer than 30,000 things" is *not* sometimes true in the actual world. It is, Russell would have to say, always false in the actual world. But in 'that case, given the reductionist translational schema provided by his official doctrine, he would have to conclude that it is *impossible* and not, as he claims, "accidental".

There is an incompatibility, then, between those occasions when Russell is trying to stick with his official, reductionist account of the modalities and those occasions when he invokes modal notions informally to mark the difference between logical and nonlogical truths. This tension, I suggest, arises out of competing dispositions in Russell's own thinking about these and related matters. On the one hand, he sometimes takes as his domain of discourse the restricted domain of *actualia*, the actual world and all its constituents. On the other hand, he sometimes takes as his domain of discourse the unrestricted domain of *possibilia*, the set of all possible worlds and all their constituents. He tries to work out the details of his logic within the confines of the restricted domain. But when it comes to giving a criterion for differentiating logic as a whole (and that part of it which, on his view, is mathematics) from other subjects, he ineluctably takes recourse to the unrestricted domain: "Pure logic," he tells us, "and pure mathematics (which is the same thing), aims at being true, in Leibnizian phraseology, in all possible worlds . . ." ([1919], p. 192).

The expressions "always true", "sometimes true", and "never true" take on wholly different meanings according to whether one takes them as ranging over the restricted domain or the unrestricted domain. Construing them in the former way, Russell's official way, leads to an actualist reduction of the modalities and enables Russell to construct an extensionalist logic totally devoid of modal notions. Construing them in the latter way yields the Leibnizian result that something is necessary if and only if it is always true within this wider domain, that is, if and only if it is true in all possible worlds; that something is possible if and only if it is sometimes true within this wider domain, that is, if and only if it is true in some possible worlds; that something is impossible if and only if it is never true in this wider domain, that is, if and only if it is false in all possible worlds. Construing them in the latter way, Russell's unofficial, off-duty kind of way, leads to a view of logic in the characterization, if not the formalization, of which modal notions play an essential part.

I think it ironic that Russell sought, and thought he had found in Wittgenstein's notion of tautologousness, a purely syntactic and metaphysically neutral characterization of the domain of logic. He writes: "the characteristic of logical propositions that we are in search of is the one which was felt, and intended to be defined, by those who said that it consisted in deducibility from the law of contradiction. This characteristic . . . we may call 'tautology' . . ." ([1919], p. 203). And, in a footnote, he comments: "The importance of 'tautology' for a definition of mathematics was pointed out to me by my former pupil Ludwig Wittgenstein, who was working on the problem. I do not know whether he has solved it, or even whether he is alive or dead." ([1919], p. 205, fn. 1). The irony lies in the fact that, although Russell apparently did not know it at the time, the notion of tautologousness that Wittgenstein was to develop as a solution to their problem was nothing other than the robustly metaphysical, Leibnizian, notion of truth in all possible worlds.

7. Wittgenstein's Account of De Dicto Modalities

As early as November 1913 Wittgenstein complained emphatically about Russell's putatively logical axioms of reducibility, infinity, and multiplication on the grounds that "*If they are true propositions they are what I shall call 'accidentally 'true and not 'essentially' true* ", and went on to explain that true logical propositions are "tautologous" (*NB* 125). The character of tautologousness, as Wittgenstein then thought of it, is made relatively clear in another letter he wrote to Russell about the same time. Complaining once more about the illegitimacy of Russell's treatment of the axiom of infinity as a proposition of logic, he invokes the Leibnizian criterion of truth in all possible worlds and claims, in effect, that since he can "imagine" a world in which the axiom of infinity is false, that proposition cannot be a true proposition of logic. In this respect, he claims, the axiom of infinity is quite unlike the propositions of logic. "All propositions of logic," he writes, "are generalizations of tautologies and all generalizations of tautologies are propositions of logic. There are no logical propositions but these." (*NB* 127). To be sure, he goes on to say "I can't myself say quite clearly yet what tautologies really are". And he also suggests that one of their most important characteristics is that their truth can be seen "in the propositional sign itself" (*NB* 127), thus leaving room for Russell to hope, as he apparently still did at the time of writing *Introduction to Mathematical Philosophy*, that the notion of tautologousness would turn out, once Wittgenstein solved "the problem", to be purely syntactical in nature. But the fact is that the notion of tautologousness, as it developed in Wittgenstein's thinking, turned out to be essentially semantic and modal in character, having to do with the actual and possible circumstances in which tautologous propositions are true.

In that part of the *Notebooks* that he wrote between 1914 and 1916 Wittgenstein not only gives several examples of propositions, or kinds of propositions, which he calls tautologies, but also advances a number of theses about tautologies in general. He claims, for instance, that identity-statements such as "a = a" are tautologies, though not in the same sense as are propositions of logic such as "p ⊃ p" (*NB* 24(6)); that there is a sense in which even a tune is a tautology since it is "complete in itself; it satisfies itself" (*NB* 40(6)); that it seems to be a tautology to say, "*Language* consists of *sentences* " (*NB* 52(4–5)); and that it is always tautological to say that one thing is part of another (*NB* 62(6)). That the range of examples he has in mind goes beyond the purely formal emerges again when we take a look at some of the propositions that he calls "contradictions", or says to be "logically impossible". Examples include the impossibility of a particle being in two places at the same time (*NB* 81(10)); the impossibility of an event's being repeated (*NB* 84(7)); and the contradiction involved in saying both that A is red and that A is green (*NB* 91(9)). Since it is always, on his view, tautologous to assert the denial of a contradiction, the denials of the preceding must also be tautologies, albeit not purely syntactical ones. Among the more general claims he makes about tautologies are the following: that "tautologies say nothing" and "are themselves logically completely neutral" (*NB* 8(10)); that tautologies may not be genuine propositions at all (*NB* 11(9)); that the answer to Kant's question "How is pure mathematics possible?" is to be given through the "theory of tautologies" (*NB* 15(3)); that definitions are tautologies (*NB* 18(9)); that in tautologies the truth-conditions "cancel one another out" so that they do not say anything about reality (*NB* 24(5)); that the logical sum of two tautologies is itself a tautology (*NB* 47(4)); that tautologies are asserted and contradictions denied by "*every* proposition" (*NB* 51(4)); that nothing follows from a tautology even though a tautology follows from every proposition (*NB* 54(7)); that in a tautology "every possibility is admitted in advance" (*NB* 55(8)); that "one cannot say of a tautology that it is true, for it is *made so as to be true*." (*NB* 55(14)); and that "all tautologies say the same thing. (Namely nothing.)" (*NB* 58(9)).

A good many of these claims survive, with little if any modification, in the *Tractatus*. One of the most important is the claim that in a tautology "every possibility is admitted in advance" (*NB* 55(8)). It points backwards, as it were, to the Leibnizian notion of a necessary truth as one that is true in all possible worlds, the notion that had been in the forefront of Wittgenstein's thinking when he had earlier criticized Russell. Yet it also points forward to the Tractarian account which holds that a proposition is to be called a tautology in the case in which the proposition is "true for all the truth-possibilities of the elementary propositions." (4.46(2)).

That the Tractarian account is a generalization of the Leibnizian notion becomes obvious as soon as we investigate what Wittgenstein means by "truth-possibilities of elementary propositions". He does not mean just the schemata that students of truth-functional logic, following Wittgenstein's lead, write out on the left-hand side of truth-tables. The truth-possibilities of elementary propositions may be *represented* by rows and columns of "T"s and "F"s, as Wittgenstein points out, "in a way that can easily be understood" (4.31). But they ought not to be identified with these schemata. Rather, the truth-possibilities of elementary propositions are, in his words, "possibilities of existence and non-existence of states of affairs." The truth-possibilities of elementary propositions, for Wittgenstein, are tantamount to totalities of possible states of affairs, that is, to possible worlds. As he puts it, "For n states of affairs, there are $[2^n]$[8] possibilities of existence and non-existence. Of these states of affairs any combination can exist and the remainder not exist." (4.27). "There correspond to these combinations the same number of possibilities of truth—and falsity—for n elementary propositions." (4.27). "Truth-possibilities of elementary propositions mean possibilities of existence and non-existence of states of affairs." (4.3). Hence, in saying that a tautology is true for all truth-possibilities of the elementary propositions, Wittgenstein is saying that a tautology is true for all possible combinations of the existence and nonexistence of states of affairs; or, as he might have put it here if he had adopted the talk of "worlds" which he uses elsewhere, they are "true in all possible worlds."

Needless to say, Wittgenstein gives corresponding accounts of the semantic conditions for ascribing contradictoriness and contingency (being a genuine proposition or "proposition with sense", as he calls it) to propositions. Summing up, he says, "A tautology's truth is certain, a proposition's possible, a contradiction's impossible." (4.464). In effect, a tautology's truth is "certain" or necessary in so far as it is true in all possible worlds, a genuine proposition's truth is "possible" (better, "contingent")[9] in so far as it is true in some possible worlds but not all, and a contradiction's truth is "impossible" in so far as it is "false for all truth-possibilities", that is, false in all possible worlds.

Not only, then, is Wittgenstein rejecting Russell's claim that modal properties can intelligibly be ascribed only to propositional functions, and not to propositions. He is also rejecting Russell's claim that the conditions for their ascription have to do solely with what I have called "the restricted domain" of the actual world. As he puts it, "It is incorrect to render the proposition '$(\exists x).Fx$' in the words, 'Fx is *possible* ', as Russell does." (5.525(1)). The properties of being "tautologous" or "certain" (that is, necessary), of being "a proposition with sense" or merely "possible" (that is, contingent), and of being "contradictory" (that is, impossible), are to be ascribed to propositions according as their truth-values are determined within what I have called "the unrestricted domain" of all possible states of affairs, and all possible totalities thereof: that is, in all possible worlds. Far from trying to reduce modal notions to the "statistical" ones of being always, sometimes, or never true, Wittgenstein takes them to be definable in terms of a Leibnizian metaphysics of possible worlds.

8. Russell's Dismissal of De Re Modalities

Immediately after the passage quoted in section 2 in which Russell described the way in which a certain kind of logical theory, that employed by Hegel and his followers, leads to metaphysical monism, Russell writes:

> Generally, one supports this theory by talking about the "nature" of a thing, assuming that a thing has something which you call its "nature" which is generally elaborately confounded and distinguished from the thing, so that you get a comfortable see-saw which enables you to deduce whichever results suit the moment. The "nature" of the thing would come to mean all the true propositions in which the thing is mentioned. Of course, it is clear that since everything has relations to everything else, you cannot know all the facts of which a thing is a constituent without having some knowledge of everything in the universe. ([1918], p. 204)

Now it is indeed true that talk about the "nature" of a thing tends to play a crucial, and often suspect, role in British Idealist arguments for monism. These arguments from "nature" take many forms. But all seem to boil down to something like the following: that if an object, Y, has properties different from those of an object, X, then Y is not identical to X; that the very identity, internal "nature", or essence, of an object, X, is therefore *constituted* by the properties that X has; that among the properties that any object, X, has are those relational properties that X has by virtue of standing in various relations to other objects; that every object stands in some relation or other to each and every other object in the universe; that if any of these relations were to be other than it in fact is then X would change its relational properties; that the very identity, internal "nature", or essence, of any given object X would change if any of its properties, relational or otherwise, were to change; and hence, by generalization, that the "nature" of *each and every* object is constituted by its relations to every other object in the universe, in such a way that no object could exist apart from its relations to everything else. Reality is an organic unity, Idealists concluded, insofar as none of its supposed parts can alter in the slightest respect without consequential alterations of its relations to other objects, hence to the relational properties, and hence to the internal natures or essences—indeed the very identity—of those other parts. The doctrine that embodied this sort of reasoning came to be known, not surprisingly, as the Doctrine of Internal Relations.

An excellent job of exposing its fallaciousness was performed by G. E. Moore

[1919]. Moore, in effect, called into question the Idealists' implicit appeal to Leibniz's Principle of the Nonidentity of Discernibles (alternatively referred to as the Principle of Indiscernibility of Identicals), the principle that if X and Y have different properties they are nonidentical.[10] He allowed that, if a thing X does indeed have properties, relational or otherwise, that Y does not have, then it *follows of necessity* that X is different from Y. But he claimed that it does not follow from this indisputable truth that if a thing Y has any properties different from those of X, Y is *necessarily* different from X in the sense of having a different essential "nature" from X. All that follows, he argued, is that Y is different from X, not that it is necessarily or essentially different.

Significantly, Moore's exposure of the fallacy is made possible only by virtue of the fact that he is able to employ a distinction that Russell cannot admit. The Idealist doctrine of internal relations, according to Moore, is made plausible by their conflation of two propositions that, when they are expressed in ordinary English, do indeed sound equivalent, but which, when they are properly disambiguated in an adequate logical notation, turn out to be quite different and such that one can easily be shown not to follow from the other. The two propositions are these:

(1) If an object X has the property P, whether this property be relational or otherwise, then it follows of necessity that if an object Y does not have P then X is not identical to Y;

and

(2) If X has P, then it follows of necessity from Y's not having P that X is not identical to Y.

Using the term "entails" to express the converse of the relation of *following from*—that relation which holds between the premises and the conclusion of a valid argument—Moore expresses the difference between (1) and (2) by means of a somewhat clumsy notation which, suitably modified, yields the result that (1) is of the form

(1)* (X has P) entails ($\sim$ (Y has P) $\supset$ $\sim$ (X = Y))

whereas (2) is of the form

(2)* (X has P) $\supset$ ($\sim$ (Y has P) entails $\sim$ (X = Y))

Propositions having the form of (1)*, Moore believes, are certainly true. Their truth, though he does not point this out, follows from the Leibnizian Principle, as the Idealists might well have claimed. But propositions having the form of (2)*, Moore argues, do not follow from propositions having the form of (1)*, despite the similarity of their ordinary English expressions, (1) and (2). The Idealists, Moore claims, think that propositions having the form of (2)* do follow from propositions having the form of (1)*. And this, according to Moore, explains why they think that Leibniz's Principle compels them to conclude that objects necessarily have whatever properties they in fact have, that is, to conclude that all properties are "internal" to the objects that have them.

The fact that propositions having the form of (2)* do not follow from propositions having the form of (1)*, Moore points out, can be made clear by means of a counter-example. For (1)* and (2)* are, respectively, of the more general forms

(1)** p entails (q ⊃ r)

and

(2)** p ⊃ (q entails r)

Let p = "All the books on this shelf are blue", q = "My copy of the *Principles of Mathematics* is a book on this shelf", and r = "My copy of the *Principles of Mathematics* is blue". Then, he points out, the proposition corresponding to (1)** is true, but the proposition corresponding to (2)** is false. Ipso facto, propositions having the form of (2)** do not follow from propositions having the form of (1)**, notwithstanding the beguiling similarity of their English expressions. The Idealists, in short, are quite unwarranted in their supposition that the doctrine of internal relations can be grounded in the indubitability of the Nonidentity of Discernibles.

Significantly, the Idealists are not the only ones, according to Moore, whose reliance on an inadequate notation debars them from recognizing and observing the crucial distinction between (1)** and (2)**. Russell, too, is unable to make that distinction. For Russell, as we have seen, fails to draw any distinction between the case where a conditional is necessary in the sense of being always true in the actual world and the case where a conditional is true in all possible worlds. That is to say, he fails to draw any distinction between the case where the antecedent of a conditional materially implies the consequent, and the case where it logically implies— or, as Moore puts it, "entails"—the consequent. He fails, that is, to recognize the distinction between material implication and logical implication. In the absence of such a distinction, (1) and (2) are indistinguishable. In a sense, therefore, Russell is in a worse position than are the Idealists. They fail to distinguish between (1) and (2) because they are, in effect, insensitive to the differences in meaning of the English sentences (1) and (2). Russell fails to distinguish between them because, given his actualist preferences, and his consequential reliance on the purely actuality-oriented notion of material implication, any differences in English disappear in his logical notation. For him, both (1) and (2) would have to be transcribed in precisely the same way, namely, as "p ⊃ (q ⊃ r)". The differences between the English sentences (1) and (2), which Moore is able to record as the difference between (1)** and (2)**, cannot be recorded at all in Russell's notation.

The expressive inadequacy of Russell's notation, then, precludes him from attacking the Idealist's doctrine of internal relations in the Mooreian way. Unable to criticize their reasoning with the finesse displayed by Moore, Russell launches a wholesale attack on the very intelligibility of talk about the "nature" of a thing. Since such talk is essential to the Idealist's argument, he suggests, we ought to give it up. Besides, as Moore had pointed out, talk about the "nature" of a thing is Idealist shorthand, as it were, for talk about the internal properties (including relational ones) that constitute that nature: a property P is said to be internal to an object X just if X possesses P "in all conceivable circumstances", that is, in all possible worlds. To the extent, therefore, that Russell's official theory of modalities precludes his talking of this unrestricted domain of worlds, it precludes his attaching any sense to the notions of internality and "nature" so defined. Russell does not, so far as I know, expressly claim that properties and relations are *never* internal to, and hence constitutive of the nature of, the objects that have them. But that seems to be his official position. In short, it seems as though he is committed not only to the rejection of de dicto modal notions but to the rejection of de re modal ones as well.

Moore has no need for such wholesale rejection of the idea that properties and relations are sometimes internal or essential to their possessors. Neither does Wittgenstein. Moore takes some pains to argue that some relational properties, for example, the relational property that he calls "having *this* for a spatial part", are indeed internal in the way that Idealists claim they are.[11] Wittgenstein would agree, even to the point of citing the same example, in *NB* 62(6) (quoted earlier). The error of the Idealists, Moore holds, lies in their insisting that *all* relational properties— and all nonrelational ones as well—are internal. This, he points out, "flies in the face of common sense." As he puts it, "It seems quite obvious that in the case of many relational properties which things have, the fact that they have them is *a mere matter of fact*: that the things in question *might* have existed without having them." (p. 289). Once more, Wittgenstein would have agreed. For Wittgenstein, as for Moore, some properties are indeed internal to, and constitutive of the natures of, their possessors; others are merely external. For him, as for Moore, though not for Russell, it is just as much a mistake to claim that no properties are internal as it is to claim that all are.

9. Wittgenstein's Acceptance of De Re Modalities

Talk of the "nature" of an object, which Russell found so suspect, appears as early as the second page of the *Tractatus* when Wittgenstein claims, "If I know an object I also know all its possible occurrences in states of affairs. (Every one of these possibilities must be part of the nature of the object.) A new possibility cannot be discovered later." (2.0123). This passage is strikingly reminiscent of some of the things which Idealists liked to say. They, too, liked to entertain the idea of our having complete knowledge of the "nature" of an object. And they, too, thought of such complete knowledge as beyond the capacity of finite human understanding. I say "they, too" because I suggest that this is how Wittgenstein also thought of it. For both parties, knowledge of the nature of an object is something which only a god (or the Absolute) could have. We humans can aspire to it, but only to the extent that we think of ourselves as aspiring to a God's-eye view of reality. The essential point that both want to make, then, is best understood as a metaphysical one about what constitutes the nature of a thing rather than an epistemic one about what we can or do in fact know of the nature of anything.

So much for the similarities between Wittgenstein and the Idealists. After that the differences begin to show. The Idealists see the nature of an object as being constituted by the actual relations into which it enters with everything else in the universe. Wittgenstein sees it as constituted not by all the actual relations, but only by the possible relations into which the object enters. For him, the actual relations in which an object stands are not at all constitutive of the nature of the object. They are not internal, but external; not essential, but accidental to its nature. Hence, to return to the epistemic mode of expression for a moment, knowledge of the nature of an object, for Wittgenstein, requires only knowledge of its possibilities of combination, not knowledge of any actual combinations into which it enters. Summing up, Wittgenstein writes: "If I am to know an object, though I need not know its external properties, I must know all its internal ones." (2.01231). He puts the point in something more like the metaphysical mode when he writes: "If all objects are given, then at the same time all *possible* states of affairs are also given." (2.0124).

Lest it be thought that I am reading too much into three passages from page 2 of the *Tractatus*, let it be noted that every single one of the eleven passages from 2.011 to 2.0141 inclusive, passages which together take up most of the first two pages of the *Tractatus*, and a bit of the third, is concerned with explaining or illustrating how the internal or essential natures of objects are connected with their de re modal possibilities of combination. These de re possibilities, Wittgenstein tells us, are "essential" to them (2.011), are "written into" them (2.012), are "in them from the beginning" (2.0121), are "a form of connection with states of affairs" (2.0122), are such that one "cannot imagine the thing" without these possibilities (2.013), are such that objects "contain" them (2.014), and are definitive of "the form of an object" (2.0141).

Wittgenstein's disagreement with Russell comes to the fore when we consider the role that de re modalities play, for Wittgenstein, in determining the domain of logic. According to Russell's official doctrine, it will be remembered, the domain of logic is the restricted one of *actualia*. In his words, "I should always wish to be engaged in the investigation of some actual fact or set of facts, and it seems to me that that is so in logic just as much as it is in zoology." ([1918], p. 216). Wittgenstein's official position, by way of contrast, views the domain of logic as the unrestricted one of *possibilia* : "Nothing in the province of logic can be merely possible. Logic deals with every possibility and all possibilities are its facts." (2.0121(3)). These possibilities, it should be noted, are not just those de dicto possibilities that correspond to propositions whose syntax pronounces them to be self-consistent. They are, as the context makes abundantly clear, the de re possibilities which are "essential to", "written into", "internal to", "contained in", or constitutive of the "natures" of Wittgenstein's metaphysically simple objects. In short, the domain of logic, for Wittgenstein, is the unrestricted one that encompasses *all* possibilities, de re as well as de dicto. It is a domain, he suggests, within which the de re possibilities of combination of simple objects in effect *determine* which states of affairs are possible, and therewith determine also which elementary propositions express de dicto possibilities. An elementary proposition, it turns out, expresses a de dicto possibility just when it asserts the existence of a possible state of affairs, where the possibility of a state of affairs is determined by the de re possibilities of combination of simple objects. In a passage that foreshadows his later metaphor of logical space, Wittgenstein tells us that "Each thing is, as it were, in a space of possible states of affairs." (2.013). The things and their de re possibilities of combination *generate* this space, this logical space. In short, for Wittgenstein the de re modal properties of things are the fundamental ones, both metaphysically and logically.

10. Recapitulation

First, we have seen that Wittgenstein does not accept Russell's restricted view of the nature of the simple objects or particulars that their two atomisms postulate. Whereas Russell regards these as actual objects of human experience, sense-data, Wittgenstein regards them as the ultimate constituents of any possible world that a god might create (*NB* 98(2) and 5.123). More generally, Wittgenstein does not accept Russell's restriction of metaphysics to the investigation of the actual world and its contents but allows himself to consider more widely the range of all possible worlds and their contents.

Second, Wittgenstein does not accept Russell's official, reductionist, account of the de dicto modalities. Whereas Russell tried to define the notions of necessity, possibility and impossibility in terms of what is always, sometimes, or never true in the actual world, Wittgenstein implicitly defined them in terms of what is true in all, in some, or in none of the set of all possible worlds. In other words, Wittgenstein does not accept Russell's account of de dicto modal notions in terms of the restricted domain but allows himself to consider the unrestricted domain.

Third, Wittgenstein does not accept Russell's dismissal of the de re modal notions. Whereas Russell gave them no role whatever in his actuality-oriented account of logic, Wittgenstein explicitly defined the domain of logic as one that studies all possibilities, de re as well as de dicto. In effect, Wittgenstein once more adopts the unrestricted domain of Leibnizian possible worlds and their constituents, possible objects, as that in terms of which logic is to be characterized. Accordingly, he sometimes "quantifies over" the objects in this unrestricted domain, sometimes saying that "there are" or "exist" such objects. When he does so, I shall say that he is using the expressions "there are" and "there exist" in the unrestricted sense.

Oddly, some six years before announcing his conversion, as it were, to the new atomistic philosophy that he claimed to have learnt from Wittgenstein, Russell had given an account of the domain of logic that explicitly rejected the idea that it is in any way restricted to that which actually exists. In *The Problems of Philosophy* [1912], Russell wrote:

> we feel some quality of *necessity* about the proposition "two and two are four", which is absent from even the best attested empirical generalizations. Such generalizations always remain mere facts: we feel that there might be a world in which they were false, though in the actual world they happen to be true. In any possible world, on the contrary, we feel that two and two would be four: this is not a mere fact, but a necessity to which everything *actual and possible* must conform [emphasis added]. (p. 78)

Not only is Russell here envisaging logical and mathematical truths as being true in the unrestricted domain of possible worlds. As the last italicized phrase suggests, he also thinks of them as being true in the unrestricted domain of possible objects. Nor is this an isolated passage. Earlier in the same work he speaks of "logic . . . where we are concerned not merely with what does exist, but with whatever might or could exist, no reference to actual particulars is involved." (p. 56). This view of logic and mathematics is precisely the one that, in both *The Philosophy of Logical Atomism*

[1918] and *Introduction to Mathematical Philosophy* [1919], Russell repudiates in favor of his official accounts of modality and existence. Yet it is also the view to which he reverts on unofficial occasions. And as I have argued, it is precisely the view of logic and mathematics that Wittgenstein held to throughout his early work.

Notes

1. The first German edition appeared in *Annalen der Naturphilosophie*, 1921.

2. The first English edition was published in the series *International Library of Psychology Philosophy and Scientific Method* (London: Routledge and Kegan Paul, 1922).

3. See Hintikka M. B. and Hintikka J. [1987], pp. 76–77.

4. Urmson J. O. [1956]. In his Introduction, Urmson gracefully acknowledges that many of his then-contemporaries were coming to doubt the accuracy of the sort of interpretation he had given and points out, "in particular they would claim that the orientation of [Wittgenstein's] thought was much more to logical and less to epistemological problems than is here suggested—for example, his *Sachverhalten* would be regarded as more akin to logical possibilities than to Russell's atomic facts." (p. ix). His somewhat lame excuse is that "it was the sort of interpretation I have given, right or wrong, which was accepted in the period under examination, and which has therefore been of historical importance and influence. For our purposes it is what Wittgenstein was thought to mean that matters." (pp. ix—x).

5. But see 5.541 for Wittgenstein's discussion of the possible exception of belief-propositions.

6. But note his discussion, in lecture IV, of "Propositions and Facts with More than One Verb; Beliefs, etc."

7. Moore [1919] refers to Leibniz's analysis of "necessary truths" and points out the need to distinguish truths that are necessary in this sense from those true universal propositions that are "mere matters of fact." (p. 302). And he explicitly invokes Leibnizian talk of possible worlds when, a few pages earlier, he tries to explicate what might be meant by saying that a property P is internal to an object A, as "anything which were identical with A would, in any conceivable universe, necessarily have P", or as "A could not have existed in any possible world without having P".

8. I here (and elsewhere) replace Wittgenstein's own formula with the much simplified one to which, as Max Black points out, it is equivalent. See Black [1964], p. 215.

9. Like Aristotle (when making his first attempts to sort out modal notions from one another), Wittgenstein often uses "possible" when he should have used "contingent".

10. The Principle of Indiscernibility of Identicals states the converse of the Principle of Identity of Indiscernibles. The former states a necessary condition of identity. The latter is supposed to state a sufficient condition: it says that X and Y are identical if they have all their properties in common. Most philosophers accept the former. Some deny the latter. Yet the Identity of Indiscernibles is necessarily true

(some would tendentiously say "trivially true") if being identical to X is counted as one of X's properties.

11. Moore claims that if a spatial complex X has Y as a spatial part then X would not be the very thing that it is were it to lack Y. Having Y as a spatial part, then, is an internal property of X such that analysis of X would reveal Y as one of its necessary constituents.

Both Moore and Wittgenstein, it seems, thought that analysis of a complex into its constituent parts yields truths about the complex that are somehow "necessary". In this respect their thinking is akin to that of Kant, who held, in effect, that if a complex subject S has predicate P as a conceptual part then analysis of S would reveal concept P as necessarily tied to it in such a way as to make the judgment that S is P "analytic" and hence necessary.

2

The Realm of Possibility

[A god] could not create a world in which the proposition 'p' was true without creating all its objects.

(WITTGENSTEIN, Tractatus)

1. Introduction

In Chapter I, I tried to loosen the grip that a certain paradigm has on the thinking of many philosophers. I mean, of course, the actualist paradigm according to which all the materials needed for our metaphysical and logical theorizing are to be found in the actual world and its constituents.[1] It is exemplified in Russell's Theory of Descriptions whose intent is to paraphrase away any apparent references to nonactual objects.[2] It exerts its influence in the tendency of many philosophers these days to dismiss the "Meinongian excess", as Russell would put it, of any theory that countenances reference to merely possible worlds or merely possible objects. It manifests itself in the currently orthodox interpretation of the logical symbolism, the existential quantifier "($\exists x$)" in particular, that Russell bequeathed us; an interpretation that treats all statements about what exists as statements about what exists actually. And, more relevantly (for our present concerns), it shows up in the standard interpretations of the early Wittgenstein's version of logical atomism, interpretations that tend to take it for granted that Wittgenstein's atomism, like Russell's, was committed to actualism.

I have tried to loosen the grip of this paradigm in two main ways. First, I've tried, by means of a brief historical excursus into the origins of the logical atomist ways of thinking, to reveal some of the quirkiness of Russell's official, actualist account of modality and existence. The spirit of his doctrines, sometimes even the letter, is still favored by many. Yet his doctrines, when viewed in an historical context, are likely to appear less than wellfounded. It can be salutary to see in them, and the somewhat confused and inconsistent thinking that led to them, the sources of what so many today take for granted.

Second, I've pointed out important and oft-neglected respects in which Wittgenstein's atomism differs from Russell's, with a view to distancing his atomism from Russell's and thereby opening the way for a fresh look at the things that Wittgenstein himself said about matters of modality and existence.

28

That is what I turn to now. In this chapter, I produce arguments and textual evidence that Wittgenstein's modal atomism treats modality and existence in possibilist terms. I know that many readers will find the prospect of being convinced disturbing for general philosophical reasons, and improbable because of the presumption that earlier scholars would have recognized Wittgenstein's possibilism if in fact it existed. To such readers I can only say, "Try to suspend your disbelief. Wait and see."

2. Three Degrees of Possibilism

Possibilism, in general, is the belief in things which are merely possible, that is, nonactual possibles. Since, in what follows, I shall be concerned only with those nonactuals that are also possible, not with those that are impossible, I shall often omit the qualifier "possible" and speak of them simply as nonactuals, whether these nonactuals are worlds, states of affairs, objects, or whatnot.

Possiblists want to say that, in the unrestricted quantificational sense of "are" and "exist" noted at the end of Chapter I, there are (or exist) possible but nonactual states of affairs, possible but nonactual complex objects, or even possible but nonactual simple objects (whatever they may be).

It is useful to distinguish three degrees of possibilism, whose differences can be illustrated in terms of the following theses:

    (1) There are some *states of affairs*, such as that of Alvin Plantinga's being the first climber to conquer Mt. Everest, which though possible, are nonactual (though the objects involved in these states of affairs are themselves actual).

    (2) There are some *complex objects*, such as "additional" persons, or planets in our solar system, that though possible, are nonactual (though the simpler objects of which these complex objects are constituted are themselves actual).

    (3) There are some *simple objects*, such as, perhaps, "additional" quarks (or whatever else, if anything, turns out to be ultimately simple), that though possible, are nonactual.

First-degree possibilists would assert (1). Second-degree possibilists would assert (1) and (2). Third-degree possibilists would assert (1), (2), and (3).

I hope to establish, in this chapter, not only that Wittgenstein is a possibilist but also that he takes his possibilism as far as it can go: to the third degree. But first, I want to say a little about the intuitive appeal of all three degrees of possibilism.

3. The Plausibility of Possibilism

Let's leave aside, for a while, the question as to precisely how the apparent existence-claims of possibilists are to be construed and think for a little about the prima facie truth of each of the three possibilist theses.

It is, I submit, undeniable that we can and do conduct much of our thinking in accord with the supposition that (1) is true. Whenever in our idle moments we entertain suppositions as to what might have been the case, might now be the case, or might someday come to be the case, then, to the extent that what we are envisaging either was not, or is not, or will not, be the case, what we are envisaging is a nonactual state of affairs. And the same holds when our speculations are not idle but serious, and the suppositions we entertain are candidates for the roles of scientific theories. What we are envisaging, to the extent that our hypotheses are self-consistent but mistaken, is the existence of certain states of affairs that are possible but nonactual. More generally, when we reflect on the choices we make between alternative courses of action, we envisage—sometimes in considerable detail—the different consequences which would ensue were we to choose to do this, that, or the other thing. What we are envisaging is different ways the world might be. Yet there is only one way the world (timelessly) is. Of the various ways the world might be, only one of them was, is, or will be, actual. All the others were, are, or will be, nonactual.

Likewise, with regard to thesis (2), we do in fact often think counterfactually about complex objects that might have existed but don't: additional children whom we might have had but didn't; new buildings, bridges, or highways that were planned but never constructed; and so on. Nor do there seem to be any problems, in principle at least, about our *naming* such nonactual possibles as these. In the cases of proposed buildings, bridges, and highways, planners—for ease of reference—name them almost every day. And even in the case of nonactual persons, it is easy enough to conceive of circumstances in which they, too, may be named. Consider, for instance, some future time in which the would-be biological parents of a planned test-tube baby have half-a-dozen or so selected sperm and ova examined under an electron microscope in order to determine, for each of the thirty-six possible pairings, which determinate features in a child would thereby be determined. Let's suppose that, in order to facilitate their thinking, they dub the individual spermatazoa "a", "b", "c", and so on, and the individual ova "u", "v", "w", and so forth. Then they can refer to the possible pairings of these gametes by means of letter-pairings: "a-w", "a-z", and so on. Moreover, they can then go on to dub each of the thirty-six possible *children* who, in the normal causal chain of events, would develop from these pairings, by such names as "Hamlet", "Ophelia", "Romeo", "Juliet", and the like. It should be noted that "Hamlet", "Ophelia", and the rest are not names of gamete-pairs; for the gamete-pairs already have their own names. Rather, they are the names of the possible children into whom the various gamete-pairs could develop. Suppose, now, that the parents decide that they want to have Juliet, that the appropriate gamete-pair is put into the test-tube, and that this gamete-pair does in fact grow to be the person to whom they antecedently assigned the name "Juliet". Then Juliet will be an actual person. Her alternates (Hamlet, Ophelia, Romeo, and the rest), however, must surely count as nonactual possible persons, who would have featured in the actual world's population had the parents chosen differently.

There is, to be sure, a currently much-favored account of naming—the so-called causal theory or historical theory—which seemingly precludes cases of the kind I have just sketched. The theory, as commonly understood, involves three main claims about ordinary names: (a) that names are normally bestowed on their bearers by means of some locutionary act whereby an object of acquaintance is "baptized", as it were, with a name (a claim about reference-introduction); (b) that, by virtue of (a), names function semantically as mere labels for their bearers (a semantic claim); and (c) that the use of a name to pick out its bearer is transmitted from one user to another by some sort of historical chain (a claim about reference-transmission). Clearly, if (a) is true, the scenario I just sketched, about naming several distinct possible nonactual children, is in trouble. For how, it may be asked, can the parents perform such acts in the absence of the *persons*, as distinct from the gamete-pairs with which they are confronted? How, more generally, can someone name an object that does not exist in the actual world but only in some other possible world? Are not causal exchanges of the postulated sort, exchanges in which an object "presents" itself to the namer and then has a name bestowed on it, possible only *within* a world, not *between* worlds? For these sorts of reasons, some proponents of causal-cum-historical accounts of naming may be inclined to say that naming of nonactual possibles is in principle impossible. But if so, then so much the worse for claim (a), the claim about reference-introduction. In any case, as has been pointed out (Bradley [1984]) there are independent reasons for thinking (a) false. For it is inconsistent with cases where names are bestowed in absentia, bestowed, that is, on objects which, since they are not present at the time of naming, are known, at that time, only by description. A paradigm case of bestowal of a name in absentia is that of the naming of Neptune, whose existence was merely postulated, as the cause of certain perturbations in the orbit of Uranus, at the time when it was named. The fact that it was then known only by description, as it were, not by acquaintance, certainly counts against (a). But it does not count against claim (b). For instance, it does not count against having the word "Neptune" function, not as a disguised description, but as a genuine proper name the sole semantic function of which is to pick out Neptune, not to ascribe any properties to it. Nor does it count against claim (c), the claim that knowledge of the name-bearer relation is transmitted from generation to generation in such a way as to enable future users of the name to refer to objects with which they themselves are not acquainted, by means of the names that were initially conferred on them. Claims (b) and (c), in short, are independent of (a), and their truth, therefore, is in no way compromised by the dubious, and unnecessary, claim (once more Russellian in character) that the original name-conferrers were themselves involved in some sort of causal interaction with, or were acquainted with, the objects named.[3]

How about thesis (3): that some simple objects, though possible, are nonactual? There can be little doubt but that we can and do sometimes think of ultimate simples as existing. We can suppose it to be the case, for instance, that quarks are indeed among the ultimate simples that make up the substance of the actual world. And we can imagine its being the case, further, that these—or whatever other candidates we cast in that role—could have been more numerous than they are. We can imagine, that is, that there might have been more quarks, or whatnot, than are contained in the world as it happens to be. Surely, there is no logical necessity for the world in which we live to be populated by just that number of quarks which it happens to contain, no contradiction involved in the supposition that it might have contained more (or fewer). Suppose the actual world contains n simple objects. Is it not possible, logically, that it should have contained n + 1 such objects? Or n + 2? Or n + 3? Or . . . ? If we can, as I submit we can, coherently conceive of such possibilities, then we are conceiving of worlds in which there are simple objects that are possible but nonactual, and we are, to that extent, third-degree possibilists. Even Russell would (sometimes) agree.

Our ordinary way of thinking about possibilities, I'm saying, does encompass all three degrees of possibilism. So, too, I'll try to show, does Wittgenstein's.

4. Wittgenstein's First-Degree Possibilism

The fact that Wittgenstein uses the expression "possible states of affairs" ("*Moglichen Sachverhalte*"), to refer to states of affairs that need not be among the actual ones which he calls "facts", is known to any reader of the Pears and McGuinness translation of the *Tractatus*, though (for reasons noted in my Preface) it might not be so obvious to someone relying on the Ogden translation. A recurring theme in the *Tractatus* is that genuine propositions, that is, propositions with sense, assert the existence of possible states of affairs. When a proposition is true, the relevant state of affairs exists (in the restricted sense). When false, the relevant state of affairs, though still possible, does not exist (in the restricted sense). Numerous passages in the *Tractatus* either assert or presuppose that this is the case. Typical examples are these: "If an elementary proposition is true, the state of affairs exists: if an elementary proposition is false, the state of affairs does not exist." (4.25); and "For n states of affairs, *there are* [emphasis added] 2^n possibilities of existence and nonexistence. Of these states of affairs any combination can exist and the remainder not exist." (4.27). The theme is articulated even more forthrightly in the *Notebooks*, where Wittgenstein says such things as the following: "The proposition points to the *possibility* [emphasis added] that such and such is the case." (*NB* 29(5)); and "The propositional sign guarantees the *possibility* [emphasis added] of the fact which it presents (not that this fact is *actually the case* [emphasis added])—this holds for the general propositions too." (*NB* 27(2)). Clearly, he is saying that propositions that are true assert the existence of possible states of affairs which in fact do exist (in the actual world), whereas significant propositions that are false assert the existence of possible states of affairs that are not "actually the case", that is, do not exist in the actual world. False propositions, in short, assert the actual existence of nonactual possible states of affairs.

Although, in the *Tractatus*, Wittgenstein doesn't actually use the expression "possible world" ("*mogliche Welt*"), in the *Notebooks*, with which most readers are less familiar, he does. There he writes: "There cannot be an orderly or a disorderly world, so that one could say that our world is orderly. In every *possible world* [emphasis added] there is an order even if it is a complicated one, just as in space too there are not orderly and disorderly distributions of points, but every distribution of points is orderly." (*NB* 83 (2)). True, he goes on to comment: "(This remark is only material for a thought.)" (*NB* 83 (3)). But the context makes it clear that what gives him pause here is not the reference to possible worlds but only his claim that their orderliness or disorderliness is not a contingent—and hence sayable—matter.

The precise form of words he uses to refer to possible worlds, however, is unimportant. What is significant is that he implicitly takes for granted the Leibnizian metaphysics of possible worlds in his use of a number of other expressions. For instance, he talks about imaginary worlds, as in, "It is obvious that an imagined world, however it may differ from the real one, must have *something*—a form—in common with it." (2.022), (a passage that entertains the idea of there being worlds which are not "real" or actual); and again in, "It is possible to imagine a world in which the axiom of reducibility is not valid. It is clear, however, that logic has nothing to do with the question whether our world really is like that or not." (6.1233); (a passage that implicitly invokes the Leibnizian notion of truth-in-all-possible-worlds as a criterion of logical truth).

He also writes, in a manner that echoes Leibniz, of worlds that might have been created by God, or by a god. In the *Notebooks* he writes: "If there were a world in which the principles of logic were true, in that world the whole of mathematics holds. No world can be created in which a proposition is true, unless the constituents of the proposition are created also." (*NB* 98 (2)). And, in a more or less parallel passage in the *Tractatus*, he writes: "If a god creates a world in which certain propositions are true, then by that very act he also creates a world in which all the propositions that follow from them come true. And similarly he could not create a world in which the proposition 'p' was true without creating all its objects." (5.123). Wittgenstein makes it clear that only one of the imagined worlds is the real one; that only one of the worlds which God might have created is the one which he did in fact create. That world he variously describes as "this world" (*NB* 72(18)), "the world we live in" (*NB* 127), "my world" (5.6), "our world" (6.1233), "the world" (1–1.11), "the real one" (2.022), "the sum total of reality" (2.063), "the whole of reality" (4.12). All the other possible worlds are nonactual.

Since the belief that there are nonactual possible states of affairs and worlds is precisely what characterizes first-degree possibilism, it follows that Wittgenstein is, at the very least, a first-degree possibilist.

5. Imaginability, Thinkability, and Logical Possibility

In citing various passages in which Wittgenstein talks about imagined worlds as evidence of his acceptance of nonactual possible worlds as well as the actual one, I have taken it for granted that the worlds that Wittgenstein calls "imagined" ones are possible ones in that sense of "possible" which has to do with logical possibility. Yet the following questions may be asked: Am I not riding rough-shod over a number of distinctions which we ordinarily think need to be preserved? Don't we ordinarily distinguish between what is thinkable or imaginable and what is possible; between what is possible in a generic sense (one that allows for various "species" such as logical, physical, moral, and legal) and what is possible in the purely logical sense; and between what is logically possible and what can be expressed by means of propositions?

The answer is: Yes, I am ignoring these important distinctions, but for good reason. The reason is that, insofar as we are concerned to understand Wittgenstein's position, we need to realize that the collapse of each of these distinctions is explicitly warranted by things that Wittgenstein says. No matter, then, how *we* would ordinarily construe the expressions involved, we won't understand Wittgenstein unless we trace *his* use of these expressions with care. This is a matter of some importance, since failure to accord with his usage, rather than our own, can lead us to attribute to him puzzles and paradoxes that are of our making, not his. (For instance, as noted earlier, Wittgenstein invites puzzlement with his use of the term "nonsensical", a use according to which all philosophical propositions, his own included, fail to have sense. But it turns out that the only propositions "with sense" are those which make contingent assertions about what he regards as "picturable", "thinkable", "imaginable", or logically possible.)

Let's start with Wittgenstein's view that imaginability and thinkability are tantamount to possibility. Surely, we are inclined to say, he is wrong about this. Are there not well-known objections to treating the realm of the possible as if it were coextensive with the domain of human imagination and thought? Our ability to imagine devising a procedure for squaring the circle does not entail that such a procedure is possible. So imaginability is not a sufficient condition of possibility. But neither is it a necessary condition. Our inability to imagine, conceive, or think of the solution to some complex mathematical problem does not entail that no solution is possible.

These objections to equating imaginability with possibility are sound enough. Yet there can be no doubt but that Wittgenstein equates the two. Indeed, he equates several notions that are prima facie distinct. According to him, thinkability = imaginability = picturability = expressibility by propositions with sense = possibility = logical possibility. This can easily be demonstrated.

In the first place, *NB* 24(1) tells us, "'A situation is thinkable' ('imaginable') *means* [emphasis added]: We can make ourselves a picture of it." From this we can infer:

(i) Thinkability, imaginability, and picturability are equivalent.

Second, 3.02(b) tells us, "What is thinkable is possible too." From this we can infer:

(ii) Thinkability is a sufficient condition of possibility.

Hence, from (i) and (ii) we may conclude:

(iii) Imaginability, thinkability, and picturability are sufficient conditions of possibility.

How about the converse of 3.02(b)? Evidence that he regards thinkability—and hence also imaginability and picturability—as a necessary condition, not just a sufficient condition, of possibility is provided by the conjunction of two further passages. First, 4.01 tells us, "A proposition is a picture of reality . . . a model of reality as we imagine it"; or, in other words, that if something is a proposition (a proposition with sense, a genuine proposition) then it pictures or models an imaginable reality. Hence

(iv) Imaginability is a necessary condition of expressibility by a proposition with sense.

Second, 5.525 tells us that the possibility of a situation is expressed by a proposition with sense; that is, that if a situation is possible then it can be expressed by a proposition with sense. Hence

(v) Expressibility by a proposition with sense is a necessary condition of possibility.

Now consider 6.375, which tells us, "Just as the only necessity that exists is logical necessity, so too the only impossibility that exists is logical impossibility". From this it obviously follows that, for Wittgenstein, the only kind of possibility is *logical* possibility. Thus we have

(vi) Possibility and logical possibility are equivalent.

We are now in a position to demonstrate the equations stated previously. From (i), (iv), (v), and (vi) we can infer

(vii) Imaginability, thinkability, and picturability are necessary conditions of logical possibility.

From (iii) and (vi) we can infer

(viii) Imaginability, thinkability, and picturability are sufficient conditions of logical possibility.

Finally, from (vii) and (viii) we can infer

(ix) Imaginability, thinkability, and picturability are equivalent to logical possibility.

Thus, despite the objections previously mentioned, Wittgenstein is indeed *equating* the logical notion of possibility with the prima facie "psychological" one of imaginability.

The preceding derivation shows, in passing, that expressibility by means of a proposition with sense is a sufficient condition of imaginability (from (iv)), and hence (by (i)) of thinkability. Is it also a necessary condition? I think so. For Wittgenstein also tells us in the *Tractatus*: "A thought is a proposition with sense." (4). And from this it seems reasonable to infer that if something is thinkable, then it is also expressible by means of a proposition with sense. Thus we have

(x) Expressibility by a proposition with sense is equivalent to thinkability.

And if this is right, then expressibility by a proposition with sense joins the other notions of imaginability, thinkability, and picturability in being both a sufficient and a necessary condition of logical possibility.

How would Wittgenstein handle the familiar objections to all this? Since he neither entertains nor addresses them, I'm not sure. Nevertheless, we do know that he is every bit as insistent as is Frege that psychological questions must not be mistaken for logical ones; and he is concerned, therefore, lest he himself fall into that very error.[4] So we must, if we are to be charitable, cast about for an interpretation that would enable him to avoid the problems.

Such an interpretation, I think, can only be this: that whenever Wittgenstein speaks of the possibility of our imagining, thinking, picturing, or expressing something, he means us to take quite literally his implied claim that the possibility in question (of imagining, of thinking, and so forth,) is *logical*. What I'm suggesting is that his claims that something—a world, a situation, a state of affairs, or whatnot—is imaginable, thinkable, picturable, or expressible amounts to the claims that it is *logically* possible for us to imagine, think of, picture, or express, it. If I'm correct, his answer to the standard objections might then be this: (a) that it is true that the powers of imagining, for example, that we *actually* possess are neither sufficient nor necessary conditions of logical possibility; (b) that there nevertheless are possible worlds in which these powers of ours are on a par with those of an omniscient being; and (c) that, in these worlds, what we can imagine, think, picture, or express as being the case is indeed coextensive with what is (logically) possibly the case. What is thinkable, imaginable, picturable, or expressible, then, is what is thinkable, imaginable, picturable, or expressible from a God's-eye point of view, not from the point of view of finite human beings. Given a God's-eye point of view, there is sound warrant for my assumption, in section 4 and elsewhere, that the imaginary worlds of which he writes in passages such as 2.022 and 6.1233 are, for Wittgenstein, genuinely possible—indeed logically possible—worlds.

6. Wittgenstein's Second-Degree Possibilism

To be a second-degree possibilist, it will be remembered, is to suppose that there are at least some complex objects which, though possible, are not actual. Prima facie evidence that Wittgenstein is a possibilist of the second degree, not just the first, is provided by some of Wittgenstein's statements about complex objects.

In most instances, Wittgenstein merely describes complex objects without naming them. But in a few cases he does assign names to them or says that names might be given to them. Examples are: Socrates (*NB* 69(9)), a landscape, the dance of motes in the air (*NB* 53(4)), a watch (*NB* 60(9)), and a book (*NB* 60(2)). Presumably, all these are intended as examples of complex objects that actually exist. How about possible complex objects that do *not* actually exist? No clear-cut examples are forthcoming in the *Notebooks* or the *Tractatus*. But elsewhere, in his later work, the *Philosophical Investigations* (p. 39), he gives an example which will suit our purposes, that of the fictional sword Excalibur.

Excalibur, he points out, "consists of parts combined in a particular way." Hence it is a complex object. And these parts are such that, as he puts it, "If they are combined differently Excalibur does not exist." Now, of course, Excalibur is only a fictional, nonactual, possible object. Even so, Wittgenstein says, "it is clear that the sentence 'Excalibur has a sharp blade' makes *sense* whether Excalibur is still whole or is broken up." Yet his position, in the *Philosophical Investigations* and the

Tractatus alike, is that a sentence or proposition makes sense only if it asserts the existence of a possible state of affairs, whether or not that state of affairs "is actually the case" (*NB* 27(2)).[5] Hence, since the proposition "Excalibur has a sharp blade" mentions the complex object, Excalibur, there must be a possible, though nonactual, state of affairs in which Excalibur both exists and has the property of having a sharp blade.

To be sure, this is not exactly the conclusion that Wittgenstein himself draws when he discusses the sword Excalibur in this passage. Rather he uses the Excalibur case to illustrate the dual errors of supposing that only simple objects can be named and of supposing that a name can have no meaning unless its bearer "still" exists. Nevertheless, the Excalibur example is relevant for our purposes insofar as it can also be used, as I have used it, to illustrate a more general point, namely, that the actual existence of an object at *any* time seems not to be a necessary condition of the possible existence of that object or of that object's being assigned a name. After all, "Excalibur" is (that is, functions as) a name; there are imaginable circumstances in which the proposition "Excalibur has a sharp blade" would be true; and these circumstances would be ones in which Excalibur would exist. Yet Excalibur does not (now) exist. Excalibur, then, would seem to be a prima facie example of a nonactual complex object whose existence, in some nonactual state of affairs, commits Wittgenstein to second-degree possibilism.

This conclusion is supported not only by the above passages from the *Philosophical Investigations*. It is also supported by both the *Notebooks* and the *Tractatus*.

In the first place, consider his *Notebooks* claim: "The propositional sign guarantees the possibility of the fact which it presents (not, that this fact is actually the case) . . ." (*NB* 27(2)). It has obvious implications for a proposition such as

(4) Excalibur has a sharp blade.

As we have seen, this proposition is one that, in the *Philosophical Investigations* (p. 39), he says "makes sense". And its sense guarantees the possibility, but not the actuality, of the state of affairs that would make (4) true. But the possible nonactual state of affairs that would make (4) true would have to be a state of affairs in which Excalibur existed. Yet Excalibur does not actually exist. Therefore, Excalibur is a nonactual possible object.

Second, consider his Tractarian claim: "A proposition that mentions a complex will not be nonsensical, if the complex does not exist, but simply false." (3.24). Proposition (4) is obviously one that mentions a complex. Hence, proposition (4) will not be nonsensical but will retain its sense even if Excalibur (the complex object mentioned in that proposition) does not in fact exist. Excalibur would not exist if, for example, no simple objects were ever brought together in the actual world in just that way which is constitutive of the fictional sword of King Arthur. We can imagine that Merlin had plans to make such a sword and even that he named the sword of his dreams "Excalibur", but never actually got around to making it. The nonexistence, in the actual world, of that particular combination of simple objects that would have been Excalibur, had Merlin carried through on his project, renders proposition (4) "simply false". Yet the proposition itself retains its *sense*, since there is a possible but nonactual world in which the complex object, Excalibur, exists and has a sharp blade. Once more, then, Wittgenstein is committed to second-degree possibilism.

7. Wittgenstein's Third-Degree Possibilism

Does it make sense, according to Wittgenstein, to imagine worlds in which there are simple objects that do not exist in ours?

Again the answer is surely, Yes. For the existence of such worlds certainly is within the bounds of our imaginative powers; hence their existence (by the argument of section 5) is logically possible.

It is sometimes suggested, however, that certain of Wittgenstein's retrospective comments on the *Tractatus* presuppose that he had there held that the *only* cases in which it makes sense to speak of imagining as existing an object that in fact does not exist are cases in which the object concerned is a complex one; that what we are doing when we imagine such a nonexistent complex object as existing is to imagine that certain actually existing simple elements were combined to produce that complex; and that we therefore cannot imagine a nonexistent simple object as existing. For instance, in *The Blue Book*, Wittgenstein writes:

> Supposing we asked: "how can one imagine what does not exist?" The answer seems to be: "If we do, we imagine non-existent combinations of existing elements." . . . . "But can't we imagine an object utterly different from any one which exists?"—We should be inclined to answer: "No; the elements, individuals, must exist. If redness, roundness and sweetness did not exist, we could not imagine them". (p. 31)

But this passage settles nothing. Note, first of all, that he is not putting forward a *doctrine* on the matter (something that the post-*Tractatus* Wittgenstein liked to avoid), but is merely making the simple observation that this is something "we should be inclined to answer" (though he himself neither asserts nor defends that answer). Secondly, the reference to "redness, roundness and sweetness" shows that Wittgenstein isn't here addressing the question at issue, namely, whether one can imagine an *object* to exist if in fact it does not. To say that one cannot imagine the nonexistence of putative simple *properties* (such as redness, roundness, or sweetness) is beside the point. He led us to expect an answer to a question about objects; but what he gives us is an answer which we would be "inclined" to give to a question about properties. True, this passage from *The Blue Book* raises some further questions: Does he intend us to take such properties as *among* the metaphysically simple objects of his Tractarian ontology? Does he, as some have argued, hold that they just *are* those metaphysically simple objects? Does Wittgenstein, at least in retrospect, think that simple properties are, in some sense, necessary existents? But these issues are left unanswered. And in any case they obviously do not bear on our present concern, namely, whether nonactual simple *objects* (in that contrastive sense of "objects" that excludes properties and relations) can be imagined, that is, whether they are, as we ordinarily think they are, logically possible.

A second objection to the supposition that Wittgenstein thought there might be simple objects in other worlds that do not exist in ours derives from the standard supposition that 2.022 and 2.023 implicitly claim the contrary. In these passages, Wittgenstein claims that all possible worlds have a form in common and that the simple objects that exist in the actual world are what "constitute" this form. Do these claims entail that all worlds have the same objects? Since the view that they do has achieved some prominence in the literature, it deserves more than passing comment; so I'll defer consideration of it until section 9 where I'll deal with it in detail.

So, back to the main question: Is there any unequivocal textual evidence, in Wittgenstein's early work, that he thought there could be, in other possible worlds, objects or things that do not exist in ours?

At one point, in the *Notebooks*, Wittgenstein uses the expressions "possible relations" and "possible things" in such a way as to suggest that there are indeed some possible relations that are not exemplified in the actual world and some possible things that do not exist in the actual world. He is talking about the conditions in which both a proposition of the form "xRy", and the possible state of affairs with which it is correlated can be said to be "of like sense" (as opposed to being "of opposite sense"). A proposition of the form "xRy" will be of like sense to a state of affairs, he claims, when the names "x" and "y" are correlated with the things x and y to which they refer, the symbol "R" is correlated with one of the possible relations which holds between the things x and y, and the possible state of affairs with which "xRy" as a whole is correlated is one in which x and y stand in the relation R. "In this way", he writes, "I extract from all possible relations the relation R, as by a name, I extract its meaning [reference] from among all possible things." (*NB* 99(1)). I take him to be saying that just as any proposition with sense is correlated with a possible, but perhaps nonactual, state of affairs, so any name or relational expression occurring in such a proposition is correlated with a possible, but perhaps nonactual, thing or relation.

That this is indeed how he thinks of matters to do with possible existence is shown conclusively by some of the things that Wittgenstein says about the multiplicity of possible worlds. He obviously thought that there are infinitely many worlds that a god might create. This follows from the fact that for any number n, greater than one (or possibly, two), it seems that Wittgenstein would allow for worlds containing that number of objects.

Thus, at one extreme, he envisages a world containing only one object: "if for example the world consisted of only one thing and of nothing else, could we say that there was ONE thing?" (*NB* 11(7)). True, this seems not to accord with his insistence, in *Tractatus* 2.01, that possible worlds involve states of affairs, and that each state of affairs consists of "a *combination* [emphasis added] of objects (things)." But, be that as it may, he certainly does allow, in the *Notebooks*, for worlds that meet all the requirements of Tractarian worlds but have fewer objects than does the actual world. For instance, he allows for worlds consisting of just *two* things: "Let us suppose, e.g., that the world consisted of the things A and B and the property F, and that F(A) were the case and not F(B)." (*NB* 14(4)). Such worlds, he clearly supposes, are genuinely possible even though, by comparison with the actual world, they are object-impoverished.

Then, at the other extreme, he envisages worlds consisting of infinitely many objects. In a passage that expands upon 6.1233 (quoted in section 4), he criticizes Russell by writing:

> it is for physics to say *whether anything exists*. The same holds of the infinity axiom; whether there are [*aleph* $_0$] things is for experience to settle (and experience can't decide it). But now for your reducibility axiom: Imagine our living in a world, where there is nothing but *things*, and besides *only one relation*, which holds between *infinitely many of these things* [emphasis added], but does not hold between every one and every other of them: further it never holds between a finite number of things. It is clear that the axiom of reducibility would certainly *not* hold in such a world. But it is also clear to me that it is not for logic to decide whether the world we live in is actually like this or not. (*NB* 127)

Clearly, then, Wittgenstein does allow for possible worlds consisting of precisely n things where n is any number greater than one. (I take it that, for Wittgenstein, a "world" containing no objects would not be a world at all.) Hence, he allows for infinitely many different worlds, worlds that are different from one another with respect to the number of objects they contain.

Now it is surely obvious that the actual world contains more objects than some others; that is, that some worlds are *object-impoverished* by way of comparison with the actual world; or, to put it conversely, that the actual world is *object-enriched* by way of comparison with some other possible worlds. But are there any worlds in comparison with which the actual world itself is object-impoverished, worlds that are object-enriched in comparison with the actual world? Are there, to put the question in David Lewis's now-fashionable locution, any possible worlds some of whose objects are "alien" to ours?

Wittgenstein nowhere addresses this question directly. Nevertheless, his answer to it can be inferred from the fact that he treats the question itself as a logically open one.

Consider, once more, the passage from 6.1233 (quoted in section 4) and its more expansive treatment in *NB* 127 (quoted four paragraphs back). The thought behind these passages is probably what forced Russell's admission that, for any number n, it is a wholly contingent matter as to whether the actual world contains n objects. Wittgenstein is giving his grounds for rejecting Russell's supposition that the infinity and reducibility axioms are propositions of logic. In both cases, his point is that it is a *logically open* (and, for that matter, an experientially undecidable) question whether the world in which we live is composed of infinitely many objects or not. But that can be true only if it is a logically open question whether there are worlds that are object-enriched by way of comparison with the actual world, worlds that contain objects "alien" to our world.

It is worth dwelling on the implications. The question can be a logically open one only if it is possible that the actual world should contain only a finite number of objects, and hence only if it is possible that there should be worlds containing more objects than exist in the actual world. It matters not how many objects the actual world *in fact* contains. If the question is a logically open one, then it has to be logically possible for there to be worlds that contain more objects than does ours. In envisaging such a possibility, Wittgenstein is envisaging the possibility of worlds that, in comparison with the actual world, are object-enriched. But to imagine that there are such worlds is nothing other than to imagine that there are worlds which contain nonactual possible objects. In imagining such worlds Wittgenstein is subscribing to third-degree possibilism.

8. Wittgenstein's General Argument for Possibilism

In both *NB* 98(2) and the parallel 5.123, Wittgenstein claims that if a god creates a world in which a certain proposition is true, then he thereby ensures that all the propositions which follow from the given proposition will be true (as he puts it) "in" that world. And he goes on to say (as a corollary) that a god could not create a world in which a proposition "p" is true without creating all its constituent objects (that is, without creating all the objects which feature in the states of affairs which would make the proposition true).

What sorts of propositions does he have in mind? The passage from the *Notebooks* restricts these to the fields of logic and mathematics. But that from the *Tractatus* does not. Rather, he allows in 5.123 for any contingent proposition whatever—any proposition, that is, which "has a sense"—to be such that God could make it true in some world or other. That, at any rate, seems to be what he is getting at when he writes: "It used to be said that God could create anything except what would be contrary to the laws of logic." (3.031(a)). True, he goes on to express this point in a theologically neutral way by explaining: "The reason being that we could not *say* what an 'illogical' world would look like." (3.031(b)). But the essential point remains the same. Whatever is not contrary to the laws of logic is possible. Any world, state of affairs, or object the supposition of whose existence does not involve a violation of the laws of logic is something God could have chosen to create. And any contingent proposition, about any object whatever, is one God could choose to make true in a world of his creation.

Here, in these passages, Wittgenstein enunciates principles that commit him to all three degrees of possibilism. This becomes clear when we apply his principles to the following propositions:

(5) Alvin Plantinga was the first climber to conquer Mt. Everest.
(6) There are twenty planets in our solar system.
(7) There are $n + 1$ elementary particles in the universe (where n = the number of elementary particles which in fact populate the universe).

Plainly, since there is no contradiction involved in any of these propositions, 3.031(a) commits Wittgenstein to saying that we can infer that worlds in which (5), (6) and (7) are true, are all possible. And if that is so, then, according to 5.123, all the propositions that *follow* from (5), (6), and (7) will be true in those worlds, including propositions asserting (or, as some would prefer, presupposing)[6] the existence of whatever objects are mentioned in (5), (6), and (7). But worlds in which (5), (6), and (7) are true are worlds in which there are (in the unrestricted sense of "are", of course) "additional" states of affairs, "additional" complex objects, and "additional" putative simple objects (elementary particles), respectively. The conjunction of 3.031(a) with 5.123, then, commits Wittgenstein to all three degrees of possibilism.

We can run the argument through again with the additional help of his claim: "A proposition constructs a world with the help of a logical scaffolding, so that one can actually see from the proposition how everything stands in logic *if* it is true. One can *draw inferences* from a false proposition." (4.023(5)). This passage is, in effect, an elaboration of the first sentence of 5.123, namely, 5.123(a), which allows us to suppose that propositions such as (5), (6), and (7) are true "in" certain of the worlds that a god might create. Which worlds? 4.023(5) implies that, at the very least, they are worlds in which all the propositions that follow from (5), (6), and (7) are also true.

Now propositions (5), (6), and (7), of course, are all false in the actual world. But this does not matter. As 4.023(5) points out, one can draw inferences from false propositions as well as from true ones. Hence there must be worlds which each of these false propositions "construct", nonactual possible worlds in which all the propositions that follow from each of these false propositions "come true" (as Wittgenstein put it). But (and here is the crucial point), as 5.123(b) makes clear, there cannot be such worlds unless there also exist, in those worlds, whatever objects are "constituents" (*NB* 98(2)) of the propositions that come true in them. And these objects, as we have already seen, must surely include nonactual ones of all three possibilistic degrees: nonactual states of affairs in worlds in which (5) is true; nonactual complex objects in worlds in which (6) is true; and nonactual (putatively) simple objects in worlds in which (7) is true.

Some critics, however, might object that Wittgenstein simply would not allow any putative propositions about nonactual objects to count as among those that a god might make true in some world or other. They would cite Wittgenstein's claim, in 3.203, that "A name means an object. The object is its meaning." And from this they would infer that, in the case of a nonactual object, any putative name, such as "Excalibur", must lack a meaning, and hence any putative proposition such as

(4) Excalibur has a sharp blade

in which that putative name occurs must also lack a meaning. Putative propositions about nonactual objects, they would say, simply don't count as genuine ones; hence the principles behind 5.123 just do not apply.

I have two main points to make in reply.

First, the objection assumes that when Wittgenstein says that the meaning of a name is an object, he means an actual object. But that is to beg the question. After all, so far as naming is concerned, the question at issue is whether Wittgenstein allows for the possibility of names being assigned, in other worlds or our own, to objects which don't exist in our own. As to that, I argued in Chapter I, section 4, that Wittgenstein's doctrine of naming is not a doctrine about how *we*, in the actual world, assign names to objects (since we obviously don't assign them to any simple objects that occur in the actual world), but rather is about the *possibility* of names being assigned to objects (simple as well as complex) by some namer or other (a "god", perhaps). (Recall his claim: "*we* cannot analyze propositions so far as to mention the elements by name" (*NB* 62(10).) And I have also argued, earlier in this chapter, that Wittgenstein does in fact treat, as making sense, propositions containing names of objects that don't exist in the actual world.

Second, I deliberately chose the propositions (5), (6), and (7) in order to circumvent any such objection as the one we are considering. I concede that the objection has some prima facie (but only prima facie) plausibility against the argument that applies 5.123 to proposition (4). At least that proposition does contain a name ("Excalibur") which has no bearer in the actual world. But the objection gets no purchase whatever on (5), (6), or (7). In (5), a name (the name "Alvin Plantinga") does occur; but it is the name of an actual object. As for (6) and (7), these propositions do not contain any names whatever. (The expression "the solar system" is the description, not the name, of a certain complex object. In any case, the object to which that description refers is an actual one.) Yet (6) and (7) refer to objects. And since they are propositions with sense, they must be such that a god could create worlds in which they are true, worlds, therefore, in which the objects to which they refer do exist, even though these objects do not exist in the actual world.

To sum up, then, the preceding general argument from 5.123 provides conclusive evidence that Wittgenstein was indeed committed to all three degrees of possibilism.

9. The Form of All Possible Worlds

The view that Wittgenstein is a possibilist, however, is inconsistent with what I have called the "standard interpretation" of the things Wittgenstein says, in the *Tractatus*, about the form that is common to all possible worlds. His precise words are: "It is obvious that an imagined world, however different it may be from the real one, must have *something*—a form—in common with it. Objects are just what constitute this unalterable form." (2.022–2.023).

Now, as F. P. Ramsey pointed out, in his insightful "Review of *Tractatus*", the following are evident:

(a) that Wittgenstein is here envisaging a multitude of possible worlds other than the real one;
(b) that Wittgenstein is claiming that all such worlds have a common form;
(c) that Wittgenstein believes this form to be somehow "constituted" by the simple objects that exist in these worlds.

However, according to Ramsey, and most other Tractarian commentators who have considered the matter, Wittgenstein also believed the following:

(d) that precisely the *same* set of simple objects is to be found in each of these possible worlds; that is, that the set of all possible worlds is *object- homogeneous*;
(e) that the form which all worlds have in common is to be *identified* with this single set of objects.

The conjunction of (a) through (e) comprises what I have called the standard (Ramseian) interpretation.[7]

I agree about (a), (b), and (c). But I disagree about (d) and (e).

As against (d), we saw in the previous section: (i) that, in the *Notebooks*, Wittgenstein portrays some worlds as having fewer, and others as having more, objects than does the actual world; and (ii) that, in the *Tractatus*, thesis 5.123 provides a general warrant for asserting that other possible worlds may contain objects that don't exist in ours. Both in the *Notebooks* and in the *Tractatus*, then, he regards possible worlds as *object-heterogeneous*. But from this it follows that he cannot without inconsistency also hold that the form of all possible worlds consists in a common set of objects. For, if possible worlds are object-heterogeneous, there is no such set.

In order to reinforce this conclusion, let's consider one of the implications of taking 5.123 seriously. Surely, if 5.123 is true then among the possible worlds that God might choose to create are ones populated by what Lycan [1979] has called "irreducibly spiritual objects" such as "ghosts, monads, or Cartesian egos." (p. 306). Indeed, there seems no logical reason to suppose that God should not create a world or worlds populated *solely* by such nonphysical entities. (Isn't Heaven supposed to be just such a place?) Yet it is evident that the actual world, in Wittgenstein's view, is *not* a purely spiritual, nonphysical one. If it were, then Newtonian mechanics could not—contrary to 6.341—offer "a possibility of describing the world"; the laws of physics could not—contrary to 6.3431—"still speak, however indirectly, about objects in the world"; and the impossibility of the simultaneous presence of two colors at the same place in the visual field, could not—contrary to 6.3751—be shown by what he calls "the analysis of physics"(*NB* 82(12). Evidently, then, Wittgenstein holds that at least some objects in the actual world are physical ones. But if there are other possible worlds that don't contain any physical objects, then the form which the actual world has in common with these other possible worlds cannot consist in a common set of objects.

In short, the consequence of accepting the standard interpretation of 2.022–2.023 is that Wittgenstein must then stand convicted of inconsistency. Surely this suggests the need for a more careful examination of what Wittgenstein means by "form".

Thus, in opposition to (e), I'll argue that the form that is common to all possible worlds consists in the set of *possibilities* generated by the set of all objects, that is, by the set of all possible objects, that is, by the union of the sets of actual objects and nonactual but possible objects. Note that this set is not to be identified with the set of all possible worlds. This set of possibilities has, as its members, possible combinations of possible objects, that is, possible states of affairs; the set of all possible worlds has, as its members, maximally consistent sets of possible states of affairs.

Finally, I'll argue that this set of possibilities is best understood in terms of the system of modal logic, S5. That logic, as it turns out, characterizes the *form* of every possibility, and hence of every possible world, within logical space.

Note, first of all, that the standard account treats 2.022 as if it claimed expressly that all possible worlds had the same *objects* in common. Yet this is not what

Wittgenstein actually *says*. What he in fact says is only that they have a *form* in common. To be sure, in the immediately succeeding passages he tells us that objects "constitute" (2.023) the form of all possible worlds, or "determine" (2.0231) this form. But these claims wouldn't make sense if objects were *identical* with form. If Wittgenstein had meant to assert that all possible worlds have the same objects in common, why didn't he say just that—or say, equivalently, that all possible worlds have the same "substance"? The fact is that he didn't say either of these things, for the fairly obvious reason that the objects which make up the world are the *substance* of the world (2.021), and the *form* of a world is not at all the same as its substance.

The standard account assumes that the object-homogeneity of all possible worlds follows immediately from the conjunction of 2.022 and 2.023. Yet such an inference is far too quick. Not only does it neglect the fact that what Wittgenstein actually tells us is that it is a common "form"—not a common set of objects—that all possible worlds share. It also neglects the fact that, quite generally, Wittgenstein regards the notion of form as equivalent to a set of *possibilities*. And it neglects the fact that a set of objects may generate, or "constitute", a set of possibilities common to all possible worlds without the objects themselves being common to those worlds in the way that the doctrine of object-homogeneity envisages.[8]

Let's therefore take a more careful look at how Wittgenstein uses the notion of form. At one point or another he attributes form, or formal properties, to each of the main items in his ontological catalogue: objects (2.0141, 2.0233, 2.0251); states of affairs (2.033); facts (5.156); pictures (2.15, 2.151); propositions (4.5, 5.47); reality (2.18); language and the world (6.12); and imagined worlds (2.022). What, in *these* instances (as opposed to others less pertinent to our present concerns), does he mean by "form"?

For two of these instances, states of affairs (2.032 and 2.033) and pictures (2.15), he takes pains explicitly to define "form" as "the possibility of structure". So we may infer:

> (i) For any item, X, which has structure, the form of X consists in the possibility of X's structure.

These passages also make clear what he means by "structure". The structure of something is simply the way that thing is put together. It is the "determinate connection of objects or elements." So we may infer:

> (ii) For any item, X, which has structure, the structure of X consists in the determinate connection of X's elements.

And, from (i) and (ii), we are entitled to infer:

> (iii) For any item, X, which has structure, the form of X consists in the possibility of the determinate connection of X's elements.

This definition of "form", however, is too restrictive. It holds only for those items, complex ones, that have structure. It does not give sense to the notion of form for the case in which an item has no constituent elements and a fortiori has no structure. In short, it does not encompass the case of *simple* objects. Yet Wittgenstein wants to say that a simple object, too, has a form.

In what, then, does the form of a simple object consist? Wittgenstein's answer is: "The possibility of its occurring in states of affairs is the form of an object." (2.0141). Thus we may infer:

> (iv) For any item X, which has no structure, the form of X consists in the possibility of the determinate connection of X with other elements.

Finally, abstracting from (iii) and (iv) so as to obtain the notion of form in general, we may conclude:

> (v) For any item, X, the *form* of X consists in the *possibility* of determinate combination of the elements of X, or of X with other elements (objects).

Now the forms of simple objects, for Wittgenstein, have logical primacy over the forms of complex items in the sense that the forms of simple objects *determine* the forms of all those other sorts of entities that have simple objects as their ultimate constituents: states of affairs; situations; facts; pictures; propositions; worlds; and so on. At one point he writes: "If all objects are given, then at the same time all *possible* states of affairs are also given." (2.0124). His thinking is that the form of a simple object determines the possible combinations into which that object can enter. Hence, if we were given all possible objects—and therewith, of course, the essential *forms* of these objects—we would thereby be given all the possibilities of combinations of objects, that is, all possible states of affairs. There is, then, a set of possibilities, namely, the set of all possible combinations of objects, that is "given" or "constituted" by the set of all possible objects. And since, by (v), the set of all possibilities of combination of objects constitutes a form, the question naturally arises as to what this form is a form of. I suggest that, provided we take the set of objects concerned to be the set of all *possible* objects, not just the set of all actual ones, the set of their possible combinations is equivalent to the form that all possible worlds have in common.

According to my interpretation of 2.022 and 2.023, then, when Wittgenstein tells us that objects "constitute" the unalterable form that is common to all worlds, real or imagined, he intends us to understand (in addition to (a), (b), and (c)) the following:

> (f) that the objects of which he is speaking are not just those that exist in the actual world, but are whatever objects exist in any possible world, that is, they are *possible* objects;
> (g) that the form of which he is speaking is the set of possibilities of combination generated by the members of the set of possible objects.

Reasons for insisting, in clause (f), that the objects referred to in 2.023 should be taken to include nonactual, merely possible, objects along with all the actual ones, are provided by *NB* 98(2) and 5.123 (discussed in the previous section).

In any case, the need for clause (f) becomes especially clear when we consider clause (g). For only if we admit the existence, in other possible worlds, of objects that do not exist in ours can we allow for the full plenitude of merely possible states of affairs that intuition licenses: states of affairs such as that of Wittgenstein's being the father of two children, that of there being more elementary particles or molecules in the universe than there actually are, that of Excalibur's having a sharp blade, that of Sherlock Holmes's sniffing cocaine, and so on. Indeed, it follows from his claim that it is "essential to things that they should be possible constituents of states of affairs" (2.011) that, if there are any merely possible objects such as Wittgenstein's children, extra particles, Excalibur, or Sherlock Holmes, these objects *must* be able to combine with others in states of affairs such as those we have envisaged. And the possibilities of their so combining must then be included within the set of all possibilities that constitute the form of which Wittgenstein speaks in 2.022.

From the God's-eye point of view that Wittgenstein adopts in both the *Notebooks* and the *Tractatus*, there is a single set of possibilities (of combinations of objects) which is, so to speak, common to all possible worlds.[9] This is the set of possible combinations of possible, not just actual, objects. Clearly, the set of combinatorial possibilities generated by all possible objects is wider than that generated by actual objects only: wide enough to encompass both the combinatorial possibilities generated within object-impoverished worlds and those generated within object-enriched worlds. Since Wittgenstein countenances object-heterogeneous worlds of both sorts, I conclude that, for him, the all-encompassing set of possibilities generated, or "constituted", by the members of the set of all possible objects *is identical with* the unalterable form that any imaginable world has in common with the real one. The conjunction of 2.022 and 2.023, therefore, poses no threat to my claim that, in both works, Wittgenstein espouses all three degrees of possibilism.

10. S5, the Logic of Wittgenstein's Metaphysics

It is clear that, for Wittgenstein, the possibilities which constitute the common form of all possible worlds are, like all possibilities, *logical* possibilities. This follows from his claim: "Just as the only necessity that exists is logical necessity; so too the only impossibility that exists is logical impossibility." (6.375). This is why he claims: "Logic deals with every possibility, and all possibilities are its facts." (2.0121(3)). The question then arises: *Which* logic—that is to say, which logical system—is it that "deals with every possibility"? Wittgenstein himself does not say. But it is clear that it cannot be, as is commonly supposed, the truth-functional logic that Russell and Whitehead, following in Frege's footsteps, had devised. Rather, if it is to deal with the modal notion of possibility, it must be a *modal* logic.

I don't know how much, if anything, Wittgenstein knew about the modal logics that some of his contemporaries—Hugh MacColl [1908] and C. I. Lewis [1918], for example—were working out in the early part of the century. And it may well be that, even if he did know something of their work, he was inclined to dismiss (or even disparage) it[10] in the same way as did Russell.[11] Be that as it may, Wittgenstein's general theory of propositional significance commits him to the modal logic that was designated, by Lewis, as "S5".

The system S5 is just one of many modal logics. This is not the place to discuss these logics in detail or to trace out their interconnections. But for those who are

unfamiliar with the field, or need their memories refreshed, the following sketch
might help.

There are many ways of constructing S5. One is to start with some axiomatiza-
tion of truth-functional propositional logic; for example, that presented by Russell
and Whitehead in *Principia Mathematica* (the axiomatic system hereafter referred to
as PM). The system PM has five axioms (of which the fourth was subsequently
shown to be dispensable since it could be derived as a theorem from the other four):

(A1) $((P \vee P) \supset P)$
(A2) $(Q \supset (P \vee Q))$
(A3) $((P \vee Q) \supset (Q \vee P))$
(A4) $((P \vee (Q \vee R)) \supset (Q \vee (P \vee R)))$
(A5) $((Q \supset R) \supset ((P \vee Q) \supset (P \vee R)))$

It also has two rules of inference for deriving the theorems of the system: the Rule of
Uniform Substitution[12]; and the Rule of Modus Ponens (or Detachment).[13] Together, the axioms and the theorems constitute the "theses" of PM. Provably, the
system is complete: its theses embrace all and only the tautologies of truth-
functional propositional logic.

In order to construct S5 on the basis of PM (or some deductively equivalent
system), we need first to enrich our logical vocabulary. PM uses symbols for the
truth-functional concepts of negation, "∼", conjunction, ".", disjunction, "v", material implication, "⊃", and material equivalence, "≡". To these we add symbols
for one or more of the modal concepts: for instance, "□" (or "L") for necessity,
"◇" (or "M") for possibility, or "∇" (or "Q") for contingency.[14] Then to the existing
axioms and rules of our basis we add one or more modal axioms and rules of
inference so as to generate one or other of a series of progressively stronger systems
of modal logic. If we add the Rule of Necessitation,[15] and the axioms

(A6) $\Box P \supset P$

and

(A7) $\Box (P \supset Q) \supset (\Box P \supset \Box Q)$

then we obtain von Wright's system M (a system which is deductively equivalent to
Fey's system T). If to M we add the axiom

(A8) $\Box P \supset \Box \Box P$

we obtain C. I. Lewis's system S4; whereas if to M we add the axiom

(A9) $\Diamond P \supset \Box \Diamond P$

we obtain Lewis's system S5 (within which (A8), and hence S4, can be derived).
Alternatively, we can obtain S5 from M by adding the axiom

(A10) $\sim \nabla \nabla P$

In the view of many philosopher-logicians, S5 is the system that best captures the
Leibnizian notions of logical necessity, possibility, contingency, and so forth, as
well as the notion of logical (as distinct from material) implication.

I will demonstrate Wittgenstein's commitment to the modal system S5 in two stages: first, by showing that he is committed to axioms (A6) and (A7), and hence to system M; second, by showing that he is also committed to axioms (A9) and (A10), the addition of either of which yields S5.

It would be difficult to find a proposition of modal logic whose truth was more analytically obvious than that expressed by axiom (A6), namely, " □ P ⊃ P". What (A6), on interpretation, expresses—or, as Wittgenstein would put it, "shows"—is that if a proposition is broadly tautologous or necessarily true, in the sense of being "true for all the truth-possibilities of the elementary propositions" (4.46), then it is true in the actual world.[16] The elementary propositions to which he is referring here, of course, are just those propositions that he sets out, in nonstandard fashion, on the left-hand side of the truth-table schemas presented in 4.31, namely,

p	q	r		p	q		p
T	T	T		T	T		T
F	T	T		F	T		F
T	F	T		T	F		
T	T	F		F	F		
F	F	T					
F	T	F					
T	F	F					
F	F	F					

But as he points out, in 5.31, "The schemata in 4.31 have a meaning even when 'p', 'q', 'r', etc., are not elementary propositions." We can therefore drop the reference in 4.46 to elementary propositions and interpret the truth-possibilities in these schemata as either elementary or nonelementary. A necessary truth, then, is simply one which is true for all truth-possibilities. But by "truth-possibilities" he just means "possibilities of existence and nonexistence [of states of affairs]" (4.27). Hence he is saying, in 4.46, that a proposition is necessarily true just if it is true for all possible combinations of states of affairs, that is, for all possible worlds. And since one of those possible combinations of states of affairs is that which constitutes the actual world, it follows that if a proposition is necessarily true, then it it is true in the actual world.

Axiom (A7), " □ (P ⊃ Q) ⊃ (□ P ⊃ □ Q)", on interpretation, tells us (or shows) that if a proposition P logically implies a proposition Q, then if P is necessarily true so is Q.[17] Consider, now, Wittgenstein's characterization of the *following from* relation. He writes: "In particular, the truth of 'p' follows from the truth of another proposition 'q' if all the truth-grounds of the latter are truth-grounds of the former." (5.12). Let's first rewrite 5.12 to make Wittgenstein's words mesh better with those I have used in interpreting axiom (A7). Then, substituting our "P" for his "q" and our "Q" for his "p", and making allowance for the fact that the following-from relation is the converse of the relation of logical implication, we obtain the following simplification of 5.12: "P logically implies Q if all the truth-grounds of P are truth-grounds of Q." Does Wittgenstein think that containment of P's truth-grounds in Q's are a necessary as well as a sufficient condition of P's logically implying Q? I think so. For 5.121, when given a parallel rewrite, makes the

equivalence clear: "The truth-grounds of the one [P] are contained in those of
the other [Q]: P logically implies Q." Thus 5.12 and 5.121 in conjunction yield the
conclusion that P logically implies Q if and only if the truth-grounds of P are
"contained" in the truth-grounds of Q. So far, so good. But what exactly does
Wittgenstein mean by "truth-grounds"? And in what sense can the truth-grounds of
one proposition be "contained" in those of another? The truth-grounds of a proposition, he tells us in 5.101, are "those truth-possibilities of its truth-arguments which
make it true." Hence, by 4.3, the truth-grounds of a proposition are the possible
states of affairs in which it is true. As to the second question, I think the answer can
only be this: that the truth-grounds of P are "contained" in those of Q just when the
set of possible state of affairs in which P is true is included in (is a subset, not
necessarily a proper subset, of) the set of possible states of affairs in which Q is
true.

Now axiom (A7) is logically equivalent[18] to

(A7)* $(\Box (P \supset Q) \, . \, \Box P) \supset \Box Q$

Hence another way of expressing axiom (A7) is to say that if a proposition P
logically implies a proposition Q *and* P is necessarily true, then so is Q. We are now
in a position to show that Wittgenstein is committed to (A7)*, and hence also to
(A7). For suppose, as in the antecedent of (A7)*, that P logically implies Q *and* that
P is necessarily true. Then from the second conjunct, the supposition that P is
necessarily true, it follows (given 4.46) that P will be "true for all truth-
possibilities", that is, will be true in all possible states of affairs. And from the first
conjunct, the supposition that P logically implies Q, it follows (given 5.121) that the
set of possible states of affairs in which P is true (P's truth-grounds, that is, the
truth-possibilities that make it true) is included in the set of possible states of affairs
in which Q is true (Q's truth-grounds). But if P is true in all possible states of affairs,
and the set of possible states of affairs in which it is true is included in the set of
possible states of affairs in which Q is true, then Q must also be true in all possible
states of affairs. Hence, from the antecedent of (A7)* we can infer its consequent,
viz., that Q is necessarily true. Wittgenstein is committed to (A7)*, hence to (A7),
and hence, given his previously established commitment to (A6), is committed to
the modal system M.

It remains for me now to demonstrate Wittgenstein's commitment to either, or
both, of axioms (A9) and (A10).

His commitment to (A9) can be read into a passage from the second page of the
Tractatus: "If I can imagine objects combined in states of affairs, I cannot imagine
them excluded from the *possibility* of such combinations." (2.0121(5)). Recall from
section 5 that, for Wittgenstein, all possibility is logical possibility, and that imaginability is both a sufficient and a necessary condition of logical possibility. Make
the appropriate substitutions of talk about logical possibility for talk about what can
be imagined, and alter syntax a little. We then obtain: "If it is logically possible that
objects should combine in such and such states of affairs, then it is logically
impossible that they should not possibly combine in such states of affairs."
(2.0121(5)*). Now, to say—as in the consequent of 2.0121(5)*—that it is logically
impossible that something not be the case, is to say that it is logically necessary that

it be the case. Hence, 2.0121(5)* is equivalent to, "If it is logically possible that objects should combine in such and such states of affairs, then it is logically necessary that it is logically possible that objects should combine in such states of affairs." (2.0121(5)**). But 2.0121(5)**, expressed in standard symbolism, is a thesis having the form of (A9): $\Diamond P \supset \Box \Diamond P$.[19]

What all this means, of course, is that in the very passage in which he is talking about the possibilities of objects combining in states of affairs—possibilities that, I argued earlier, "constitute" the form of all possible worlds—Wittgenstein makes a claim which, when it is taken together with his commitment to M, establishes his commitment to S5. It means, too, that for him S5 is the logic that all possible worlds have in common, the logic that pervades the whole of logical space.

Wittgenstein's commitment to the alternative axiom (A10) has been demonstrated by G. H. von Wright [1982]. Von Wright's case rests on the fact that Wittgenstein endorses each of the following theses: (a) A significant proposition, or "proposition with sense", is a contingent one, one that is both possibly true and possibly false. (b) P is a contingent proposition if and only if ~P is a contingent proposition. (c) Such facts as that a given proposition is contingent, that another is necessary, or that still another is a contradiction, are facts that cannot be "said" by contingent propositions but can only be "shown" by noncontingent ones. Theses (a) and (b) tell us, in effect, what is involved in Wittgenstein's talk about "propositions with sense". Thesis (c) tells us, in effect, that would-be assertions about the modal status of a proposition—attempts to say that they are contingent, necessary, or impossible—are always noncontingent, and hence not "sayable" in contingent propositions.

Evidence that Wittgenstein holds all three theses abounds, as von Wright shows. I shan't duplicate that evidence here, but will give my own independent evidence.

As to (a), Wittgenstein comes close to endorsing it explicitly when, in the course of a discussion of how propositions with sense, significant propositions, differ from tautologies, he writes: "In order for a proposition to be capable of being true it must also be capable of being false." (*NB* 55(7)). More generally, he holds that whereas with tautologies "every possibility is admitted in advance" (*NB* 55(8)), significant propositions allow certain possibilities and exclude others. To say this, of course, is just to say that significant propositions are always contingent.

As to (b), Wittgenstein expresses it in the form, "Just as we can see that ~P has no sense, if P has none; so we can also say P has none if ~P has none." (*NB* 117(5)). This is Wittgenstein's version of what has sometimes been called the Principle of Significant Negation.

As to (c), this is what Wittgenstein is getting at when he tells us, "The certainty, possibility, or impossibility of a situation is not expressed by a proposition, but by a proposition's being a tautology, a proposition with sense, or a contradiction" (5.525(2)). Given that a proposition with sense always expresses the possibility of (that is, the possible existence of) a situation or state of affairs, and that the existence or non-existence of a state of affairs is always accidental (something that "can be the case or not the case" (1.21)), it follows that a proposition with sense, that is, a contingent proposition, can never express a logical "fact" such as that this or that expression is a tautology or is a contradiction or even a proposition with sense. In short, contingent propositions can never say anything about the necessary truth, necessary falsity, or contingency of any other propositions. Noncontingent "pseudo-propositions", such as tautologies (in that broad sense of that word to which I drew attention in Chapter I, section 7) can show such logical facts. But contingent ones cannot. Thus, one of the consequences of (c) is that the contingency of a proposition P is always a noncontingent matter. But this consequence is just that which is expressed by axiom (A10), namely, $\sim \nabla \nabla P$.[20] And axiom (A10), when added to M, yields the modal system S5.

11. Problems about the Existence of Possibilia

We have seen that Wittgenstein believes, or at least is committed to believing, that in some sense or other "there are" or "there exist" possible worlds, possible states of affairs, and possible objects, that—by virtue of the fact that they are not identical with our world or any of its constituent states of affairs or objects—are nonactual. But what is this sense? Does it in fact make good philosophical sense to entertain a belief in mere possibilia?

Many contemporary philosophers, following Russell, claim that it doesn't make sense, or even that it is self-contradictory. It is very easy to argue that there can't be things which don't exist. One need only insist: (i) that all "There are . . ." or "There is . . ." statements should be treated as existence-claims, formalizable in predicate calculus by the existential quantifier "$(\exists x)$"; and (ii) that to say that something is nonactual is to say that it does not exist. It will then follow that the claim "There are some things which, though possible, are nonactual" is self-contradictory, a form of Wittgensteinian nonsense.

Equally, however, one need only reject either, or both, of (i) and (ii) to render such a claim self-consistent. And, on reflection, it is surely evident that neither (i) nor (ii) is a truth of logic. Their adoption is a notational convenience at best, a matter of entrenched dogma at worst. Does not the very fact that the regimentation of language by a currently preferred logical notation prevents us from saying things that are prima facie intelligible and true cast doubt on the expressive adequacy of that notation? Why should we insist, for instance, on recasting all "there are" statements as "there exist" statements? Why should we accept the strictures of a notation that demands that we express both sorts of statements in terms of a single existential quantifier "$(\exists x)$" and then go on to read the latter as ranging only over *actualia* ? Ought not our suspicions to be aroused by the fact that this sort of regimentation is precisely that insisted on by those who, like the early Russell, have a metaphysical axe to grind, those who, like him, want to inject a "realistic bias" into both metaphysics and logic? Is there any way in which we can coherently assert that there are indeed many things that do not really exist?

Two main strategies for avoiding even the appearance of contradiction have recently been explored. One is that adopted by contemporary defenders of Meinong, such as Richard Routley (now Richard Sylvan) and Terence Parsons. Their strategy—which allows us, if we like, to encompass impossibilia as well as possibilia and actualia—reads the existential quantifier "(∃x)" as "There are" or "For some" and introduces an existence-predicate, "E" or "E!", to mean "There exists". As against those who still think that Kant's doctrine "Existence is not a predicate" is somehow sacrosanct, they would point out that what Kant in fact argued was only that "existence" is not a "real" or "determining", that is, not an ordinary predicate.[21] On their accounts, formulae such as Routley's "∼(x) E(x)" and Parsons's "(∃x) ∼E!x" are self-consistent. They read them in English as "some things don't exist" and "there are things which don't exist", respectively (a difference that makes no difference). For both Routley and Parsons, the so-called existential quantifier "(∃x)" ranges not only over things which exist in the actual world (actualia) but also over things that exist in other possible worlds (mere possibilia), and even—much more radically—over things that do not exist in any possible world (impossibilia).

The neo-Meinongian's strategy can be diagrammed thus (where "there are" is symbolized as "(∃x)" and "there exist" as "Ex" or "E!x"):

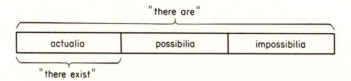

In effect, Routley and Parsons reject (i) while retaining (ii). They want to say that "there are" all sorts of entities or "objects" ("*Gegenstand*", as Meinong called them) that do not exist or even subsist (subsistence, for Meinong, being the mode of being which belongs to things like properties and relations). After all, they would say, we can refer to both possibilia and impossibilia alike and can readily provide examples of each. So there are such objects (of reference). Nevertheless, such objects are not actual. And since, for neo-Meinongians, actuality is one and the same as existence, they conclude that there are these nonactual objects that don't "exist".

A second strategy is to accept (i) but reject (ii). That, in effect, is David Lewis's way. In his "Counterpart Theory and Quantified Modal Logic" [1986] he allows both the English expressions "There are" and "There exist" to be symbolized by the existential quantifier "(∃x)". But he interprets the latter unrestrictedly, as ranging over all possible objects, and introduces an actuality-predicate "A" for those restricted cases in which we want to talk only about those objects that exist in the actual world. As he explains, in his *Counterfactuals* :

> Our idioms of existential quantification may be used to range over everything without exception, or they may be tacitly restricted in various ways. In particular, they may be restricted to our own world and things within it. . . . It would be convenient if there were only one idiom of quantification, say "there are . . .", that was firmly reserved for the unrestricted use and another, say "there actually exist . . .", that was firmly reserved for the restricted use. Unfortunately, even these two idioms of quantification can be used either way; and thus one can pass indecisively from equivocating on one to equivocating on another. All the same, there are the two uses . . . and we need only to keep track of them to see that the argument [against possibilia] is fallacious. (p. 185)

As for the neo-Meinongian claim that "there are" impossibilia as well as possibilia and actualia, Lewis retorts that there neither are nor do there exist any such things as impossibilia.

The second strategy, then, can be diagrammed thus (where both "there are" and "there exists" are symbolized as "$(\exists x)$" and "there actually exist" is symbolized as "$(\exists x)Ax$"):

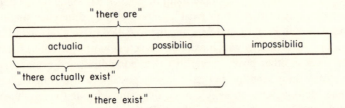

This strategy, too, renders possibilist discourse coherent. For given the distinction between the restricted domain of actualia and the unrestricted domain of both actualia and possibilia, one can express the claim that there "are"—or that there "exist"—things that are nonactual by writing "$(\exists x) \sim Ax$", a formula in which there is not even a hint of self-contradiction.[22]

The second type of strategy can be implemented in other ways as well. One that I think particularly pertinent to Wittgenstein's position is that provided by John Crossley and Lloyd Humberstone in their paper "The Logic of 'Actually'" [1977]. Although it is not their deliberate intent to provide expressive resources whereby to rescue possibilists from the charge of inconsistency, the logic that they devise, an actuality-enriched extension of the standard modal system S5, can be put to that end. This is the logic which they call "S5A".

Technically, Crossley and Humberstone's actuality-logic is very different from Lewis's counterpart theory. Lewis's counterpart theory builds on standard quantificational logic by adding four primitive predicates (including "Ax" for "x is actual") and eight postulates (including "Nothing is in two worlds", a postulate that repudiates the notion of identity across possible worlds and substitutes for it the notion of a counterpart). Crossley and Humberstone's actuality-logic, S5A, builds on S5 by adding an actuality operator (such that "Ap" is to be read as "In the actual world, p", or more simply "Actually p") and the following axioms:

(A11) $A(Ap \supset p)$
(A12) $A(p \supset q) \supset (Ap \supset Aq)$
(A13) $Ap \equiv \sim A\sim p$
(A14) $\Box p \supset Ap$
(A15) $Ap \supset \Box Ap$

The main differences between Crossley and Humberstone, on the one hand, and Lewis on the other, are philosophical. Lewis's counterpart theory rules out the possibility of any individual's occurring in more than one world, whereas S5A does not. And Lewis's theory treats "is actual" as indexical, that is, as such that any world is actual from the point of view of its inhabitants, whereas Crossley and Humberstone's S5A treats "actually" as a rigid designator that picks out just one world from the rest.

More of all this in due course. For the moment, the most relevant point is that although Crossley and Humberstone do not deal explicitly with matters of quantification, the expressive resources of S5A, when applied straightforwardly to sentences of predicate-logic, enable one to say that a thing having the property F exists without in any way appearing to contradict the claim that that thing nevertheless does not actually exist. For the formula p ⊃ Ap is not a thesis of S5A. Hence one can, without contradiction, assert p while denying Ap. And, as a substitution-instance, one can also without contradiction assert (∃x) Fx and deny A(∃x) Fx. In effect, then, S5A provides us with another way of distinguishing between two domains of quantification and thereby provides another way of rescuing possibilists—Wittgenstein among them, in my view—from the charge of contradiction.

In Chapter V, section 6, I'll argue that Crossley and Humberstone's S5A provides a better overall fit for Wittgenstein's possibilism than does Lewis's counterpart theory. This is because his views on the possibility of one and the same individual's existing in more than one world, and on the unique status of the actual world, are not only contrary to Lewis's but are best accommodated by S5A.

But, for now, I want to draw attention to how Wittgenstein, in ways that I think accord with S5A, handles the notion of existence. And, in order to do that, I first want to outline the way in which Russell handles it so that Wittgenstein's way can be contrasted with his and the standard presumption of his agreement with Russell on this issue can be laid to rest.

12. Russell's Treatment of Existence

I pointed out in Chapter I, section 6, that the expressions "always true", "sometimes true", and "never true" take on very different meanings according to whether one takes them, as Russell does on official occasions, as ranging over the restricted domain of what actually exists, or takes them, as Russell does on unofficial occasions, as ranging over the unrestricted domain of Leibnizian possible worlds and their constituents. As a consequence, I argued, each of the expressions "necessary", "possible", and "impossible", respectively, also takes on a different meaning according to the strictures, or latitude, of the occasion.

So, too, for Russell, does the expression "exists". According to him existence is no more to be predicated of individuals than possibility or other modal notions are to be predicated of propositions. Both, he tells us, are properties of propositional functions. Indeed, it turns out, somewhat surprisingly, that the putative properties of existence and of possibility are one and the same. Both are properties of a propositional function when that propositional function is "sometimes true". As he puts it [1918], "It will be out of this notion of *sometimes*, which is the same as the notion of *possible*, that we get the notion of existence. To say that unicorns exist is simply to say that '(x is a unicorn) is possible'." (p. 232). In short, the following formula, which I shall call "Russell's Formula", determines the conditions under which existence and possibility alike may be ascribed:

"Fs exist" = "(∃x) Fx = (Fx) is possible" = "(Fx) is sometimes true".

As an example of the application of Russell's Formula, we have

> "Unicorns exist" = "($\exists$x) x is a unicorn" = "(x is a unicorn) is possible" = "(x is
> a unicorn) is sometimes true".

Clearly, just as the meaning of "possible" varies according to whether "sometimes true" ranges over a restricted domain or over an unrestricted one, so, too, does the meaning of "exists".

Once more, Russell's official position takes the restricted domain as the basis for interpretation of existence-claims.[23] Yet this official position leads him into difficulties. As with his official doctrine of modalities, he finds it hard to maintain in the face of his own contrary intuitions and ways of speaking.

Existence, he tells us, can never significantly be attributed to individuals, but only to propositional functions or (derivatively) to classes. ([1918], 233). It follows, for Russell [1918], that "to say that the actual things that there are in the world do not exist . . . is utter nonsense . . [and] to say that they do exist is also strictly nonsense." (p. 233). Yet this is a hard thesis to maintain. At one point, for instance, he acknowledges, "It is obviously a perfectly significant statement, whether true or false, to say that Romulus existed." (p. 242). And we are left to wonder how this can be if it is strictly nonsense to assert or deny the existence of things. Russell's answer is that it is significant to assert or deny Romulus's existence only insofar as we treat "Romulus" not as a proper name but as an abbreviated description of certain properties. When we do this, of course, we treat "Romulus" as shorthand for one or more predicate-expressions, such as "the founder of Rome". We treat the putative proposition "Romulus exists" as a misleading way of expressing what is better expressed by saying, "The propositional function 'Fx' is sometimes true", where "F" abbreviates some definite description such as "the founder of Rome". It is in this way that Russell preserves, or tries to preserve, our intuition that it makes perfectly good sense to assert or deny the existence of Romulus. But he does so at a cost. The cost is that, in his view, ordinary proper names such as "Romulus", "Socrates", and "Scott" really do not function as names at all but only as descriptions. This is a cost that many philosophers, Wittgenstein among them, are not prepared to pay (though, for Russell, and many other so-called descriptivists, it is not a cost at all). [24]

Russell's official account of existence also poses problems for our understanding of such expressions as "there are". How, for instance, are we supposed to understand this expression as it occurs in Russell's own claim, quoted previously, that "to say that the actual things in that there are in the world . . . do exist" is just as nonsensical as to deny it? Not, I suggest, as "there exist", since this would make the assertion of their existence patently tautological and the denial of their existence patently self-contradictory. Although Wittgenstein would be happy to call such tautologies and contradictions "nonsensical", Russell would not. So what exactly are we to make of this expression?

What, for that matter, are we to make of Russell's use of the related expression "there will be" as it occurs in a sentence such as "Among 'possible' worlds, in the Leibnizian sense, there will be worlds having one, two, three, . . . individuals."? ([1919], p. 203). Is he saying that such worlds timelessly exist? He can hardly mean that the propositional functions "x is a world and x contains one [two, three, . . .]

individuals" is sometimes true in the actual world. For that would be false, and hence—by his official doctrine—such worlds would be impossible.

Our puzzlement deepens even further when we ask what, according to his official doctrine, it might mean to say that "there are" worlds in which "there are" exactly 30,000 things, worlds in which "there are" fewer than 30,000 things, and worlds in which "there are" more than 30,000 things. ([1918], p. 240). The trouble is, of course, that Russell is impelled to say all these things when he is trying to characterize the difference between logical propositions and all the rest.

The fact is that Russell's official account of existence is as impossible to maintain as is his official account of modality. And for the same reason. Russell's Formula defines both possibility and existence in terms of the notion of *being sometimes true*, a notion that he usually wants to construe narrowly but sometimes has to construe broadly. When he construes the expression "sometimes true" as ranging over the restricted domain of the actual world and all its constituents, he is led to suppose that the only things that "there are", or that "exist", are things that are values of the variable "x" in propositional functions of the form "Fx" when these are "sometimes true" *in the actual world*. When he construes the expression "sometimes true" as ranging over the unrestricted domain of Leibnizian worlds, the domain that Russell feels impelled to consider when characterizing the status of logic, he is led to suppose that the only things that "there are", or that "exist", are things that are values of the variable "x" in propositional functions of the form "Fx" when these are "sometimes true" *in the set of all possible worlds*. Russell tries always to construe "sometimes true" in the former way, since only then can he maintain his "realistic bias". But when he has more important concerns at heart, he is forced to construe it in the latter way, and hence is forced to take account of possibilia.

Obviously, what I have been calling the restricted and unrestricted domains are in fact two domains of quantification. Take the formula "(∃x)Fx" and read it in any of the usual ways: for instance, as "There is an x such that Fx", "There exists an x such that Fx", or "For some x, Fx". It then becomes clear that these readings are simply alternates to Russell's reading: "(Fx) is sometimes true". And since this latter, as Russell uses it, is equivocal between "is sometimes true in the actual world" and "is sometimes true in the set of all possible worlds", the distinction between these two domains affects the meaning we give to each of these "readings". We can, and do, sometimes use the expressions "There is (are) . . .", "There exists . . .", "For some . . .", in the way dictated by Russell's official account of modality and existence. When we so use them, we are (as logicians say) "quantifying over" the restricted domain of actual entities and the notion of existence is thought of as tantamount to that of actual existence. It is in this way—as Terence Parsons has pointed out ([1980], pp. 5–9)—that students of logic these days are taught to use or read the existential quantifier "(∃x)". But this is not the only way in which the existential quantifier can be understood. We can, and do, sometimes use that quantifier, and these related English expressions, in the way to which Russell takes recourse when he is off-duty. When we so use them, we are quantifying over the unrestricted domain of possible entities and the notion of existence becomes tantamount (though not identical) to that of possible existence. I take it that it is in this unrestricted quantificational sense that Russell wants to claim that "there are" Leibnizian possible worlds in which "there are" n individuals, where n is any number from one to infinity; or again that "there are" worlds in which "there are" exactly 30,000, more than 30,000, or fewer than 30,000 individuals; and so on. Otherwise these claims are just plain false.

We need to be on guard, then, against letting Russell's realistic bias in metaphysics, and his consequent preference for a restricted reading of existence-claims, become enshrined as a seemingly indubitable matter of logic. Even Russell, as we have seen, is unable to stick with the restricted reading when he is talking about the status of logic itself.

13: Wittgenstein's Treatment of Existence

How does Wittgenstein think of existence? For a start, there are conclusive reasons for holding that he does not agree with Russell's official account of this notion.

(1) Unlike Russell, he does not claim that existence can be attributed only to propositional functions. Whereas Russell rejects as strictly nonsensical any talk of the existence of things or individuals, Wittgenstein does not. On the contrary, he is perfectly happy to make existence-claims regarding such entities as states of affairs (2), complexes (3.24), a logical place and a proposition with sense (3.4), internal properties and relations (4.122), propositions (5.131), and situations (5.135). In none of these cases does he suggest that we should, or could, translate out this talk in the way Russell's official theory would dictate. To be sure, Wittgenstein implicitly treats existence as a "formal" property (4.1272), one that cannot be predicated of an object by a significant (that is, a contingent) proposition. And accordingly, he claims, in words that sound like Russell's, "one *cannot say* [emphasis added], for example, 'There are objects', as one might say 'There are books'." (4.1272(5)); or again, "it is *nonsensical* [emphasis added] to speak of the total number of objects." (4.1272(6)). But this does not mean that existence-claims cannot be made in any way at all. On the contrary, the existence of objects, though it is something that cannot be asserted or *said* (said by a contingent proposition, that is) is nevertheless something that can be *shown*. It can be shown by means of the existential quantifier "(∃x)". And it can also be shown by the presence in our notation of names for such objects (5.5535).

I think that Wittgenstein is much misunderstood on this point. It is often supposed that, for him, the presence of "a" in the propositional sign "fa" somehow guarantees the actual existence of a. But all it guarantees is the existence of *possible* a in the *possible* state of affairs that "fa" represents. We need to remember that "fa" may in fact be false, either because a does not actually exist or because it does actually exist yet fails to have the property f.

Again, it sometimes supposed that, for Wittgenstein, "fa" would not make sense if a did not exist. But this is just as confused as it would be if we were to argue that "fa" would not make sense if the state of affairs of a's having f did not exist. All that is required, for him, in order that "fa" have sense, is that a's having f be a *possible* state of affairs (and a fortiori, that f be a *possible* property, and that a be a *possible* object).

An associated misunderstanding arises from the fact that Wittgenstein regards expressions such as "a exists" as nonsense. Ramsey, for instance, seems to think that it follows from "'a exists' is nonsense" that "a is a necessary existent". In his "Review of Tractatus" he argues: "It is an unusual view that any imaginable world must contain all the objects of the real one; yet it seems to follow from his principles, for if 'a exists' is nonsense, we cannot imagine that it does not exist, but only that it does not have some property." (p. 22). But it does not follow. For according to Wittgenstein there are at least two kinds of nonsensicality, and only one of these has to do with the kind of considerations to which Ramsey is appealing. We can allow that a proposition about an object, a, will indeed count as nonsensical if that proposition is true in all possible worlds; and we can allow that in this case—the sort of case of which Ramsey is thinking—a's nonexistence is something that "we cannot imagine". But there is also another kind of nonsensicality, according to Wittgenstein. It is that which arises when we try to say of an object a that it falls under a formal concept (a concept such as those expressed by the words "object", "number", "complex", or—more pertinently—"exists"): "When something falls under a formal concept as one of its objects, this cannot be expressed by means of a proposition. Instead, it is shown in the very sign for the object. (A name signifies an object, a sign for a number that it signifies a number, etc)." (4.126(3)). As he explains, whenever we try to use a formal concept as if it were a proper concept-word—of the kind that he would represent in logical notation by means of a predicate-constant or predicate variable—"nonsensical pseudo-propositions are the result." (4.1272(4)). Thus the reason why "a exists" is nonsense is not—as Ramsey thinks, along with many others—that "we cannot imagine that it [a] does not exist". Rather the reason is that existence is a formal concept and, as such, cannot significantly be attributed to a in a correct conceptual notation, but can only be shown in that notation by the presence of "a" itself.[25]

(2) Wittgenstein would see neither the need nor the point of Russell's claim that apparent assertions and denials of the existence of an individual like Socrates need to be explained away in accordance with Russell's Theory of Descriptions. That theory involves, among other things, replacing a name such as "Socrates" with a description and then treating that description as a predicate-expression in a propositional function that we can then say is sometimes true (in the case where we would otherwise be tempted to say that Socrates exists), or can say is never true (in the case where we would otherwise be tempted to say that Socrates does not exist). But, as I have already shown, Wittgenstein gives a very different account of the kind of description by means of which complexes are "given". A complex is represented by a *propositional* description of the concatenated simples that are their constituents. And a complex exists if these simple constituents are concatenated in the way the propositional description says they are: "the complex: *a in the relation R to b* . . . is just that which 'exists' if that proposition is true." (*NB* 48(4)). Moreover, Wittgenstein sees no reason why we should not name this existent complex. For he continues: "It seems as if we could designate this something, and what's more with a

real 'complex sign'—the feelings expressed in these sentences are quite natural and unartificial, so there must be some truth at the bottom of them." Not surprisingly, therefore, Wittgenstein doesn't share Russell's aversion to treating ordinary names, such as "Socrates", as if they were genuine names of individuals. The *Notebooks* makes this particularly clear. Not only does he give examples, for example, of naming a book "A" (*NB* 50(2)) or "N" (*NB* 60(1)); he also discusses, at length, the whole business of naming what he calls "complex spatial objects" and observes: "the designation of them by means of names seems to be more than a mere trick of language," (*NB* 47(11)). Likewise, in the *Tractatus*, he does not shy away from treating, for example, "Green" as "the proper name of a person." (3.323(3)). By way of contrast, Russell's epistemology prevented him from treating ordinary names as genuine ones. According to that epistemology our knowledge of complex objects is always knowledge by description, not by acquaintance. But no such epistemological considerations stood in Wittgenstein's way. According to Wittgenstein, it is complex objects such as Socrates and books with which we are acquainted, and simple ones that we know only by description. Hence Wittgenstein would neither need nor want to give a reductive analysis of apparent existence-claims regarding Socrates, Romulus, or anyone else, in the way that Russell proposed.[26]

(3) Whereas Russell only rarely (on what I have called "unofficial" occasions) concedes that there are possible worlds and possible objects that are nonactual, Wittgenstein, in both the *Notebooks* and the *Tractatus*, makes it clear that, for him, there are infinitely many such possibilia that a god could "create" and thereby bring into existence. To repeat: whereas Russell is an (official) actualist, Wittgenstein is a third-degree possibilist. When Wittgenstein entertains the idea of a god's creating a world, he entertains the idea of a god's bringing that world into *existence*. And not only that: he thereby entertains the idea of a god's bringing into *existence* all the objects which are the substance of that world. For suppose, in the vein of 5.123, that a god were to create a world in which the proposition "Fa" were true. Then, in so doing, he creates a world in which any proposition that is identical with "Fa" is true. But as Wittgenstein points out: "'Fa' says the same thing as '$(\exists x)$ Fx . x = a'." 5.47(2). It follows that, in creating a world in which the proposition "Fa" is true, a god would be creating a world in which the proposition "$(\exists x)$ Fx . x = a" is true: a world in which *there exists* an x which is identical with the object, a.

All three considerations discussed count conclusively against the supposition that Wittgenstein treated existence-claims in accordance with Russell's official theory. And the last of them makes it clear that although Wittgenstein sometimes thought of the existential quantifier as ranging over only those objects that are constitutive of the actual world, he also thought of it as sometimes ranging more widely over any possibilia that a god might create.

Further reasons for concluding that Wittgenstein treats existence-claims differently from Russell are to be found in 4.27. There he tells us that for n states of affairs, "there are" 2^n possibilities of existence and nonexistence and that any combinations of these states of affairs "can exist and the remainder not exist." A possibility of existence, then, just is a possible combination of states of affairs—just is, in other words, a possible world. And "there are"—he tells us—such possibilities, such possible worlds. Thus, he is saying that for n states of affairs, there exist (in the unrestricted quantificational sense) 2^n possible worlds; and further, that any one of these possible worlds can exist, in the restricted quantificational sense (that is, can be actual) while the remainder do not exist, again in the restricted sense, (that is, are not actual). He is saying, in other words, that these 2^n possible worlds exist as possibilia (have existence in the unrestricted domain), and that they are such that a god could create any one of them, that is, bring any one of them into actual existence (give it existence in the restricted domain).

Quite generally, then, Wittgenstein is committed—by his views on the metaphysics of modality (his possibilism) and the associated ontological commitments that these views involve—to the recognition of two domains of quantification: an unrestricted domain of objects that exist as possibilia and a restricted domain of actualia.

As I said earlier, it seems to me that Wittgenstein's treatment of existence-claims is more readily regimented by Crossley and Humberstone's logic, S5A, than by David Lewis's counterpart logic. Nevertheless, Lewis's remarks capture nicely the equivocal character of Wittgenstein's unregimented usage. When Lewis writes, "Our idioms of existential quantification may be used to range over everything without exception, or they may be tacitly restricted in various ways", he might well be taken to be describing Wittgenstein's idiom. Likewise, when he comments, "one can pass indecisively from equivocating on one to equivocating on another." For this, it should now be clear, is just how Wittgenstein uses the term *"Bestehens"* (which Pears and McGuinness translate sometimes as "there are", sometimes as "there exist"). His talk of existence needs to be examined carefully in context in order to determine, for each occurrence, whether he is using the term in the one way or the other. But, as Lewis would point out, we need only to "keep track" of these two uses in order to prevent confusion.

Notes

1. The actualist paradigm has taken on the character of something like what Kuhn calls a "normal science", as Terence Parsons points out ([1980], esp. pp. 2 and 5). I am indebted to Parsons for this way of seeing the situation, though not for my Wittgensteinian way of redressing it.

2. The Theory of Descriptions was first proposed by Russell [1905]. It has often been described as "a paradigm of analytical philosophy". But, as I shall argue, the kind of analysis it proposes is very different from that of Wittgenstein.

3. I have also argued, in Bradley [1984], that (b) is independent of (c), and hence that the semantic doctrine that names are mere proxies for, or rigid designators of, their bearers is in no way compromised by any failure of (c).

4. See, for example: "Does not my study of sign-language correspond to the study of thought-processes, which philosophers used to consider as so essential to the philosophy of logic? Only in most cases they got entangled in unessential psychological investigations, and with my method too there is an analogous risk." (4.1121(3)).

5. Wittgenstein's claim, that "Excalibur has a sharp blade" makes sense, sets him in opposition to those causal theorists who, like Saul Kripke, believe that in the case where an object does not in fact exist, we wouldn't even know what it would be like for it to exist. Kripke claims that, if there never had been, in the actual world, any unicorns "we just can't say under what circumstances there would have been unicorns." Likewise, with regard to Sherlock Holmes, Kripke holds, "granted that there is no Sherlock Holmes, one cannot say of any possible person that he *would have been* Sherlock Holmes, had he existed." (These passages occur on pp. 24 and 158, respectively, of [1980]). My own intuitions regarding this issue, are in support of Wittgenstein, not Kripke. But the issue is too large, and too tangential to our present concerns, to be dealt with adequately here. It should be noted, however, that Kripke's reservations about the semantic function of mythological and fictional names do not count against his claim that in other possible worlds "some actually existing individuals may be absent while new individuals . . . may appear." (p. 158). Kripke, in short, seems to allow for possible but nonactual individuals, despite the fact that he doesn't think that we can name them.

6. Strictly, Wittgenstein would not allow that there can be any propositions "asserting" the existence of anything. But that is because of his idiosyncratic use of "asserts" which he will not allow with respect to any proposition that predicates a formal property, such as that of existence, of its subject. I am using the term "asserting", then, not in the strict Wittgensteinian sense, but in its usual sense, one that suffers from no such unusual restrictions. (For more on this point, see Chapter IV, section 2.)

7. Some of Ramsey's reasons for attributing object-homogeneity to Wittgenstein are quite independent of the passages about the form of all possible worlds. Thus he writes: "It is an unusual view that any imaginable world must contain all the objects of the real one; but it seems to follow from his principles, for if 'a exists' is nonsense, we cannot imagine that it does not exist, but only that it does or does not have some property." (I discuss this passage later in section 13.)

8. The standard account also entails that an Idealist-type world that is a single organic unity, is not (for Wittgenstein) a possible world. But although Wittgenstein believes the actual world to be wholly different from the way the Idealists think it is, it is doubtful that he would regard Idealist-type worlds as logically impossible. And if that is so, then he could not without inconsistency claim that all possible worlds are made up of the same set of simple objects as the actual world.

9. The existence of a single set of such possibilities is, of course, *compatible* with the supposition of object-homogeneity. For if all possible worlds contain precisely the same objects then the possibilities of their configurations in any given world will be the same as those in any other. But, contrary to what is often supposed, it does not *entail* object-homogeneity. For the existence of a single set of possibilities is also compatible, as we have just seen, with object-heterogeneity.

10. That the incomprehension was not one-sided is evident from a letter that C. I. Lewis wrote to Professor Woodbridge (then editor of the *Journal of Philosophy*) on 2 January 1923, in which he asks whether Woodbridge has looked at Wittgenstein's new book and comments: "I am much discouraged by Russell's foolishness

in writing the Introduction to such nonsense. I fear it will be looked upon as what symbolic logic leads to; if so, it will be the death of the subject." I am indebted to Leonard Goddard for bringing this letter to my attention.

11. For a fascinating, and revealing, account of Russell's "baneful influence" on the development, and recognition, of modal logic, see Nicholas Rescher [1979]. At one point, Rescher advances the standard view that "the ideology of truth-functionality . . . received its canonical formulation in Wittgenstein's *Tractatus Logico-Philosophicus*" (p. 144). But a little later he does justice to the seminal influence of Wittgenstein when he writes: "Modal logic remained in the shadows for a long time. It did not really begin to come into its own until the development of modern modal semantics, largely under the influence of Rudolph Carnap (erecting a structure of his own on foundations laid by Wittgenstein and Tarski)" (p. 146). And again:

> There is no fundamental historical reason why modern symbolic modal logic could not have developed substantially sooner. The basic tools forged by MacColl and Lewis lay to hand by 1920, as did those hints of Wittgenstein's *Tractatus* . . . from which Carnap first systematized the possible-worlds interpretation of modal logic. There is no reason of historical principle why the logic of modality which surged up shortly after Carnap's *Meaning and Necessity* (University of Chicago Press, 1947) could not have begun soon after 1920. (p. 144)

12. The Rule of Uniform Substitution may be expressed as: "If X is a thesis (an axiom or a theorem) and Y results from uniformly substituting a well-formed formula for some variable in X , then Y is a thesis." In effect this rule relies on the fact that the Ps and Qs of our formulae are *variables* in order to give us a licence to derive as a theorem any formula that is a special case (substitution-instance) of an axiom or a previously derived theorem

13. The Rule of Modus Ponens may be expressed as: "If X is a thesis and X $\supset$ Y is a thesis then Y is a thesis." This rule gives us a licence to derive as a theorem any formula that is the consequent of an axiom or theorem whose antecedent is also an axiom or theorem. The rule corresponds to a well-known valid form of argument that often goes by the same name.

14. These symbols, and their corresponding concepts, are interdefinable (with the help of truth-functional symbols or concepts). For instance, "$\Box$P" may be defined as "$\sim \Diamond \sim$P", "$\Diamond$P" as "$\sim\Box\sim$P", "∇P" as "$\Diamond$P. $\Diamond \sim$P", and so on. Likewise for their Polish-notational equivalents, "LP", "MP", and "QP".

15. The Rule of Necessitation may be expressed as: "If X is a thesis, then $\Box$X is a thesis". This rule relies on the fact that since any formula derivable as a thesis is (on interpretation) either a necessary truth of truth-functional logic (a tautology) or a necessary truth of modal logic, the modal statement that says (or, as Wittgenstein would have it, *shows*) that it is a necessary truth must itself be a thesis.

16. To be sure, Wittgenstein says that a proposition that is true for all truth-possibilities is a "tautology" and that tautologies are "certain" rather than "necessary". But this is a terminological matter of no substance. In any case, see my discussion of this terminological point in Chapter III, section 14.

17. Here I take for granted, as against so-called relevance logicians, that S5 gives an adequate analysis of logical implication.

18. The familiar rule of inference known as Importation gets us from (A7) to (A7)*, while Exportation gets us back from (A7)* to (A7)).

19. It is worth noting, further, that the notation "$\Diamond P \supset \Box \Diamond P$" expresses, especially aptly, the sense in which S5 possibility is "absolute" possibility, possibility from the "God's-eye point of view", possibility "sub specie aeternitatis". Freely interpreted in possible-worlds locution, it amounts to saying that if a state of affairs is possible at all, insofar as it exists in any possible world, then its possibility holds "absolutely" from the point of view of all possible worlds. Wittgenstein obviously adopts this point of view when he writes: "(The thought forces itself upon one): The thing seen *sub specie aeternitatis* is the thing seen together with the whole of logical space. As a thing among things, each thing is equally insignificant; *as a world each one equally significant* [emphasis added]." (*NB* 83(11–12)). Thus, according to the absolutist point of view, whatever is possible in any world is possible "in" every world.

Consider, for instance, a world in which both Sherlock Holmes and cocaine exist and in which the state of affairs of Sherlock Holmes's nose being configured in a certain way with a quantity of cocaine also exists. Call this world (strictly, set of worlds) W_1. Then the state of affairs of Sherlock Holmes's sniffing cocaine is possible, not just relative to the constituents of W_1, but absolutely in the sense that the existence of this possible state of affairs must be recognized in every possible world.

To be sure, we sometimes think in terms of a weaker sense of "possible": a sense in which what is possible is relative to the constituents of a given world. This is the sense in which we might want to say that the proposition that Sherlock Homes sniffs cocaine is possibly true in W_1, but that it is not possibly true in worlds (like our own) in which Sherlock Holmes does not exist, nor possibly true in worlds (unlike our own) in which cocaine does not exist. But the sense of "possible" that is thus relativized to worlds and their constituents, I suggest, is not Wittgenstein's. Arguably, it is that which is captured by the system S4, not S5. Nor is it the sense that usually predominates in our own thinking. Rather, to say that such a proposition is possibly true, or that the state of affairs whose existence that proposition asserts is possible, is to say something that is independent of the constitution of the world we live in—or, for that matter, of the constitution of any other particular world.

20. Within S5 we can also deduce various other consequences of thesis (c) (using "Q" for "it is contingent that", "L" for "it is necessary that', and "M" for "it is possible that"), viz., $\sim Q \sim QP$ (the noncontingency of P is a noncontingent matter), $\sim QLP$ (the necessity of P is a noncontingent matter), $\sim QMP$ (the possibility of P is a noncontingent matter), $\sim Q \sim LP$ (the nonnecessity of P is a noncontingent matter), $\sim Q \sim MP$ (the impossibility of P is a noncontingent matter), and—more generally still—$\sim Q\$P$ (where \$ is any modal property whatever).

21. See, e.g., Richard Routley [1980], pp. 180–186; Terence Parsons [1980], p. 216; George Nakhnikian and Wesley Salmon [1957].

22. Still another strategy would be to reject both (i) and (ii) in the manner displayed on the following figure:

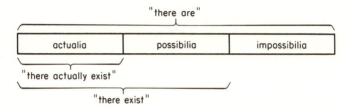

By virtue of rejecting (i), this strategy would enable us to drive a wedge between talk of what things "there are" and talk of what things "exist", thereby accommodating the neo-Meinongian claim that it makes perfectly good sense to say that "there are" impossible worlds, impossible states of affairs, and impossible objects, even though no such impossibilia "exist". By virtue of rejecting (ii), this strategy would enable us to drive a wedge between talk of what "exists" and talk of what "actually exists", thereby accommodating David Lewis's claim that it makes perfectly good sense to say that "there exist" possible worlds, possible states of affairs, and possible objects, even though many of these possibilia do not "actually exist". Clearly, then, this third strategy offers expressive resources greater than those of either of the other two. Yet, since I do not know of any philosopher who explicitly adopts it, I shall say no more about it here.

23. His official view can be depicted thus:

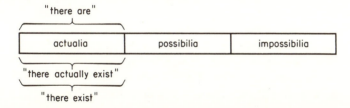

24. According to descriptivists—those who, like Frege, Russell, Strawson, and Searle, hold that ordinary proper names function as disguised descriptions of their bearers—it is one of the merits of their theory that it provides so easy a solution to the problem of how to construe negative existential statements such as "Romulus did not exist." Referentialists—those who, like Mill, Wittgenstein, Kripke, and Donnellan, hold that proper names function not as descriptions but solely as labels of their bearers—have to find some other way of accounting for the intuition that negative existentials can make perfectly good sense when the object named does not exist. See, for instance, Donnellan [1974].

25. Surprisingly, Ramsey himself draws attention to this special class of showable, but unsayable, propositions. But he seems not to realize that its existence vitiates his own reasoning.

26. To be sure, Wittgenstein, like Russell, thought that both complex objects and their names needed to be *analyzed*. But, for Wittgenstein, analysis of complex objects leads to metaphysically simple objects and analysis of the names of complex objects leads to structured combinations of the names of metaphysically simple ones. For Russell, analysis of ordinary names leads to descriptions. For Wittgenstein, analysis of ordinary names leads to more names.

3

The Essence of The World

My whole task consists in . . . giving the nature of all being.
(WITTGENSTEIN, *Notebooks 1914–1916*)

1. Introduction

In the present chapter, I have two main goals. First I try to show that Wittgenstein's metaphysics is an *atomistic* one insofar as all the complex items in his ontology are constructed from those possibilia which he calls "simple objects". Second, I try show how his atomism is *essentialistic* in character insofar as each of his simple objects has an internal nature, constituted by its de re necessary ("essential") properties, which makes it possible for the object to enter into certain combinations and impossible for it to enter into others. The essential properties of his atoms provide the blueprints for the construction of all the other items in his ontology: complex objects, complex properties, complex relations, states of affairs, and possible worlds.

This elaboration of Wittgenstein's metaphysics goes hand-in-hand with a further elaboration of the kind of logic to which he is implicitly committed. In Chapter II, we saw that he is committed to the propositional (de dicto) modal logic known as S5. In the present chapter, I'll argue that he is also committed to the (de re) modalities of quantified S5. As I observed in the Introduction, when Wittgenstein claims, in 2.0121(3), "Logic deals with every possibility and all possibilities are its facts", he really does mean *all* possibilities (and all necessities, impossibilities, and so forth), not just the de dicto (propositional) ones but the de re (essentialist) ones as well. The fact that the logic he is talking about in 2.0121(3) is *primarily* one that deals with de re possibility is evident from the fact that 2.0121(3) is a comment on 2.012: "In logic nothing is accidental: if a thing *can* occur in a state of affairs, the possibility of the state of affairs must be written into the thing itself." He is not merely saying that the nonaccidental character of an object's possession of combinatorial potential belongs to the "province of logic" (2.0121(3)). He is also saying that the possibility of any state of affairs (something that would be asserted by a de dicto necessary proposition) is grounded in certain simple essential properties of objects (their de re necessary possession of these properties). This passage also makes it clear that he regards objects as being pregnant not only with the possibility of occurring in states of affairs but with those states of affairs themselves. As he puts it in 2.0124, "If all objects are given, then at the same time all *possible* states of affairs are given." The de dicto modalities are grounded in the de re (essentialist) properties of the atoms of his ontology, his "simple objects".

2. "Objects": its Shifting Uses

Before we get into the details of Wittgenstein's essentialistic atomism, we need to ask, What exactly are these simple objects? I know of no exegetical question regarding the early Wittgenstein that is more difficult, and more vigorously debated, than this. The reason is that Wittgenstein's use of the term "object"—like his use of the terms "property" and "relation"—is far from univocal. Indeed, in 4.123(3) he himself explicitly alerts us to what he himself calls "the shifting use" that he gives all three of these words. My first task, therefore, must be to sort out what these shifting uses are.

Like most of us, Wittgenstein sometimes uses the terms "object" and "thing" (the German terms *"Gegenstand"* and *"Ding"*) in an all-embracing, *omnibus* way such that anything and everything counts as an object—whether it be, for instance, a physical object, a putative mental object, an abstract object, an event, a process, a states of affairs, or even a property or a relation. Thus, in the *Notebooks* the terms *"Gegenstand"* and *"Ding"* encompass such things as the following: objects that have length (38(2)); pencil-strokes and steamships (43(5)); points and parts of the visual field (45(12)); parts of space (47(10)); complex spatial objects (47(11)); ongoing events such as the moon circling round the earth and in so doing moving round the sun (49(1)); a tune, a spoken sentence; a knife or a letter (49(3)); temporal complexes (49(8)); a book (50(2)); a landscape, the dance of motes in the air (53(4)); a watch (60(9)); anything that is a possible referent of the demonstrative "this" (61(1)); relations and properties (61(2)); material points (67(8) and 69(5)); Socrates and the property of mortality (69(9)); a rod and a ball (70(8)); humans and animals(82(10)); and worlds (83(12)). And in the *Tractatus*, *"Gegenstand"* and *"Ding"* encompass such things as these: spatial objects (2.0131(1)); a speck in the visual field or a tone in the auditory field (2.0131(2)); tables, chairs and books (3.1431(1)); and shades of blue (4.123(2)).

An object, individual, or thing, in this omnibus sense, is whatever is, so to speak, one of the possible "objects of the thought" (3.2), whatever exists in a possible world, whatever is self-identical, or again, whatever is a possible value of an individual variable "x" (4.1272(1)), a predicate variable, "F", or a relational variable,"R" (*NB* 63(9)).[1]

Of the examples listed, that of *NB* 49(1) deserves special attention since it shows just how all-encompassing his use of the term "thing" can be. There Wittgenstein writes: "We can even conceive a body apprehended as in movement, *and together with its movement*, as a thing. So the moon circling around the earth moves round the sun. Now here it seems clear that this reification is nothing but a logical manipulation—though the possibility of this may be extremely significant." He makes his point, in more general terms, a page or so earlier when he tells us, "complex spatial objects, for example, seem to me in some sense to be essentially things—I as it were see them as things—and the designation of them by means of names seems to be more than a mere trick of language." (*NB* 47(11)). What is remarkable about the moon-earth-sun case, of course, is that it is more than just a "complex spatial object". It is, so to speak, a "complex spatial-cum-temporal object", a complex of spatial objects undergoing specific sorts of changes in spatial relations over a period of time. Even complexes such as these, he is saying, can be, and are, thought of as "things". As he comments, shortly thereafter, "A complex just is a thing!" (*NB* 49(4)). Admittedly, our disposition to think of complexes as things does involve what he calls "reification". But this reification, he himself notes, "may be extremely important". It is important because the reification of such complexes provides the warrant, as *NB* 47(11) points out, for our use of ordinary names in the designation of the complex objects that we know by acquaintance. It is important, too, because it also provides the warrant for the application of logic to the ordinary propositions in which ordinary names occur:

> But logic as it stands, e.g., in *Principia Mathematica* can quite well be applied to our ordinary propositions, e.g., from "All men are mortal" and "Socrates is a man" there follows according to this logic "Socrates is mortal" which is obviously correct although I equally obviously do not know what structure is possessed by the thing Socrates or the property of mortality. Here they just function as simple objects. (*NB* 69(9))

Surely Wittgenstein is right about this. Thinking of complexes as things, we must surely agree, *does* involve more than a logical manipulation, and designating them by means of names *is* more than a mere trick of language. If we could not think of complexes in this way, and use names in this way, neither language nor logic, as we ordinarily understand them, would be possible. Wittgenstein's omnibus use, in short, is essential to our whole conceptual system.

Another general claim deserving attention occurs in *NB* 61(2), when he tells us, "Relations and properties, etc., are *objects*, too." This explains why, in *NB* 69(9), he speaks of the property of mortality as if it were, or could "function as", an object. As he pointed out to his student, Desmond Lee [1980], many years later, his use of "objects"—in 2.01—"also includes relations" (p. 120).

Wittgenstein's omnibus use of "*Gegenstand*" and "*Ding*", then, is a *noncontrastive* use, one which encompasses properties and relations as well as what we call individuals.

When he uses these terms in a more restrictive sense, that in which objects, things, or individuals[2] are to be contrasted with properties and relations, I shall sometimes speak of its *contrastive* use.

3. The Simple/Complex Distinction

All three categories of entity—objects, properties, and relations—Wittgenstein believes, may be either simple or complex. But what are his criteria of simplicity and complexity? And what would count, for him, as examples of the simple and the complex?

He operates with three criteria for distinguishing complexity from simplicity. Something is complex if it is divisible into simpler parts, is analyzable into constituents, or has a structure. By the same token, something is simple if it is indivisible, is unanalyzable, or lacks a structure.

The distinction between what is divisible and what is not applies fairly straightforwardly to objects. Clearly, an object that is divisible into simpler parts must be complex, whereas one that is indivisible must be an ultimate simple, an "element". This link between simplicity and indivisibility is particularly evident in the *Notebooks* where he tells us that he cannot avoid supposing "that there is some simple indivisible, an element of being, in brief a thing." (*NB* 62(9)).

So far as properties and relations are concerned, talk of divisibility and indivisibility into parts seems inappropriate. But the related talk of analyzability and unanalyzability into constituents plays much the same role. In the *Notebooks*, he links the idea of the complex with "the idea of analysis" (*NB* 60(4)), saying that the idea of the simple is "contained", as a sort of polar opposite, in both. And in the *Tractatus* he links the notions of simplicity and unanalyzability when he tells us that the elements of "completely analyzed" propositions, elements that must themselves not be susceptible of further analysis, are his "simple signs" (3.201).

The distinction between what is structured and what is unstructured can be applied to all three kinds of entity: objects, properties, and relations alike. For, as 2.032 and 2.15 make clear, to say that something is structured is just to say that it has a "determinate" connection of "elements". Being structured is not only a sufficient condition of complexity; it is a necessary condition too. According to Wittgenstein, *any* complex involves a connection of simpler elements and *any* connection of simple parts or elements must be a definite or determinate connection. As he says, "the world must be what it is, it must be definite." (*NB* 62(10)). Since something is complex if and only if it is structured, we can infer that any object, property or relation which has no structure must be simple.

What, then, would count as examples of simples and complexes for each of our three categories?

So far as objects are concerned, it is easy to give examples of complex ones: almost all the members of the list of objects given at the beginning of section 2. These, it will be remembered, range from things like pencil-strokes, steamships, and Socrates, in the *Notebooks*, to tables, chairs, and books, in the *Tractatus*.[3] And it is easy to add still more. Anything that has a structure and which is neither a property nor a relation must be a complex object. Examples are pictures (2.15), propositional signs (3.14), states of affairs (2.032), facts (2.034), propositions (4.1211), and the world (*NB* 62(11)). The problem, notoriously, is to give examples of *simple* objects, of what Wittgenstein would call "real simple things" (*NB* 43(4)). As to that much-debated and controversial question, I'll leave it for discussion in section 5. There we will consider in some detail the rival claims of the only two kinds of candidate that are even hinted at in Wittgenstein's writings: phenomenological objects such as points in our visual field and physicalistic objects such as the material points (point-masses as Pears and McGuinness call them) postulated by physics.

So far as *properties* are concerned, his criteria yield clear enough examples of complex ones. In *NB* 65(2) he refers to the property of circularity (the "circular form" of a circular patch) as a structural property, indeed "an infinitely complicated structural property" and says that its finite extension has "an infinitely complex structure."[4] And a little later, in *NB* 69(9), he speaks of the property of mortality as having a structure. Both circularity and mortality, then, are complex properties, properties capable in principle of analysis into simpler constituents. In *NB* 81(8) he refers to "a difference of structure between red and green." And in *NB* 82(12) he talks about colors, in general, as being susceptible to "the analysis of physics". Still more generally, any of his so-called "material properties"—properties such as *being red*, *being loud*, and *being hard* (2.0131)—must be complex since they are produced "only by the configuration of objects" (2.0231). All these, therefore, must be considered complex.

But what would count as an example of a *simple* property? He does not tell us. Arguably, however, some of the "formal" properties which he ascribes to simple objects, for instance, *being an object* , *being in space*, and *being in time*, will count as simple.[5] They don't seem to be analyzable in Wittgenstein's sense: there seem not to be any simpler properties of which one could say that they, in combination, make up the properties of *being an object*, *being self-identical*, and so on.

So far as *relations* are concerned, Wittgenstein actually obliges with an example of a simple one, but not with examples of complex ones. His example is that of *naming* as it holds between a simple sign and a simple object. This he calls a "simple relation" (*NB* 49(13)). An even more important example of a simple relation must surely be that of *combination*: the relation in which the simple individuals of his ontology stand to one another when they constitute states of affairs. Arguably it does not itself have structure, and since it features in the ultimate analysis of the notion of structure, it is not itself analyzable. Be that as it may, Wittgenstein says quite explicitly that some of the ultimate simples that his atomism postulates are relations. The possibility of comparing reality with propositions, he tells us in *NB* 111(7), "depends upon the conventions by which we have given meaning to our simples (names *and relations*) [emphasis added]." And in *NB* 61(3) he claims that, although we ourselves may be incapable of completely analyzing propositions, "I certainly seem to know that if the analysis were completely carried out, its result would have to be a proposition which once more contained names, *relations, etc.* [emphasis added]." A proposition (or propositional sign) that is completely analyzed, of course, can contain only signs for simples.

4. Simples: Metaphysical, Semantical, and Epistemological

So far I have been proceeding as if, for Wittgenstein, the notion of simplicity were solely a *metaphysical* one, having to do with objects, properties, and relations considered as the ultimate building-blocks of all that is or might be. But Wittgenstein doesn't always use the term in this way. Sometimes he uses it in what I shall call the *semantical* sense, and sometimes he uses it in what I shall call the *epistemological* sense. Since it seems to me that much confusion has arisen among commentators because of their uniform failure to attend to these further senses of "simple", I'll say a bit about all three.

(i) *Metaphysical Simplicity*

In the metaphysical sense of "simple"—the sense that has been predominant so far—an object, relation, or property, is complex if it has constituents or parts and is simple if it does not (that is, if it is not structured and hence cannot be divided or analyzed into simpler parts). It is of these that Wittgenstein is thinking when he tells us, "the WORLD must consist of elements." (*NB* 62(9-10)). And it is of these that he is thinking again when he tells us: "Objects make up the substance of the world. That is why they cannot be composite." (2.01). Metaphysically simple objects, along with metaphysically simple properties and metaphysically simple relations, are the ultimate atoms of his ontology. They are the elements out of which everything actual or possible is constructed.

(ii) *Semantical Simplicity*

At one point, in (*NB* 59(12)), Wittgenstein refers to a sense of "simple" that he regards as in some ways even more "fundamental" than the metaphysical sense. This is the sense in which *anything* whatever—be it a complex object, a complex property, a complex relation, or a complex sign standing for one of these—may be *treated*, for purposes of language and logic alike, as simple. I shall call this the semantical sense of "simple". This is the sense in which we regard something as simple when, as Wittgenstein puts it, "*Its composition* becomes completely *indifferent*. It disappears from view." (*NB* 69(4)). It is in this sense that Wittgenstein uses the term when he describes the following complex *objects* as "simple": a watch as it lies ticking on the table (*NB* 60(9)); a sign (*NB* 69(2-4)); and Socrates (*NB* 69(9)). Likewise, it is in this sense that he uses the term when he describes the complex *property* of mortality (*NB* 69(9)) as "simple". The semantical sense of "simple", then, is as all-encompassing as is the omnibus sense of "object". Indeed, the all-encompassing senses of the two words come together in *NB* 69(9) when he claims that the thing Socrates and the property of mortality "just function as simple objects."

Here are some of Wittgenstein's thoughts about this sense of the word:

> What is my fundamental thought when I talk about simple objects? Do not "complex objects" in the end satisfy just the demands which I apparently made on the simple ones? If I give this book a name 'N' and now talk about N, is not the relation of N to that "complex object" [the book], to its form and contents, essentially the same as I imagined only between name and simple object? (*NB* 59(12))

> For N.B.: even if the name 'N' vanishes on further analysis, still it indicates a *single common* thing. (*NB* 60(2))

It is quite clear that I can in fact correlate a name with this watch just as it lies here ticking in front of me, and that this name will have reference outside of any proposition in the very sense I have always given that word. And I feel that that name in a proposition will correspond to all the requirements of the "names of simple objects". (*NB* 60(8))

From this it would now seem as if in a certain sense all names were *genuine names*. Or, as I might also say, as if all objects were in a certain sense simple objects. (*NB* 61(11))

As I understand him, the "certain sense" to which he is referring is that in which, notwithstanding any complexity in a sign such as "Socrates" or "mortality" and notwithstanding any complexity in the object, property, or relation named, all "objects"—in the omnibus sense of that word—may "function as", or may be "treated" as, simple. The "certain sense" is the semantical sense. The name of an object functions as a semantically simple name when "*its composition* becomes completely *indifferent.*" (*NB* 69(4)). Correspondingly, an object functions as a semantically simple object in our thinking when, in talking about it or reasoning about it, we ignore any complexity in the object and treat it as a "*single common* thing" (*NB* 60(2)). It is by virtue of our ability to think of things and their signs as simple in the semantical sense, remember, that we can apply the logic of *Principia Mathematica* to the propositions of ordinary language (*NB* 69(9)). We can treat the name-variables and predicate-variables, name-constants and predicate-constants, of that logic as if they had metaphysically simple objects or metaphysically simple properties as their values, even in the cases where their values are in fact not simple at all but are metaphysically complex objects like Socrates or metaphysically complex properties like that of mortality. Little wonder, then, that Wittgenstein speaks of this as the "fundamental" sense of "simple".[6]

I shall return to the notion of semantical simplicity and note its connections with Kripke's notion of rigid designators in Chapter 4, section 5. (Roughly, to say that an object, property or relation is semantically simple in Wittgenstein's sense is to say that it is something that is designated by a Kripkean rigid designator.)

(iii) *Epistemological Simplicity*

On a couple of occasions Wittgenstein uses the term "simple" in an *epistemological* sense, as a way of describing the simplest sort of thing we can be acquainted with in experience. In *NB* 45(12) he confesses: "As examples of the simple I always think of points of the visual field (just as parts of the visual field always come before my mind as typical composite objects)."[7] And in *NB* 64(7) he tells us: "It seems to me perfectly possible that patches in our visual field are simple objects, in that we do not perceive any single point of a patch separately: the visual appearances of stars even seem certainly to be so."

The passages just quoted establish beyond all doubt that Wittgenstein sometimes speaks of the sort of items with which we may be immediately acquainted in experience as "simple". But are these items of acquaintance, these *phenomenological* simples, to be *identified*, as some have claimed, with the simple objects which "make up the substance of the world" (2.021)? Are they one and the same as his metaphysical simples? Or are his metaphysical simples more plausibly to be thought of as physicalistic in character? These are the questions that I'll address in the next section.

But before turning to them, I want to draw attention to the fact that Wittgenstein was not alone in allowing his talk of objects and simples to shift between the various senses laid out. The same melange of different notions is also to be found in Russell [1918].

For a start, Russell sometimes thinks of objects, as does Wittgenstein, in what I have called the noncontrastive, omnibus kind of way: he allows the notion of a simple object (a "logical atom" or "particular", in his terminology) to range not only over individuals but also over both properties ("predicates", as he calls them) and relations. In his words; "Some of them [logical atoms] will be what I call 'particulars'—such things as little patches of color or sound, momentary things—and some of them will be predicates or relations and so on." (p. 179).

Then, too, his talk of simplicity can be disambiguated in much the same sort of threefold way as can Wittgenstein's.

(i) Russell is thinking of metaphysically simple objects when he speaks of the "ultimate simples out of which the world is built" (p. 270), and says of them that each "has that sort of self-subsistence that used to belong to substance." (p. 201f). Like Wittgenstein, he takes unanalyzability to be a criterion of metaphysical simplicity when he talks about them as "the sort of last residue of analysis" (p. 179).

There are times when Russell, like Wittgenstein, is inclined to be agnostic about which things actually satisfy this criterion for being simple: "It remains to be investigated what particulars you can find in the world, if any. The whole question of what particulars you actually find in the real world is a purely empirical one which does not interest the logician as such." (p. 179). But he also, like Wittgenstein, sometimes succumbs to the temptation to provide actual examples, e.g., (in his case) the patch of white with which one is acquainted when one sees a piece of white chalk (p. 209).

(ii) Russell is thinking of objects as being *semantically* simple when he refers to Socrates as a "particular thing" and comments, "I am here for the moment treating Socrates as a 'particular' . . ." (p. 182). Russell defends the propriety of treating a complex object like Socrates as a simple object in his [1919], when he writes: "If, as may be the case, whatever seems to be an 'individual' is really capable of further analysis, we shall have to content ourselves with what may be called 'relative individuals', which will be terms that, throughout the context in question, are never analyzed and never occur otherwise than as subjects." (p. 173). For Russell, Socrates may count as a relative individual even if he is not an absolute individual. As I read him, Russell is making the same sort of move here as Wittgenstein makes when, in *NB* 69(9), he treats Socrates as a semantical simple. Alternatively, we may say that Wittgenstein is treating Socrates as a relative individual.

(iii) Russell is thinking of *epistemologically* simple objects when he cites such things as little patches of color or sound and "momentary things" as examples of particulars, and again when he claims: "One can use 'this' as a name to stand for a particular with which one is acquainted at the moment. . . . It is only when you use 'this' quite strictly, to stand for an actual object of sense, that it is really a proper name." ([1918], p. 201).

The parallels between Russell and Wittgenstein, here as elsewhere, are striking. But the differences are even more so. For Russell, the distinction between metaphysical and epistemological simplicity collapses: his simples just *are* his objects of acquaintance, and the substance of the world, for him, is to be identified with experienced particulars. Not so for Wittgenstein. Rather, for him, that which is epistemologically simple is always metaphysically complex: his metaphysical simples are never objects of acquaintance, and the substance of the world, for him, is to identified (probably) with unexperienced point-masses. Or so I will now argue.

5. Metaphysical Simples: Phenomenological or Physical?

Most commentators who have tried to determine what Wittgenstein meant by "simple objects", seem to me to have gone astray. They have done so in one or more of three ways.

First, nearly all have ignored Wittgenstein's shifting uses of both "simple" and "object". Their failure to recognize that he uses both terms with the multiplicity of senses outlined in section 4 has usually led them either to give up on the enterprise or to seize upon just one of these senses and then suppose it to be what Wittgenstein *always* means "simple objects". As against them, I hold that although Wittgenstein's usage is confusing, it can be disambiguated, and that when it sorted out it is easy to see not only that the objects that are basic to Wittgenstein's atomism are those that I have called "metaphysically simple objects", but also that many of the objects that are simple in some other sense (namely, the semantical or the epistemological senses) are in fact metaphysically complex.

Second, some have adopted what (in Chapter II, section 9) I called "the standard interpretation" of what Wittgenstein means when he talks of a form common to all possible worlds and have concluded that if the actual world is constituted of a certain range of metaphysically simple objects, then other possible worlds must also be constituted of those very same objects. Their failure to recognize that Wittgenstein's worlds are object-heterogeneous has led them to suppose that the simple objects that feature in our world can differ neither in number nor in kind from those that feature in others, and hence to conclude that if nonphysicalistic objects such as objects of acquaintance qualify as basic in any world they must also qualify as basic in ours. As against them, I hold that there is no bar to our recognizing Wittgenstein's commitment to physicalistic items as the metaphysical simples out of which the *actual* world is constructed, while recognizing that other possible worlds may well contain nonphysicalistic items (such as sense-data, Cartesian souls, or the Absolute) as well, or even solely. We need, that is, to separate the question as to what sorts of objects might plausibly be regarded as ultimate in some other possible world from the question whether Wittgenstein regards those sorts of objects as among the ultimate constituents of our world .

Third, some have taken at face value Wittgenstein's admission, in the *Note-*

books, that although he kept on speaking of simple objects, he was "unable to mention a single one" (*NB* 68(11)), and his subsequent protestation to Norman Malcolm [1958] that at the time when he was writing the *Tractatus*, "his thought had been that he was a logician; and that it was not his business, as a logician, to try to decide whether this thing or that was a simple thing or a complex thing, that being a purely empirical matter." (p. 86). Their failure to recognize that Wittgenstein's diffidence about making a final commitment to the natures of his metaphysical simples does not entail his wholesale ignorance of what might count as *possible* examples has led them to declare the question a pointless or unanswerable one. As against them, I hold that, though he is coy about the character of his simple objects, Wittgenstein is not wholly agnostic about them. And I further hold that of the two main candidates for the role of metaphysical simples in the *actual* world—phenomenological items such as points in our visual field and physicalistic items such as the material points—only the latter can satisfy the three criteria of simplicity previously noted: indivisibility, unanalyzability, and structurelessness.

Now for the question itself: Are Wittgenstein's simple objects phenomenological or physicalistic items?

According to Merrill Hintikka and Jaakko Hintikka [1986], they are the former. Reviving an account that was orthodox up until the 1950s but has been held suspect by most since then, they claim that the simple objects that make up the world of the *Tractatus* are to be *identified* with Russell's objects of acquaintance (p. 55).

Now it is true that early in the *Notebooks* Wittgenstein toys with the notion that phenomenological items might be examples of his "simple objects". He asks: "Is a point in our visual field a simple object, a thing?" (*NB* 3(4)). He confesses, in *NB* 45(12), that he does "think" of points of the visual field as examples of simple objects. And he claims, in *NB* 64(7), that there is indeed a sense in which it is "perfectly possible" that patches in our visual field should be simple. But do these passages demonstrate anything more than a passing flirtation with the phenomenological interpretation?

Hintikka and Hintikka think so. Yet even a brief examination of the textual evidence they cite shows that their interpretation is unwarranted. In fact, much of the evidence they adduce, when given in full and taken in context, actually counts against—rather than for—their view. Consider, once more, the passage on which they place most emphasis: "It seems to me perfectly possible that patches in our visual field are simple objects, *in that we do not perceive any single point of a patch separately*: the visual appearances of stars even seem certainly to be so." [emphasis added] (*NB* 64(7)). The italicized qualification (which for some reason they omit when they quote the passage) explains in just what *sense* Wittgenstein is prepared to allow the possibility of visual patches' being simple objects. Visual patches are simple "*in that we do not perceive any single point of a patch separately:*" This qualification makes sense, however, only if we take him to be allowing that, although such visual patches may be *epistemologically* simple, they are nevertheless in fact *metaphysically* complex, being made up of even simpler single points. The immediate context makes this abundantly clear. In the very next paragraph, Wittgenstein goes on to claim that such patches or spots in one's visual field have an "infinitely complex structure" (*NB* 65(2)). But structure ("the connection of its elements" (2.15)), we have already seen, is something that only a complex object can have. In any case, Wittgenstein has already said explicitly, in another passage that Hintikka and Hintikka overlook or ignore, that visual objects are always complex: "We can single out a part of our visual field, for example, and we see that it is always complex, that any part of it is always complex but is already simpler, and so on--." (*NB* 50(9)).

Hintikka and Hintikkas' discussion, as I see it, is bedevilled by their failure to distinguish between epistemological simplicity and metaphysical simplicity. It is bedevilled, too, by their failure to distinguish between structure (something that only complex items can possess) and form (something that simples as well as complexes can possess). By virtue of treating "structure" and "form" as synonyms throughout their book (see, especially, pp.40–41), they fail to recognize that Wittgenstein's claim that parts of the visual field always have structure *implies* that they are always complex.

Hintikka and Hintikka make much of various statements from the *Tractatus* which Wittgenstein makes about the "world" of the solipsist, the "world" of life, and the "world" of death. On their view, in each of these cases Wittgenstein is talking about the *real* world. Accordingly, they quote Wittgenstein's claim, in 5.62, that "the world is my world" and then comment:

> The passage makes little sense unless it is the case that the objects are in some strong sense mine. Otherwise the fact that the world is determined by the totality of objects would not turn the world into my world. (Cf. 5.63: "I am my world", and also 5.632 and 5.641). It is indeed the case that such a relation to myself is intrinsic to objects on the interpretation defended here. If we construe Tractarian objects as objects of acquaintance, the only objects I have are the objects of my acquaintance. And if these objects define the world, then the world cannot but be my world. Hence Wittgenstein's qualified solipsism becomes not only understandable but positively predictable on this interpretation. (p. 65)

Now it must be admitted that when Wittgenstein talks about the world of the solipsist, he is talking about a *possible* world, and further that the possible world of the solipsist is one that is populated solely by objects of acquaintance. But this does not mean that the possible world of the solipsist, namely, the phenomenological world, is to be identified with the *actual* world. Nor does it even mean that objects of acquaintance are *among* the metaphysical simples that make up the substance of the actual world.[8] Hintikka and Hintikkas' discussion of these passages, as I see it, is bedevilled by their failure to recognize that other possible worlds may be populated by objects that do not feature in ours.

It is easy to demonstrate that, on Wittgenstein's view, no phenomenological object is metaphysically simple in the actual world. He holds, to the contrary, that every phenomenological object—paradigmatically such things as specks in our visual field, tones in our auditory field, or objects of the sense of touch—is metaphysically *complex*. For 2.0131 tells us that specks "must have some color", that tones "must have some pitch", that objects of the sense of touch "must have some degree of hardness", and so on. But determinate colors, tones, degrees of hardness, and so on, Wittgenstein holds, are all what he calls "material properties", such as are produced "only by the configuration of objects" (2.0231). Moreover, just as colors have structure, according to 6.3751, so too, presumably, do other phenomenological properties. Hence, notwithstanding the fact that such objects may be the simplest ones with which we can be acquainted, they must still be metaphysically complex.

Perhaps the most compelling textual evidence for distinguishing between, rather than identifying, epistemological and metaphysical simples is to be found in two passages in the *Notebooks*. In *NB* 50(5), Wittgenstein writes: "But it seems certain that we do not infer the existence of simple objects from the existence of particular simple objects, but rather know them—by description, as it were—as the end-products of analysis, by means of a process which leads to them." And three entries later he continues: "Even though we have no acquaintance with simple objects we *do* know complex objects by acquaintance, we know by acquaintance that they are complex." (*NB* 50(10)). Far from embracing Russell's views about the fundamental objects of knowledge, Wittgenstein here explicitly rejects them. Wittgenstein's metaphysical simples are known only as the end products of analysis, never by acquaintance. It follows that his metaphysical simples cannot be identical with Russellian objects of acquaintance.

In a revealing passage Wittgenstein comments, "It always seems as if there were something that one *can regard as a thing*, and *on the other hand* real simple things" (*NB* 43(4)). Phenomenological objects, it seems fair to conclude, can indeed be regarded as "things", even as "simple" things (in the epistemological sense of "simple"). But for the reasons given, they cannot be the "*real* simple things" out of which the world is constructed.

So what are these real simple things? I think Wittgenstein's answer is absolutely clear and unmistakable. He says straightforwardly, "The division of the body into *material points*, as we have it in physics, is nothing more than analysis into *simple components*." (*NB* 67(8)); and again, "It always looks as if there were complex objects functioning as simples, and then also the *really* simple ones, like the material points of physics, etc." (*NB* 69(5)). If anything is to count, for him, as one of the ultimate building-blocks of reality, it must be physicalistic in character, not phenomenological. That, at any rate, is what I'm now going to argue.

In the first place, it is to the material points of physics, Wittgenstein claims, that analysis of phenomenological object leads. Both in the *Notebooks* (*NB* 81(8-11)) and in the *Tractatus* (6.3751) Wittgenstein treats points and patches of color—both of which, remember, are paradigms of phenomenological simplicity—as susceptible to what (in the former work) he calls "the analysis of physics" (*NB* 82(12)). It is by means of the analysis of physics, for example, that "a difference in structure between red and green" is revealed, by means of the analysis of physics that "the true structure of the objects [red and green] is brought to light." (*NB* 81(8-9)). Here Wittgenstein is presupposing that points and patches of color are complex. And he is asserting that their "true structure" is revealed when the material points whose configurations "produce" these material properties (2.0231) are displayed as standing to one another in certain determinate relations. These material points themselves, however, he thinks of as unstructured and hence incapable of further analysis and division. To repeat, "The division of the body into *material points*, as we have it in physics, is nothing more than analysis into *simple components*." (*NB* 67(8)). The kind of analysis provided by physics, then, isn't just a model for analysis of complex objects into simple components. It *is* such an analysis.

Second, it is arguable that when Wittgenstein speaks of the "material points" or "point-masses" (the renderings of "*materiellen Punkte*" given, respectively, by Anscombe, in her translation of the *Notebooks* and by Pears and McGuinness in their translation of the *Tractatus*) of physics, he is thinking of mass-possessing but strictly extensionless spatiotemporal points of the kind that Einstein envisaged in 1915 and that contemporary physicists call "singularities". This would not be surprising, given that Wittgenstein's understanding of physics owes much to his reading of Heinrich Hertz's *The Principles of Mechanics*. Since anything that is extensionless is *necessarily* indivisible, point-masses, on this account, would have to be among the ultimate simples which make up the substance of the world.

Note—since I don't want to be misunderstood on this point—that I'm not saying that Wittgenstein's metaphysical simples are physical *atoms*, or any other material *particles*. He chooses his words, here, rather carefully, speaking of *points* rather than particles. The "material points"—or "point-masses"—of physics are different both from atoms (as traditionally conceived) and from particles (as currently conceived). They are such that one cannot even conceive of their being divided into parts. They are extensionless points, and hence, for purely logical reasons, they are indivisible. His putative examples of metaphysical simples, then, are about as good as anyone could give.[9]

Third, there is historical evidence that Wittgenstein regarded the language of the *Tractatus* as having been physicalistic in character, one that in the last analysis makes reference to physical items. Writing to Schlick in 1932, Wittgenstein protested that it was he, not Carnap or Neurath, who should get the credit for developing the basic ideas of physicalism (albeit "with the same brevity with which the entire *Tractatus* is written.").[10]

Fourth, several passages in the *Tractatus* itself show quite clearly that Wittgenstein did indeed think of his simple objects in physical terms. He explicitly asserts both that the science of mechanics "supplies the bricks for building the edifice of science" (6.341) and that the propositions of natural science, the propositions whose bricks mechanics supplies, tell us everything that can be "said" about the actual world (*NB* 91(2) and 6.53). "Mechanics," he says, "is an attempt to construct according to a single plan all the *true* propositions that we need for the description of the world." (6.343). When he goes on to claim, in the very next passage, "The laws of physics, with all their logical apparatus, still speak, however indirectly, about objects in the world" (6.3431), we ought—I believe—to take him seriously. He may well be judiciously agnostic about whether this or that physical object is one of his ultimate simples, just as contemporary physicists may prudently reserve judgment about whether the current repertoire of "elementary particles" will prove to be the simplest achievable. But there can be little doubt that he believed that, notwithstanding the fact that other kinds of objects might feature as the simples of other possible worlds, the ultimate building-blocks of the actual world must be physical objects of some kind—be they "material points" or something else.[11]

6. Atomism and Basic Ontology

In Chapter II we saw that Wittgenstein is committed to a possibilist ontology. This ontology, it should be noted, includes nonactual possible relations (explicitly) and nonactual possible properties (implicitly), as well as nonactual possible things (objects). Confirmation that he included possible relations along with possible things is provided by Appendix I to the *Notebooks*, where he writes: "I extract from all possible relations the relation R, just as by a name, I extract its meaning from all possible things." (*NB* 99). As for nonactual possible properties, although he does not explicitly mention them, their inclusion would seem to accord with the general tenor of his thinking. After all, from the conjunction of 3.031 and 5.123 (the source for our general argument for possibilism, noted in Chapter II, section 8) we can infer that a god can create *any* constituent of a possible state of affairs—not just any possible object and any possible relation, but any possible property as well.

Now, Wittgenstein's atomism consists in the fact that from combinations of these three kinds of possibilia he can construct everything else in his ontology. Given all possible simple objects and the de re necessary simple properties that are part of (internal to, essential to, de re necessary to) their natures, he has on hand all the items he needs in order to construct, with the help of the simple relation of combination, the remaining items. All possible complex objects "consist" (*NB* 50(8)) of, or have as their "constituents" (2.0201), simple objects standing in relations of combination to one another. All possible material properties of complex objects are "produced" by the structured combinations of simple objects (2.0231). Structured combinations of simple objects likewise "produce" (2.0272) all *possible* states of affairs (2.0124). And *possible* combinations[12] of possible states of affairs produce those totalities that Wittgenstein refers to in the *Tractatus* as "imagined worlds" (2.022) and in the *Notebooks* as "possible worlds" (*NB* 83(2)). He needs only to import the notion of existence (in the restricted sense, noted in Chapter 2) in order to derive further the items that he calls "facts" (that is, existing states of affairs (2)) and the "real" (2.022) or actual world (that is, the totality of facts (1.1), or the totality of existing states of affairs (2.04)).

Wittgenstein's atomism, however, must not be thought of as a sort of Meccano-set construction out of simple objects, simple relations, and simple properties. These ultimate constituents are all to be thought of as analytical postulates, items postulated as "the end-products of analysis, by means of a process which leads to them." (*NB* 50(5)). Simple objects, simple properties, and simple relations do not, as it were, lie around waiting to be put together: objects are always propertied and always stand in relation to other objects. What is primary, for him, is always something complex: an object's having a property, or two or more objects' standing in a relation, in short, a state of affairs. Another way of expressing the point is to say that the metaphysically simple objects of Wittgenstein's ontology are not to be thought of as what Copi once called "absolutely bare particulars". Rather, each simple object, as we shall now see, is indissolubly and polygamously wedded to several *formal* properties, each of which is "part of the nature" of that object.

7. Formal Properties in General

What does it mean, in general, to say that something $\emptyset$ is a form of, that is, a formal property of, an item x? I believe that Wittgenstein would hold that $\emptyset$ is a formal property of x if and only it satisfies the following conditions:

(1) $\emptyset$ is a "characteristic" (4.126(5)) that x has when x falls under the corresponding formal concept $\emptyset$;

(2) $\emptyset$ is an internal property of x;

(3) x's having $\emptyset$ determines or is made manifest in the combinatorial potential of x to combine with other items (in the case where x is simple) or the combinatorial potential of x's own elements (in the case where x is complex);

(4) x's having $\emptyset$ cannot be expressed, or "said", *by* means of a proposition with sense (a contingent proposition) but expresses itself, or "shows" itself, *in* the proposition in the kind of sign employed for x.

Each of these conditions requires some explanation.

Condition (1) explicates what Wittgenstein says in 4.126 through 4.1274 about the connection between formal properties and formal concepts (pseudo-concepts, as he sometimes calls them). In 4.1272 he lists a number of words that, he says, "signify formal concepts", namely, the words "object" ("thing"), "complex", "fact", "function", and "number". Since he ends the list with "etc.", it is clear that still other concepts qualify for the same formal status. Arguably, the list could be extended to include, at the very least, "simple", "self-identity", "property", and "relation". The first, "simple", must surely signify a formal concept if "complex" does. And the remainder are all formal ones, in a fairly intuitive sense of that word. Moreover, the formal properties corresponding to these concepts—those of *being a simple*, *being self-identical*, (*being identical with*, of course, is not a formal property but a formal relation), *being a property*, and *being a relation*—all satisfy each of the remaining conditions (2) through (4). And Wittgenstein himself provides some further examples of formal properties in 2.126 when he writes: "Space, time, and color (being colored) are forms of objects." Thus, *being in space*, *being in time* (of which *being an event* is a special case), and *being colored* must also be counted as formal properties.

Condition (2) reminds us that a necessary condition of $\emptyset$'s being a formal property of x is that it be an *internal* property, that is, a de re necessary property of x. 4.122 makes it clear that formal properties, together with structural ones, *comprise* the set of internal properties, just as formal relations, along with structural ones, *comprise* the set of internal relations. Any formal property, therefore, must a fortiori be an internal one. Formal properties, then, along with structural ones, are always internal to their possessors.[13] Now a property is internal to an object, Wittgenstein says, "if it is unthinkable that its object should not possess it." (4.123).

But (as we saw in Chapter II, section 5) unthinkability, for Wittgenstein, is equivalent to logical impossibility. Hence, a property is internal if it is logically impossible that its possessor should lack it: if it is logically necessary that its possessor should have it. However, the logical necessity which binds an internal property to its possessor is de re necessity. Condition (2), then, entails that if $\varnothing$ is a formal property of x then $\varnothing$ is a de re necessary property of x in the sense that x has $\varnothing$ in every world in which x exists.

Condition (3) is, in effect, a recapitulation of two of our earlier findings (Chapter II, section 5): (a) that the form of (and hence any formal property of) a simple item determines, or is made manifest in, the set of possible combinations into which that item can enter; and (b) that the form of (and hence any formal property of) a complex item determines or is made manifest either in the set of possible combinations into which that complex can enter or in the set of possible combinations into which the elements of that complex can enter. Claim (a), it may be remembered, is a generalization of 2.0141: "The possibility of its occurring in states of affairs is the form of an object"; and (b) is a generalization from 2.032, 2.033, and 2.15 in which Wittgenstein makes it clear that the form of a complex item is "the possibility of structure", where structure is "the determinate connection of objects or elements."

Condition (4) has to do with the *expression*, in Wittgenstein's preferred conceptual notation, of formal properties and of the formal concepts that objects fall under when they possess these formal properties.[14] In 4.126 Wittgenstein draws attention to "the confusion between formal concepts and concepts proper, which pervades the whole of philosophy." Formal concepts, he tells us in 4.1272, are "pseudo-concepts" that should not be represented, in the manner of Frege and Russell, by means of symbols for functions or classes. What he is getting at, I think, is this: that just as there is a difference in logical function between a proposition proper (a proposition with sense that says something contingent about how the world happens to be) and a logical pseudo-proposition (a tautology that shows something noncontingent about how every world must be), so too there is a difference in logical function between a concept proper (that ascribes to any object falling under it some property which that object may have or fail to have) and a logical pseudo-concept (which ascribes to any object falling under it a property which that object must have). And he wants to record this difference of logical function by means of a conceptual notation which will, all by itself, *show* this difference. Only a conceptual notation which records this sort of distinction can, in Wittgenstein's view, be truly adequate to the logical purposes that it is supposed to serve, that of being "a mirror-image of the world." (6.13).

How, then, would such a conceptual notation record the difference in logical function between genuine concepts (and genuine properties) and pseudo-concepts (and pseudo-properties)? Two cases have to be taken into account: that in which variables occur in such a conceptual notation and that in which names (or individual constants) occur.

For the case of variables, Wittgenstein's way of showing that an object falls under a given formal concept is, apparently, to use a variable (perhaps subscripted) that will *show* what formal property is being ascribed to the object. "The expression for a formal property", he says, "is a feature of certain symbols." (4.126(6)). For instance, "The variable name 'x' is the proper sign for the pseudo-concept *object*." (4.1272(1)). That, of course, represents no departure from the standard notation; and in this particular case no subscript is needed. But how about variables for other pseudo-concepts, such as the pseudo-concept expressed by the word "number"? For an answer, we have to consult what Wittgenstein said many years later, in 1930, when he explained his meaning to students in his classes at Cambridge. According to notes taken by John King and Desmond Lee [Lee 1980], his view was that just as one should not write "($\exists$x) . x is an object", so one should not write "($\exists$x) . x is a number". What one should write instead is, for the former case, simply "($\exists$x)", and, for the latter case, "($\exists x_{number}$)". As he puts it, "The pseudo-concept occurs inside the $\exists$ bracket." Here is what he says in full:

> There are no logical concepts, such for example as "thing", "complex", or "number". Such terms are expressions for logical forms, not concepts. Roughly speaking, a concept can be expressed as a propositional function: e.g. $\emptyset$ ( ) = ( ) is a man. But we cannot say $\emptyset$ ( ) = ( ) is a number. Such logical concepts are pseudo-concepts and cannot be predicated as ordinary concepts are. They are properly expressed by a variable together with the rules applying to it, the rules for obtaining its values. So I cannot write ($\exists$x) . x is a number or ($\exists$x) . x is a thing. If I use this notation I must write ($\exists x_{number}$). $\emptyset$x, meaning that there are certain variables to which specified rules apply: the pseudo-concept occurs inside the $\exists$ bracket, the true concept outside. All apparent logical concepts are to be expressed by a variable plus the grammatical rules governing its use. (p. 10)

As I understand him, he would say that "($\exists$x)" is a radically shortened form of "($\exists x_{object}$)", which in turn is short for "There are objects". "($\exists x_{complex}$)" will be short for "There are complexes", "($\exists x_{fact}$)" for "There are facts", and "($\exists x_{function}$)" for "There are functions". If I am right about the way in which his list of formal concepts can be extended, "($\exists x_{simple}$)" will be short for "There are simples", "($\exists x_{property}$)" for "There are properties", "($\exists x_{relation}$)" for "There are relations", and so on.[15] In each case, the subscript associated with the variable indicates the range of its possible values, the "grammatical rules governing its use".

Now the concept of existence, for Wittgenstein, is a formal concept, that is, a concept whose "characteristic" is a formal property. Like Kant and countless others, he holds that "exists" is not what Kant would call a "real" or "determining" predicate. Accordingly, the concept of existence can *not* be expressed, as can an "ordinary" concept, by means of what he called (in his comments to Lee) a "propositional function", that is, by means of a predicate-expression "$\emptyset$" which lies "outside the $\exists$ bracket". Rather, the concept of existence *expresses itself* in a proposition in one or other of the two ways previously distinguished: either (for the case of a name) in the name (or individual constant) which is the sign for the object itself, or (for the case of an individual variable in a closed formula) in what he calls "the $\exists$ bracket", that is, in the sign for what we call "existential quantifier". Wittgenstein writes: "In fact elementary propositions themselves contain all logical operations. For 'fa' says the same thing as '($\exists$x).fx . x = a'." (5.47(2)).[16] His point is that the existence of an object a *shows itself* in our symbolism either in the presence of the "$\exists$ bracket" (together with the sign for identity and the name "a") or, equivalently, in the simple presence of the name "a".

Before proceeding further, I wish to draw attention to some of the major points to emerge so far from our discussion of formal properties and the implications of those points.

In the first place, when discussing condition (1), I argued that the list of formal properties could be extended beyond that given by Wittgenstein himself. I have just added the property of *existence*. Let me now add still further properties to the list. Consider the formal property of *being a number* (one that features on Wittgenstein's own list). Obviously, anything that has that formal property (falls under the corresponding formal concept) is itself a number, and its being a number will be signified, Wittgenstein tells us (4.126(3)), by the sign for a number (that is, by a numeral). But, arguably, any given number must itself have certain formal properties, such as *being odd*, *being even*, *being prime*, etc. So these too must be added to the list. Consider, next, the formal property of *being a property,* which, though it does not feature on Wittgenstein's own list, must—I have already argued—be in any extension of his list. Obviously, anything that has that property is itself a property, and its being a property will be signified by the sign for a property, for instance, "F". But again, arguably, any given property must itself have certain "second-order" formal properties, such as *being a formal property*, *being a material property*, *being a structural property*, *being an internal property of its possessors*, and *being an external property of its possessors*. Likewise, anything that has the formal property of *being a relation*, must itself *be* a relation, and so must have have certain second-order formal properties of relations: *being symmetrical*, *being asymmetrical*, *being nonsymmetrical*, *being transitive*, *being intransitive*, *being nontransitive*, and so on, (though, of course, only certain combinations of these). The list can be extended still further so as to include, as I shall argue, such repeatable properties as *being an event*, and such nonrepeatable relational ones *as being identical to a*, and *being identical to b*. If I am right about this, there is no kind of item—be it an object, a property, a relation, a simple instance of one of these, or a complex instance of one of these—that does not have formal properties (indeed several formal properties).

Second, it should now be evident that, as condition (2) requires, all of the formal properties on our extended list are internal to their possessors in the sense that none of their possessors would be what they are were they to lack the relevant properties. A metaphysically simple object, since it is logically incapable of division into simpler elements, is essentially simple; a metaphysically complex object, since "its nature" is to have simpler objects as its constituents, is essentially complex; the number seven, which is prime and odd, is essentially prime and essentially odd; the relation of implication, which is nonsymmetrical and transitive, is essentially nonsymmetrical and transitive; and so on.

Third, as condition (3) requires, an item's having any of the formal properties in our extended list determines, and is made manifest by, the range of combinations—with other objects, properties, or relations—into which it can enter. Having certain formal properties precludes having certain other properties and standing in certain relations. Something that has the formal, and hence essential, property of *being an event*, for instance, is thereby precluded from having the property of *being colored* and is likewise precluded from having the relational property of *being put into a hole* (or, if you like, of standing in the relation *being put into* to a hole). The number seven, by virtue of being essentially odd and essentially prime, is thereby precluded from having the property of *being even*, and is likewise precluded from having the relational property of *being divisible by two* (of standing in the relation of *being divisible by* to two). To appropriate Wittgenstein's own terminology, "the internal nature of [an item] comes into view" (*NB* 70(8)), or is made manifest, in the range of combinations with other items (objects, properties, or relations) into which it is possible for it to enter; and having certain of these formal properties as part of its nature will mark out a given item as belonging to what Wittgenstein calls "a particular logical kind." (*NB* 70(9-10)). If I am right about this, Wittgenstein's doctrines regarding formal properties and logical kinds serve, for him, as a sort of substitute for Russell's theory of types (a theory that, he said, "must be wrong" (3.331)). They provide a nonarbitrary basis for determining which combinations of items are ontologically possible, and therewith for determining which combinations of symbols, in language and logic, are significant.

8. Formal Properties of Metaphysically Simple Objects

In section 7, we have been considering formal properties in general; and we have seen that their possessors may be any sort of item whatever, an object, a property, or a relation, be that item simple or complex. It is now time to consider the formal properties that metaphysically simple objects may possess, since—on the account I am going to give—the possibilities of combination for simple objects are constrained by certain of these formal properties.

The formal properties of objects are of three main kinds: some are undiscriminating in so far as all metaphysically simple objects must have them; some discriminate between different "logical kinds" of simple object; and some are sufficient, by themselves, to individuate each of the individual members of the set uniquely.

(1) All metaphysically simple objects, 2.011 tells us, are "possible constituents of states of affairs." And 2.0141 tells us, "The possibility of its occurring in states of affairs is the form of an object." I shall therefore refer to this possibility as the formal property of *being able to combine with other objects so as to produce a state of affairs*, or more briefly as the formal property of *combinatorial potential*. This formal property, which has to do with the "possibility" of configuration, is a modal property of its possessors. Moreover, it is "essential" to (2.011), "part of the nature of" (2.0123(2)), or "internal" to (2.01231) its possessors. Hence it is a de re necessary modal property of all metaphysically simple objects.

2.0121(5) asserts the internality of *combinatorial potential* in another way: "If I can imagine objects combined in states of affairs, I cannot imagine them excluded from the *possibility* of such combinations." Recall, from Chapter 2, section 5, that imaginability is both a sufficient and a necessary condition of logical possibility. I argued subsequently (in Chapter 2, section 10) that if one makes the appropriate substitutions—of talk about (logical) possibility for talk about what can be imagined—one obtains, "If it is possible that objects should combine in such and such states of affairs, then it is necessary that it is possible that objects should combine in such states of affairs", which—when analyzed in terms of the expressive resources of propositional modal logic—has the form of the distinctive thesis of S5: $\Diamond P \supset \Box P$. I now wish to point out that, when this same thesis is analyzed in terms of the more ample expressive resources of quantified modal logic, it has the form (x) $\Diamond Fx \supset \Box \Diamond Fx$. Quantified S5, therefore, is needed for the expression of Wittgenstein's view that the simple objects of his ontology have certain de re necessary (essential) properties, such as the essential formal properties of being able to combine with other simple objects to constitute all possible states of affairs.

Other formal properties that all simple objects have are the trivial ones of *being an object* and (arguably) *being self-identical*. That *being an object* is a formal property of simple objects, as well as complex ones, follows from what we have already said about 4.126 through 4.1272.[17] That Wittgenstein is committed to endowing all his simple objects with the essential property of *self-identity* follows, by generalization, from the fact (established in (3) later) that he is committed to endowing each object with its own individual essence: a with the property of *being identical with a*, b with the property of *being identical with b*, and so on.

(2) We have already noted that, according to 2.0251, *being in space*, *being in time*, and *being colored* are among the formal properties of objects. Of these, the first two but not the third are presumably among those that metaphysically *simple* objects can have. Note: I do not say that *being in space* and *being in time* are formal properties that all possible metaphysically simple objects possess. But if the point-masses of physics are, as I suggested earlier, plausible candidates for such status in the actual world, then they must surely possess the formal properties of *being in space* and *being in time*. And if they do possess them, then they possess them essentially. This is clear from 2.0121(4): "Just as we are quite unable to imagine spatial objects outside space or temporal objects outside time, so too there is *no* object that we can imagine excluded from the possibility of combining with others." Not only does he take it for granted that *being in space* and *being in time* are essential to any of their possessors; he asserts that they are essential to their possessors in just the same sort of way as combinatorial potential is essential to all objects.

It seems to be Wittgenstein's view that formal properties such as *being in space* and *being in time* mark out their possessors as belonging to different (though not necessarily exclusive) "logical kinds". He nowhere says this explicitly. Nevertheless, it seems to be implicit in *NB* 70(9) when he speaks in quite general terms of "the logical kind of an object", and when, in 2.0121(4) he uses the sortal terms "spatial objects" and "temporal objects" to mark out the possessors of these formal properties. It seems, then, to accord with Wittgenstein's thinking to suppose that he regards objects that fall under the formal concept "spatial object" as being of one logical kind, and objects that fall under the formal concept "temporal object" as belonging to a different, but not incompatible, logical kind. The internal natures of spatial objects sort them out into one logical kind; the internal natures of temporal objects sorts them out into another logical kind; and so on, for all the different internal natures that objects have by virtue of possessing formal properties.

Now the internal nature and corresponding logical kind of an object determines the range of the object's combinatorial possibilities. In *NB* 70(8), Wittgenstein uses the example of two complex objects, a rod "A" and a ball "B", to illustrate. He writes: "I can say that A is leaning against the wall, but not B. Here the internal nature of A and B come into view." It is by virtue of its internal nature that A can stand in the relation of *leaning against* to the wall, and by virtue of its internal nature that B cannot stand in that relation to the wall. They belong to different logical kinds. Hence their combinatorial potentials are different. To be sure, these examples all involve complex objects. But his thesis is a quite general one, applying to simple objects as well: "It is clear that the object must be of a particular logical kind; it just is as complex, *or as simple* [emphasis added], as it is." (*NB* 70(10)).

In an interesting passage a few pages later, Wittgenstein writes: "If I can imagine a '*kind* of object' without knowing whether there are any such objects, then I must have constructed their proto-picture for myself." (*NB* 74(4)). It seems, then, that the list of possibilia allowed for in his ontology includes not only possible objects, possible relations, and possible objects, but also those merely possible (uninstantiated) properties by virtue of which objects may be classified as belonging to different logical kinds. All that is necessary, he seems to be saying, is that we can construct their proto-pictures for ourselves, that is, that we can imagine what it would be like for an object to have a property that in fact nothing does have and imagine it as therefore belonging to the logical kind defined by that property. As usual, he gives no examples. But once more, with a little imagination, we can provide our own. For instance, it seems that we can imagine that *kind* of object that many persons call "disembodied spirits" without knowing whether there are any such objects. People can, and do, construct their "proto-pictures" for themselves. Other prima facie examples would seem to be angels, devils, celestial spheres, perpetual motion machines, and various exotic kinds of elementary particles. If in our conceptual scheme there is logical space, as it were, for merely possible objects, then there would seem also to be logical space for merely possible *kinds* of objects as well.

(3) Wittgenstein's formal properties of the sorts (1) and (2) are repeatable ones in as much as they can be instantiated by more than one object: all objects in case (1), only some in case (2). But it is arguable that Wittgenstein would also want to include among the formal properties of simple objects those nonrepeatable ones that, according to so-called haecceitists,[18] constitute the "individual essences" of objects. Those who believe in individual essences would say that a given object a has the nonrepeatable property of *being identical to a*, that object b has the non-repeatable property of *being identical to b*, and so on.

One way of distinguishing between someone who provides for haecceitist properties in his ontology and someone who does not is to suppose that we are given nothing but simple objects a and b along with the simple properties F and G; and to suppose further that in possible world, W_1, a has F as its sole repeatable property and b has G, while in possible world, W_2, a has G and b has F.[19] Is W_2 the very same world as W_1, or is it numerically different? Someone who does not believe in haecceitist properties would argue that since there are no properties other than F and

G by virtue of which a and b may be distinguished, b in W_2 just is a in W_1 while a in W_2 just is b in W_1, and so would conclude that W_2 is not really distinct from W_1 after all. Someone who believes in haecceitist properties, by way of contrast, would insist that among the properties which are constitutive of the identity of objects a and b are those of *being identical with a* and *being identical with b*, respectively. Since, for the haecceitist, a in W_1 has a property (namely, *being identical to a*) that b in W_2 lacks, b in W_2 is numerically distinct from a in W_1 notwithstanding the fact that these objects are otherwise indiscernible.[20] Hence, for the haecceitist, W_2 is distinct from W_1.

I believe that Wittgenstein would want to say that W_1 and W_2 are indeed different, and that he is therefore committed to haecceitism. Consider 5.53, which tells us, "Identity of object I express by identity of sign . . . Difference of object I express by difference of sign." Wittgenstein holds that a name such as "a" rigidly designates the very same object in each of the "propositional formations" (*NB* 50(2)) in which it occurs, independently of which of these propositional formations is true, and independently therefore of which corresponding world—for example, W_1 or W_2—actually obtains.[21] Hence, for Wittgenstein, a in W_1 will not be identical to b in W_2 notwithstanding the fact that a in W_1 has all and only the repeatable properties that b has in W_2, namely, the single repeatable property F. 5.53, remember, guarantees both that a in W_1 is identical to a in W_2 and that b in W_1 is identical to b in W_2. So, too, does 4.1211, in which Wittgenstein tells us, "two propositions 'fa' and 'ga' show that the same object is mentioned in both of them." Thus the propositional formation "Fa & Gb", for Wittgenstein, is by no means the same as "Ga & Fb"; the former will be true in W_1, the latter true in the numerically distinct W_2. And this can only be because a in W_1 has the property of *being identical to a*, whereas b in W_2 lacks that property.

9. External Properties of Metaphysically Simple Objects

It should not be forgotten that metaphysically simple objects may have properties other than internal ones: properties, that is, that are "external" to their possessors in the sense that it is *not* unthinkable, not de re impossible, that their objects should possess them. Such properties are not essential but merely "accidental", not de re necessary but "merely possible". As such they are, of course, excluded from what Wittgenstein calls "the province of logic" (2.0121(3)), and so are of little relevance to my present argument. Nevertheless, there has been some confusion about what sorts of properties might count as external to simple objects. So a brief digression seems called for.

It has sometimes been supposed, for example, by Max Black [1964], that any property that is not internal but external must be a material property. Now if Black were right, then, since material properties are produced only by the "configuration" of simple objects and hence are possessed only by complex objects, it would follow that the only properties possessed by simple objects are internal ones. Commenting on Wittgenstein's claim, in 2.0232, "In a manner of speaking, objects are color-less", Black tells us that "objects themselves have neither color nor any other contingent (= 'material, external') properties. Objects are propertyless." (p. 64). That objects are entirely "propertyless" is, of course, an exaggeration, and Black himself would allow it to be so since he recognizes elsewhere that simple objects have formal properties. Let us, then, take him to mean only that simple objects have no "contingent", external properties. Even so, this conclusion is mistaken and derives from muddled thinking. It stems from his conflation of the "for-mal/material" distinction with the "internal/external" one. As the preceding quota-tion makes clear, he *identifies* being material with being external. And elsewhere he *identifies* being formal with being internal: he tells us that material properties are "contrasted with 'formal' (= 'internal') properties". (p. 63). But both identifica-tions are mistaken. That "internal" does not mean the same as "formal" is evident from the fact that Wittgenstein distinguishes between "formal" and "structural" and regards structural properties as internal too.[22] That "external" does not mean the same as "material", with respect to either properties or relations, is evident from the fact that (as we shall see in a moment) some of Wittgenstein's objects have relation-al properties, such as *being combined with a*, properties that though external are not material. Quite generally, we need to remember, a property is external to an object, simple or complex, when it is possible to conceive of the object lacking it; and we can conceive of objects lacking many other properties besides their material ones. There is conceptual space in Wittgenstein's way of thinking for external properties which are not material, just as there is for internal properties that are not formal.

It is sometimes supposed, for instance, by Anscombe, and again by Goddard and Judge, that $\varnothing$ is an external property of a simple object a just when $\varnothing$ is the relational property that a has by virtue of *actually* being combined with certain other objects to produce a state of affairs S. Thus Anscombe [1959] writes, "The only 'external properties' his simple objects have, of course, are those of actually occur-ring in certain facts." (p. 11). And Goddard and Judge [1982] write, "What is possible constitutes the essential characteristics of an object, and what is actual constitutes the accidental attributes." (p. 10). Although this view isn't as badly mistaken as Black's, it still doesn't get Wittgenstein's position quite right. We need to be careful here. Recall that all that is necessary for $\varnothing$ to be one of a's external properties is that it be thinkable, and hence de re possible, that a should lack $\varnothing$, not that in addition a should actually have $\varnothing$. Suppose simple object a is combined with simple object b in possible but not actual state of affairs S'. Then in S' a has two properties: the property of *being combined with b* and the property of *being able to be combined with b* (the "possibility" of combining with b). The latter property, of course, is an internal, indeed a formal, property of a. But the former is not. We can easily imagine a's lacking that property and having some other property instead, for example, that of *being combined with c* in possible but not actual state of affairs S". Hence *being combined with b* is an *external* property of a. Yet since by hypothesis S' is a nonactual state of affairs, the property of *being combined with b* is not an *actual* property of a. It follows that not all the external properties of simple objects are the ones they actually have. Some are merely possible.

10. Combinations: Possible and Impossible

It is sometimes supposed, by Goddard and Judge, for instance, that there are absolutely no restrictions on the combinations into which Wittgenstein's simple objects can enter, that they are, as it were, totally promiscuous.[23] But I shall now argue, to the contrary, that certain of the formal properties to which they are initially wedded, namely, those that sort them out into different logical kinds, place curbs upon their other liaisons. Some combinations of simple objects are possible, namely, those that yield the complex entities mentioned; but other combinations are not.

An abundance of textual evidence, involving passages in which Wittgenstein advances an interesting blend of ontological and linguistic considerations, shows this to be the case.

In the first place, consider again Wittgenstein's own example of a rod A and a ball B, whose respective internal natures are made manifest by the fact that "I can say that A is leaning against the wall, but not B." (*NB* 70(8)). The reason why I can *say* the one but not the other, Wittgenstein believes, is not a consequence of some arbitrary doctrine of a grammarian's devising. It is, he claims, because of the internal natures of the objects being talked about; because A has an internal nature, and belongs to a logical kind determined thereby, that permits it to stand in that relation to the wall whereas B does not. This is why, as he says in the very next entry, "A name designating an object thereby stands in a relation to it which is wholly determined by the logical kind of the object . . ." (*NB* 70(9)).

Note that in talking of different "logical kinds" he is not just talking about the basic ontological categories of objects, properties, and relations. These latter, of course, do indeed mark out differences of logical kind. But the logical kinds that Wittgenstein is talking about here are more specific. They are to be drawn within the category of objects itself, not just between that category and the categories of properties and relations.

Second, Wittgenstein immediately goes on to give another example of impossible combinations when he writes, " 'The watch is *sitting* on the table' is senseless!" (*NB* 70(11)). Significantly, in calling the sentence "senseless", he is using the very same term, "sinnlos", which he uses in the *Tractatus* 4.461 to characterize any contradiction which attempts to express what he calls the "impossibility of a situation." (5.525). I think it likely that he regards the senselessness of this sentence as simply a special case of logical impossibility, the de re logical impossibility of the watch's standing in the relation of *sitting on* to the table, and that he is trying, by means of this example, to illustrate the general point that belonging to a particular logical kind restricts the logically possible liaisons into which an object, simple or complex, can enter.

Third, in Appendix II to the *Notebooks* (his "Notes Dictated to G. E. Moore in Norway, April 1914"), Wittgenstein gives another example of an object belonging to a logical kind such that it is thereby precluded from standing in certain sorts of combinatorial relationships to other objects: "An illogical language would be one in which, e.g., you could put an *event* into a hole." (*NB* 107(5)). Events, I take him to be saying, belong to the logical kind that, in the *Tractatus*, he calls "temporal objects" (2.0121). They are of such a logical kind that in no intelligible language could it be said that an instance of that logical kind has the relational property of *being put into a hole*. It is de re impossible for an event to have that relational property.

Fourth, Wittgenstein's doctrine of logical kinds is carried through into the *Tractatus* even though the terminology is not. As we have seen, he classifies certain objects as belonging to the logical kind that he calls "temporal objects" and others as belonging to the logical kind that he calls "spatial objects". These logical kinds obviously encompass simple and complex objects alike. Certain other logical kinds that he mentions, namely, "specks in the visual field", "tones", and "object of the sense of touch" (2.0131), encompass complex ones only. What is important is that all these logical kinds of object—like those explicitly discussed in the *Notebooks*—are defined by their object's possession of corresponding de re necessary properties, properties that, he says, the objects "must have": *being in time, being in infinite space, having some color, having some pitch*, and *having some degree of hardness*, respectively. And their possession of these essential properties rules out their possession of certain others.[24]

Fifth, many years later, some time during 1931–32 to be more precise, Wittgenstein confirmed that this had indeed been his view in the *Tractatus*. He was explaining to Desmond Lee [1980] the import of 2.012 in which he had written: "if a thing *can* occur in a state of affairs, the possibility of the state of affairs must be written into the thing itself." Presumably Lee wanted to know whether Wittgenstein's emphasis on "can" was intended to carry the suggestion that there are states of affairs within which a given object can *not* occur. Wittgenstein's answer, though couched in the linguistic mode, was unambiguous: "If you know how to use a word and understand it you must already know in what combinations it is *not* allowed [emphasis added], when it would be nonsense to use it, all its possibilities." (p. 120). The possibilities and impossibilities of combination for words *mirror* the possibilities and impossibilities of combination for objects.

Finally, the idea that some combinations of objects are possible whereas others are not carries through into the *Philosophical Investigations* as well. He writes: "Compare 'logically possible' with 'chemically possible'. One might perhaps call a combination chemically possible if a formula with the right valencies existed (e.g., H-O-O-O-H). Of course, such a combination need not exist, but even the formula HO_2 [sic] cannot have less than no combination corresponding to it in reality" (p. 521). Needless to say, a formula will be chemically *possible*, whether or not it depicts some actual chemical substance, only if the atoms it symbolizes have the right "valencies", that is, the possibility of combining in the way depicted. And this will evidently depend on what *kinds* of atoms are being depicted. Just as a combination will be chemically impossible if the chemical atoms are not of the right chemical kinds, so a combination will be logically impossible if its "logical" atoms (the atoms of logical analysis) are not of the right logical kinds.

In 5.525 Wittgenstein talks about "impossible situations". These, on the account I am giving, not only encompass the de dicto impossibilities recognized in the contradictions of truth-functional logic. They encompass also the de re impossibilities of combining objects of certain logical kinds with objects of incompatible logical kinds. When objects belong to incompatible logical kinds, their putative combinations yield impossible states of affairs. Only when they belong to compatible logical kinds do their combinations yield possible (though not necessarily actual) states of affairs.

11. Complexes, Supervenience, and Emergence

As an atomist, Wittgenstein believes that his metaphysical simples suffice for the construction of everything else that exists or might exist. Among the complex entities that, he claims, the configurations of his atoms "produce" are not just states of affairs but complex objects (*NB* 50(8)) and complex properties, including material ones (2.0231), as well.[25] All these complexes, of course, have structures, and the properties of having just the structures they do are internal to them.

In order to understand what these claims amount to, I want initially to address two questions: (1) How exactly are complex objects supposed to differ from states of affairs? (2) What does Wittgenstein mean by "material properties"; and how, if at all, do material properties differ from other complex properties? That done, I'll turn to the more substantive question: (3) In what sense are complex properties supposed to be "produced" by the configuration of simple objects? Finally, in subsection (4), I'll explain the distinction between the expressions "structured property" and "structural property" and give an account of why Wittgenstein holds that all structural properties (though not all structured properties) are internal to their possessors.

(1) It seems that the distinction between complex objects and states of affairs, for Wittgenstein, is merely one between two ways of thinking of the same complex. On the one hand, he claims, "A complex just is a thing!" (*NB* 49(4)). On the other hand, a complex, he would also say, can be thought of as a state of affairs, as a thing having a property, or as two or more things standing in relation to one another. Consider the complex which consists of the moon, the earth, and the sun and their changing relations to one another. This complex, he says, "We can even conceive of . . . as a *thing*." [emphasis added] (*NB* 49(1)). But equally, we can conceive of the moon's circling round the earth and thereby moving round the sun as a state of affairs (as our use of the gerund clause makes clear).

Now if I am right in supposing that Wittgenstein treats the distinction between states of affairs and complex objects as a function of how we think of complexes, then it follows that everything that Wittgenstein says about the internal properties, formal and structural, of states of affairs applies mutatis mutandis to complex objects.[26] Consider, for instance, some complex, C, of simple objects that "stand in a determinate relation to one another" (2.031). By virtue of being a "combination of objects (things)", C (according to 2.01) is to be regarded as a state of affairs. Call this complex, qua state of affairs, S. Then by virtue of having constituents standing in determinate relations to one another, S (according to 2.032) has a certain structure and hence has corresponding structural properties. However, let us suppose that this very same complex, C, is the thing to which we customarily refer by the name "Socrates". Then since Socrates is identical with complex, C, and C is identical with state of affairs S, it will follow that any structure of S will ipso facto be a structure of Socrates. Thus we find Wittgenstein speaking about the structure "possessed by the thing Socrates" (*NB* 69(9)). For any complex whatever, that complex, qua state of affairs, has certain structural properties that are internal to it, and qua object, has the very same internal structural properties.

(2) As we saw earlier, Wittgenstein holds that some properties are complex. What he calls "material properties" are obviously cases in point, since they are produced "only by the configuration of objects" (2.0233). But wherein lies the difference between material properties and other complex ones? Since neither Wittgenstein nor, to my knowledge, any of his commentators explains the difference, one might easily succumb to the idea that they are one and the same. Nevertheless, there is a distinction to be drawn here; and an important one at that.

The best way of demonstrating this, and of getting clear about the criteria for being a material property, is to invoke the distinction between internal and external properties. By common consensus among commentators, the term "material properties" encompasses, at the very least, such paradigms as *being on my table, occurring at 1500 hrs on 17 July 1989, being red, having the same pitch as middle C, having the hardness of a diamond, being 10cm long*, and *being 28 degrees Celsius*. By common consensus, too, all such material properties are external, or accidental, to their possessors. (Recall that Max Black even goes so far as to suggest that "material" and "external" are synonyms.) But, according to Wittgenstein, some *complex* properties are internal to their possessors. Thus, although the determin*ate* property of *being red* is external to its possessors, the corresponding determin*able* property of *being colored* is internal to anything—a visual point or patch, for instance—that has that property: a speck in my visual field, he tells us, "though it need not be red, must have *some* color" (2.0131(2)). Likewise, he goes on, with tones that "must have *some* pitch"; with objects of the sense of touch that "must have *some* degree of hardness"; and so on. More generally, any of what Wittgenstein's philosopher-friend at Cambridge, W. E. Johnson, called the "determinables" under which determinate material properties fall, will be internal, on Wittgenstein's account, to their possessors. But if so, then these determinable properties, though obviously complex (since they have structure (as 6.375(1) makes clear), cannot themselves be material properties.[27] In short, since material properties are always accidental properties of their possessors, whereas some complex properties are not, there must be some complex properties that are not material.[28]

But precisely where, within the class of complex properties, are we to draw the line between material and nonmaterial? Is the property of *mortality*, which we know from *NB* 69(9) to be complex since it has a structure, a material property? How about so-called mental properties such as the property of *being intelligent* or spiritual ones such as *having a soul*?

We simply do not know what Wittgenstein's answers to any of these questions would be. We can allow that conventional interpretational wisdom is correct in counting *being red, being hard, being loud, being hot*, and so on, as paradigms of material properties. But we don't know how to go on extending the list. And Wittgenstein's one-time use of the term "material properties" (in 2.0231) doesn't help much. All it tells us is that simple objects do not themselves possess material properties (or, as he puts it in 2.0232, that they are, in a manner of speaking, "colorless"), and that material properties are somehow "produced" by the configuration of simple objects.

Fortunately, we don't need to determine the precise boundary between material and nonmaterial properties in order to be able to address the next, more interesting, question: What does it mean to say that material properties are "produced" by the configuration of simple objects? It is to this that I now turn.

(3) There are two ways in which Wittgenstein's talk of properties' being "produced" may be construed: temporally or atemporally.

Viewed atemporally, the claim that material properties are produced by the configuration of simple objects amounts to the claim that they are supervenient on the simple properties (the formal ones) of those simple objects when they are related or configured in certain ways. By this I mean, roughly, that any two complexes whose constituents are configured in the same way must have the same material property even though the same material property may be instantiated by a variety of different configurations.[29] The idea that macroproperties, quite generally, are in this sort of way "supervenient" on microproperties is currently receiving a lot of attention in the philosophy of science (in particular, the philosophy of biology) and the philosophy of mind. It would do no violence to the history of ideas to suggest that Wittgenstein, in 2.0231, was himself promoting some such an idea, albeit somewhat vaguely. At the very least, what he has to say about the production of material properties is consistent with this construal.

Viewing the "production" of complex properties in terms of supervenience, however, leaves out an important temporal dimension. I suspect that it would not be at all out of keeping with Wittgenstein's way of thinking about complex properties to say that from a historical point of view they are "emergent". Here, once more, I am admittedly invoking an expression which Wittgenstein himself does not employ. Yet the concept of emergence may help us understand the way his thinking goes. Let me explain.

One way of elucidating the concept of an emergent property is to invoke a distinction between those properties that, in an atomistic scheme of things, are possessed by the most *elementary* objects and those that aren't. Clearly, if atomism is to afford some sort of explanatory account of how the world comes to be as it is, any properties that complexes have but simples do not must somehow be accounted for in terms of what happens when the simples are combined with one another. And one way of describing this is to say that these properties (any that complexes alone possess) "emerge" from the structured configuration of propertied simpler elements. Now clearly, some of the properties of complexes are ones that their simple constituents also have. The property of *being in space* is a case in point: if a complex object is in space then its elementary constituents must also be in space. The property of *being in space* is therefore *not* an emergent one. But equally, some of the properties that complexes have are not ones that their constituents have. The property of *being red*, for instance, is a property that many complexes such as the surfaces of cherries, fire-engines, and rosy cheeks possess. Yet as a matter of fact, the simple elements out of which cherries, fire-engines and rosy cheeks are compounded (elementary particles, according to contemporary physics) do not possess that property. Rather, the property of *being red* may be said to "emerge", and may then be attributed to the complex object, once the simple elements of the complex are configured in a determinate, and hence structured, way. Just how many simple elements must enter into configuration, just how complex their structured configuration must be, or in just what relations the structured configuration must stand to other structured configurations,[30] in order for the property of *being red* to emerge, is something for physicists to decide. But, as philosophers, we can recognize the distinction between emergent and nonemergent properties and bring it bear on our ontology.

That, I believe, is what Wittgenstein is doing when he tells us, in 2.0231, that although the substance of the world—the set of metaphysically simple objects that make up the actual world—does not by itself determine any material properties, it is by means of the configuration of those simple objects that make up the substance of the world that material properties—and complex properties, more generally—"are produced". Remember that, for him, metaphysically simple objects have no accidental (external) properties apart from certain of their relational ones. They have essential, formal properties only. The simple objects that populate the actual world have such simple formal properties as *being in space* and *being in time*; but they do not in themselves have material properties such as *being red*, *being hard*, *being loud*, and *being hot*. The latter are produced by, that is, emerge from, the structured configurations of the metaphysical simples that he seems most to favor as the ultimate constituents of the actual world: material points.[31]

Now I admitted earlier that it is extremely hard to determine from anything that Wittgenstein says just where the line of demarcation, if any, between material and nonmaterial properties lies. But so far as the concepts of (atemporal) supervenience and (temporal) emergence are concerned it matters not. For the supervenience or emergence of *all* properties not possessed by metaphysically simple objects is a corollary of Wittgenstein's version of atomism. Accordingly, since the property of *mortality* is complex (since it has structure (*NB* 69(9)) and cannot plausibly be attributed to simple objects (since they are "unalterable and subsistent" (2.0271)), it must be emergent. So, too, with mental properties such as those of *being intelligent*, and spiritual ones such as *having a soul*. They are all properties that, in this world at least (though not necessarily in all worlds), are "produced"—arguably, during the course of evolution (in the case of species) and in the course of embryological development (in the case of individuals)—by the configuration of the metaphysically simple objects that make up the substance of our world.[32] More particularly, if my general argument in support of a physicalistic interpretation of these simples is correct, all complex properties, material and immaterial alike, are emergent from point-masses or whatever other simples are eventually decided upon by the analysis of physics. (Little wonder, if this be so, that Wittgenstein thought of Carnap's and Neurath's physicalism as a case of near-plagiarism.)

(4) In section 3, I pointed out that *being structured* (that is, having a determinate connection of simpler, and ultimately absolutely simple, constituents) is a sufficient and necessary condition of complexity. It follows that any complex—whether it be a complex object or a complex property (or, for that matter, a state of affairs or a world)—may be said to be structured. For the case of complex properties this warrants our talking about such properties as "structured properties" (where, by that expression, we mean "property that has a structure"). Serious confusion can arise,

however, if we fail to distinguish between "structured properties", as so defined, and what Wittgenstein calls "structural properties". The reason is that, in Wittgenstein's usage, all structural properties are internal to their possessors, whereas structured properties may well be merely external to their possessors.

Let us suppose that some complex object X consists of simpler parts a, b and c standing in triadic relation R, and that by virtue of having these parts standing in that determinate connection, X has the material property of *being red*. Then the structure of the complex object X consists of Rabc[33]; and the structural property of X consists in *having a, b, and c in relation R*. Having that structural property, according to Wittgenstein, would be essential to X insofar as X would not be what it is if it lacked that property. Now complex properties, too, have structures and hence structural properties. In what would the structure of an instance of the complex property *being red*, that X possesses, consist? The answer that I am inclined to give draws on the fact, noted already, that since no object can exist wholly unpropertied, each of the simpler parts in X, namely, a, b, and c, must have its own property or properties. Let us suppose that a has F, b has G, and c has H. Then, the structure of this instance of the property of *being red* may be said to consist in *having an F-part, a G-part, and an H-part standing in relation R* ; and the property of having that determinate structure will be essential to this instance of *being red*.[34]

We can now see why it is important to distinguish between "structured property" and "structural property". All complex properties are structured. But not all complex properties are structural. The property of *being red* is structured, as we have seen. Yet it certainly is not internal to all its possessors. Rather, like other material properties, it is always external to the objects that have it. The structural properties of *having a, b, and c in relation R*, and *having an F-part, a G-part, and an H-part standing in relation R* , by way of contrast, certainly are internal to their possessors, namely, to X and a certain instance of *being red*, respectively.

12. States of Affairs: Their Structures and Forms

States of affairs, in general, are the kind of thing that we normally refer to in English by means of gerund clauses such as "the rod's leaning against the wall", "the ball's leaning against the wall", "the watch's lying on the table", and "the watch's sitting on the table". Some of these gerund clauses, e.g., the first and third, make sense; the corresponding states of affairs are possible. Others, for example, the second and fourth, do not make sense (according to Wittgenstein)[35]; the corresponding states of affairs are impossible. Now a *possible* state of affairs, we have seen, is produced by a *possible* configuration of metaphysically simple objects, a configuration, that is, that is possible given the essential forms of the constituent objects. In such a state of affairs the constituents "fit into one another like the links of a chain" (2.03). An impossible state of affairs, by way of contrast, would be one whose constituent objects have forms that do not permit them to fit into one another like links of a chain.

A mere combination of simple objects, it is clear, will not count as a state of affairs any more than a mere "medley" of corresponding words will count as a proposition (3.141). Just as the elements of a proposition (words) are "articulated", so too are the elements of a state of affairs (objects). In both cases, it is necessary not just that certain elements be combined with one another, but that they be combined with one another in certain ways, that is, have a particular mode of combination. A complete description of a state of affairs, then, must go beyond saying that its constituent objects are "combined". It must tell us in what *determinate* way they are combined. We are not told enough, for instance, if a state of affairs is described merely as one in which a ball is "combined" with a wall or a watch with a table. For descriptions such as these do not discriminate between the *possible* modes of the objects' combination (e.g., the ball's resting next to the wall or the watch's lying on the table), and the *impossible* ones (such as the ball's leaning against the wall or the watch's sitting on the table). (To be sure, these examples have to do with combinations of complex objects, not simple ones. But for simple objects the same principle must also hold.) What is required, for the combination of simple objects, as well as of complex ones, in states of affairs is that the precise or *determinate* mode of combination be given. As Wittgenstein puts it, "In a state of affairs objects stand in determinate relations to one another." (2.031). And this determinate way in which objects are connected in a state of affairs, he goes on to tell us, is what he will call the *structure* of the state of affairs (2.032). States of affairs, in short, are not just combinations of propertied objects; they are structured combinations of such objects.

Now states of affairs have form as well as structure. How do these differ, and in what does each consist? Two main accounts have been given. Each account meshes quite well with some of the things that Wittgenstein says, but not so well with others. So, before expressing a final judgement, I'll review the main merits and defects of both. Let's start with what each has to say about *structure*.

According to one account, which I'll call the A-account, the structure of a state of affairs is a function not only of the particular *mode* of connection but also of the particular *objects* connected. On this account (which is favored by F. P. Ramsey, Max Black, and B. F. McGuinness), the structure (or structural property) of a state of affairs is uniquely individuating.[36] Hence no two states of affairs can have precisely the same structure.

This, it is argued, is the view to which Wittgenstein is committed by virtue of what he has to say about the linguistic analogues of states of affairs, namely, propositions. For propositions, too, have structures. And in a number of passages (4.1211(2), 5.13, 5.2, and 5.22) Wittgenstein claims that it is primarily the structures of propositions which determine their logical interrelationships. Of these it is 4.1211(1) that seems to me to provide the most compelling evidence for the A-account. There he tells us, "two propositions 'Fa' and 'Ga' show that the same object is mentioned in both of them". Since he goes on, in the very next sentence, to connect this remark with his views about structure ("If two propositions contradict one another, then their structure shows it; the same is true if one of them follows from the other"), it seems clear that he believes it to be the *structures* of "Fa" and "Ga" which show that a is mentioned in both of them. But if this is the case, then the name "a" must be essential to the structures of both propositions, and correspondingly the object for which that name stands must be essential to the structures of both states of affairs.

The essence of the A-account can be brought out by considering some state of affairs S in which object a stands in the determinate relation R to object b. On the A-account, the structure of aRb is in no way different from aRb itself. Hence the structure of S is to be represented, as is S itself, by "aRb". As McGuinness acknowledges, the A-account makes the claim that the state of affairs aRb has the structure aRb "trivial" and talk of the structure of a state of affairs strictly redundant.[37] This result is somewhat counterintuitive insofar as we ordinarily think of the structure of something, not as identical to that thing, but as a property of that thing. It is also counterintuitive in so far as we ordinarily think of the structure of something not as a property which that thing alone can possess, but as a property which that thing can share with other things. Yet the A-account treats the structural properties of states of affairs as uniquely individuating individual essences, that is, as haecceitist properties of their possessors.[38]

These somewhat counterintuitive results are avoided by what I shall call the B-account. According to the B-account (that favoured by James Griffin), the structure of a state of affairs is a function of the mode of connection only. On this account, talk of the structure of a state of affairs is by no means redundant. Rather, when Wittgenstein tells us in 2.032 that the structure of a state of affairs is the "determinate way in which objects are connected", he means just that; he is talking only about the *mode* of their connection, not about the objects connected. It follows, on this account, that it is perfectly possible for states of affairs with different constituent objects to have their structure in common. For instance, consider two states of affairs, S (=aRb, as before) and S' (=cRd). The B-account would hold that although S and S' are different states of affairs, they have the same structure. They have the same structure insofar as their different constituent objects are configured in the same manner, by the relation R. In saying what this common structure is, we are abstracting from the particularity of the objects in the two states of affairs and considering only their common mode of configuration. Thus, on the B-account, there is just one structure that is common to both aRb and cRd, and this structure may be represented, with the help of variables, by "xRy".

The B-account, then, fits nicely with our ordinary understanding of the word "structure". But does it fit with Wittgenstein's? This is not so clear. In the first place, it doesn't accommodate the apparent implications of 4.1211, in which he seems to imply that particular objects do feature in the structures of states of affairs. And in the second place, it leaves us wondering how, either in Wittgenstein's usage or our own, "structure" is supposed to differ from "form". After all, "xRy" displays what we (and he, according to the A-account) would probably be disposed to call the *form* that both aRb and cRd have in common. But in that case, the term "structure" itself would seem to be redundant.

Note that no matter which account we give, some things remain the same. In the first place, in Wittgenstein's terminology, the structure of a state of affairs is a *structural property* of that state of affairs. In the second place, Wittgenstein regards structural properties, whether of states of affairs or of other items, as internal to their possessors, as is evident from 4.122(2) in which Wittgenstein observes, "Instead of 'structural property' I also say 'internal property'." It follows that the structure of a state of affairs is internal to it. No matter which account we give, it is easy to see why. On the A-account, the structure of S is *identical* with S itself. It would be "unthinkable", therefore, that S should not possess the structure that it has, for then it would not be itself. It would be unthinkable, that is, for S not to have the property of *being a standing in R to b*.[39] On the B-account, the structure of S is not identical with S but is still an essential property of S. For again, it would, in Wittgenstein's view, be unthinkable that S should not have the property of *having some object x standing in relation R to some object y* ; any state of affairs that lacked that property would not be S but a different state of affairs.

The A- and B-accounts differ about *form* as well as structure. According to the A-account, the form of a state of affairs is what the B-account would call its structure. It is a function not of the particular objects but solely of the mode of their connection. As McGuinness [1956] puts it, "two facts or pictures are of different structure if their objects (or elements) are arranged in the same way, but are different objects; in such a case however they will have the same form." (p. 143). However, according to the B-account, the form of a state of affairs is a function neither of the particular objects nor of the particular mode of their connection but solely of the *forms* of the constituent objects. As Griffin [1964] says, "to put it roughly, the form of a state of affairs is the amalgam of the forms of the objects constituting it." (p. 76).

Both accounts try to explicate what Wittgenstein means by the puzzling assertion that the form of a state of affairs is "the possibility of [its] structure." (2.033). (I put "its" in brackets because the German text, *"Die Form ist die Moglichkeit der Struktur"*, according to Black, warrants only "the possibility of structure".) Both accounts take some liberties with the syntax of 2.033 to make their respective stories sound plausible. On the A-account (which Griffin dubs the "variable interpretation"), 2.033 tells us, for instance, that the structure (that is, the state of affairs) aRb is a possible way of instantiating the specific *form* "xRy"—and, for that matter, other increasingly more general forms such as "$\emptyset(x,y)$" (where the adicity of $\emptyset$ is left open) and "P" (that is, the most general propositional form "This is how things stand" (4.53(5)). In short, "its form is the possibility of structure" is taken to be short for something like "its form is something of which structure is a possible instantiation". On the B-account, "its form is the possibility of structure" is short for something like "its form is the possibility of its constituents being in a structure", where the possibility of being in the kind of determinate connection that Wittgenstein calls a structure is something which belongs to simple objects by virtue of their forms. This accords well with the account I gave earlier (in Chapter II, section 9) when, generalizing from a number of cases in which Wittgenstein talks about the forms of complex items, I said: "For any item, X, which has structure, the form of X consists in the possibility of the determinate connection of X's elements." Since, according to 2.0141, the possibility of determinate connection in some state of affairs or other is identical to the form of an object, 2.033 may be taken as asserting that the form of a state of affairs consists in, or is a function of, the forms of its elements, that is, the forms of its constituent objects. This comes very close to what

Griffin [1964] is getting at when he says, "to put it roughly, the form of a state of affairs is the amalgam of the forms of the objects constituting it." (p. 76). If I understand him correctly he is claiming that we can think of the form of a state of affairs as the set of forms of its constituent objects, and hence as the set of all possible ways in which its constituent objects could be combined to produce possible states of affairs.

Admittedly, the A-account seems best to accommodate our ordinary understanding of "form", since "xRy", "$\varnothing(x,y)$", and "P" are all what we ordinarily would call forms of aRb. On the other hand, the B-account—at least as I have construed it here—seems best to accommodate the overall view of Wittgenstein's modal atomism that I have been advancing throughout this chapter. Let me explain.

On the B-account, 2.033 implies that the form of a state of affairs is a function of the formal properties of the metaphysically simple objects that are its constituents. This, of course, is what we should expect given that it is, as we have seen, the forms of simple objects that determine how they can combine. Consider S again. Suppose that a and b have different forms (and hence different possibilities of combination); that a has the formal property F and b has the formal property G; and that these formal properties F and G are repeatable ones such that still other objects may possess them. Then, in giving an account of the form of S, there is no need for us to mention the particular objects a and b. For if the form of S is a function of the *forms* of its constituent objects, all we need mention is their formal properties F and G. Neither is there any need for us to mention the particular relation R in which a and b stand in S. For presumably R is not the only *possible* relation in which objects of the forms F and G can stand to one another. Hence if the form of S is the set of *possible* ways in which objects of forms F and G can be combined, then all we need mention is that an object of the form F can stand to an object of the form G in some relation $\varnothing$. On the B-account (as I am construing it), what Wittgenstein would call "the" form of the state of affairs S might be expressed by something like "$\varnothing(Fx,Gy)$". This, of course, is not how Wittgenstein himself would represent it. If he were to use his 1930–32 subscripting device, then presumably he would write something like "$\varnothing(x_F, y_G)$". And if he were to use the notation of the *Tractatus*, in which he sanguinely supposes that the form of an object "is given immediately any object falling under it [the corresponding formal concept] is given" (4.12721), it would seem to suffice simply to write "$\varnothing(x,y)$".[40] In any case, the use of the individual variables "x" and "y" and of the functional variable "$\varnothing$" would suffice to show that there are many possible ways in which this form may be instantiated, many different possible values that the variables can take. Thus, on the B-account, whereas the representation of the *structure* of S (as "xRy") doesn't have to show the particular objects a and b, but does have to show the particular determinate relation R in which they stand, the representation of the *form* of S (as "$\varnothing(Fx,Gy)$" or "$\varnothing(x_F, y_G)$" or "$\varnothing(x,y)$") doesn't have to show anything particular about either the objects or the relation, but does have to show what *possible* relations objects having the same *forms* as a and b might stand in. Roughly speaking, then, we know what "the" form of a state of affairs is (its *specific* form, that is) when we know the possible states of affairs in which objects having the same forms as its constituents can combine.

One way of summarizing the differences between the A- and B-accounts of both structure and form is to consider the state of affairs S and the series of expressions that might be used to represent it: "aRb", "xRy", "∅(x,y)", "P". On the A-account, "aRb" counts as the (nonshareable) structure of S, and those following it in the series count as its increasingly general forms. On the B-account, "aRb" counts merely as a representation of S itself but not of its structure, "xRy" as the (shareable) structure of S, and those further to its right as its increasingly general forms. Thus the B-account turns out to involve a systematic shift of the structure/form distinction one place to the right (as it were) along the preceding series of expressions. I have said that the B-account fits most easily into the general story I am telling. But I also recognize that there is nothing in the A-account that is inconsistent with my overall view.

In the end, then, the credentials of these two accounts turn on the question of what Wittgenstein really meant by "structure" and by 2.033. And as to that, it must be acknowledged that his meaning is very elusive indeed. In fact, in a couple of passages (4.1273 and 4.1252) he refers to the first of the expressions in the above series, viz., "aRb" as a *form*, thereby effectively collapsing the "structure"/"form" distinction altogether. So it may be that that the best thing to do is to avoid any dogmatic stance whatever and admit simply that his use of these expressions is every bit as "shifting" as is his use of "object", "property" and "relation" (4.123).

Be all that as it may, the point that I wish to emphasize right now is that, no matter which account we give, the forms of states of affairs, like their structures, are internal to them; or, more precisely, that the formal properties of states of affairs, like their structural properties, are internal properties of their possessors. On the B-account, for instance, it is as unthinkable that S should lack the formal property of *having an F-part standing in some relation ∅ to a G-part* as it is that S should lack the structural property of *having a standing in relation R to b*. Since, according to Wittgenstein, "a formal concept is given immediately any object falling under it is given" (4.1274), *having an F-part*—on the assumptions given we have been making about the forms of a and b—follows from *having a as a part*, and *having a G-part* follows from *having b as a part*. The unthinkability of the lack of the formal property, then, *follows from* the unthinkability of the lack of the structural one.

Two corollaries regarding the formal properties of states of affairs are worth noting. In the first place, that states of affairs possess certain internal formal properties is not something that can be *said* by means of a genuine proposition but rather—like all that is noncontingent—is something that can only be *shown*. In 4.122(1), Wittgenstein says that there is a "certain sense" in which we can talk about the formal properties of states of affairs. But this sense, of course, is that in which we can talk about these formal properties showing themselves, making themselves manifest, or expressing themselves "in", the relevant propositions. Thus he goes on: "It is impossible, however, to assert by means of propositions that such internal properties and relations exist: rather, they make themselves manifest in the propositions that represent the relevant states of affairs and are concerned with the relevant objects." (4.122(4)). In the second place, the way in which the internal property (whether formal or structural) of a state of affairs is made manifest in a proposition is by an internal property of the proposition itself: "The existence of an internal property of a possible situation is not expressed by means of a proposition: rather, it expresses itself in the proposition representing the situation, by means of an internal property of that proposition." (4.124(1)). Here we have an intimation of one of the main themes (which I'll pursue in Chapter 4) of Wittgenstein's theory of language, namely, that the internal structures and forms of propositions are expressions of the internal structures and forms of the states of affairs which they represent, and—in both cases—that these internal properties are functions of the formal properties of simple objects.

13. The Myth of Independence

Notoriously, Wittgenstein asserts that states of affairs are independent of one another in the sense that "from the existence or non-existence of one state of affairs it is impossible to infer the existence or non-existence of another" (2.061–2.162); or, as he says more generally, "There is no possible way of making an inference from the existence of one situation to the existence of another, entirely different one." (5.135). Correspondingly, he asserts the logical independence of those propositions, elementary propositions, that assert the existence of states of affairs: "The simplest kind of proposition, an elementary proposition, asserts the existence of a state of affairs. It is a sign of a proposition's being elementary that there can be no elementary proposition contradicting it." (4.21–4.211). I say "notoriously" because the doctrine of independence, to my mind, is indefensible: I know of no account that makes it plausible, and even Wittgenstein eventually came to recognize that it was a mistake.

It is somewhat remarkable that he should ever have thought the doctrine sound. There is no hint of it in the *Notebooks*. It is not needed as support for any other doctrines (not even that of truth-tables) in the *Tractatus* .[41] And given what he says in both works about the internal logical properties of states of affairs and of the elementary propositions that represent them, there is a powerful prima facie case against it.

In developing the case against the doctrine of independence I shall, for the most part, set aside considerations having to do with the internal properties of states of affairs and elementary propositions and concentrate instead on arguments having to do with (1) the requirement that the constituent objects in states of affairs be configured in *determinate* ways, and (2) the requirement that elementary propositions be *complete* descriptions of the states of affairs they represent.

(1) The Argument from Determinateness

Simple objects are combined or configured with one another to produce states of affairs (2.01 and 2.0272). But not just any combination or configuration, remember, will do. Any combination must be a *determinate* one that is possible for objects of the logical kinds concerned, so that spatial objects must combine in determinate ways, temporal objects in determinate ways, and so on. Consider, then, a state of affairs consisting of three spatial objects, a, b, and c. In what does the determinateness of their connection consist? It will not do to say merely that they are "combined" with one another in space. That would in no way distinguish between their forming a mere collection or aggregation and their forming a state of affairs in which the objects "fit together like the links of a chain." (2.03). Nor would it distinguish between various possible *modes* of their combination in states of affairs. If they are spatial objects, and therefore necessarily "situated in infinite space" (2.0131), they must be related to one another in spatially determinate ways. Among their possible spatially determinate relations would be linear ones. And for linear relations there are three possibilities: one is that the three objects should be combined linearly so that a is between b and c; another that b should be between a and c; still another that c should be between a and b. Each such spatial relation is a determinate one, and to each there corresponds a different possible state of affairs. But, as should be obvious, these different possible states of affairs are not independent of one another. Rather, since we are talking here of specific individuals, not types of individuals, no two of these states of affairs can exist at the same time, and the inference from the existence of one to the nonexistence of either of the others would be perfectly valid.

We can, of course, run the same argument through again for the case of temporal objects. Such objects, for example, events, are necessarily related to one another in time. Once more it will not do to say merely that event e_1 is temporally related to event e_2. For if the temporal relation between them is to be a determinate one then it must either be one in which e_1 precedes e_2, or one in which e_2 precedes e_1, or one in which e_1 and e_2 occur simultaneously. But, once more, these three possible states of affairs are incompatible and hence not independent.

The argument from determinateness can be generalized. Despite his feigned agnosticism as to which objects in the actual world are to count as metaphysically simple, Wittgenstein makes it clear that in his view the actual world contains objects that are located in space and in time (2.0251). These objects must, therefore, stand in determinate spatial and temporal relations to one another. But among the determinate spatial and temporal relations that are possible as between simple objects are some that are asymmetrical. Let R' be such an asymmetrical relation. Then the possible state of affairs aR'b is incompatible with its converse, the possible state of affairs bR'a. Hence the doctrine that states of affairs are independent of one another is false.

Note that it won't help to suppose that when, in 2.051, Wittgenstein tells us that being in space and being in time are forms of objects, he means only that they are forms of complex objects. For all the constituents of a complex spatial object must themselves be spatial objects. Hence any simple objects that are spatially and/or temporally related to one another in the actual world must be so related in determinate ways that will sometimes be asymmetrical. So the problem of satisfying the requirement of determinacy for the spatial relations between them arises all over again.

Clearly Wittgenstein intends his metaphysics to be realistic, one that will give an account of they way the world is, not just of ways worlds might be. But the real world, he recognizes, is a spatiotemporal world. And the spatiotemporal world, I have been arguing, is one in which there are simple asymmetrical spatial and temporal relations between objects. It follows that states of affairs, in such a world, cannot always be independent of one another.

Neither can states of affairs always be independent of one another if the world is, as Wittgenstein again believes it to be, one in which names stand for objects. For the semantic relation of naming is essentially an asymmetric one. Let N stand for the relation of naming as it holds between simple name "a" and its bearer, simple object a. Then, since N is an asymmetrical relation, "a"Na is incompatible with aN"a", and these two states of affairs are not independent of one another.

A determined defender of the doctrine of independence might reply to these criticisms by reminding us that it is supposed to hold only between *elementary* states of affairs—those in which the only objects, properties, and relations that occur are simple and unanalyzable—and then suggesting that at a deeper level of analysis the asymmetrical spatio-temporal and semantic relations to which I have drawn attention might somehow be analyzed away. But, in the first place, this defense isn't available to Wittgenstein since, on his own account, the relation of naming is a "simple", and hence unanalyzable, one (*NB* 49(13)). By hypothesis, then, both "a"Na and aN"a", in the previous paragraph have only simple constituents and hence are elementary states of affairs. And secondly, the defense merely replaces one myth (that of independence) with another: that of the ultimate reducibility, in ways seemingly nondemonstrable and certainly never demonstrated, of asymmetrical relations to ones which are either symmetrical or nonsymmetrical.

(2) The Argument from Completeness

I have directed the argument from determinateness against the doctrine that elementary states of affairs are independent, though that argument could with equal (if not greater) felicity have been directed against the associated doctrine that elementary *propositions* are independent. The argument from completeness is directed against the latter doctrine only. In pressing it, I shall set aside all considerations to do with the irreducible asymmetry of certain spatiotemporal and semantic relations, and (for the sake of the argument) suppose counterfactually that the only simple relation required by Wittgenstein's ontology is the simple, symmetrical, one of combination. Even if this were the case, I shall now argue, the doctrine of independence would still be doomed.

Wittgenstein holds that an elementary proposition gives us a *complete* description of the state of affairs it represents in the sense that (a) in it "the elements of the propositional sign correspond to the object of thought" (3.2) so that the two "possess the same logical (mathematical) multiplicity" (4.04), and (b) in it the configuration of the simple signs corresponds to the configuration of simple objects in the state of affairs (3.21). An elementary proposition, then, is a complete description of an elementary state of affairs and hence will contain neither fewer nor more simple signs than there are objects in the state of affairs. Let "aRb" be an elementary proposition in which "R" stands for the simple symmetrical relation of combination. Then the possible state of affairs that "aRb" represents must be one in which simple object a is combined with simple object b, *and* (given that "aRb" has the same mathematical multiplicity as the state of affairs it describes) *with no other object*. To be sure, the elementary proposition "aRb" does not itself assert the italicized clause. But that is not only because, being elementary, it cannot contain any conjuncts; it is also because, in saying all that *is* the case it implies what is *not* the case. As Wittgenstein puts it, "If all the positive statements about a thing are made, aren't all the negative ones already made too?" *NB* 33(5). Now, if "aRb" is an elementary proposition then "aRc" (where "c", too, is the name of a simple object) must surely also be one. And in that case, "aRc" will completely describe a possible state of affairs—this time one in which the very same object a is combined with c, *and with no other object*. But if both "aRb" and "aRc" are complete descriptions of a's involvements, then it cannot be the case that, *at one and the same time*, both "aRb" and "aRc" are true. Just as from the truth of "Tom is legally married to Jane" we can (given society's insistence on monogamy) infer the falsity of "Tom is legally married to Sue", so also from the truth of the elementary proposition "aRb" we can (given Wittgenstein's insistence on what I call the Principle of Descriptive Completeness[42]) infer the falsity of the elementary proposition "aRc". Hence elementary propositions may fail to be independent of one another just as the states of affairs they represent may.

I think that Wittgenstein eventually came to see that this was so. More than twenty years after he had finished the *Tractatus* , in his 1929 paper "Some Remarks on Logical Form", he considered the doctrine of independence again and concluded that, contrary to his earlier opinion, propositions about elementary states of affairs can, as he then put it, "exclude" one another. His examples are not very well-chosen since he writes as if attributions of determinate degrees of length, pitch, color, temperature, and other such material properties could be asserted by elementary propositions.[43] But that aside, the reasons he gives in 1929 for abandoning the doctrine of independence are closely related to those I have just given concerning the completeness requirement. In his words

> If someone asks us "what is the temperature outside?" and we said "Eighty degrees", and now he were to ask us again, "And is it ninety degrees?" we should answer "I told you it was eighty." We take the statement of a degree (of temperature, for instance) to be a *complete* description which needs no supplementation. Thus, when asked, we say what the time is and not also what it isn't. (pp. 34–35)

The moral of the story is obvious. As applied to our presumed examples of elementary propositions, the proposition "aRb" tells us that a is combined with b; and, given that it is a complete description which needs no supplementation, we are entitled to infer that a is not also combined with c. Thus the putative elementary propositions "aRb" and "aRc" exclude one another just as effectively as do the propositions "It is eighty degrees outside" and "It is ninety degrees outside". To repeat: "If all the positive statements about a thing are made, aren't all the negative ones already made too?" (*NB* 33(5)).

An explicit recognition of the fact that the doctrine of independence is incompatible with the completeness requirement is to be found in a work composed about the same time as "Some Remarks on Logical Form", namely, in his *Philosophical Remarks* [44] (composed between February 1929 and April 1930). There Wittgenstein eventually came to recognize that the fact that two elementary propositions, f(a) and f(b), *can* contradict one another is, as he put it, "connected with the idea of a complete description" (sections 77–78, p. 106). Thus, he explains: "'The patch is green' describes the patch completely, and there's no room for another color." And he later adds: "Besides, the position is no different for colors than for sounds or electrical charges. In every case it's a question of the complete description of a certain state at one point or at the same time." (§81, p.109).

Now, if the doctrine of independence is so demonstrably a myth, why should Wittgenstein ever have supposed otherwise?[45] As far as I know, Wittgenstein never explained why. So I can only speculate. But our speculation need not be wholly idle. In the course of it I want to touch on a couple of points of interest and importance.

One possible answer is that he took himself to be reaffirming the Humeian doctrine that there is no logical nexus between events, or his own doctrine that "all that happens and is the case is accidental." (6.41(2)). It is possible, then, that he did not realize that Hume's doctrine does not require that there can be no inference from the existence of one state of affairs to the existence or nonexistence of another, but only that there can be no such inference from the existence of a state of affairs to the existence or nonexistence of another *entirely different* one. Interestingly, Wittgenstein gets it right at one point when, writing about situations in general, he claims: "There is no possible way of making an inference from the existence of one situation to the existence of another, entirely different situation." (5.135). Elsewhere, however, he omits the "entirely different" qualification. Were it—or its equivalent for elementary propositions—included in 1.21, 2.061, 2.062, 4.211, 4.27, 4.28, 4.42, 4.45, and 5.134, these independence-claims as thus amended would be true.[46] When thus amended, the false doctrine of the independence of elementary propositions and states of affairs would yield to the true doctrine of the independence of entirely different elementary propositions and entirely different states of affairs.

Another possible explanation of why Wittgenstein was led to espouse the unqualified independence doctrine is that he took it to be a precondition of the deservedly famous, because original, truth-tabular account of truth-functional logic that he gave in 4.31. Interestingly enough, it is usual even today to maintain the fiction that the so-called "truth-possibilities" set out on the left side of a *standard truth-table* (i.e., a truth-table which has 2^n lines for n variables) are truth-possibilities for propositions that are both elementary and independent. Yet they need not be either. Nor need they even be genuine truth-possibilities, genuine possibilities of combination for the propositions represented. Wittgenstein himself pointed out in the *Tractatus*, "The schemata in 4.31 have a meaning even when 'p', 'q', 'r', etc. are not elementary propositions." (5.31). And it is certainly not required, for truth-tables in modified form to be effective, that the propositions there represented be independent; we can modify the standard truth-tables so as take account of failures of independence. Wittgenstein himself eventually came close to seeing this. He notes, in "Some Remarks on Logical Form", that there may be cases in which two propositions—such as "Patch P is red at time t" and "Patch P is blue at time t"—exclude one another. In such a case, he points out, one of the lines in the truth-table gives the conjunction of these two propositions "a greater logical multiplicity than that of the actual possibilities." (37).[47] That is to say, there would be fewer than 2^n (that is, fewer than four in this case) genuine truth-possibilities. But he thinks this demonstrates some "deficiency" of his notation, and presumably also of his way of setting up truth-tables, and supposes that "rules of syntax" need to be laid down in order to prevent such awkward results, these rules of syntax being ones which we will be able to formulate only when "we have actually reached the ultimate analysis of the phenomena [for example, the phenomenon of color-exclusion] in question." Presumably, the sorts of rules of syntax he has in mind are akin to those at which he hints in his discussion of the different formal concepts under which objects fall and of the various ways in which corresponding differences of formal properties might be recorded in a correct conceptual notation (for instance, by the subscripting device within the "∃-bracket"). But, as we have already seen, his own suggestions as to how these rules might go are inadequate. And in any case he seems not to realize that we have no need to await an adequate formulation of such rules of syntax or the successful completion of any such "ultimate analysis". It suffices that we have sound philosophical reasons to *strike out* any of the lines in which the 'p's, 'q's, and 'r's, etc., on the left side are *not* independent of one another—perhaps because a line represents what he calls "an impossible combination", or because some other logical relations (for instance, of implication, equivalence, or subcontrariety) hold between them. Then since independence will be preserved on the remaining lines, the *reduced truth-table* (one in which fewer than 2^n lines remain) will still do the job it is supposed to.[48] In short, we do not need to maintain the fiction that all noncompound, elementary propositions are logically independent of one another in order to employ truth-tables as a decision-procedure for truth-functional propositional logic. All we need to do is to forbear from applying truth-tables in an unreflective, purely mechanical way. We need only determine in advance what are the internal structures of the propositions represented, what are their consequential internal relations to each other, and hence what are the genuine truth-possibilities for their combination.

I think it likely that had Wittgenstein paid more attention to the fine-grained structures of states of affairs and elementary propositions, and to the internal properties of both, as determined by the simple objects they contain or name, respectively, he would never have propounded the doctrine of independence in the first place. A major flaw in the *Tractatus*, and a major barrier to our understanding of the essential features of his metaphysical and logico-linguistic doctrines, would thereby have been avoided.[49]

14. Situations: Possible, Impossible, and Necessary

In the *Tractatus*, Wittgenstein advances several important theses about the complexes that he calls "*Sachlagen*" (translated by Pears and McGuinness as "situations"). *Sachlagen* (situations) may be possible, impossible, or certain; of those which are possible, some exist while others do not; and "entirely different" situations are logically independent of one another. But what exactly are *Sachlagen*? And how, if at all, do they differ from other Tractarian complexes?

Our efforts to find out are likely to be frustrated by differences in translation. If we read Anscombe's English translation of the *Notebooks*, we find that the word "situation" occurs frequently enough; yet it turns out that this is her rendering of the German term "*Sachverhalt*", not "*Sachlage*", and that the latter term does not occur at all in that work. Complicating matters still more, we find that both Ogden (in his original translation of the *Tractatus*) and Black (in his *Companion*) render "*Sachlage*" as "state of affairs" and "*Sachverhalt*" as "atomic fact", while Pears and McGuinness, as we have seen, translate these as "situation" and "state of affairs", respectively. As a contribution to clarification, I try to sort out this translational mess and the confusions that it promotes in the following table:

English translations

	Of the *Tractatus*		Of the *Notebooks*
German term	Ogden and Black	Pears and McG.	Anscombe
Sachverhalt:	Atomic fact	State of affairs	Situation
Sachlage	State of affairs	Situation	—

[As noted, throughout this book I adopt the Pears and McGuinness translation.]

But what does "*Sachlage*" *mean*? Despite the fact that the term doesn't appear in the *Notebooks*, we can establish what Wittgenstein means by it, when he uses it in the *Tractatus*, if we pair off certain passages in the two works. The following table displays the correlations (where the expressions in square brackets are those given by Pears and McGuinness and adopted here):

Tractatus passages		*Notebooks* passages
Sachlage	=	*Sachverhalte* [= state of affairs]
4.031	=	8(4)
4.032	≈	8(7)
4.04	≈	37(2)
4.462	=	8(10)
Sachlage	=	*Tatsache* (= fact)
5.156	=	61(10)
Sachlage	=	*ein Welt* (= a world)
4.031	=	7(3)

These correlations show, and a general reading of the *Tractatus* confirms, that Wittgenstein uses the term "*Sachlage*" as a general-duty term to refer to one or more states of affairs, to one or more facts, or to one or more whole worlds.[50] It follows, then, that situations (*Sachlagen*) may fall under the same range of concepts, may have the same sorts of properties, as these other items: like states of affairs, for example, they may be possible or impossible, and they may exist or fail to exist.

It comes as no surprise, then, to find that Wittgenstein allows for this when he talks, in 5.525(2), of certain situations as being possible and of others as being impossible. Two kinds of possible situations may be distinguished: those in which metaphysically simple objects enter into possible combinations with one another to produce possible elementary states of affairs; and those in which two or more possible states of affairs are combined with one another to produce, as it were, a compound state of affairs or (as we are now to call such) a possible situation. Likewise, two kinds of impossible situations may be distinguished: those in which the forms of metaphysical simples preclude them from combining to produce possible states of affairs; and those in which two or more possible states of affairs fail to be compossible, for instance, the sort of case envisaged in section 13 ("The myth of independence") in which a's being in R to b precludes a's being at the same time in relation R to c, or in which a patch's being green precludes it from being at the same time red.

What may come as a surprise, however, is to find Wittgenstein's referring, in 5.525(2), to the "certainty" ("*Gewisheit*") of certain situations when he writes, "The certainty, possibility, or impossibility of a situation is not expressed by a proposition, but by an expression's being a tautology, a proposition with sense, or a contradiction." What can Wittgenstein mean, here, by "certainty"?

Anscombe argues that the certainty he is talking about is epistemological rather than logical. Yet the context surely suggests otherwise. The trichotomy "certain/possible/ impossible", both here and in 4.464, corresponds to the trichotomy "tautology/proposition with sense/contradiction". These trichotomies would not be exhaustive, as they are plainly intended to be, were "certain" here not to be understood as meaning "logically necessary". If I am right, Wittgenstein is telling us, in 5.525(2), that the logical necessity, logical possibility, or logical impossibility of a situation is shown by an expression's being a tautology, a proposition with sense (a contingent proposition), or a contradiction, respectively. This is clearly what, on other grounds, we would expect him to say. But it still leaves us with the puzzle. What can it possibly mean to say that a *situation* is logically necessary?

A clue is to be found in 5.152(3), where Wittgenstein talks about the "certainty [i.e., logical necessity] of a logical inference" as being a limiting case of probability, and goes on to link this to the notion of tautologousness. What he is getting at would seem to be that in the case where the truth of a proposition P may validly be inferred from the truth of a proposition Q, the probability of P given Q is 1 ("certain"), and the corresponding conditional statement of the form "If Q then P" is logically necessary. Suppose, for instance, that the proposition Q asserts the existence of the situation in which both of two states of affairs, S_1 and S_2, exist, and that the proposition P merely asserts that S_2 exists. Then the conditional statement "If Q then P" may itself be viewed as asserting the existence of a hypothetical situation: that in which if both S_1 and S_2 exist, then S_2 exists. And the certainty of the inference from Q to P may then be said to be a function of the necessity, or certainty, of this hypothetical situation.

Consider the following passage, in which Wittgenstein sets out conditions whose satisfaction suffices for the truth of a proposition P following (of logical necessity) from the truth of a proposition Q:

> If all the truth-grounds that are common to a number of propositions are at the same time truth-grounds of a certain proposition, then we say that the truth of that proposition follows from the truth of the others. In particular, the truth of a proposition "P" follows from the truth of another proposition "Q" if all the truth-grounds of

the latter are truth-grounds of the former. The truth-grounds of the one are contained in those of the other: P follows from Q. (5.11–5.121)

Recall (from our discussion in Chapter II, section 10) that by "the truth-grounds" of a proposition, Wittgenstein means the possible states of affairs, or possible situations, that would make that proposition true. For instance, in the case we have been considering, the truth-grounds of Q are the possible states of affairs S_1 and S_2, while the truth-grounds of P are the possible state of affairs S_2. Clearly, the truth-grounds of Q are "contained" in the truth-grounds of P in the sense that all possible worlds in which both S_1 and S_2 obtain are worlds in which S_2 obtains. Hence P follows from Q. This can be illustrated by means of the following worlds-diagram:[51]

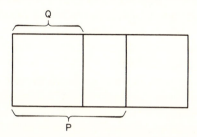

Here we let the rectangle represent the set of all possible worlds, and the brackets for P and Q represent the worlds in which P and Q, respectively, are true. These brackets, then, represent what Wittgenstein calls the "truth-grounds" of P and Q. And our diagram shows in what sense it can be said that the truth-grounds of Q are "contained" within the truth-grounds of P: the set of possible states of affairs in which Q is true is included in (is a subset of) the set of states of affairs in which P is true. Thus the logical necessity of the hypothetical situation envisaged when we assert "If Q then P" consists in the conditional necessity that relates the truth-grounds of Q to the truth-grounds of P when the former are "contained" within the latter.[52] If I'm right about all this, Wittgenstein's talk, in 5.525(2), of the "certainty" of situations has nothing to do with epistemology. Rather, like his talk of the possibility of some situations and the impossibility of others, it plays a central role in his explication of the metaphysical foundations of logic.

Another range of concepts under which situations (as well as states of affairs) fall is that of existence and nonexistence. That situations can exist or fail to exist is presupposed by 5.135, in which Wittgenstein enunciates the appropriately qualified, and entirely sound, doctrine of the independence of *entirely different* situations. Just as the class of possible states of affairs needs to be subdivided into those that exist (in the restricted quantificational sense) and those which do not, so, too, with situations. Existing situations, like existing states of affairs, are *facts*.

15. Facts, Realities, and the Actual World

On the account I gave in the Introduction and have been presuming ever since, states of affairs are possibilia that, when they actually exist, are facts (*Tatsachen*). Thus I agree with Erik Stenius [1960], who claims, "a Sachverhalt is something that could *possibly* be the case, a Tatsache something that is *really* the case." (p. 31). All *Tatsachen* are *Sachverhaltes*. But not all *Sachverhaltes* are *Tatsachen*, since *Sachverhaltes* may either exist or fail to exist, and only those that actually exist are to be counted as *Tatsachen*.

The evidence, cited by Stenius, for regarding the expressions "facts" and "existing states of affairs" as virtual synonyms is compelling. These expressions are contextually defined as meaning the same on two occasions: first, in the parallelism of "The world is the totality of facts . . ." (1.1) with "The totality of existing states of affairs is the world." (2.04); and secondly, in the parallelism of "For the totality of facts determines what is the case, and also what is not the case." (1.12) with "The totality of existing states of affairs also determines which states of affairs do not exist."(2.05). Moreover, Wittgenstein tells us quite explicitly (though with a slight change of grammar), that facts are existing states of affairs: "What is the case—a fact—is the existence of states of affairs." (2).

This account of the relation between *Sachverhalte* and *Tatsachen* is best captured by the Pears and McGuinness translation of "*Sachverhalt*" as "state of affairs" and of "*Tatsache*" as "fact". But it does not fit at all well with the original Ogden translation of these expressions as "atomic fact" and "fact", respectively, a translation which strongly suggests that the former are a subclass of the latter rather than the other way round.

Now I admit that a certain amount of textual evidence seems to give trouble for my and Stenius's account, and for the Pears and McGuinness translation which promotes it. The following passages from the *Tractatus*, in particular, therefore call for some explanatory comment: "Even if the world is infinitely complex, so that every fact consists of infinitely many states of affairs . . ." (4.2211), and "If an elementary proposition is true, the state of affairs exists: if an elementary proposition is false, the state of affairs does not exist." (4.25). So does Wittgenstein's explanation of the relationship between a *Sachverhalt* and a *Tatsache*, as offered to Russell: "Sachverhalt is, what corresponds to an Elementarsatz if it is true. Tatsache is what corresponds to the logical product of elementary props when this product is true." (*NB*129). In each case—and, for that matter, in 2 as well—Wittgenstein appears to be saying that a fact (*Tatsache*) may be made up of more than one state of affairs; that facts (*Tatsachen*) have states of affairs as their constituents; and that *Tatsachen* are nonelementary, "nonatomic", logical products of *Sachverhaltes* whereas the latter are always elementary or "atomic". Hence it is plausible to argue that *Sachverhaltes*, as the constituents of the complex entities which Wittgenstein calls *Tatsachen*, must themselves have the status of facts, being differentiated from *Tatsachen* only by virtue of being "atomic", whereas *Tatsachen* are "molecular". So, the argument goes, the Ogden translation of "*Tatsache*" as "fact" and "*Sachverhalt*" as "atomic fact" is the right one after all.

I don't deny that in a number of passages Wittgenstein speaks of facts as having states of affairs as their constituents. But it does not follow that *all* facts are complexes of states of affairs. Nor does it follow that *all* states of affairs are constituents of facts. Nor, for that matter, is it absolutely clear that Wittgenstein thinks of *all* states of affairs as elementary in anything other than a relative sense.[53] I'll deal with these points in turn.

As to the question whether all *Tatsachen* are complexes of *Sachverhaltes*, I think it significant that, in the one case (*NB* 129) where he directly addresses the issue, Wittgenstein speaks of facts as corresponding to the "logical products" of elementary propositions, where the expression "logical product", as he certainly knew, allows for the degenerate case where a true elementary proposition is its own logical product. He explicitly makes reference to another "degenerate" case when he observes, "The logical product of a tautology and a proposition says nothing more nor less than the latter by itself." (*NB* 8(10)). Hence, a *Tatsache* may well correspond to a true elementary proposition, namely to an elementary proposition that is true by virtue of asserting the existence of an elementary state of affairs that does in fact exist.

As to the question whether all *Sachverhaltes* are constituents of *Tatsachen*, here the evidence to the contrary (1.12 and 2.05) is quite conclusive. We have already seen that some states of affairs, though possible, do *not* actually exist. Clearly, however, any possible state of affairs which does not actually exist must count as one of those things which are *not the case*, that is, that are *not* facts. Hence, not all *Sachverhaltes* are constituents of *Tatsachen*.

As to the question whether *Sachverhaltes* are always elementary, I think it important to note that Wittgenstein explicitly licences us to treat states of affairs which are not really elementary *as if* they were elementary, just as (in *NB* 61(11)) he licenses us to "treat" objects that are not simple as if they were simple. Remember that in 5.31 he comments that the schemata he has given for his truth-tables (in 4.31) "have a meaning even when 'p', 'q', 'r', etc., are not elementary propositions", and—he might well have added—even when the corresponding truth-possibilities (which he identifies, in 4.3, with "possibilities of existence and non-existence of states of affairs") are not really truth-possibilities of elementary states of affairs. Here we encounter, once more, his deliberate policy of making provision for the transfiguration, as it were, of much that he says about the atomic level—of simple objects, of simple states of affairs, of simple names, and of simple propositions—to the nonatomic level of quite ordinary objects, ordinary states of affairs, ordinary names, and ordinary propositions.

Wittgenstein also uses another pair of terms to refer to those states of affairs that exist, that is, to whatever is the case or is a fact. These are the terms "*Realität*" and "*Wirklichkeit*", both of which are usually translated as "reality". [54]

His use of these terms is a little unusual. There is some disposition for speakers of English to use the word "reality" as an abbreviation for "the (real or actual) world". So used, the question, How many realities are there? admits of only one answer: there is only one reality. Yet Wittgenstein repeatedly uses both "*Wirklichkeit*" and "*Realität*" as if there could be many realities—or even no reality. For instance, he uses the expressions "any reality [*jede Wirklichkeit*]" (2.171), "no reality [*keine Wirklichkeit*]" (*NB* 29(8)), "the reality [*die Wirklichkeit*]" (*NB* 22(7)), "the reality [*die Realität*]" (*NB* 31(7)), "the realities [*die Realitaten*]" (*NB* 31(10)), "this reality [*Wirklichkeit*]" (*NB* 37 (7)), and "the sum-total of reality [*die gesamte Wirklichkeit*]" (2.063). I think, therefore, that the only way to make sense of these uses of *"Wirklichkeit"*, *"Realität"*, and *"Realitaten"* is to construe them as synonymous with "fact" or "facts", to construe them, that is, as referring to one or more of those entities the totality of which comprises the whole of reality.

If I am right, Wittgenstein's claim, "The sum-total of reality is the world" (2.063), which has mystified many, amounts to the assertion that the actual world is the sum-total of all realities, that is, facts. In short, 2.063 is just another statement of his claim that the real or actual world is the sum-total of existing situations: "is the totality of facts" (1.1), is "the totality of existing states of affairs." (2.04).

16. Worlds as Possible Totalities

We have seen that, at every stage in his atomistic construction, Wittgenstein has had to take recourse either explicitly or implicitly to the notion of possibility. Possible metaphysically simple objects, possessing de re necessary formal properties, are the ultimate elements of his analysis. From their possible combinations he constructs possible states of affairs. And from possible combinations of possible states of affairs he constructs possible worlds. The actual world is a possible combination of existing (and a fortiori possible) states of affairs; other, nonactual, possible worlds are possible combinations of possible states of affairs, one or more of which do not exist.

Possible worlds, however, are not just possible (consistent) combinations of possible states of affairs, actual or nonactual. They are, as Wittgenstein conceives them, always totalities or sum-totals of such consistent combinations. He thinks of them, that is, not just as consistent combinations of states of affairs but as *maximally consistent* combinations thereof.

Now, according to certain contemporary theorists, a set of states of affairs is maximally consistent just when it is a consistent set of states of affairs such that, for any possible state of affairs, S, either S is a member of that set or S is inconsistent with it. On this view, a possible world, W, is a consistent set of states of affairs such that, for any S, either S is a member of W or S is inconsistent with W.[55]

It might be thought that this latter-day conception cannot be reconciled with Wittgenstein's commitment, noted in Chapter 2, to the possibility of worlds having n objects, where n ranges from 2 to infinity. Consider the two-object world (call it W_1) that he describes in *NB* 14(4). It seems to involve two consistent states of affairs. But, it might be asked, in what sense are these two states of affairs *maximally* consistent? W_1, it may be remembered, consisted of two states of affairs: S_1, in which object A has property F; and S_2, in which object B does not have F. Can we not imagine S_1 and S_2 being combined with another state of affairs, S_3, in which object C has property G? The combination of S_3 with S_1 and S_2 will, to be sure, constitute a different world—say W_2—from W_1. But does this mean that W_1 is *inconsistent* with S_3? Does it mean that W_1 is a *maximally* consistent—or, as it is sometimes called, a "complete"—world?

The answer to these questions is that it all depends on how possible worlds are specified: with or without a completeness condition (what is sometimes called a "closure condition", a "that's all"-clause). Suppose W_1 for instance, is taken to be specified by saying that it has S_1 and S_2 as members, and no closure clause is added. Then since it is clear that S_1 and S_2 are *not* inconsistent with S_3, it will follow that W_1, even if it does not have S_3 as a member, is nevertheless not inconsistent with S_3. W_1, when thus specified, will be a consistent set of states of affairs. But it will not be a maximally consistent one. If, however, W_1 is taken to be specified by saying that it has S_1 and S_2 alone as its members—if, that is, we think of W_1 as being *completely* described in *NB* 14(4)—then, of course, W_1 *is* inconsistent with S_3, and hence is a maximally consistent set of states of affairs after all.

Wittgenstein, I shall argue, regards possible worlds in general—not just the actual world—as being specified in the second sort of way: as completely determinate totalities of states of affairs; as totalities, that is, whose complete description is such that, for any state of affairs, S, S is given either as a member of that totality or as something excluded by it.

In the first place, in *NB* 14(4), he is surely saying that the states of affairs asserted by "F(A)" and "not F(B)" are *all* the states of affairs that exist in that world, that their possible combination constitutes the totality of possible states of affairs that exist in that world. And if this is what he is saying then he is implicitly saying, with respect to any other possible states of affairs such as G(C), that their nonexistence in that world is thereby determined. This follows, of course, from the Principle of Descriptive Completeness: "If all the positive statements about a thing are made, aren't all the negative ones already made too?" *NB* 33(5).

Second, the maximal consistency of worlds follows from Wittgenstein's claim that worlds are determinate (or "definite", as he sometimes calls it). In *NB* 62(10), he holds that "the world must be what it is, it must be definite", claiming that any uncertainty, indefiniteness, or indeterminateness can be only a feature of the way we think or talk about the world, but not a feature of the world itself: "what vacillates is our determinations, not the world." This, of course, is a claim about *the* world, the actual world. Yet, clearly, he takes it to hold of other possible worlds as well: "A proposition constructs *a world* [emphasis added] with the help of a logical scaffolding, so that one can actually see from the proposition how everything stands in logic *if* it is true. One can *draw inferences* from a false proposition." (4.023(5)). He is saying that the inferences one validly draws from a proposition are determinate whether or not the states of affairs whose existence is asserted by the propositions inferred are ones that exist in the actual world. And if the propositions inferred are determinate, then so also must be the states of affairs and worlds whose existence these propositions "construct." Admittedly, Wittgenstein nowhere tells us exactly what he means by "determinate." But it seems plausible to suppose that he would say that a world, W, is determinate just in case for every proposition, P, either P is true in W or P is false in W. If this is what he means, then he certainly is committed to the complete determinateness of the actual world: "A complete description of the world is given by listing all elementary propositions, and then listing which of them are true and which false." (4.26). And we might reasonably expect him to hold that other possible worlds are likewise determinate insofar as they may be completely described by listing all elementary propositions, and then listing which of them are true and which false in those worlds. This is, of course, precisely the way in which he does describe, for example, his two-object world.

If this is right, then no doubt whatever should remain as to whether possible worlds, for Wittgenstein, are maximally consistent sets of states of affairs. For it is easy to see that determinateness (as defined in the previous paragraph) and maximal consistency amount to the same thing. Suppose, on the one hand, that a possible world, W, is maximally consistent. Then, by definition, for any possible state of affairs, S, either S is in W or S is inconsistent with W. Let P_1 be a proposition that asserts that S exists in W. Then if S exists in W, P_1 is true in W; and if S is inconsistent with W, P_1 is false in W. Generalizing, if W is maximally consistent then, for any proposition, P, either P is true in W or P is false in W. Conversely, suppose that a possible world, W, is determinate. Then, since one member of every contradictory pair of propositions will be true in W, there can be no further proposition, added to the set that truly describes W, that is not inconsistent with a proposition already in that set. Any further proposition, after all, would have to contradict a proposition already in the set. But that is just to say that for every proposition, P (and for every state of affairs whose existence P asserts), either P is a member of the set that truly describes W (and S is a member of the set of states of affairs that constitutes W) or else P is inconsistent with the set that truly describes W (and S is inconsistent with the set of states of affairs that constitutes W).

Notes

1. As he says in the *Notebooks*: "We portray the thing, the relation, the property, by means of variables . . ." (*NB* 63(9)). See also 4.1252(3), 4.1273, and 4.24. Note that predicate variables and relational variables feature in his examples of fully analyzed elementary propositions, "Fx" and "aRb".

2. He employs the term "individual" just once in the *Tractatus*, (viz., in 5.553). And there he seems to reserve it for what I have called the contrastive sense of "object". It would have been nice had he reserved it for that use throughout his writings.

3. I say "just about all" of the items listed because it must, for the moment, remain an open question as to whether some of them—such as points and parts of the visual field, and material points—might not count as simple.

4. For reasons that I'll give later, we need to distinguish between structured properties and structural properties. Structural properties, according to 4.122, are always essential or "internal" properties of whatever has them. Structured properties need not be. Thus, structural properties are a proper subclass of structured ones. Wittgenstein's claim in *NB* 65(2) that the circularity and finite extension of a circular patch are structural properties, not just structured ones, entails that he thinks of them as essential to the circular patch.

5. See section 7 for more on the formal properties of objects, complex as well as simple.

6. It is fundamental in another way as well. For it is in this sense of "simple"

that we must construe his unqualified claim in 2.02 that [all] "objects are simple". Otherwise 2.02 is manifestly inconsistent with the many examples he gives in both the *Notebooks* and the *Tractatus* of objects that are metaphysically complex.

7. The distinction between points and parts of space—be it visual space, physical space, or logical space—is systematically preserved throughout Wittgenstein's early writings.

8. Strangely, Hintikka and Hintikka themselves seem to recognize this. On p. 59 they write: "The objects which determine the world (in the sense in which he is speaking of the world here, not in the sense of 1.1) are the objects of one's immediate experience, and in a reasonably good sense they can be said to constitute one's life." Yet the reference to 1.1 ("The world is the totality of facts, not of things") gives the game away. It explicitly alerts us to the fact that, in the sense of 1.1—and, for that matter, the sense of 2.021 ("Objects make up the substance of the world")—the world that is Wittgenstein's main concern throughout the *Tractatus*, is *not* the world of immediate experience.

9. There is, of course, a conceptual tension involved in the supposition that something might at once be both an extensionless spatiotemporal point and a possessor of mass. Nevertheless, talk of extensionless masses is not just a mathematical fiction. As the German physicist, Karl Schwartzschild pointed out in 1916, Einstein's general relativity theory of 1915 allows for mass to be squeezed into an infinitely small space, into a so-called "singularity". For a discussion of some of the conceptual difficulties involved in the contemporary notion of a point-mass—and, more generally, in the ontology of contemporary physics—see Leonard Goddard and Brenda Judge [1982].

10. See Hintikka and Hintikka [1986], p. 146, for a discussion of Wittgenstein's insistence on this point and the correspondence he conducted with Schlick about it. Curiously, Hintikka and Hintikka seem not to recognize the import of these revelations for their own phenomenological account of Wittgenstein's "simple objects".

11. Recall, however, that this does not mean that physical objects of some sort must be the building-blocks of all possible worlds. Such a conclusion would follow only if Wittgenstein held that all possible worlds were object-homogeneous. But, as I showed in Chapter 2, that was not his view.

12. Note that the combinations must be *possible* ones, that is to say, must be such that the propositions asserting the existence of these states of affairs are consistent. Wittgenstein thinks that this requirement of consistency is automatically satisfied insofar as all elementary states of affairs are, on his account, independent. But, as I'll argue in section 13, the thesis of their independence is false. Hence, there can be inconsistent as well as consistent combinations of states of affairs. A combination of states of affairs will count as a possible world, then, only if it is a consistent combination.

13. Formal properties, it should be remembered, are internal properties ascribable to simple and complex items alike, whereas structural properties are internal ones ascribable only to complex items.

14. As will become obvious, neither in formulating conditions (1) through (4) nor elsewhere do I adopt Wittgenstein's preferred notation. For ease of exposition in

formulating these conditions, I use the expression "$\emptyset$" in such a way that its admissible values include formal properties. Wittgenstein probably would not allow this but would insist that only "ordinary", nonessential, properties may properly be so symbolized.

15. In the notation of variables, the correct way of expressing the *self-identity* of an object, I presume, would be the same as for expressing the *existence* of that object, viz., to write "$(\exists x)$". When it comes to names, the correct way of expressing the *self-identity* of an object a is to use the name of the object itself, viz., the self-same name "a", a notation that also shows the *existence* [unrestricted sense] of a.

16. In 4.441, Wittgenstein speaks of the "vanishing" of the logical constants in the case of "$(\exists x).fx \, . \, x = a$", which "says the same thing" as "fa". The so-called logical constants (here, the formal concepts) that vanish in the transformation from the former to the latter are those of *existence* and *self-identity*.

17. In 4.1272 he also lists *being a complex*, *being a fact*, *being a function*, and *being a number*, as formal concepts (that is, as what formal properties are "characteristics of" (4.126)). But the first two are clearly formal properties of complexes only; and it is unlikely that Wittgenstein thinks of the bearers of the formal properties of *being a number* and *being a function* as objects of the kind that "make up the substance of the world" (2.021).

18. The term "haecceitism" has been used by David Kaplan, [1975], Robert Merrihew Adams, [1979], and others, to refer to the doctrine that objects have uniquely individuating essences. Understandably, many philosophers object that since properties are traditionally regarded as universals, and universals are, as it were by definition, capable of being instantiated in more than one individual, there cannot be any such thing as a property that is instantiable by only one individual. This is not the place to try to settle the issue that is thereby generated. Three quick points will have to suffice: First, it does seem to be truly predicable of an individual a that a is identical to a. Of course, it might then be questioned as to whether whatever is truly predicable of some thing is a genuine property of that thing. Second, so far as Wittgenstein is concerned, the question whether *being identical to a* is a genuine property is largely beside the point since for him it is a formal property and *no* formal property, on his account, is a "genuine" one. Third, those who would reject haecceitist properties are obliged to say how they would deal with relational properties such as *being the successor of the number six*. Reference to such properties as these is seemingly indispensable in number theory. Yet this property, like infinitely many others in number theory, is not only uniquely individuating in the sense that just one thing happens to possess it; it is necessarily uniquely individuating since one and only one thing *can* possess it. There is a powerful case, then, for saying that haecceitist properties are unavoidable, and hence admissible, in number theory at least. And if they are admissible there, why not elsewhere?

19. Here I draw upon, and modify, David Armstrong's way of sharpening up the issue between haecceitists and their opponents [1986]. For the sake of simplicity, I ignore Armstrong's distinction between stronger and weaker forms of anti-haecceitism.

20. On the haecceitist's account, of course, they are not wholly indiscernible

with respect to their properties. For they differ from one another with respect to what Plantinga calls their "world-indexed" properties: such properties as *being identical to a in W_1* and *being identical to b in W_2*.

21. See also 3.3442, which parallels *NB* 50(2). Although in both cases Wittgenstein is talking about names of complex objects, it is clear that he holds to the same thesis for names of simple ones as well.

22. Black [1964] is also inclined to conflate "formal" with "structural". He writes: "Wittgenstein's distinction between 'structure' and 'form' has troubled commentators as able as Ramsey. It is doubtful whether it is needed." (p. 66).

23. For detailed criticisms of this and other of their claims, see my [1987].

24. Presumably, the division of objects into simple and complex is itself a division into logical kinds, since there are properties of the complexes that simples cannot have. For example, the property of *having some color*, which is essential to all [complex] visual objects, is impossible for simple objects since it is—so Wittgenstein tells us in 2.0231—the sort of property that only "configurations" of simple objects can have.

25. For the sake of simplicity, I omit any discussion of complex relations other than to observe that, since Wittgenstein—as we have seen (in section 3)— recognizes certain relations as simple, he presumably recognizes others as complex.

26. For more on the formal and structural properties of states of affairs, see section 12.

27. Like all accidental properties, material properties are determinate ones, never determinables. But not all determinate properties are accidental. *Being the successor of the number six*, for instance, is a determinate property falling under the determinable, formal, property of *being a number*. Yet this determinate property, I am sure Wittgenstein would say, is an essential property of the sole object that possesses it, that is, of the number seven. (It is, in fact, both a uniquely individuating, and—more narrowly still—a haecceitist property of the number seven.) Being a determinable property of an object, then, is a sufficient but not a necessary condition of being an essential property of that object.

28. Note that some determinable, and hence internal, properties would seem to be simple ones. The properties of *being situated somewhere in infinite space* (2.0121(4) and 2.0131(1)), of *occurring at some time or other* (2.0121(4)), are cases in point.

29. For more on the concept of supervenience, see Kim [1979], pp. 31–49.

30. I add this third consideration in order to draw attention to the fact that certain emergent properties such as *being red* may ultimately prove to be relational, requiring an account to be given (for example) of how the cherries stand in relation to some light-source (for the physicalistic property) or of how the cherries stand in relation to some observer (for the corresponding phenomenological property). Clearly, a lot more needs to be said about this than is possible here.

31. It is, of course, an odd consequence of Wittgenstein's terminology that if the simples out of whose configuration material properties are produced are material points, then these material points or point-masses cannot themselves be said to have material properties. But this is a merely terminological matter of no philosophical consequence.

32. This, I suspect, is why Wittgenstein claims, "there is no such thing as the soul—the subject, etc.—as conceived in the superficial psychology of the present day. Indeed a composite soul would no longer be a soul." (5.5421). He is saying, as I understand him, that since souls are neither among his metaphysically simple objects nor among the complex objects produced by configurations of simple ones (since souls are, as it were, "by definition" simple), talk about having a soul is best construed in terms of a somewhat complex sort of organism having certain sorts of soulful *properties*. If so, then he is indeed (as his apparent espousal of physicalism suggests) subscribing to something like an emergent-property theory of mind and soul alike.

33. For the sake of simplicity, I am here presuming the soundness of what, in the next section, I shall call "the A-account" of structure.

34. This instance of the property of *being red* may be said to be supervenient on that structured relation between those simpler properties. Other instances of *being red* may, of course, be produced by different structures of different base-properties and instantiated by different micro-objects.

35. The soundness of Wittgenstein's linguistic intuitions here might be disputed. But it matters not whether these particular examples are good ones. For other examples, such as "an event's being put in a hole", suffice to make the point.

36. Ramsey [1923] writes: "it seems from remarks later in the book that the structure of the fact is not merely the way in which the objects hang together but depends also on what objects they are, so that two different facts never have the same structure." (p. 10). What Ramsey calls "facts" here are what Pears and McGuinness call "states of affairs".

Black [1964] writes: "Two distinct facts can have the same form: can they also have the same structure? The correct answer seems to be that distinct facts [Sachverhalten] must have distinct structures, even in a case in which the facts have the same form." (p. 66). Black gives no reasons for his conclusion, but he may have had in mind those that I go on to give.

McGuinness [1956], on the other hand, does give reasons, ones that are akin to those that I adduce. See especially p. 143, fn. 3.

37. McGuinness [1956]: "to assert the existence of the structure is nothing other than to assert the existence of the fact, and it will also seem that to say that a fact has a certain structure is to say nothing beyond what one has already said in asserting the fact. It does not seem to me, however, that this triviality is an objection to my interpretation of 'Struktur'." (p. 144).

38. To my knowledge no proponents of the A-account have drawn attention to the fact that this is a logical consequence of their account.

39. Incidentally, the A-account of structural properties throws some light on Wittgenstein's remark, "to say that one thing is part of another is always a tautology." (*NB* 62(6)). Like Moore, it seems, Wittgenstein thought that the property of *having such and such as a part* is an internal property of any complex that has it; that having such a property is de re necessary to, and hence (so to speak) tautologously attributable to, all its possessors. Consider the object a as it features in the complex state of affairs S. On the A-account, S has the property of *having a as a part*. And just as the structural property of *having a standing in relation to b* is

internal to S, so too *having a as a part*—which is essential to S's having that structural property—is also internal to S. More generally, on the Moore/Wittgenstein account, it will always be "tautologous" to say that a complex has such and such as a part. Note, however, that Moore (and presumably Wittgenstein as well) would deny that the correlative relational property of *being part of such and such a complex* is internal to its possessors. To use an earlier example, although S could not be what it is if it did not have a as a part, a could very well be what it is without being a part of S.

40. Recall that when quantifiers are involved we are supposed to put the symbol for the corresponding pseudo-concept "inside the ∃ bracket", and that I argued that we need a similar device for names and individual constants. Presumably in such a subscripted notation, the form of the state of affairs aRb (where a has the formal property F and b has the formal property G) would be given by something like "$\emptyset(x_F, y_G)$" (where "F" and "G" appear in the subordinate places appropriate to pseudo-concepts). However, in the *Tractatus*, Wittgenstein did not think such subscripts were needed. For the case of variables, he writes: "Every variable is the sign for a formal concept. For the variable represents a constant form that all its values possess, and this can be regarded as a formal property of those values." (4.1271). Illustrating, he writes: "Thus the variable name 'x' is the proper sign for the pseudo-concept *object*." (4.1272(1)). As for names and individual constants, he tells us that a name "shows that it signifies an object" (4.12(3)), and that "in the limiting case the variable becomes a constant" ((3.313(2)). This makes it clear that, at the time of writing the *Tractatus*, Wittgenstein did not think that an adequate conceptual notation requires subscripts so as to show the formal properties of the elements. Thus the variables "x" and "y" are supposed to show by themselves what formal concepts they fall under, and thereby show also their admissible values. My main reservation would be that, as I explained before, it would be all too easy to overlook the forms of the elements in a notation that lacks the explicit subscripting suggested by Wittgenstein in his Cambridge lectures. (Indeed, I suspect that the Ramsey and McGuinness *interpretation* does in fact overlook these forms since in presenting it they make no mention of them.) The notation employed is unimportant so long as we do not forget the essential role played by the forms of simple objects in determining the forms of the states of affairs of which they are constituents.

41. It is, however, presupposed by some of the things he says *about* truth-tables, for instance, that for n possible states of affairs there are 2^n possibilities of their existence and nonexistence. For an explanation of why truth-tables can get along without the myth of independence, see section 13.

42. The Principle of Descriptive Completeness is obviously connected with what (in Chapter 4, section 15) I call his Same-Multiplicity Principle and his consequent commitment to the referential completeness of propositions. Together they help to explain why he makes such remarks as, "the totality of facts determines what is the case, and also whatever is not the case." (1.12). When one has said exactly what is the case, it is redundant to say also what is not the case.

43. I say "determinate" degrees because it is important to realize that so-called "determinable" properties, such as *having some length or other, having some pitch or other*, or *having some color or other*, are not to be considered as material

properties. Determinable properties are always essential to their possessors; determinate ones, of which material properties are a subclass, need not be.

44. See also Waismann's notes (Appendix 2) in which Wittgenstein explains that when he was working on the *Tractatus*, he was "still unaware of all this".

45. In asking this question, of course, I am seeking not a psychological explanation but a philosophical one: I want to know what philosophical reasons he might have had for espousing the doctrine. As to the psychological question, the answer may very well be that, since he composed the *Tractatus* in the remarkably short period of about three months, he simply did not think out the implications of the doctrine carefully enough.

46. Two further amendments are also needed. We should amend 5152(2) to read: "Two *entirely different* elementary propositions give one another the probability 1/2". Likewise we should amend 6.3751(3) to read: "(It is clear that the logical product of two *entirely different* elementary propositions can be neither a tautology nor a contradiction. .)."

47. As a consequence, the number of truth-possibilities for n elementary propositions cannot be generated with quite the liberality he supposed in 4.27 and presupposed in 4.42 and 4.45.

48. For a detailed account of how truth-tables work when the independence myth is abandoned, and other logical relations besides contrariety are admitted between the values of the 'p's, 'q's and 'r's on the left side, see Bradley and Swartz [1979], pp. 294–301.

49. It seems to me particularly unfortunate, therefore, that many interpreters of the *Tractatus* begin with the presumption that the doctrine of independence is indispensable to the rest of the work and then either try to construe all other doctrines in such a way as to preserve its truth, or (if that fails) reject other doctrines on the grounds of their incompatibility with the doctrine of independence, or (lamenting their failure to effect a reconciliation between these other doctrines and the doctrine of independence) conclude that the *Tractatus* suffers from the fatal flaw of logical inconsistency. Far from letting the doctrine of independence drive my interpretation, I have recognized its indefensibility from the start and have concentrated on showing how the rest of Wittgenstein's Tractarian doctrines hang together.

50. Again, the near-parallelism between "a completely analyzed proposition contains just as many names as there are things contained in its reference" (*NB* 11(2)) and "In a proposition there must be exactly as many distinguishable parts as in the situation it represents." (4.04(1) suggests that "situation", in the *Tractatus*, also serves as a stand-in for what, in the *Notebooks*, he calls "the reference of a proposition" (i.e., "the sense of a proposition" in the *Tractatus*).

51. For a detailed account of worlds-diagrams and their use as a decision-procedure for propositional logics, modal and nonmodal, see Bradley and Swartz [1979].

52. It is very easy indeed to be confused by this talk of containment, especially since Wittgenstein goes on, in the very next passage, to say: "If P follows from Q, the sense of 'P' is contained in the sense of 'Q'." (5.122). Since we are told in 4.031 ("Instead of, 'This proposition has such and such a sense', we can simply say, 'This proposition represents such and such a situation'.") that talking about the sense of a

proposition is tantamount to talking about the situation which the proposition represents, we might have expected Wittgenstein to say that where P follows from Q, the sense of P contains (rather than is contained by) the sense of Q. The apparent inconsistency can be resolved only if we suppose that Wittgenstein has in mind here a rather different sense of "is contained". This is the sense in which, in the case before us, since S_2 (the sense of P) is a *member* of the set (the sense of Q) of which S_1 and S_2 are members, he says that S_2 is "contained in" the latter set, and hence, more generally, that where Q implies P the sense of P is "contained in" the sense of Q. Here the "containment" is that of set-membership displayed in Figure 3.2.

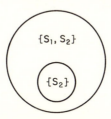

Two senses of "contained in" are involved. As Black observes, Wittgenstein's use of the expression is "an impediment to clarity".

53. As Stenius puts it: "it is not obvious that a Sachverhalt is always to be taken as 'atomic' in an absolute sense; as we shall see later it will in some contexts be more convenient to take the 'atomicity' in only a *relative* sense, relative, that is, to some fixed context." (p. 33).

54. See Anscombe's translation of the *Notebooks*, and both the Ogden and the Pears and McGuinness translations of the *Tractatus*. Plochmann and Lawson, however, prefer to reserve "reality" for *"Realitat"* and use "actuality" for *"Wirklichkeit"* [1962]. Max Black seems to follow Plochmann and Lawson for the adjective *"wirklich"*, which he translates as "actual", while following everyone else in his rendering of both the nouns *"Wirklichkeit"* and *"Realitat"*.

55. My account is very similar to that offered by Plantinga [1974] when he writes: "a state of affairs S is *complete* or *maximal* if for every state of affairs S', S includes S' or S precludes S'. And a possible world is simply a possible state of affairs that is maximal." (p. 45).

4

Propositions and the
Mirror of the World

My *whole* task consist in explaining the nature of the proposition. That is to say,
in giving the nature of all facts, whose picture the proposition *is*.

(WITTGENSTEIN, *Notebooks 1914–16*)

To give the essence of a proposition means to give the essence of all description,
and thus the essence of the world.

(WITTGENSTEIN, *Tractatus*)

Logic is not a body of doctrine, but a mirror-image of the world.

(WITTGENSTEIN, *Tractatus*)

1. Introduction

In Chapter 3, I argued that Wittgenstein's ontology is an atomistic one and that it is
infused throughout by modal properties and relations. Not only do his "atoms", that
is, his metaphysically simple objects, have de re necessary, internal natures or forms
that determine the range of their possible combinations in more complex entities
(complex objects, states of affairs, facts, situations, and whole worlds); each of
these complex structured entities, too, has its own essential structural and formal
properties and stands in internal relations to other structured entities.

Now among the complex, structured entities that Wittgenstein's ontology em-
braces are linguistic items, namely, propositional signs, the principal function of
which is to *represent* any item in Wittgenstein's ontology (other than themselves),
and in so doing to *mirror* the modal properties of these items and the modal relations
in these items stand.

Propositional language, too, is infused with modal properties. Not only do the
"atoms" of language, the simple signs that he calls "names", have forms (matching
those of the simple objects for which they stand) which determine the range of their
possible combinations in propositional signs (thereby determining the rules of logical syntax with which their combinations must comply); each of these propositional
signs has its own essential structural and formal properties and stands in internal
relations to other propositional signs. "Thus a language which can express everything *mirrors* certain properties of the world by these properties which it [language]

122

must have; and logical so-called propositions show *in a systematic way* those properties." (*NB* 107(6)).

My aim in the present chapter is bring out the ways in which the modal atomism of Wittgenstein's metaphysical theory is reflected in the modal atomism of his account of language and logic.

2. The Propositional Core of Language

In the *Tractatus*, Wittgenstein writes as if language comprises nothing other than propositions that represent or say how things stand in this or some other possible world. "The totality of propositions," he says (as if making an identity-statement), "is language." (4.001). Each proposition represents "the existence and non-existence of states of affairs" (4.1) and thereby "constructs a world with the help of a logical scaffolding, so that one can actually see from the proposition how everything stands in logic if it is true." (4.023(5)).

But what does Wittgenstein mean by "proposition" (Pears and McGuinness's translation of "*Satz*")? The question eludes a univocal answer.[1]

In the first place, although some passages suggest that a Satz is simply a *sentence-token*, others seem to require that a Satz be something like the *content* of a sentence-token (something like a *Fregean proposition* , the kind of thing that may be "expressed" by a sentence but is not to be identified with a sentence).

Supporting the sentential interpretation, favored by Stenius and some others, is the fact that Wittgenstein claims that in a *Satz* "a thought finds an expression that can be *perceived by the senses*" [emphasis added] (3.1), and that a *Satz* is made up of "words" in articulation (3.141), where these words are "names" (3.142), or "simple signs" (3.202). Obviously, if a Satz is a perceptible combination of signs, it must be something physical, a "spatial arrangement" of "spatial objects" (3.1431).

In support of the contrary, Fregean propositional interpretation, favored by Pears and McGuinness and most others, is the fact that in passages contiguous to or in the immediate context of those just cited—such as 3.14, 3.143, 3.1431, 3.2— Wittgenstein often employs the term "*Satzzeichen*" (which Pears and McGuinness translate as "propositional sign" but which might equally well be translated as "sentence-token") to refer to the kinds of complexes of which words and names are constituents, and reserves the term "*Satz*" for something different, namely, what a *Satzzeichen* "expresses". Significantly, in 3.1431 it is propositional signs, not propositions, that he compares with spatial arrangements of spatial objects; and it is these, he claims, that function in the same way as written sentences insofar as they "express the sense of the proposition." Thus, when he is being careful, he seems to embrace the view that a *Satzzeichen* is a propositional sign or sentence-token, something physical that is "the perceptible sign of a proposition (spoken or written)" (3.11), whereas a *Satz* is a proposition that may be expressed by a propositional sign, that is, is "a propositional sign in its projective relation to the world." (3.12).[2]

For my own part, I am content to stick with the Pears and McGuinness translation of "*Satz*" as "proposition" and "*Satzzeichen*" as "propositional sign", but think it important to point out that on most occasions when Wittgenstein uses "*Satz*", he should—and would, were he being careful—have used "*Satzzeichen*". For many of the properties that he attributes to propositions are more properly conceived of as belonging to what Pears and McGuinness call propositional signs, that is, sentence-tokens. Among the more important properties of propositional signs or sentence-tokens are the following: (i) being physical items of the sort that might be set out in writing or in print; (ii) having sense; and (iii) being used to express a thought, that is, to say or show that something is the case. By way of contrast, Fregean propositions are usually thought of as (i) nonphysical items, (ii) the senses that sentence-tokens have on particular occasions of their use, and (iii) what is or may be expressed, that is, said or shown, by the use of a sentence-token. When we attend to these categorial differences between sentence-tokens and propositions, we can see that, strictly speaking, Wittgenstein is right about attributions of type (i) when he speaks of propositional signs as being expressed "in writing or in print" (3.143(1)), but wrong when he speaks of propositions as being "set out on the printed page" (4.011). He is right about attributions of type (ii) when he speaks of our understanding "the sense of a propositional sign" (4.02) but wrong when he claims,"Every proposition must already have a sense" (4.064). And he is right about attributions of type (iii) when he says that a propositional sign is that "with which we express a thought" (3.12) but wrong when he tells us that a proposition "*shows* how things stand if it is true" and "*says that* they do so stand" (4.022).

Clearly, then, Wittgenstein uses "*Satz*" in an extraordinarily sloppy way. Having drawn the distinction between propositional signs and what they express, he then—for the most part—ignores it and switches from talk of the one to talk of the other. (Sometimes he even makes the switch within the compass of a single section. For example, in 3.143 he speaks first of propositional signs as being the sorts of things that occur "in writing or print", but then immediately goes on to speak of a "printed proposition.") There is, however, some warrant for this. For strict observance of the distinction in contexts where nothing hangs on it can be tedious and lead to cumbersomeness of expression. What is important is only that, having been alerted to the distinction, we bring it to bear when necessary. In what follows, therefore, I shall only occasionally (usually just as a reminder) effect the disambiguation that the distinction makes possible.

The second initial barrier to our understanding of what Wittgenstein means by "*Satz*" stems from the fact that although some passages seem to allow the term "*Satz*" to encompass the noncontingent claims of logic (5.43(2)), mathematics (6.2321), and philosophy (4.003), others seem to require that a Satz should always say something merely contingent (6.53), that is, that all *Satze* be "*Satze der Naturwissenschaft*" ("propositions of natural science"). In support of the view that Wittgenstein sometimes thinks of propositions as a genus of which the contingent and the noncontingent alike are species is the fact that 4.46 not only refers to tautologies and contradictions as "propositions" but also tells us that these propositions are "true for all the truth-possibilities of the elementary propositions" and "false for all the truth-possibilities", respectively. If being truth-valued is the mark of a proposition, then the claims of logic, mathematics, and philosophy are assuredly propositional in nature. However, it is clear that Wittgenstein sometimes takes a more restrictive view of propositions. He asserts that a proposition is a "picture of reality" (4.01), that every proposition must "have a sense" (4.064), and that a proposition that has sense "states something" (6.1264), and denies—in 4.462 (1), 4.461(3), and 4.461(1), respectively—that the claims of logic have any of these properties. The claims of logic are not alone in this respect. Those of mathematics, also, "do not express a thought" (6.21), "state nothing" (4.242), and "do not have a sense" (4.243(3)). And likewise for the claims of philosophy (including his own in the *Tractatus*): they are excluded from the domain of what can be said (6.53), are "nonsensical" (6.54), and are among those that we must "consign to silence" (7). When he is thinking in this restrictive vein, he thinks of a genuine proposition as always being contingent, that is, as being true for some truth-possibilities and false for others. Wittgenstein sometimes, but regrettably not always, draws the distinction between contingent propositions and noncontingent ones by referring to the former as "real propositions" (*NB* 108(5)) or "propositions with sense" (5.525(2)) and the latter as "so-called propositions" (*NB* 107(1)) or "pseudo-propositions" (6.2(2)).

Clearly, Wittgenstein's use of the term "*Satz*"—like his use of the terms "*Gegenstand*" ("object"), "*Eigenschaft*" ("property"), "*Relation*", and "*einfach*" ("simple"), remarked upon in Chapter 3—is a shifting one. What we need to do, then, is to avoid becoming preoccupied with any one use and simply try to keep track of what he means on any given occasion. Usually the context provides the necessary disambiguation. But when it does not, I often refer to propositions in the restricted sense as "contingent propositions", "significant propositions" (Ogden's expression), or "propositions with sense", and allow the unqualified term "proposition" to range over contingent propositions and noncontingent ones alike.

Running through all Wittgenstein's uses of the term "*Satz*", however, is a single thread. Whether he thinks of a *Satz* as a sentence-token or as a Fregean proposition, and whether he thinks of a *Satz* as always contingent or as sometimes noncontingent, one thing remains constant: a *Satz* or proposition is always some sort of *truth-valued* item.

But that generates a problem. If propositions are always truth-valued, then his claim in 4.001 that the totality of propositions "is" language is manifestly false. Not only that: it was known by Wittgenstein, at the time of writing these words, to be false. This is evident from the fact that, much earlier, in his "Notes on Logic" of September 1913, he had made the point, which he was to reiterate in his *Philosophical Investigations* of 1953, that language in fact contains many other constructions, besides truth-valued, propositional, judgment-making ones, for example, constructions for issuing commands and asking questions. "Assertion", he writes, "is merely psychological. There are only unasserted propositions. Judgement, command and question all stand on the same level; but all have in common the propositional form, and that alone interests us. What interests logic are only the unasserted propositions." (*NB* 96(2)).

The reasons for his oversimplified Tractarian claim about the propositional nature of language would seem to be twofold. First, he believes that there is a common propositional element shared by judgments, commands, and questions (and presumably also by wishes, commendations, and so forth). His view seems to be that the common propositional form "This is how things stand" (4.5(3)) is shared by all complete speech-acts of natural language, presumably in something like the following way:

Judgments:	I judge (assert, state): *this is how things stand.*
Commands:	Bring it about that: *this is how things stand.*
Questions:	Is it the case that: *this is how things stand?*
Wishes:	Would that it were the case that: *this is how things stand.*
Commendations:	It would be good if it were the case that: *this is how things stand.*

This seems to me to be an important insight (one that has been developed by a number of later philosophers) and to be arguably correct.[3]

Second, it seems to be his view that everything in these speech-acts, other than their common propositional element, is "merely psychological", and hence of no import for logic. "Psychology", he says, "is no more closely related to philosophy than any other natural science." (4.112(1)). Thus, he rejects the use of the assertion-sign, by Frege, Russell, and Whitehead, on the grounds that "It only shows . . . that these authors hold the propositions so indicated to be true." (*NB* 96(2)).

If we are to be charitable, therefore, we shall regard his claim that the totality of propositions *is* language as a sort of persuasive definition in which he stakes out that aspect of language in which he, as a philosopher and logician, is interested. He is not unaware of the nonassertive functions of language but is deliberately ignoring them in order to concentrate on the element that, in his view, is common to assertive and nonassertive functions alike.

For Wittgenstein, then, propositions are to be regarded as the essential logical core of language. And those of them that have sense represent possible states of affairs, possible situations, or possible worlds. They say how things are or might be.

3. The Sayable and the Showable

Now a contingent proposition—more strictly, a propositional sign that expresses such a proposition—not only *says* (truly or falsely) "This is how things stand". It also *shows* the logical form of the state of affairs that it depicts. It shows that the state of affairs depicted is a "possibility of structure" for the objects that are its constituents, that is, is a possible way of structuring those objects (2.15–2.151). This contrast between these two functions is emphasized in such passages as the following: "Propositions can represent the whole of reality, but they cannot represent what they must have in common with reality in order to be able to represent it—logical form. In order to be able to represent logical form, we should have to be able to station ourselves with propositions somewhere outside logic, that is to say outside the world." (4.12); and "Propositions cannot represent logical form: it is mirrored in them. What finds its reflection in language, language cannot represent. What expresses *itself* in language, we cannot express by means of language. Propositions *show* the logical form of reality. They display it." (4.121).

Significantly, the propositions he is talking about in these passages are all propositions with sense, contingent propositions. Such propositions (propositional signs), Wittgenstein is saying, enable us to do two things at once. They enable us to say, *by* language, something contingent about the existence or nonexistence of states of affairs. And they enable us to show, *in* language, something noncontingent about the "essence of the world" (5.4711) or "the nature of all being" (*NB* 37(9)).

Noncontingent propositions, the tautologies of logic, the identities of mathematics, and the nonsensical propositions that philosophical analyses yield, also show something. They "show the formal—logical—properties of language and the world." (6.12). But this is their only function. Unlike propositions with sense, they *say* nothing. In other words, they say nothing about the actual world that would distinguish that world from any other possible world (for the simple reason that all worlds share the same "formal—logical—properties").

Wittgenstein's distinction between these two aspects of propositional language has mystified many. But the essential point of the saying/showing distinction seems to me both simple and sound. Consider some proposition with sense such as his *Notebooks* example "The watch is lying on the table". Leave aside the fact, which he notes, that this propositional sign contains "a lot of indefiniteness" (*NB* 69(11)) and that the state of affairs it describes (roughly, the "sense" of the propositional sign) is "more complicated than the proposition itself." (*NB* 69(12)). "All the same," he points out, if the proposition is true there must exist a complex of objects consisting of a watch lying on a table such that "this proposition is a picture of that complex." (*NB* 70(6)). Now what this proposition *says* is something contingent, namely, that this complex exists. But it also *shows* something noncontingent that it does not say, namely, that this complex is a *possible* one for the objects concerned (is a possibility of combination for its constituents—the watch, the table and the relation of lying on—given their respective forms).

It might seem, on the face of it, that there is no reason why the possibility of these objects' combining with one another should not be asserted by another proposition, the proposition "It is possible for the watch to lie on the table". Yet Wittgenstein seems expressly to rule this out by his dictum: "What *can* be shown, *cannot* be said." (4.1212). How are we to understand this?

I think we need to distinguish between two ways of understanding it: a weaker and stronger. The weaker thesis is merely that what can be shown by a given proposition cannot be said *by that very same proposition*. The stronger thesis is that what can be shown by a given proposition cannot be said *by any [contingent] proposition whatever*.

The need to distinguish between these two versions of the sayable/showable distinction is made clear by an early passage from "Notes to G. E. Moore in Norway" (Appendix II of the *Notebooks*). There he writes:

In any ordinary proposition, e.g., "Moore good" [sic], this *shows* and does not say that "Moore" is to the left of "good"; and here what is shown can be *said* by another proposition. But this only applies to that *part* of what is shown which is arbitrary. The *logical* properties which it shows are not arbitrary, and that it has these cannot be said in any proposition. (*NB* 110(4))

When he concedes that the proposition (more accurately, propositional sign or sentence-token) "Moore [is] good" shows but does not say something which *can* be said by another proposition, namely, that the word "Moore" is to the left of the word "good", and insists that this applies only to that part of what is shown that is arbitrary, he is advancing the weak thesis. He is conceding that the purely contingent features of a given proposition (more accurately, propositional sign) *can* be both shown and said but insisting that they can be said only by *another* proposition.

However, in this same passage he also advances the stronger thesis. Indeed, the point he wishes to emphasize is that the proposition "Moore [is] good" has logical properties as well as contingent, arbitrary ones, and that these *logical properties cannot be said by any proposition, that is, by any proposition with sense, whatever.* What are these logical properties? Wittgenstein does not tell us. But I'm inclined to think that they include such broadly logical-cum-formal features as that Moore belongs to the right *logical kind* to have a property such as goodness, that this determinate combination of the object Moore with the property of goodness is a *possible* one, and perhaps that having Moore as a constituent is *internal* to (because it features in the structure of) the proposition.[4] These features are all what he would call "internal properties" of the possible situation of Moore's being good and so cannot be said (by means of a proposition with sense) but only shown. As he puts it in the *Tractatus*, "The existence of an internal property of a possible situation is not expressed by means of a proposition: rather, it expresses itself in the proposition representing the situation, by means of an internal property of that proposition." (4.124).

As I understand it, then, the sayable/showable distinction amounts to the following: Consider some contingent proposition such as "Moore is good." The propositional sign expressing this proposition plays two roles: it says something, and it shows something. What it *says* is simply something contingent, namely, that Moore has the property of being good. But what it *shows* is twofold.

First, it shows something contingent: that the word "Moore" in this propositional sign stands to the left of the word "good". This accidental or arbitrary feature of the propositional sign results from "the particular way in which the propositional sign is produced" (3.34(2)). It is something that could well have been "different in different sign-languages" (*NB* 17(2)). That "Moore" stands to the left of "good" in the propositional sign is something that the propositional sign itself does not say to be the case—indeed *cannot* say to be the case, since "a propositional sign cannot be contained in itself" (3.332). Yet it is something that another propositional sign *can* say to be the case. Thus, where what is shown by a propositional sign is something contingent, this contingent feature of the propositional sign cannot be said by that very same propositional sign, though it can be said by some other propositional sign. This is the weak thesis.

The second thing that the propositional sign "Moore is good" shows is something noncontingent, for instance, that Moore's being good is a possible situation.

This (or any other) noncontingent feature obviously cannot be said by the propositional sign for any contingent proposition whatever. It obviously isn't *said* by the propositional sign "Moore is good" itself. Neither is it *said* by the propositional sign for any other contingent proposition. For the propositional sign "It is possible that Moore is good" expresses a noncontingent proposition, not a contingent one. Thus in the case where what is shown about a situation is something noncontingent, formal, or logical, this noncontingent feature of the situation cannot be said by any proposition with sense whatever. This is the strong thesis.

If I am right about this connection between the sayable/showable distinction and the contingent/noncontingent distinction, then the dictum "What *can* be shown, *cannot* be said" requires careful disambiguation. On one reading we may take it to assert the weak thesis that where what can be shown by a given propositional sign is something contingent, that which is shown cannot be said by that same propositional sign (though it can be said by some other propositional sign). When so construed, 4.1212 is evidently true, for the simple reason that Wittgenstein himself gives, namely, that "a propositional sign cannot contain itself." (3.332).[5] On another reading, we may take it to assert the strong thesis that where what is shown by a given propositional sign is something noncontingent, that which is shown cannot be said by that propositional sign or by any other propositional sign for a contingent proposition. When so construed, 4.1212 is once again evidently true, for the simple reason that noncontingent matters are never assertable by any contingent propositions whatever.

Interestingly, Wittgenstein appeals to both theses in his rather perfunctory dismissal of Russell's theory of types. He writes: "No proposition can make a statement about itself, because a propositional sign cannot be contained in itself (that is the whole of the theory of types)." (3.332). It is, of course, widely held that Wittgenstein's account of the theory of types is superficial and his proposed alternative inadequate. But as we shall see in section 13, this judgment may be too hasty. For the moment it suffices to make his general intent clear. He wants to say, (i) that, by virtue of the weak thesis, the kind of self-referential paradoxes which Russell's theory tried to preclude cannot even be expressed in a proper notation; and (ii) that, by virtue of the strong thesis, since what Russell's theory of types tries to say is something noncontingent about which types (logical kinds) of expressions can combined so as to produce significant propositions, it tries to say something that can only be shown.[6]

It is the strong thesis that features most prominently in Wittgenstein's account of language. Consider, for example, the important points he makes in the two entries that immediately precede his statement of the dictum. Having told us, "Propositions *show* the logical form of reality" (4.121(4)), he continues, "Thus one proposition 'fa' shows that the object a occurs in its sense, two propositions 'fa' and 'ga' show that the same object is mentioned in both of them." (4.1211(1)). Here is a case where the strong thesis applies. For the fact that the object a occurs in the sense of both "fa" and "ga" is, in his view, a logical fact, a fact to do with an internal, logical, property of the structures of the possible situations that "fa" and "ga" represent. Accordingly, as 4.124 later tells us, the existence of this de re necessary property of these situations cannot be *asserted* by a proposition with sense. Rather, he says, "it expresses itself in the proposition representing the situation, by means of an internal property of that proposition" (4.124), namely, the occurrence of the name "a" in the structures of the propositions "fa" and "ga".

Having just made this point about the way in which the logical *properties* of situations are shown by the logical properties of the propositions that represent them, Wittgenstein goes on to make a similar point about logical *relations*: "If two propositions contradict one another, then their structure shows it; the same is true if one of them follows from the other. And so on." More generally, he writes, "The existence of an internal relation between possible situations expresses itself in language by means of an internal relation between the propositions representing them." (4.125). It follows, by the strong version of 4.1212, that the existence of such internal, logical relations cannot be said by any genuine proposition at all.

It is a commonplace of Tractarian exegesis that Wittgenstein sometimes couches the distinction between what is sayable and what is showable in terms of other locutions: what is sayable can be "asserted" (4.122, 6.2322), can be "put into words" (3.221, 4.116), and can be "expressed *by* language" (4.121(3), 4.124, 4.126); what is only showable cannot be asserted, cannot be put into words, and cannot be expressed by language but can "make itself manifest" (4.12, 6.522), can be "mirrored in propositions" (4.121) and can be "expressed *in* a proposition" (4.124).

What is not so often observed is that the notion of what is showable is also connected with the notion of what propositions "contain". Consider, for instance, the following passages: "A picture contains the possibility of the situation that it represents" (2.203); "A thought contains the possibility of the situation of which it is the thought" (3.02); "A proposition does not actually contain its sense, but does contain the possibility of expressing it" (3.13(3)); and "A proposition contains the form, but not the content, of its sense" (3.13(5)). Many have been perplexed by this talk of what propositions contain. Yet an early passage from the *Notebooks* makes clear how it should be construed. Wittgenstein writes, "The proposition must *contain* (and in this way show) the *possibility of its truth*." (*NB* 16(7)). This establishes the required connection. Substitute talk of showing for talk of containment, and all becomes clear. As the strong thesis insists, noncontingent modal features of the world, such as the possibility (or form) of a situation, can be shown—but not said—by pictures, thoughts, and propositions, respectively.

4. The Picture Theory of Language

The underlying presupposition of everything Wittgenstein has to say about saying and showing is that these dual features of propositional language reflect dual features of his ontology. Objects, states of affairs, and so on, have both logically contingent features and logically noncontingent ones. The logically noncontingent features are functions of the internal (de re necessary, formal) properties of simple objects (how they *can* combine in possible states of affairs). The logically contingent features are functions of their external properties (how they *do* combine in possible states of affairs). What is logically contingent about possible states of affairs and their constituents is both sayable and showable *by* language. What is logically noncontingent is only showable *in* language. Propositional language, then, is constructed along the same lines as—has the same general features as—his ontology. And the essentialistic atomism of the latter is reflected in the essentialistic atomism of the former.

Wittgenstein's so-called Picture Theory of Language guarantees that this should be the case. The theory, as I understand it, involves six main principles that, taken together, guarantee that features of the simplest elements of language (names) and of the complexes which result from their combination (propositions) are isomorphic with features of the simplest elements of his ontology (metaphysically simple objects) and of the complexes that result from their combination (the possible states of affairs that propositional language represents). These principles may be briefly stated as follows:

(1) **The Proxy Principle:** A name "goes proxy for" a simple object.
(2) **The Form-Signalizing Principle:** Names "signalize" the forms of the objects for which they stand and thereby themselves take on corresponding forms.
(3) **The Generalized Compositionality Principle:** A proposition is a function of the names contained within it.

Principle (3), as we shall see, turns out to a generalization of two quite distinct functional principles: (i) that the *sense* of a proposition is a function of the *references* of its constituent names; and (ii) that the *form* of a proposition is a function of the *forms* of its constituent names. Each of these has its own epistemic corollary, namely, (iii) that our *understanding* of a proposition is a function of our *understanding* of its constituent names; and (iv) that our *knowledge* of the syntactical rules governing the formation of a propositional sign is a function of our *knowledge* of the syntactical rules governing the signs that are its components.

(4) **The Compositional-Freedom Principle:** In a proposition with sense, names are connected experimentally in such a way as to represent a possible state of affairs, situation, or world.

This principle, which emphasizes what combinations of names are possible in propositions with sense, is an elaboration of the second of the functional theses encompassed by the Compositionality Principle but is worth stating in its own right.

(5) **The Compositional-Constraints Principle:** The connection of the propositional components, namely, names, in a proposition must be possible for the objects they represent (where what is possible for the objects is, of course, a function of the forms of the objects).

This principle, which emphasizes what combinations of names are *not* possible in propositions with sense, is also an elaboration of the second of the functional theses encompassed by the Compositionality Principle but again is worth stating in its own right.

(6) **The Same-Multiplicity Principle:** There must be as many distinguishable names in a proposition as there are objects in the possible state of affairs that the proposition represents.

In much of the rest of this chapter I shall try to trace the ways in which these principles determine the construction of propositional language and, as a special case, the construction of logic.

5. The Proxy Principle

Wittgenstein emphasizes the primacy of the Proxy Principle as a precondition of propositional language both in the *Notebooks*, where he tells us, "The possibility of propositions is, of course, founded on the principle of signs as GOING PROXY for objects" (*NB* 37(8)), and in the *Tractatus*, where he makes the similar claim that "The possibility of propositions is based on the principle that objects have signs as their representatives." (4.0312(1)).

The principle itself is declared in both works: "In the proposition the name goes proxy for the object" (*NB* 37(11)) and "In a proposition a name is the representative of an object." (3.22).

Wittgenstein makes a point of the fact that the relation between a name and the object that it goes proxy for is always a conventional, "arbitrary", or "accidental" one. The assignment of names, he writes, "must take place by means of arbitrary stipulations." (*NB* 17(2)). Again: "The arbitrary correlation of sign and thing signified . . . is a condition of the possibility of the propositions." (*NB* 25(8)). The arbitrary nature of the assignment of names to objects, he points out, is reflected in certain features of the propositions in which those names occur. "Every proposition must accordingly contain features with arbitrarily determined reference." (*NB* 17(2)). These are the features of propositions that, in the *Tractatus*, he calls "accidental" and distinguishes from the so-called "essential" ones (to which I shall draw attention in section 8). The accidental ones have to do with "the particular way in which the propositional sign is produced." (3.34(2)).

Wittgenstein's claim that names are assigned in a purely conventional manner, is uncontentious. Not so his claim, to which the Proxy Principle commits him, that names have a purely referential function and are wholly lacking in sense or descriptive content.

In espousing the Proxy Principle, Wittgenstein sets himself squarely against the descriptivist tradition of semantic analysis. Descriptivists hold, roughly: (i) that names have sense as well as reference; (ii) that the sense of a name is given by a description (or a cluster of descriptions) of the properties we associate with the name; and (iii) that the bearer of the name (the reference—or better still, the *referent*—of the name) is to be identified as that object, if any, which satisfies the description of those properties. The descriptivist tradition is one to which, with varying degrees of fidelity, such philosophers as Frege, Russell (officially), Strawson, and Searle have subscribed.

Wittgenstein would want to reject all three of these claims. He would reject (iii), I suspect, because he would regard it as no part of his business as a logician to concern himself with epistemological questions about *how* the referent of a name is to be identified. "Theory of Knowledge," he tells us, "is the philosophy of psychology" (4.1121(2)); and psychology, he would remind us, is not one of his concerns.

He would reject (ii), as it stands, for much the same reason, since the question of what descriptions we "associate" with a name is also a psychological one. And if a descriptivist were to try to avoid psychologism by identifying the relevant set, or cluster, of descriptions with those that the bearer of the name *actually* satisfies (as opposed to those that we *think* it satisfies), Wittgenstein would still object. He would argue, to the contrary, that many of the descriptions that an object in fact satisfies are purely accidental to the object and hence are ones that the object does *not* have in some of the merely possible, nonactual states of affairs in which the object occurs. (In effect, he would invoke what I shall later call "the argument from counterfactual truth-conditions".)

As for (i), he would reject this on the grounds that, for him, sense (*Sinn*) is something that belongs only to whole propositions, never to names. Names don't have sense, he would say, but only reference (*Bedeutung*).[7] Thus he claims: "Objects I can only *name*. Signs go proxy for them. I can only speak *of* them, I cannot *express* them." (*NB* 51(9-10)); and again, "Objects can only be *named*. Signs are their representatives. I can only speak *about* them: I cannot *put them into words*." (3.221). Were it the case, as Frege and other descriptivists hold, that names had a sense as well as reference, that sense would be capable of being expressed or put into words, as a description of the object. But according to Wittgenstein, nothing about objects *can* be expressed or put into words. Hence names do not have sense.

Wittgenstein is by no means alone in subscribing to the Proxy Principle. John Stuart Mill [1883] had articulated it with some care, as a thesis about ordinary proper names, when—in a passage that is something of a locus classicus of the view—he wrote: "Proper names are not connotative: they denote the individuals who are called by them; but they do not indicate or imply any attributes as belonging to those individuals." Mill goes on to point out that although a certain town may originally have been named "Dartmouth" because it was, at the time of naming, situated at the mouth of the Dart, it is "no part of the signification . . . of the word Dartmouth, to be situated at the mouth of the Dart." After all, he argues, "If sand should choke up the mouth of the river, or an earthquake change its course, and remove it to a distance from the town, the name of the town would not necessarily be changed. That fact, therefore, can form no part of the signification of the word; for otherwise, when the fact confessedly ceased to be true, no one would any longer think of applying the name." Generalizing, he concludes: "Proper names are attached to the object themselves, and are not dependent on the continuance of any attribute of the object." (p. 20).[8]

Even Bertrand Russell, whom many regard as the arch-descriptivist, claimed that *genuine* proper names (which, for reasons to do with his anti-Meinongian stance in metaphysics and his empiricist epistemology, he identified with demonstratives such as "this" and "that") are "merely means of getting through to things". He even went so far as to allow that ordinary proper names such as "Scott" are sometimes so used, that is, are sometimes used "*as* names" (his emphasis) rather than as truncated descriptions. When so used, he said, "the name itself is merely a means of pointing to the thing, and does not occur in what you are asserting, so that if one thing has two names, you make exactly the same assertion whichever of the

two names you use, provided they are really names and not truncated descriptions."
([1918], p. 245).

More recently, Saul Kripke [1980] has revived the Proxy Principle for objects by claiming that names, in general, are what he calls *rigid designators*. "Let's call something a *rigid designator*," he writes, "if in every possible world it designates the same object, a *nonrigid* or *accidental* designator if this is not the case. . . . One of the intuitive theses I will maintain in these talks is that names are rigid designators." (p. 48).[9]

Now I think that Kripke's claim that names are rigid designators involves more than just the Proxy Principle. It involves, as well, the claim that the objects that names rigidly designate can preserve their identity across different possible worlds. The thesis that names are rigid designators, then, is grounded in two highly plausible intuitions: that objects can occur in states of affairs other that those in which they actually occur and that names can be used, and standardly are used, simply to stand for, or go proxy for, those objects regardless of the states of affairs in which they occur. The first of these intuitions is embodied in the particular view of possible worlds to which both Wittgenstein and Kripke subscribe. And it is plausible, I think they would both say, insofar as it is plausible to think or talk about objects as existing in states of affairs which are not actual, that is, to think counterfactually of them as being connected in merely possible states of affairs "as they do not have to be in reality" (*NB* 13(2)). The second intuition, of course, is that which is embodied in the Proxy Principle, to which Mill, Russell (on unofficial occasions, as it were), Wittgenstein, and Kripke subscribe. It is plausible, I think they would all say, insofar as it is plausible to suppose that human beings have the ability to invent linguistic devices for *merely* referring to objects without thereby describing the properties of those objects, and in so far as it is also plausible to suppose that *names* were invented to serve just that purpose (though Russell thinks that they nevertheless usually fail to serve it).

6. Arguments for the Proxy Principle

Adherents of the Proxy Principle have advanced two main arguments for saying that names, in natural language, function as mere proxies and have no descriptive content.

The first is that given by Mill. In effect, he points out that if the word "Dartmouth" had the sort of descriptive content that it might plausibly be thought to have, namely, of signifying the town that satisfies the description "the town at the month of the river Dart" (the description of a property which Dartmouth *in fact* has), then in a counterfactual situation in which the town's position is changed with respect to the mouth of the river, "no one would any longer think of using the name." But, he argues, we *would* continue to use that name even if the counterfactually envisaged changes to its position were to occur. Hence "Dartmouth" does not have this—or, by generalization, any other—descriptive content.

A second argument, also involving appeal to what one would say in counterfactual situations, has been offered by Kripke. He considers not only whether we would continue to use the same name for the same object but also whether we would be disposed to say that some property that we had originally attributed to the object would, in the counterfactually envisaged situation, belong to some *other* object. He invites us to consider the statement that Aristotle was fond of dogs and see in what circumstances this would be counted as true if the descriptivist account were correct. Suppose the descriptivist were to assign to the name "Aristotle" the descriptive content of the expression "was the last great philosopher of antiquity". Now consider a counterfactual situation in which someone other than Aristotle would have had that property. Then, he points out, the descriptivist would be obliged to make that *other* person's fondness for dogs the relevant issue for the correctness of the statement that Aristotle was fond of dogs! (pp. 6–7). But, Kripke argues, this is absurd. We would not in the slightest degree be disposed to count the statement that Aristotle was fond of dogs as true on the grounds that the person who (counterfactually) was the last great philosopher of antiquity was fond of dogs. Rather we would count it as true if and only if *Aristotle*, not that other person, was fond of dogs. Hence "Aristotle" cannot have the assigned descriptive content—or, by generalization, any other.

It should, perhaps, be emphasized that these two arguments—Mill's regarding *counterfactual naming-conditions*, and Kripke's regarding *counterfactual truth-conditions*—have to do solely with the *semantic role* of names and hence are independent of any stories that might be told about why or how a given name happens to be assigned to a given object. Causal stories about how or why a name comes to be bestowed on its bearer, or about how the name is subsequently transmitted from one speaker to another, may be true (or false). But they have to do only with what Wittgenstein, Kripke, and even Mill (despite his aversion to the essential/accidental distinction) would regard as merely *accidental* features of the name concerned and as in no way bearing upon its *essential* role as a simple proxy or representative.[10]

7. Are Ordinary Names Mere Proxies?

There can be no doubt that Wittgenstein subscribed both to the Proxy Principle and to the stronger thesis of rigid designation regarding names. Yet it may be questioned whether the expressions to which they apply include, for Wittgenstein, as they do for Kripke,[11] the ordinary names that occur in natural languages. Might it not be his view that they apply only to names for what we have called metaphysically simple objects? Might he not hold, with Russell, that the names we ordinarily use need analysis of the kind provided by Russell's Theory of Descriptions? In short, might he not be a descriptivist after all, with respect to the only names that we in fact use: the ordinary names of natural language?

I think not. In the first place, when Wittgenstein explicitly addresses questions about the semantic role played by ordinary names, he concludes, "we quite instinctively designate those objects by means of names" (*NB* 48 (1)). And a little later he observes that the ordinary name for an ordinary complex object such as a watch will satisfy "all the requirements of the 'names of simple objects'." (*NB* 60 (10)).

As he puts it, quite generally, "it would seem as if in a certain sense all names were *genuine names*." (*NB* 61 (11)). There is no good reason to suppose that his position in the *Tractatus* is any different. There he writes, without any qualms, about "the name Julius Caesar" (5.02) and claims, "In the proposition 'Green is green' . . . the first word is the proper name of a person . . ." (3.323). Clearly, "Green" and "Julius Caesar" are not names for metaphysically simple objects, such as occur "only in the nexus of an elementary proposition" (4.23). But he calls them names nonetheless, presumably because he holds that they go proxy for (and rigidly designate) the complex objects that are their bearers.

Second, although it is true that both Wittgenstein and Russell believed that ordinary names need to be analyzed if we are to understand the full implications of their use, the idea that they both thought of analysis in the same way does not withstand serious examination. According to Russell, a proper name such as "Socrates" is seldom used *as* a name for, that is, as a proxy for, a thing. Rather, such a name is ordinarily used as a proxy for a definite description, for instance, "the person called 'Socrates'" or "the teacher of Plato". For him, the analysis of a name like "Socrates" involves two stages: (i) that in which "Socrates" is taken to be equivalent to, for example, "the teacher of Plato"; and (ii) that in which the definite description given in (i) is itself given a further analysis. Now an expression such as "the teacher of Plato", Russell would claim, is an incomplete symbol: it does not, he holds, have a meaning all by itself, but admits of being analyzed only in the context of its use in a proposition. Thus if we start with the sentence "Socrates was human", we obtain, at the first stage of analysis, "The teacher of Plato was human." And then, invoking the analytical schema provided by the Theory of Descriptions, we obtain at the second stage, "There is one and only one object which taught Plato, and anything which taught Plato is human." Sentences like the latter are the ultimate products of analysis.

However, the sort of analysis envisaged by Wittgenstein is quite different and produces totally different results. Significantly, nowhere in the *Notebooks* or the *Tractatus* does Wittgenstein use the kind of analysis provided by Russell's Theory of Descriptions. Rather, Wittgenstein thinks that complexes are to be analyzed by giving a complete account of their constituent parts and of how these parts are related. Taking physics and chemistry as his models, he holds that a complex object like Socrates can in principle be analyzed into a structured configuration of simple parts (*NB* 69(9)), and suggests that a familiar substance like water can be analyzed into a structured configuration of two parts of hydrogen to one part of oxygen ([1986], p. 521). This is how complex *things* are to be analyzed. And it also sets the pattern for how the *names* for such objects are to be analyzed. The names of ordinary objects "disappear on further analysis" (*NB* 61(3)). But they give way, when analyzed, to *more* names (in configuration). They do not give way, as in a descriptivist account, to expressions containing predicates of ordinary language.[12] I conclude that, for Wittgenstein, the Proxy Principle applies without qualification to names for metaphysically simple and metaphysically complex objects alike. This conclusion accords, of course, with that of Chapter 3, section 4, in which we saw that a metaphysically complex object, when named, may be treated as *semantically simple* in just the same way as a metaphysically simple one: "Its *composition* becomes completely *indifferent*. It disappears from view." (*NB* 69(4)).

8. Identity-Problems for the Proxy Principle

Despite the apparent plausibility of the Proxy Principle, it is well known that any such strictly referentialist account of names—any account, that is, that holds that the sole semantic function of a name is that of referring to its bearer—is faced with problems involving the notion of identity.

The problems arise like this. According to a referentialist theory, the proposition that is expressed by the sentence

(1) "Scott is identical to Scott"

is the very same proposition as that which is expressed by the sentence

(2) "Scott is identical to Sir Walter".

For suppose it to be true—as indeed it is—that "Sir Walter" is just another name for Scott. Then, if the only function of "Sir Walter" in (2) is to pick out its bearer, namely, Scott, it must surely follow that (2) *says* no more than (1) *says*, namely, that a certain object, Scott, is identical to itself. But, the objection goes, the proposition expressed by (1) *cannot* be identical with that expressed by (2) since the proposition expressed by (1) may have different properties from that expressed by (2). For instance, the proposition expressed by (1), it would be said, is uninformative whereas that expressed by (2) is not. And again, it would be said, the proposition expressed by (1) may have the property of being believed by someone, for example, King George IV, whereas that expressed by (2) does not have that property.

What generates these sorts of problems for the Proxy Principle, of course, is Leibniz's Principle of the Indiscernibility of Identicals (sometimes called the Substitutivity of Identicals[13]). For Leibniz's Principle, to which Wittgenstein subscribes, tells us that, if an object x has a property F, then any object y that is identical with x also has F. And from this it plainly follows that if y does not have a property F which x has, then y is *not* identical to x.

Let's look at the problems in a little more detail.

Problem I: Consider, first, the case where x = the proposition expressed by (1), y = the proposition expressed by (2), and F = the property of *being uninformative*. Then, it is often said, since it is true that

(3) The proposition expressed by (1) is uninformative

and, according to the referentialist theory, it is also true that

(4) The proposition expressed by (2) is identical to the proposition expressed by (1)

it must, by Leibniz's Principle, follow that

(5) The proposition expressed by (2) is uninformative.

Yet (5), it is claimed, is in fact false. Hence, given the undisputed truth of (3), it is argued (by antilogism) that the referentialist theory that leads us to adopt (4) must be abandoned.

Problem II: A parallel problem arises when we turn to so-called belief-contexts.[14] Consider the case where x = the proposition expressed by (1), namely,

    (6) Scott is identical to Scott

y = the proposition expressed by (2), namely,

    (7) Scott is identical to Sir Walter

and F = the property of *being believed by George IV* . And suppose it to be true that

    (8) George believes that (6).

Then, since it is true, on the referentialist theory, that

    (9) (6) is identical to (7)

it must, by Leibniz's Principle, follow that

    (10) George believes that (7).

Yet (10), it is often claimed, may well be false even in circumstances in which (8) is true. Hence, given the truth of (8), it is argued that the referentialist theory that leads us to adopt (9) must be abandoned.

Both problems, or "paradoxes" as they are sometimes called, share a common structure: each apparently derives a certain manifestly false proposition—(5) in the case of Problem I, (10) in the case of Problem II—from two other propositions, each of which is taken to be true. Not surprisingly, therefore, each paradox invites the same range of responses.

One common kind of reply is to say that Leibniz's Principle is not universally valid since it does not apply within so-called nonextensional contexts. A second is to say that predicates such as " . . . is uninformative" and " . . . is believed by George" do not express genuine properties and hence are not admissible substituends for the predicate variable "F" in our formulation of Leibniz's Principle. A third kind of response is to say that propositional designations and proper names like "Scott" and "Sir Walter" are not admissible substituends for the variables "x" and "y" in Leibniz's Principle. This last kind of response, of course, entails a rejection of the referentialist view that designations of propositions such as "(6)" and "(7)" and ordinary proper names such as "Scott" and "George" function as mere proxies for their bearers. And it is, in effect, the response that Frege and other descriptivists have offered. Thus Frege and his followers would diagnose the source of the problems as a failure, by referentialists like Wittgenstein, to recognize that names and other designators have senses as well as referents.

In "On Sense and Reference", Frege [1966] recognizes that, if identity were a relation only between that which two names "a" and "b" refer to (that for which they are Wittgensteinian representatives or proxies), then provided that a is indeed identical to b, the statement that a = b could *not* differ in cognitive value from the statement that a = a. For, as he puts it, "A relation would thereby be expressed of a thing to itself, and indeed one in which each thing stands to itself but to no other thing." (p. 66). The evident difference of cognitive value, he therefore suggests, is to be explained by the fact that the two signs "a" and "b" are different "modes of presentation" of the same object. And these different modes of presentation, he claims, entail different senses for each sign. Thus, of the examples given, he would want to say that the differences in informative content between (1) and (2), and of belief-status between (6) and (7), are consequences of the fact that "Sir Walter" has a different *sense* from "Scott", in spite of the fact that both names have the same referent.

Wittgenstein is certainly not unaware of the problem. Early on in the *Notebooks* he discusses what he calls "the old old objection against identity in mathematics." This, he explains, is "the objection that if 2 × 2 were really the *same* as 4, then this proposition would say no more than a = a." (*NB* 4(5)). And he mentions the problem once again, this time in the *Tractatus*, when he writes: "Roughly speaking, to say of *two* things that they are identical is nonsense, and to say of *one* thing that it is identical with itself is to say nothing at all." (5.5303).

Unfortunately, however, he does not give the problem its proper due but dismisses it as a pseudo-problem that is generated solely by our adoption of a faulty notation, that is, by our use of a notation in which redundant names occur. In a correct conceptual notation, he insists, problems like this would not arise. We would use only one sign for one object, two for two objects, and so on. (See, especially, 5.533–5.535).

Now it is all very well for Wittgenstein to claim that if we were to use only one name for the actual author of *Waverley*—say "Scott"—and so were to abjure sentences such as "Scott is Sir Walter", there would be no apparent differences of cognitive value to explain away. But this does nothing whatsoever to answer the problems that seemingly force themselves upon us when we *do* use more than one name for a single object. Nor does it do anything to answer questions about identity in mathematics. It does not explain why "2 × 2 = 4" seems to tell us more than "4 = 4". And, more generally, it does not explain what would remain of mathematics were mathematicians to abide by his injunction to use one sign only for one number. What, for instance, would become of the *equations* of mathematics? Treating the "old, old problem of identity in mathematics" (and elsewhere) as a pseudo-problem simply will not do. How, we must ask, is the problem to be solved, given the general parameters that Wittgenstein has set for himself? How is it to be solved given his rejection of Frege's sense-reference distinction for names and his insistence (in the Proxy Principle) that names have reference only?

In the next section, I'll try to show that, although he does not avail himself of them, Wittgenstein in fact has on hand—in his distinctions between propositional signs and propositions, and between saying and showing—most of the materials needed for still another response (one that both is different from and seems to me more promising than any of the three just sketched).

9. A Wittgensteinian Response to the Identity-Problems

The first point that needs to be made is that if we are going to be careful (as, unfortunately, Wittgenstein often fails to be) about the distinction between propositional signs or sentence-tokens, on the one hand and propositions, on the other, then we shall want to insist that the properties of *being informative* or *being uninformative* are properly ascribed only to the former, not to the latter. Strictly speaking, *sentences* are the vehicles of communication, *propositions* the items of information (sometimes called the informational "content") conveyed. More specifically, it is sentences that convey information, by *saying* or *showing* something to be the case, and propositions that are the items of information conveyed, by being *said* or *shown* to be the case.

Given this distinction between sentences and propositions and the categorially admissible properties of each, we are well on the way to solving Problem I. Thus we can, as a first step, allow that the *sentence*

(1) "Scott is identical to Scott"

is uninformative, whereas the *sentence*

(2) "Scott is identical to Sir Walter"

is informative. But this is in no way inconsistent with the claim that the proposition that (1) expresses, namely,

(6) Scott is identical to Scott

is identical with the proposition which (2) expresses, namely,

(7) Scott is identical to Sir Walter.

Nor is it inconsistent with the belief that Leibniz's Principle is universally applicable. For that which has the property of *being uninformative* plainly is not identical to that which does not. Sentence (2) is *different* from sentence (1), even though (2) expresses the very same proposition as (1).

But exactly what is the information that (2) conveys but (1) does not? By way of an answer, we can, as a second step, invoke the weak form of Wittgenstein's Tractarian distinction between that which a sentence *says* and that which a sentence *shows*. What sentence (2) *says*—or, as it is usually put, "expresses"—is that proposition (7) is true. And this proposition is identical, on the referentialist theory, with the proposition (6), which sentence (1) says to be true. But what sentence (2) *shows* (in this case, something contingent) is not identical with what sentence (1) shows. Sentence (2) shows, though it does not say, something that is said by the sentence

(11) "The name "Sir Walter" is another name for Scott".

That is to say, sentence (2) shows that the proposition

(12) The name "Sir Walter" is another name for Scott

is true. Sentence (1), however, neither says nor shows that (12) is true. The propositional information, (12), that (2) conveys by showing is not conveyed in any way by

(1). We can retain Leibniz's Principle without qualification and explain the difference in informative content between (1) and (2) without recourse to Frege's sense/reference distinction and hence without compromising the referentialist theory of designation in any way.[15]

To deal with Problem I it sufficed for us to distinguish carefully between sentences and propositions, to insist that the role of carrying information (whether by saying or by showing) is performed by the former but not by the latter, and thereby to challenge the presupposition, on which Problem I rests, that propositions can properly be said to be informative or uninformative. The conceptual resources on which we drew here, however, will not suffice for a treatment of Problem II since the latter involves the concept of belief also. Nevertheless, a similar strategy may work. What we need to do in this case, I suggest, is to distinguish once more between sentences and propositions, insist that the property of being believed may be possessed by the latter but not by the former, and challenge the common presupposition—on which I think Problem II rests—that a person's assent to or dissent from a sentence is a reliable guide to what that person believes.

Let's begin by asking what grounds we have for supposing that George IV believes the proposition

(6) Scott is identical to Scott

but does not believe the proposition

(7) Scott is identical to Sir Walter

despite the fact that, on a referentialist account, (6) is the very same proposition as (7). Surely, it would be said, we can judge George's beliefs by his linguistic behavior: if George is disposed to assent to the *sentence* "Scott is identical to Scott" but not to the *sentence* "Scott is identical to Sir Walter" and is a nonreticent speaker of English, then we have good grounds for supposing that he *believes* (6) but not (7). If this is our answer then we are subscribing to what Kripke [1976] calls the Disquotational Principle, a principle that he formulates thus: "A normal English speaker who is not reticent will be disposed to sincere reflective assent to 'p' (any appropriate English sentence) if and only if he believes that p." (p. 249).

Does the Disquotational Principle really provide an accurate account of our criteria for belief-attribution? I think not. For it ignores the fact that it is a necessary condition of a person's understanding *what* proposition is expressed by a given sentence, and hence a necessary condition of his giving sincere and reflective assent to that sentence, that the person know the signification of any name that is featured in that sentence, that is, recognize exactly what object the name stands for. The Disquotational Principle would have us say that George IV does not believe that Scott is Sir Walter, on the grounds that George does not behave appropriately towards the sentence "Scott is Sir Walter". But these grounds surely do not suffice. We would be entitled to draw that conclusion only if we also had reason to believe that George knew to whom the name "Sir Walter" referred. If George IV does not know to whom "Sir Walter" refers, it is not at all surprising that he will not assent to the sentence "Scott is Sir Walter", even though he willingly assents to the sentence "Scott is Scott". The explanation is simply that he does not know what proposition "Scott is Sir Walter" expresses.

More precisely, I think the Disquotational Principle must be rejected for the following reasons: (i) I take it to be a necessary condition of a speaker S's understanding what proposition is expressed by a statement-making sentence, "p", that S should know in what possible circumstances "p" says something true, and in what possible circumstances "p" says something false. S needs, at the very least, to know how things would stand if "p" said something true. (ii) It is surely a necessary condition of S's knowing how things stand if "p" says something true, that S should know which thing or things are being said by "p" to stand in what way, that is, *which* thing or things are being said to have such and such properties or to stand in such and such relations to other things. Hence, (iii) it is a necessary condition of a speaker S's knowing, for any statement-making sentence "p", which proposition "p" expresses, that for any name (or designator) "N" that occurs in "p", S should recognize "N" as a name (or designator) of its referent (or designation).

Now the conclusion just reached, namely, clause (iii), is what I shall call the Recognition Principle. It is not explicitly enunciated by Wittgenstein. But since it follows from (i) and (ii), both of which are clearly theses to which Wittgenstein would subscribe, he is committed to it. In any case, it may plausibly be viewed as a corollary of his claim that "it [is] not permissible to recognize more or less in the sign than it signifies." (*NB* 3(1)). It is also a corollary of what Gareth Evans [1982] has called Russell's Principle, namely, "a subject cannot make a judgment about something unless he knows which object his judgment is about." (p. 89).

As I see it, then, the connection between linguistic behavior and belief is not quite as straightforward as Kripke's Disquotational Principle makes it out to be. Indeed, that principle needs to be replaced by the conjunction of two others, both of which incorporate the important insight of the Recognition Principle. They are: (1) The Belief-Expression Principle, "If a normal nonreticent English speaker, A, believes that p, then A will be disposed to sincere and reflective assent to 'p' (any appropriate English sentence) only if A recognizes exactly what the signification is of any name that occurs in 'p'"; and (2) The Belief-Attribution Principle, "If a normal nonreticent English speaker, A, is disposed to sincere and reflective assent to 'p', and A recognizes exactly what the signification is of any name that occurs in 'p', then A may be credited with the belief that p."

Return, now, to the case of George. Let us suppose that he is a normal nonreticent speaker of English, that he assents to the sentence

(1) "Scott is identical to Scott"

and that he recognizes "Scott" as a name of Scott.[16] Then the Belief-Attribution Principle gives us a warrant for attributing to him the belief that the proposition

(6) Scott is identical to Scott

is true. Yet George, as we all know, may well fail to assent to the sentence

(2) "Scott is identical to Sir Walter"

even in the case where "Sir Walter" is just another name for Scott. Does this mean that, while believing (6), he nevertheless does not believe the proposition

(7) Scott is identical to Sir Walter

which, on the referentialist account, is identical to (6)? In other words, does this mean that

(10) George believes that (7)

is false? According to the Disquotational Principle, this is what we are obliged to infer. But the Belief-Expression Principle provides no warrant for any such inference. George's failure to assent to (2), according to this principle, is perfectly compatible with his believing (7). That is to say, his failure to assent to (2) is compatible with the *truth* of (10). The referentialist theory is in no way threatened once we see that the connection between beliefs and linguistic behavior is given by the Belief-Attribution Principle and the Belief–Expression Principle rather than by the Disquotational Principle.

Indeed, once we see that the conditions under which a speaker will use a sentence "p", to *express* the belief that p, are those given in the Belief-Expression Principle, rather than those given in the Disquotational Principle, we can explain *why* it is that George may fail to assent to the sentence (2) even though he in fact believes that (7), namely, the proposition that (2) expresses, is true. The explanation is that one of the necessary conditions of his giving assent to that sentence is not satisfied. He simply does not recognize the *name* "Sir Walter" as a name of Scott. His verbal behavior in failing to assent to sentence (2) *shows* this. It shows that he fails to believe what sentence (2) shows (but does not say), namely, that the proposition

(12) The name "Sir Walter" is another name for Scott

is true. Hence, by the Recognition Principle, he does not understand what proposition (2) is ordinarily used to express, and a fortiori does not understand that this sentence is ordinarily used—by those who do know the reference of "Sir Walter"—to express the very same proposition as is expressed by sentence (1). George, then, has different cognitive attitudes toward the *sentences* (1) and (2). He believes that (1) expresses the proposition that Scott is identical to himself while failing to believe that (2) expresses that same proposition. But there is no paradox here. For the proposition

(13) Sentence (1) expresses the proposition that Scott is identical to himself

is not the same proposition as

(14) Sentence (2) expresses the proposition that Scott is identical to himself.

Hence the propositions

(15) George believes that (14)

and

(16) George does not believe that (13)

may well be true together. Their joint truth poses no threat to universal applicability of Leibniz's Principle. Since (13) and (14) are not identical propositions, one of them may very well have a property—such as that of being believed by George—

which the other lacks. The view that expressions like "George believes that . . ." expresses genuine properties is in no way compromised. Neither is the referentialist claim that ordinary proper names like "Scott" and "Sir Walter" have, as their sole semantical function, that of going proxy for objects.[17]

I suspect that Wittgenstein would agree with the foregoing explanation of why George may fail to assent to the sentence (2) even though he in fact believes that (7), namely, the proposition that (2) expresses, is true. (The explanation, remember, is that one of the necessary conditions of his giving assent to that sentence is not satisfied. He simply does not recognize the *name* "Sir Walter" as a name of Scott.)

Indeed Wittgenstein himself hints at an independent argument in support of my diagnosis. In 4.243 he asks two questions: "Can we understand two names without understanding whether they signify the same thing or two different things?—Can we understand a proposition [propositional sign] in which two names occur without knowing whether their reference [*Bedeutung*] is the same or different?" His answer to both questions is "No". And his argument is, "Suppose I know the reference of an English word and of a German word that has the same reference: then it is impossible for me to be unaware that they have the same reference; I must be capable of translating each into the other." (4.243(2). His argument here takes for granted what I called the Recognition Principle: that it is a necessary condition of a speaker, S, knowing, for any statement-making sentence "p", which proposition "p" expresses, that for any name "N" that occurs in "p", S should recognize "N" as a name of its referent. Presuming its truth, he argues (by modus tollens) in 4.243(2), that if am unaware that two words have the same reference (and am consequently incapable of translating each into the other) then (i) I *don't* know the reference of one of the words (don't recognize the name "N" as a name of its referent), and hence further, (ii) that I *don't* understand the proposition sign (for instance, the propositional sign "Scott is identical to Sir Walter") in which both names occur.

Let's now return to the old, old question of why "$2 \times 2 = 4$" tells us more than "$4 = 4$". I asked how is it to be solved, given Wittgenstein's rejection of Frege's sense-reference distinction for names, and his insistence (in the Proxy Principle) that names have reference only. The answer, by now, should be obvious: "$2 \times 2 = 4$" tells us more than "$4 = 4$" just by virtue of the fact that although both *say* the same thing, the former *shows* what the latter does not: that "2×2" and "4" have the same reference.

It is worth noting that the paradoxes of identity that we are here discussing arise in many different forms. One, which especially troubled G. E. Moore [1968], has come to be known as "the Paradox of Analysis". Moore expresses his perplexity thus:

> I think that, in order to explain the fact that, even if "To be a brother is the very same thing as to be a male sibling" is true, yet this statement is *not* the same as the statement "To be a brother is to be a brother", one must suppose that both statements are in *some* sense about the expressions used as well as about the concept of being a brother. But in what sense they are about the expressions I cannot see clearly; and therefore I cannot give any clear solution to the puzzle. (p. 666)

The solution which eluded Moore is really quite simple, and avails itself of the same conceptual resources as those employed in our treatment of Problem I above.

It lies in recognizing that a sentence may *convey* information about an expression which the sentence is not "about"; in particular that a sentence can convey information about an expression even when it is not *about* that expression but merely *uses* it. Clearly the sentence "To be a brother is the very same thing as to be a male sibling" is about the *concepts* of being a brother and being a male sibling (it truly asserts their identity) and not at all about the *expressions* "to be a brother" and "to be a male sibling" (which plainly are not identical). Nonetheless, this sentence *uses* these expressions to say something true about the concepts that they express, and, in using them, conveys the information that they may be used to express one and the same concept. That is to say, this sentence *shows* (though it does not say) what can be said by the sentence "The expression 'to be a brother' expresses the very same concept as does the expression 'to be a male sibling'." By virtue of what it *says*, the sentence "To be a brother is the very same thing as to be a male sibling" expresses a necessarily true statement of identity and hence expresses a correct analysis of the concept of brotherhood. By virtue of what it *shows*, it is informative.

It is one of the ironies of history that the distinction between saying and showing, which Wittgenstein first introduced in notes dictated to Moore in 1914, and which he illustrated by means of the example "Moore [is] good", suffices (when taken together with a careful observance of the sentence/proposition distinction) for a solution to the paradox that gave Moore so much trouble more than half a century later.

Having thus responded, in a Wittgensteinian way, to some of the objections that might be made to the first of the principles involved in Wittgenstein's Picture Theory, namely, his Proxy Principle, let's now turn to the second.

10. The Form-Signalizing Principle

The role of names (for individuals) as the bedrock of propositional representation is vividly conveyed in the *Notebooks* when Wittgenstein asks himself, "Could one then manage without names?", and immediately answers: "Surely not. Names are necessary for an assertion that *this* thing possesses *that* property and so on. They link the general propositional form with quite definite objects. And if the general description of the world is like a stencil of the world, the names pin it to the world so that the world is wholly covered by it." (*NB* 53(7-10)).

But names don't only go proxy for individuals and thereby pin a proposition to the world. They also, in so doing, go proxy for the *forms* of those objects, or in his words "signalize" those forms. In other words, the presence of a name in a proposition not only shows what object occurs in the state of affairs that the proposition represents; it also, when taken together with its syntactical use, shows the possibilities of combination (the form) of that object and at the same time shows its own possibilities of combination with other names.

This second principle of propositional representation may be extracted from three passages in the *Notebooks*: "Names signalize what is common to a single form and a single content. Only *together with* their syntactical use do they signalize *one particular* logical form." (*NB* 53(5)); "We have become clear, then, that names may and do stand for the most various forms, and that it is only the syntactical application that signalizes the form that is to be presented." (*NB* 59(10)); and a passage in which the "component parts" of a proposition,that is, names themselves, are spoken of as having corresponding forms (*NB* 23(1)). The Form-Signalizing Principle, then, involves the conjunction of three theses: (i) that names stand for, and thereby signalize, the forms of the objects that they name; (ii) that names themselves have forms (combinatorial possibilities) corresponding to the forms of the objects that they name; and (iii) that both the forms of the objects and the forms of their names are shown in the syntactical rules that the names must obey when they are concatenated in propositions (propositional signs).

Claim (i), that a name shows the form of an object (not just the content, that is, which object it goes proxy for), is reiterated in the *Tractatus* when he writes, "An expression is the mark of a form and a content." (3.31(4)). Claim (ii) is presupposed in claim (iii). And claim (iii), that one must also take into account the syntactical application of the name to determine the particular form of the object, is also reiterated in the *Tractatus*: "A sign does not determine a logical form unless it is taken together with its logico-syntactical employment." (3.327).

Now we saw earlier that the Proxy Principle assigns names to objects in a purely arbitrary way, and that this arbitrary manner of their assignment explains what Wittgenstein calls the "arbitrary" or "accidental" features of propositions. By way of contrast, the Form-Signalizing Principle assigns formal or syntactical roles to names in a way that explains what he calls the "logical" or "essential" features of propositions. "The proposition," he claims, "is a formation with the logical features of what it represents." (*NB* 17(2)). What are these logical features? They are, he would say, the formal features of the objects whose names are the constituents of propositions. Given that an object has certain formal features—given, that is, that an object has certain possibilities of combination in possible states of affairs—so, too, the name for an object has corresponding formal features (corresponding possibilities of combination in any proposition that purports to represent a possible state of affairs). And these logical features, as he puts it in the *Tractatus*, are essential to the proposition; they are "those without which the proposition could not express its sense." (3.34(2)). (These essential, logical features of names as they occur in propositions, we shall see later, play a crucial role in determining which combinations of names yield propositions with sense.)

Both the Proxy Principle and the Form-Signalizing Principle have to do with the role of names, the atoms of propositional representation. They are the twin pillars— semantic and syntactic, respectively—upon which Wittgenstein erects his theory of language. Or, to change the metaphor again, semantics and syntax get their grip on the world at the "atomic" level of simple names.

Now, just as the Proxy Principle holds for ordinary names as well as the names of metaphysical simples, so too does the Form-Signalizing Principle. There are two grounds for saying this.

First, when Wittgenstein tells us, in the passage quoted, "names may and do stand for the most varied of forms, and that it is only the syntactical application that signalizes the form that is to be presented" (*NB* 59(10)), it is clear from the context that he in fact thinks this to be quite unproblematic for the case of *ordinary* names of complex objects, but not so clear for the case of simple names. For he immediately goes on to ask, rhetorically, "Now what is the syntactical application of simple names?" (*NB* 59 (10)). And later he observes, "the syntactical employment of the names [e.g., the name for a watch] completely characterizes the form of the *complex* [emphasis added] objects which they denote." (*NB* 61 (6)). In these passages it is the application of the Form-Signalizing Principle to *simple* names (names for metaphysical simple objects) that he is calling into question, though in other passages—such as 3.327—it is clear from the context that he takes it to have application to simple names as well.

Second, the applicability of the Form-Signalizing Principle to ordinary names is also made clear in the three consecutive *Notebooks* passages in which he discusses logical kinds: "If, e.g., I call some rod 'A', and a ball 'B', I can say that A is leaning against the wall, but not B. Here the internal nature of A and B comes into view." (*NB* 70(8)). "A name designating an object thereby stands in a relation to it which is wholly determined by the logical kind of the object and which signalizes that logical kind." (*NB* 70(9)). "And it is clear that the object must be of a particular logical kind; it is just as complex, or as simple, as it is." (*NB* 70(10)). Three points are worth noting here.

Note, first and foremost, that in *NB* 70(9) Wittgenstein speaks of names as signalizing the *logical kind* of an object, not just the form of the object. This, however, is not surprising. It is to be expected given that the forms of objects (the only internal properties that simple objects can possess) *determine* the logical kinds to which the objects belong. Thus the Form-Signalizing Principle might, with equal felicity, be called the Kind-Signalizing Principle.

Note, second, that—as *NB* 70(8) and (10) tell us—the objects to which he is referring may be either simple or (as in the cases of the ball and the rod) complex. This establishes the application of the Form-Signalizing Principle to ordinary names as well as Wittgensteinian simple ones.

Note, third, that—as *NB* 70(8) asserts—what makes manifest the internal nature, form, and logical kind of an object (simple or complex) is the syntactical application of the name for that object. This establishes the all-important connection between the forms, and consequent logical kinds, of ordinary objects and the rules of logical syntax for the construction of propositions with sense from the names for those objects. The form of an object "comes into view" (as he puts it in the *Notebooks*), or is *shown* (as he puts it in the *Tractatus*) by the syntactical rules for its use in propositions with sense. It is shown by what we can or cannot significantly *say*.

11. The Generalized Compositionality Principle

Wittgenstein is often said to have subscribed to some sort of compositionality principle regarding the relationship between propositions and the names that are their constituents. Hintikka and Hintikka [1987], for example, tell us that among the leading principles that Frege and Wittgenstein both accepted was what they refer to as "The compositionality principle, also known as the functional principle or the

Frege principle." This, they say, is the principle according to which "the meaning of a complex expression is a function of the meanings of its constituent expressions." (pp. 90–1). In support of their attribution of this principle to Wittgenstein, they cite 3.318, in which he asserts: "Like Frege and Russell I construe a proposition as a function of the expressions contained within it."

Now 3.318 certainly does show that Wittgenstein accepted *some* sort of functional or compositionality principle. But, equally certainly, it can't be either the principle that Hintikka and Hintikka formulate or the principle that Frege states.

In the first place, it cannot be the principle that Hintikka and Hintikka give. For if "meaning", in their formulation, means what Wittgenstein calls "*Sinn*", then Wittgenstein would reject their account on the grounds that only propositions, not names, have *Sinn* (that is, sense). And if "meaning" in their formulation means what Wittgenstein calls "*Bedeutung*" (which Pears and McGuinness infelicitously translate as "meaning" when Anscombe's "reference" would be clearer), then Wittgenstein would reject their account on the grounds that only names, not propositions, have *Bedeutung* (that is, reference).[18] Neither interpretation of their expression "meaning" will do.

Second, it cannot be the principle to which Frege himself subscribed. For Frege's principle, insofar as it can be read into his writings,[19] amounts to the second of the interpretations which we have just rejected: the view that the reference of a whole proposition is a function of the references of its constituents. Wittgenstein, to repeat, would reject it on the grounds that propositions have only sense, not reference.[20]

I think there are in fact four quite distinct functional principles, having to do with the properties of propositions and of the names out of which they are composed, to which Wittgenstein subscribes: (i) that the *sense* of a proposition (propositional sign) is a function of the *references* of its components; (ii) that the *form* of a proposition (propositional sign) is a function of the *forms* of its components; (iii) that *our understanding* of a proposition is a function of *our understanding* of the words out of which it is composed; and (iv) that our *knowledge* of the syntactical rules governing the formation of a propositional sign is a function of our *knowledge* of the syntactical rules governing the signs which are its components. I take 3.318 to express the generalization of the first two of these functional principles; hence my talk of 3.318 as a Generalized Compositionality Principle. The third and fourth state the consequences of the first and second, respectively, for our knowledge or understanding of how propositions function.

The first functional principle—that the *sense* of a proposition (propositional sign) is a function of the *referents* of the names that are its components (what, in the *Tractatus*, he calls the "contents" of the names)—is Wittgenstein's linguistic correlate of his ontological claim that a state of affairs is produced by the combination of objects (2.01, 2.0272). It presupposes the referential role of names asserted by the Proxy Principle and asserts that the sense of a proposition (which, in 4.031(2), Wittgenstein implicitly identifies with the state of affairs it represents) is compositionally determined by the references of its constituent names (the objects for which these names go proxy).

The second functional principle—that the *form* of a proposition is a function of the *forms* of its components—is Wittgenstein's linguistic correlate of his ontological claim that the form of a state of affairs is determined by the forms, that is, possibilities of combination (2.0141), of its constituent objects. It presupposes the form-presenting role of names as asserted by the Form-Signalizing Principle and asserts that the form of a proposition is compositionally determined by the forms of its constituent names. It is a thesis that Wittgenstein asserts quite explicitly: "The logical form of the proposition must already be given by the forms of its component parts. (And these have to do only with the *sense* of the propositions, not with their truth or falsehood)." (*NB* 23 (1)).

The third functional principle—that *our understanding* of a proposition is a function of *our understanding* of the words out of which it is composed—is an epistemic corollary of the first. It seems likely that this is the principle in respect of which he claims, in 3.318, to be following Russell. For Russell [1918] had written: "You can understand a proposition when you understand the words of which it is composed even though you never heard the proposition before." (p. 193). Wittgenstein, accordingly, tells us, "it [a proposition] is understood by anyone who understands its constituents." (4.024(3)). As I see it, (iii), like (i), is parasitic upon the Proxy Principle.

The fourth functional principle—that our *knowledge* of the syntactical rules governing the formation of a propositional sign is a function of our *knowledge* of the syntactical rules governing the signs which are its components—is an epistemic corollary of the second principle. I take it that this is what Wittgenstein is saying when he writes, "The rules of logical syntax must be obvious when we know how each individual sign signifies." (3.334). Like Max Black, I take him to be saying that in order to understand the grammatical rules for the construction of a complex expression we don't need to know *what* a particular sign within it signifies, that is, what its reference happens to be, but only *how* that sign behaves—where its behavior is determined by the formal properties (and corresponding logical kind) of that sign. Recall that Wittgenstein says, "If I know an object I also know all its possible occurrences in states of affairs. (Every one of these possibilities must be part of the nature of the object.) A new possibility cannot be discovered later." (2.0123). If I did not know how a name signifies, but only what it signifies, I would know only the external properties of the name (the accidental fact that this name has been arbitrarily correlated with this object), but I would not know the essential, logical features of the name (the features "without which the proposition could not express its sense" (3.34)). As I see it, (iv), like (ii), is parasitic on the Form-Signalizing Principle.

Taken together the third and fourth functional principles assert that to understand a proposition or propositional sign we must understand both the *semantic* and the *syntactic* roles of its constituent names.

Now, of the above four functional principles, the second assumes a special role in Wittgenstein's theory of propositional representation. It implies both, (a) that certain combinations of names, by virtue of the forms and syntactical roles of those names, are impossible; and (b) that certain other combinations of names—those that are not precluded by their forms and syntactical roles—are possible. That is to say, it implies both the Compositional-Constraints Principle (corresponding to (a)), and the Compositional-Freedom Principle (corresponding to (b)). These principles, though not independent of the second version of the Generalized Compositionality Principle (or of the Form-Signalizing Principle which that principle in turn presupposes), are worth emphasizing in their own rights.

Let's start with the Compositional-Freedom Principle.

12. The Compositional-Freedom Principle

The Compositional-Freedom Principle emphasizes the freedom we have in putting words together provided that we observe the constraints of logical syntax. Wittgenstein first hints at it in the *Notebooks*: "In the proposition a world is put together experimentally. (As when in the law-court in Paris a motor-car accident is represented by means of dolls, etc.)" (*NB* 7(3)).[21] He expresses it more fully when he writes, "In the proposition we—so to speak—arrange things as they do *not* have to be in reality; but we cannot make any unlogical arrangement." (*NB* 13(2)).

Three points are worth noting. First, in making these remarks Wittgenstein has in mind only genuine propositions, that is, contingent propositions or "propositions with sense", as opposed to propositions of logic and mathematics. On his view only the former can be said to present something about the world or reality. Second, he believes that provided we do not make "any unlogical arrangement" of the kind prohibited by the rules of logical syntax, any propositional sign that we put together out of words can be *guaranteed* to to represent a possible situation or even a whole world. Third, he holds that compliance with the rules of logical syntax does *not* guarantee that the propositional sign will express anything true, that is, will represent a situation that in fact exists.

The last two points are made explicit when Wittgenstein says, "The propositional sign guarantees the possibility of the fact which it presents (not, that this fact is actually the case)." (*NB* 27(2)).[22] On the one hand, then, compliance with the rules of logical syntax enables us to construct "a model of reality as we imagine it" (*NB* 20(4) and 4.01). But on the other hand, since that model may represent things as they "do not have to be in reality", our model may be, as it were, false to the facts. No proposition with sense can guarantee its own truth.

Propositions with sense, then, are those that we are free to construct within the range that is left open by the rules of logical syntax, and that tell us—truly or falsely—how things stand in the world. Their truth isn't guaranteed by their constructability. Being logically contingent, they are only possibly true, not necessarily so.

13.   Truth, Truth-Conditions, and Understanding

Obviously, Wittgenstein owes us some sort of account of what it is for a proposition with sense to be true. So what, in his view, is truth? Or rather, to make the question more manageable, under what circumstances would he want to say that a picture, or a proposition with sense, is true?

Wittgenstein's first answer, couched in terms of the generalized notion of "pictures" but equally applicable to propositions with sense ("logical pictures", as he calls them), is that a picture is true or false according to whether it "agrees with reality or fails to agree with it" (2.21).

This, of course, is a version of the so-called Correspondence Theory of Truth. Accordingly, it is prone to the standard objections to such theories: that it is difficult, if not impossible, to give independent accounts of the two terms of the correspondence relation, namely, "true propositions" on the one hand, and "reality" or "the facts", on the other; and that it is difficult, if not impossible, to give a clear account of the relation of correspondence or agreement. In the minds of many, the initial attractiveness of the theory tends to evaporate when these objections are pressed.

But Wittgenstein also gives a second answer, one that accords well with the basic intuitions that make correspondence theories so appealing but that does not seem prone to the same problems. A proposition, he says, "is true if we use it to say that things stand in a certain way, and they do." (4.062).

Unfortunately, this will not do as it stands. For, if we are to observe the sentence/proposition distinction, we shall want to say that it is not propositions but sentences or propositional signs that we "use" to say that "things stand in a certain way". However, especially since this is a distinction that Wittgenstein himself acknowledges, we can invoke it so as to provide the following acceptable formulation:

> "Propositional sign 'p' expresses a true proposition" $=$ $_{def.}$ "For some proposition p, 'p' is the propositional sign that says that p, and p."

An alternative formulation, one given by John Mackie ([1973], p. 247), following William Kneale [1972], allows for the view that a proposition may be true whether or not it is expressed by any propositional sign[23]:

> "X is true" $=$ $_{def.}$ "For some proposition p, X is the-proposition-that-p, and p."

Both formulations seems to me to capture the essence of Wittgenstein's account in 4.062. Moreover, both have the added virtue of applying not only to contingent propositions (the domain that Wittgenstein had in mind) but also to noncontingent ones.[24]

The claim that a proposition is true just if things stand as the proposition says they do lends itself to talk of the *truth-conditions* of propositions. A proposition is true just if conditions or circumstances are as the proposition says they are: that is, just if its truth-conditions obtain. This is a *semantic* thesis.[25]

Corresponding to this semantic thesis is an *epistemic* one about our *understanding* of propositions. Wittgenstein expresses it in two ways: First he writes, "To understand a proposition means to know what is the case if it is true." (4.024(1)). (He adds, as a clarificatory aside, "One can understand it, therefore, without knowing whether it is true." (4.024(2)).) Then a little later he writes: "In order to be able to say, ' "p" is true (or false)', I must have determined in what circumstances I call 'p' true, and in so doing I determine the sense of the proposition." (4.063(2)).

Of these two formulations, I think the second is better. In 4.024(1) he blurs the sentence/proposition distinction by speaking about understanding a proposition when arguably it is propositional signs that require understanding. But in 4.063 he gets it a little clearer. There, as I construe him, he is saying that we can determine what proposition with sense a propositional sign "p" expresses by determining in what conditions we would say that "p" expresses something true. And since "determining" here is a rough synonym for "understanding", this means that we can understand what a propositional sign "p" says by understanding in just what conditions "p" would say something true.

His claim that our understanding of a propositional sign is a function of our understanding of the circumstances in which it would say something true is different from, but certainly not incompatible with, his claim (discussed earlier, as the third functional principle) that our understanding of a propositional sign is a function of our understanding of the words out of which it is composed, that is, that it is "understood by anyone who understands its components." Rather, as is evident from the fact that both claims are made in 4.024, Wittgenstein sees the latter as an explication of the former. For us to understand the components of a propositional sign for a contingent proposition we must, as a minimal condition, understand their reference, that is, what objects they go proxy for. Now if that is so, then given his further claim, "only in the nexus of a proposition does a name have a reference [*Bedeutung*]" (3.3), it follows that in order to understand the components of a propositional sign one must understand the connections or nexus in which they stand to one another. But if we understand both what *objects* are named by the components of a propositional sign and in what *connections* those objects are said to stand to one another, then ipso facto we understand *how things stand* if the propositional sign says something true; that is to say, we understand the circumstances in which the proposition expressed by the propositional sign is true.

Historically speaking, Wittgenstein's account of truth had its genesis in Aristotle's dictum "to say of what is that it is, or of what is not that it is not, is true" and is part of a long tradition of attempts (of which Kneale's and Mackie's are among the latest) to preserve Aristotle's insights without getting caught up in difficulties about the notion of correspondence. Wittgenstein's contribution to this tradition was neither very original nor particularly influential.

His truth-conditional account of propositional sense wasn't wholly original, since it owes a good deal to Frege, but it certainly has proved enormously influential. This is shown by the proliferation within the past three decades of so-called "truth-conditional semantics" and "truth-conditional theories of meaning" (often generated by philosophers who seem unaware of Wittgenstein's germinal ideas on the matter).

By way of contrast, his account of the preconditions of both truth and sense, that is, his theory of logical syntax and of its ontological grounding, though highly original and (in my view) deserving of attention, seems to have had almost no influence at all.

It is to his theory of logical syntax, and its expression in the second of his compositionality principles, that I now turn.

14. The Compositional-Constraints Principle

Wittgenstein expresses the Compositional-Constraints Principle most clearly in the *Notebooks*: "The logical connection [between names in a proposition with sense] must, of course, be one that is possible as between the things that the names are representatives of . . ." (*NB* 26(12)); and again: "the connection of the proposition-al components must be possible for the represented things" (*NB* 26(13).

This principle states explicitly the all-important connection between ontology and logical syntax. Just as objects cannot be combined in just any way to yield possible states of affairs, so words cannot be combined in just any way to yield propositions with sense. Indeed, the restrictions that the forms of objects impose on the formation of states of affairs *determine* the restrictions that the forms of names impose on the formation of propositions with sense. Impossible combinations of objects—those that are precluded by the de re necessary properties of the objects concerned—are reflected in impossible combinations of their names. They are, that is to say, reflected in the senseless linguistic constructions that are prohibited by what he calls "logical grammar" or "logical syntax" (3.325)). We cannot *say*, for example, that the watch is "sitting" on the table (*NB* 70(11)) or that the ball is "leaning against" the wall (*NB* 70(8)). Both constructions, in his words, are "sense-less". (*NB* 70(11)).

Wittgenstein's use of the word "grammar" in this context is likely to mislead. For it might give the impression that what prohibits these senseless constructions is something arbitrary, something solely to do with the ways *we* choose to use words. Yet this is certainly not what he wants to say. To be sure, some of the prohibitions on which grammarians insist are within the realm of the arbitrary, having to do with accidental features of "the particular way in which the propositional sign is pro-duced." (3.34(2)). For instance, he suggests in 5.4733, we could have chosen to give the sign "is identical" as it features in the propositional sign "Socrates is identical" an adjectival meaning. Had we done so, that propositional sign would have had a sense. Hence, its *not* having sense is a result of our purely arbitrary choice not to give it that sort of meaning. But, as he puts it in the reports of his 1930 lectures (Lee [1980]), "grammar is not entirely a matter of arbitrary choice. It must enable us to express the multiplicity of facts, give us the same degree of freedom as the facts do." (p. 8). His point is, of course, that *logical* grammar—as opposed to what we might call *conventional* grammar—has to do with *essential* features of language, "those without which the proposition could not express its sense" (3.34(2)), and that these have to do ultimately with the logical possibilities and impossibilities of combination for the objects that make up the world. That a particular mode of signifying has been agreed to by conventional grammar is "unim-portant", he says. But that a particular mode of signifying is revealed by logical grammar to be a *possible* one, is "always important". For, in his words, "the *possibility* of the individual case discloses something about *the essence of the world* [emphasis added in both cases]." (3.3421).[26]

The fact that the possibility of certain modes of signifying, together with the corresponding impossibility of others, "discloses" something about *the world* is connected with the saying/showing distinction. Since all possibility and impossibility, for Wittgenstein, are logical, and matters logical can only be shown, not said, it follows that the possibilities and impossibilities of combination for objects and words alike can only be shown, never said. This has implications for all putative propositions. Thus, according to Wittgenstein: (i) Propositions with sense can only show, not say, what these possibilities and impossibilities are. "Propositions [with sense] show the logical form of reality. They display it." (4.121(4-5)). (ii) Likewise with the propositions of logic and mathematics: "The fact that the propositions of logic are tautologies *shows* the formal–logical–properties of language and the world." (6.12).[27] And again: "The logic of the world, which is shown in tautologies by the propositions of logic, is shown in equations by mathematics." (6.22). (iii) Likewise, also, for the rules of logical syntax: Syntactical rules for the manipulation of symbols, he tells us, are identical with (or "=", as he puts it) the rules of logic. (*NB* 116(5)). Hence they, too, must show the formal properties both of language itself and of the world—any world—that language represents.

Now Wittgenstein claims not only that it is necessary for the Compositional-Constraints Principle to be satisfied but also that its satisfaction is a *sufficient* condition of a combination of names yielding a proposition with sense. He writes: "Then in order for a proposition to represent a state of affairs it is *only* necessary [emphasis added] for its component parts to represent those of the state of affairs and for the former [the constituents of the proposition] to stand in a relation which is possible for the former [the objects which are the constituents of the state of affairs represented]" (*NB* 27(1)).[28]

I take Wittgenstein to be saying that there are two necessary conditions for propositional representation of a possible situation: (i) It is necessary for the constituent names in the proposition to "represent those of the state of affairs". (ii) When a proposition is composed of these names, it is necessary that the arrangement of names should respect the forms of the objects in such a way that their names are arranged in only those ways that mirror the arrangements that are possible for those objects. Conditions (i) and (ii) correspond, of course, to the Proxy Principle and the Compositional-Constraints Principle, respectively (where the latter, as we have seen, is itself a function of the Form-Signalizing Principle and the second thesis of the Generalized Compositionality Principle). And I take him to hold, further, that satisfaction of these two conditions is *all* that is necessary for propositional representation, that is, that satisfaction of these conditions is *sufficient* for the expression of a proposition with sense. In his words, "In this way the proposition represents the state of affairs—as it were off its own bat." (*NB* 26(12)).

15. The Same-Multiplicity Principle

The final principle governing propositional representation that we are to consider is first expressed in the *Notebooks*: "The trivial fact that a completely analyzed proposition contains as many names as there are things contained in its reference; this fact is an example of the all-embracing representation of the world through language." (*NB* 11(2)). (In speaking of the "reference" of a proposition, he is of course speaking of what he later, in the *Tractatus*, came to call its "sense", that is, the situation that the proposition represents.[29]) He reiterates the principle in the *Tractatus*: "In a proposition there must be exactly as many distinguishable parts as in the situation it represents. The two must possess the same logical (mathematical) multiplicity." (4.04).

He would allow, of course, that the principle doesn't have immediate application to propositions which are not completely analyzed. This is why an ordinary, un-analyzed proposition such as "This watch is lying on the table" (in which the names "watch" and "table" stand for complex objects, objects that in principle admit of analysis into metaphysically simpler components) contains "a lot of indefiniteness". (*NB* 69(11)). In cases where propositions are about complexes, he allows, the sense of the proposition (the states of affairs it represents) "is more complicated than the proposition itself." (*NB* 69(12)). Nevertheless, he believes, "Every statement about complexes can be resolved into a statement about their constituents and into the propositions that describe the complexes completely." (2.0201). A proposition in which the elements of the propositional sign (here he at last gets the *Satz/Satzzeichen* distinction right) correspond in a one-to-one way with the constituents of the objects is just what he calls a "completely analyzed" proposition. (3.2-3.201).

The relation in which the constituents of a completely analyzed propositional sign stand to the constituents of the represented state of affairs, in Wittgenstein's view, is an *internal relation*: neither term of the relation would be what it is were the constituents of both to be of the same logical multiplicity. This means that given one term of the relation together with the relation itself, one can infer the character of the other. For instance, given the structural and formal properties of a certain propositional sign, together with the relation of *having the same logical multiplicity*, we can immediately infer what structural and formal properties are possessed by the state of affairs. Generalizing to language as a whole, Wittgenstein says: "Since language stands in *internal* relations to the world, *it* [language] and these relations determine the logical possibility of facts. If we have a significant sign it must stand in a particular relation to a structure. Sign and relation determine unambiguously the logical form of the thing signified." (*NB* 42(11)).

Now the Same-Multiplicity Principle has consequences for both the semantics and the syntax of language. Among these consequences are the semantic and syntactical *completeness* of each individual proposition, together with the complete sayability of all that is contingent about the world and the complete showability of all that is noncontingent about it.

First, from the Same-Multiplicity Principle in conjunction with the Proxy Principle it follows that every proposition either is, or is analyzable into a proposition that is *referentially complete*, that is, is such that it gives a complete description of which objects are related in which ways to one another in the state of affairs that the proposition represents. It is for this reason that a propositional sign can, indeed must, "describe reality completely." (4.023). What a propositional sign *says* about the way things stand in reality it says completely.[30] And given, further, that "If all true elementary propositions are listed, the world is described completely" (4.26), it follows that *all* contingent aspects of the world can be represented by means of propositional signs.

Second, it follows from the Same-Multiplicity Principle in conjunction with the Form-Signalizing Principle that every proposition either is, or is analyzable into, a proposition that is *syntactically complete*, that is, is such that its constituent names have forms that completely mirror in language the forms of the objects in the state of affairs that the proposition represents. It is by virtue of this that a propositional sign can, and must, "*show* the logical form of reality." (4.121(4)). What a propositional sign *shows* about the logical form of the world it shows completely. And given the fact that the names that are constituents of the true elementary propositional signs that describe the world completely all have forms, and that these forms generate the forms of all the complexes into which they can or do enter, it follows that *all* noncontingent, formal, aspects of the world can be shown by means of propositional signs.

16. Logical Syntax and Logical Types

Now if propositional language, by itself, shows or mirrors—in the syntactical rules that propositions must satisfy in order to be significant—all the formal properties of the world, then there can be no need, according to Wittgenstein, for anything like Russell's Theory of Types. Russell's theory was intended to prevent language from becoming dislocated, as it were, in ways that generated nonsense or paradox: in ways, that is, that would preclude it from saying anything true or false about the world. But according to Wittgenstein, such a theory tries to say what logical syntax as he conceives it already shows. Indeed, he held that Russell's whole project of trying to proscribe, by means of his type-theory, the construction of paradox-generating sentences in everyday language and logic alike, was misconceived from the start.

Russell was concerned about paradoxes such as those of Epimenedes the Cretan who said that everything a Cretan says is false (from which it follows that if what he says is true then it is false, whereas if what he says is false then it is true) and those of set-theory which apparently allows us to talk about the class of all classes which are not members of themselves (from which it follows that certain classes are members of themselves if and only if they are not members of themselves). Such paradoxes, he thought, can be avoided only if we lay down the principle that a totality of any sort cannot be a member of itself (the so-called Vicious Circle Principle) and then account for why this is so in terms of a hierarchy of types of entities—starting with individuals as the lowest type, classes of individuals as the second, classes of classes of individuals as the third, and so on—such that no predicates or functions can univocally and significantly be attributed to all entities in the hierarchy. Russell argued that the Vicious Circle Principle (which he seemed to think entailed the illegitimacy of self-reference) would prevent both sorts of paradoxes from arising. His complaint was, in short, that since ordinary language does not preclude paradoxes,[31] it needs to be reformed so as to observe the theory of types and avoid vicious circles.

Wittgenstein will have little of this. His criticisms of Russell cluster about four main issues.

First, he does not agree with Russell's conclusion that everyday language is a logical mess. To be sure, when he says, "Language disguises thought . . . because the outward form of the clothing is not designed to reveal the form of the body" (4.002(4)), and "Most of the propositions and questions of philosophers arise from our failure to understand the logic of our language" (4.003(1)), he is echoing Russell's own sentiments about the dangers of taking ordinary language at face value. But he thinks that a proper understanding of the logic of everyday language is to be found, not in the kind of revision that Russell's theory of types would impose on it, but in a more careful attempt to think out for ourselves the *sense* of what is being said by means of the sentences of everyday language. "In fact," he says, "the propositions of our everyday language, just as they stand, are in perfect logical order." (5.5563). If they seem to us otherwise, Wittgenstein believes, this is only because we fail to note the ways we *use* these sentences and the signs that are their components. It is easy, he allows, to so concentrate on the surface-grammar of sentences that we are beguiled into supposing that sameness of sign carries with it sameness of meaning. Thus we may, for instance, come to confuse the "is" of predication with the "is" of identity, or either of these with the "is" of existence (3.323). "In this way," he says, "the most fundamental confusions in philosophy are easily produced (the whole of philosophy is full of them)." (3.324) But we can avoid these confusions, he claims, if we observe what he calls "the different modes of signification" (3.322) that a single sign, such as "is", may have. In order to recognize what a sign symbolizes "we must observe how it is used with a sense." (3.326).

Wittgenstein doesn't deny that some advantage might be gained by adopting a sign-language like that of Russell's or Frege's, a conceptual notation within which different signs would be used for different symbols. For such a language would more *obviously* be governed by logical grammar, that is, logical syntax. (3.325). But this doesn't mean that the propositions of everyday language, *as they are used and properly understood*, violate the rules of logical syntax. If we attend to the different modes of signification of an individual sign or to the possible circumstances in which a whole propositional sign is used to say something true or false (that is, attend to its truth-conditions), then we will see that the rules of logical syntax are in fact being complied with and that any possible sign or sentence, just as it stands, is "in perfect logical order."

Second, Wittgenstein does not agree with Russell's conception of what he is up to in constructing his theory of types: (i) In his investigation of logical types, Russell thinks that, as Wittgenstein put it, "he had to mention the references of signs when establishing the rules for them." (3.331). (ii) Not surprisingly, therefore, Russell [1918] thinks of himself as embarking on an *empirical* enquiry which will issue in an "inventory" or "zoo" of what he describes as "the different logical sorts of facts that there are in the world."(pp. 216–7). (iii) Accordingly, Russell thinks of the results of his investigation as being reportable in *significant* propositions about things, properties, relations, functions, types, and so forth.

As Wittgenstein sees it, however, Russell is wrong on all three scores. As to (i), Wittgenstein holds, "In logical syntax the reference of a sign should never play a role. It must be possible to establish logical syntax without mentioning the *reference* of a sign; only the description of expressions may be presupposed." (3.33). I take it that by "the description of expressions" he means the description of *how* they function in propositions with sense, that is, a description of their formal properties. This is evident from a passage in the *Notebooks* : "How usually, logical propositions do show these properties [the logical properties of the world] is this: We give a certain description of a kind of symbol; we find that other symbols, combined in certain ways, yield a symbol of this description; and *that* they do shows something about these symbols." (*NB* 107(7)). He denies that the reference of a sign (something determined arbitrarily by us) needs to be taken into account. But at the same time he points out the need to take account of a sign's form or combinatorial potential (something essential to its role). He would not deny that signs of different forms mark out entities of different forms but would insist that since his Same-Multiplicity Principle ensures that the former correspond to the latter, all we need to do is look at the way signs function logically in significant propositions.[32] This is connected with the second point. Thus, as to (ii), Wittgenstein would insist that an investigation of the logical roles of signs can never be an empirical one. The form of a sign is its *logical* form, and its logical form is determined ultimately (as his Compositional Constraints Principle makes clear) by the logical form and corresponding logical kind of the object it stands for. Hence—like all matters logical—it lies outside the domain of empirical investigation. Remember that for Wittgenstein, concepts of the sort that feature in Russell's theory of types—concepts such as *individual, property, relation, fact, function, complex,* and *number*—are all what he calls "formal concepts". And, on his view, "we do not derive these ideas from particular cases that occur to us, but possess them somehow a priori." (*NB* 65(9)). As to (iii), Wittgenstein argues that the logico-syntactical properties of a sign, and of the thing signified, can only be *shown*, not said by means of significant propositions. When an object falls under one of these formal concepts, he argues, "this cannot be expressed by means of a proposition. Instead it is shown in the very sign for the object. (A name shows that it signifies an object, a sign for a number that it signifies a number, etc)." (4.126). That an object belongs to this or that logical kind or type, then, is *shown* in language by the sign for that object together with that sign's mode of signification. And since, according to the dictum of 4.1212, what *can* be shown, *cannot* be said, the existence of different logical types in the constitution of the world and of corresponding logical types of expressions in language cannot be *said* by any contingent proposition whatever.

Third, Wittgenstein points out that Russell's theory of types cannot be stated without violating the very rules that it tries to lay down. This criticism, unlike the previous one, does not presuppose Wittgenstein's own view of what can be said by propositions with sense. Rather it takes Russell's theory at face value and points out that, even by its own say-so, it is self-refuting.

Russell's theory claims that no predicate or function can univocally and significantly be attributed to all entities without violating Russell's hierarchy of types. Yet, as has often been noted, this very claim itself uses the words "predicate" and "function" in a univocal way without introducing distinctions of type. Moreover the theory defines identity of type in such a way that two entities are said to be identical in type if a predicate that can significantly be affirmed or denied of one can also significantly be affirmed or denied of the other. But this means that if we were to try to say, in accordance with the theory, that a certain entity M is of the same type as another entity N while being of a different type from entity O, we would immediately be led into contradiction. For, if our claim is true, then M is of a different type from O. Yet equally, if our claim is true, since there is at least one predicate (viz., "being of the same type as N") that can significantly (because truly) be affirmed of M and significantly (because falsely) denied of O, it follows that M and O must be of the same type. Considerations like this, though expressed somewhat less perspicuously, led Wittgenstein to conclude that, whether it be construed as a theory about types of things or as a theory about types of symbols, "a theory of types is impossible". (*NB* 108(10)).

Fourth, and most importantly, Russell's theory of types—even if it could be "said" by means of significant and self-consistent sentences—would, according to Wittgenstein, be superfluous. He makes this point at the beginning of the *Notebooks*: "If syntactical rules can be set up *at all*, then the whole theory of things, properties, etc., is superfluous." (*NB* 2(2)).

Wittgenstein regards Russell's theory as superfluous because he thinks his own account of language already *shows* how syntactical rules are "set up" and does so in a way that is free from the difficulties that beset Russell's account. The way in which they are set up, of course, is given inter alia in his Picture Theory of Language. The rules of logical syntax, for individual signs and propositional signs alike, are generated within language itself insofar as: (i) names signalize the forms of the objects for which they stand, and thereby themselves take on corresponding forms (the Form-Signalizing Principle); (ii) the form of a proposition is a function of the forms of its constituent names (the second application of the Generalized Compositionality Principle); (iii) the combination of names in a proposition must be possible for the objects for which they stand (the Compositional Constraints Principle); and (iv) every proposition either is, or is analyzable into, a proposition that is syntactically complete insofar as its constituent names have forms that completely mirror the forms of the objects in the possible state of affairs that the proposition pictures (a consequence of the Same-Multiplicity Principle in conjunction with the Form-Signalizing Principle). It is *these* principles that generate the rules of logical syntax, not ones (like the Proxy Principle, other applications of the Compositionality Principle, and the Compositional Freedom Principle) having to do directly with the referential role of signs. We can set up these syntactical rules not by attending to *what* we use signs to refer to but by attending to *how* we use a sign with sense, that is, how we use a sign in the expression of a significant proposition. The way in which we use signs in the expression of significant propositions will *show* the rules of logical syntax for the employment of that sign. To repeat, "The rules of logical syntax must be obvious, once we know how each individual sign signifies." (3.334). That an object belongs to a certain logical type is already "signalized" by the expression for the object and is shown by what we can and cannot *say* about the object. (*NB* 70(8-9)). The rules of logical syntax, remember, are nothing other than rules for the combination of signs. And the rules for the combinations of signs, as these principles show, are nothing but reflections of the possibilities of combination of the objects of linguistic representation. The rules are *shown* in language, and neither need to be, nor can be, said by language, as Russell had supposed.

Russell had thought of his theory of types as providing a body of *doctrine* that would ensure that language doesn't get into difficulties with the paradoxes. But this, according to Wittgenstein, is the wrong way to think of the matter. Language doesn't need a life-guard. Language, like logic, can and must "look after itself" (*NB* 2(2) and 43(8); 5.473). All we have to do is to "recognize *how* language looks after itself" (*NB* 43(8)). And this we can do, he would say, if we observe his Recognition Principle and its injunction *not* "to recognize more or less in the sign than in the thing signified." (*NB* 4(1)).[33] The important point, which Russell fails to notice but that Wittgenstein wants to emphasize, is that logical syntax, like logic itself, "is *not a body of doctrine, but a mirror-image of the world.* " [emphasis added]" (6.13).

How, then, would Wittgenstein propose to deal with paradoxes such as those of the Liar or those of set theory? He does not really say in any detail. Nevertheless, it is plausible to construe him as thinking that the solution lies in two fundamental principles of propositional representation: (i) the semantic-cum-epistemic principle that I have called the Recognition Principle, namely, that it is a necessary condition of a speaker S's knowing, for any statement-making sentence "p", which proposition "p" expresses, that for any designating expression "N" that occurs in "p", S should recognize which object "N" designates; and (ii) the syntactic-cum-metaphysical principle that a propositional sign cannot signify itself.

Suppose, for example, that Epimenedes utters the sentence

(1) "What I am now saying is false."

Since (1) contains the designation "What I am now saying", and this designation apparently refers to the sentence "What I am now saying is false" itself, (1) apparently says of itself that it is false. Hence (1) apparently says

(2) "'What I am now saying is false' is false."

Clearly then, whatever it is that (1) says, what it says is the very same as what "'What I am now saying is false' is false" says. Paradox then arises if we then ask whether what (1) says is true or false? If we take it to say something true, then it truly says of itself that it is false, and hence must be false. If we take it to say something false, then since it falsely says of itself that it is false, what it says must be true.

But, Wittgenstein would want to say, let's stop for a moment and try to determine exactly *what* it is that (1) is supposed to say, that is, what proposition the sentence "What I am now saying is false" expresses. We know that (1) says the very same thing as (2) and that (2) says "'What I am now saying is false' is false". But how can we know what (2) says? According to principle (i), I can only know what (2) says if I can determine what the propositional designation in (2), namely, "What I am now saying", stands for. But what is that? It won't do to say that "What I am now saying", in (2), stands for "'What I am now saying' is false", for then we would have to say that what (2) says is

(3) "' "What I am now saying" is false' is false"

in which we are faced once more with the propositional designation "What I am now saying", a propositional designation whose reference must in turn be determined before we can determine what (3), or therefore (2), or therefore (1), says. Obviously, we have embarked on an endless task and have no option other than to conclude that it is *impossible* for us to determine what (1) says, let alone for us to determine whether what it says is true or false. For at no point in the regress can we ever stop with the *expression* of a proposition to which one of our propositional designations refers.

What has gone wrong here, of course, is that we began with the presupposition that the sentence "What I am now saying is false" could function in such a way as to express a proposition with sense, that is, (by 4.031(2)) could represent a possible state of affairs. Give that up, recognize that a proposition must be expressed before it can be designated—or equivalently, that there must be a possible state of affairs before any representation can be given of it—and we will see that Epimenedes's sentence doesn't express any proposition at all. Hence what Epimenedes says is neither true nor false. Hence no paradox arises.

In dealing with the Liar Paradox, I have invoked Wittgenstein's Recognition Principle and the principle to which it leads, that the expression of a proposition is logically prior to its designation (Kneale's "fundamental principle of semantics").[34]

The paradox might, however, be dealt with more simply by invoking the further principle that a sign cannot signify itself. In the *Notebooks* Wittgenstein writes, "The description of the world by means of propositions is only possible because what is signified is not its own sign." (*NB* 15(2)). A propositional sign, I take him to be saying, stands in a one-to-one relation to what it signifies but is not identical with what it signifies and hence cannot signify itself. He makes the same point in the *Tractatus*: "No proposition can make a statement about itself, because a propositional sign cannot be contained in itself (that is the whole of the theory of types)" (3.332), and makes a related point regarding functional signs when he writes, "the sign for a function . . . cannot contain itself." (3.333(1)).[35]

Not only does observance of this second principle prevent the formulation of the Liar Paradox. It also, according to Wittgenstein, prevents what he refers to as "Russell's Paradox" from arising. Apparently the paradox he was referring to was not that generated by the supposition that the designation "class of all classes that are not members of themselves" referred to a genuine class but that generated by the supposition that a predicate such as "is predicable of itself" can be predicated of itself, or more generally that a function can be its own argument.

His argument is supposed to proceed by reductio. "Let us suppose," he writes, "that the function F(fx) could be its own argument: in that case there would be a proposition 'F(F(fx))', in which the outer function F and the inner function F would have different references [Bedeutung] . . . Only the letter 'F' is common to the two functions, but the letter itself signifies nothing." (3.333(2)). I say "supposed to proceed" because it is not at all clear to me, or to any other commentators of whom I am aware, exactly what is going on here.

Whether or not Wittgenstein's argument is sound is a question that needn't concern us. What is important is only that we understand in general terms *why* he thinks that his own account of language makes it unnecessary to invoke Russell's theory of types. His reason is made clear enough, I think, by his whole treatment of that theory. Russell thinks that language permits combinations of signs that generate paradox. Wittgenstein answers that they will seem to do so only if we fail to attend to the way each sign is used with a sense. If we observe how a sign is used with a sense, then we will "recognize a symbol by its sign" (3.326). We will understand that what seems to be said is not in fact being said, and that the rules of logical syntax simply do not allow us to make "any unlogical arrangement" (*NB* 13(2)) of these signs *as we usually use them and as they are properly understood*.

17. Logic as the Mirror-Image of the World

Now that we have seen just how, according to Wittgenstein, *language* "takes care of itself" (*NB* 43(8)), it is time to consider logic. For it, too, in his view, needs no doctrinal safeguards to prevent it from going wrong. "In a certain sense," Wittgenstein says, "we cannot make mistakes in logic." (5.473(3)). Again: "Logic takes care of itself; all we have to do is to look and see *how* it does it." [emphasis added] (*NB* 11(4)).

So how *does* logic do it? Wittgenstein's answer is that logic looks after itself in the same way as, and by virtue of the fact that, language does. He rejects the traditional idea that self-evidence is the ultimate guarantor of logical truth—"Self-evidence, which Russell talked so much about, can become dispensable in logic"— and goes on to explain that this is "only because language itself prevents every logical mistake." (5.4731).

On the face of it both claims are preposterously false. Surely people do make mistakes in logic and do make mistakes in language.

To raise this objection, however, would be to misunderstand the "certain sense" in which mistakes in both language and logic are impossible. What he is getting at in both cases, I think, is that if we use language to represent how things stand, then we will ipso facto be using language in ways that respect the constraints that the form of the *world*, a form that our world has in common with every other possible world, puts on the way we combine words. And if we do that, then illogical thought or language will be an impossibility. As he puts it, completing his explanation of how language prevents every logical mistake, "What makes logic a priori is the *impossibility* of illogical thought." (5.4731).

There is another connection, too, between the way in which language takes care of itself and the way in which logic does. In the *Notebooks*, Wittgenstein explicitly *identifies* the rules of logical syntax with the rules of logic: "rules of logic = rules for the manipulation of symbols" (*NB* 116(5)). And in the *Tractatus* he writes: "If we know the logical syntax of any sign-language, then we have already been given all the propositions of logic." (6.124).

But in what sense, we want to know, are the propositions of logic "given" by the logical syntax of sign-languages?

Before even trying to answer this question we need to remind ourselves of two things: first, that the propositions of logic aren't "real" or "genuine" propositions, that is, aren't "propositions with sense", but are merely "logical so-called propositions" or "pseudo-propositions"; second, that the propositions of logic fall into two main classes: those having to do with de re modal properties and relations, and those having to do with de dicto modal properties and relations.

The first of these points was established in section 2. The second was sketched in Chapter 3, sections 1 and 7, but deserves a little more attention before we proceed.

In his wonderfully perceptive "Review of Tractatus", Ramsey pointed out, "not all apparently necessary truths can be supposed, or are by Mr. Wittgenstein supposed, to be tautologies. There are also [logical propositions about] the internal properties of which it is unthinkable that their objects do not possess them." ([1923] p.18). Although subsequent interpreters of Wittgenstein seem almost universally to have ignored the existence of what might be called "Ramseian necessary truths" (that is, non-tautological necessary truths), I think Ramsey is absolutely right to draw attention to them. The domain of logic, Wittgenstein insists right at the beginning of the *Tractatus*, has to do with everything that is possible, impossible, or necessary, including the de re possibilities, impossibilities, and necessities that have to do with the objects that make up the substance of the world. To be sure, it also has to do, of course, with the de dicto properties and relations that express themselves in truth-functional tautologies and contradictions. But the domain of logic certainly isn't exhausted by the latter.

Now if this is right, then an account of how the rules of logical syntax generate the propositions of logic must apply to both the de re (Ramseian) cases and the de dicto cases of such propositions.

For the de re cases, the story has already been told, inter alia, in the account I have given of the Form-Signalizing Principle and the Compositional-Constraints Principle. In effect, it is that these principles guarantee that any significant proposition (any proposition with sense, any real proposition) not only *says* how things stand but also *shows* some logical property of the world, for example, that such and such an object has such and such a de re necessary nature or stands in such and such an internal relation to the complexes into which it can or does enter. In Wittgenstein's words, "Every *real* proposition *shows* something, besides what it says, about the Universe: *for*, if it has no sense, it can't be used; and if it has a sense, it mirrors some logical property of the Universe." (*NB* 107(9)). To be sure, *that* the universe, or some object within it, has a given logical property, is something which cannot be said by a *real* proposition. But this doesn't preclude formulating Ramseian necessary truths in such *pseudo-propositions* as Wittgenstein's own generalizations: "If things can occur in states of affairs, this possibility *must* be in them from the beginning" (2.0121(2)); "A spatial object *must* be situated in infinite space" (2.0131(1)); "A speck in the visual field . . . *must* have some color" (2.0131(2)); and "Tones *must* have *some* pitch, objects of the sense of touch *some* degree of hardness, and so on." (2.0131(2)) [emphasis being added to "must" in each case]. None of these Ramseian necessary truths *says* anything about the world, in Wittgenstein's sense of "says". But in trying to say what can only be said, each *shows* something about the logical properties of the world. Wittgenstein's claim, "Logical so-called propositions *show* [the] logical properties of language and therefore of the Universe, but *say* nothing" (*NB* 107(1)), applies to Ramseian de re necessary truths just as much as it does to the necessary truths of truth-functional logic and those of modal propositional logic.

It remains to explain how logical syntax generates the de dicto (non-Ramseian) cases of necessary truths.

As I see it, the story goes like this. Any significant proposition, P, Wittgenstein tells us, "must point to a region of logical space (*NB* 31(12)), that is, to a set of possible worlds (totalities of possible states of affairs) in which it is true. And its negation, ~P, "actually points to the negated domain" (*NB* 26(4)), that is, to the set of possible worlds in which P is false. Consider, now, the tautological propositional sign "P v ~P". In it the sign "P" is a propositional sign that, (by hypothesis) expresses something significant. It therefore plays a representational role in language and by virtue of that must comply with the rules of logical syntax for each of its representing components, namely, names. The rules of logical syntax, remember, get their direct grip on the "atoms" of language, and their indirect grip on language as a whole, by virtue of the fact that names go proxy for objects and have the forms of the objects named. But how about the signs "~" and "v"? These are logical constants and hence, according to Wittgenstein, have no representational role at all. "My fundamental thought," he says, "is that the 'logical constants' are not representatives; that there can be no representatives of the logic of facts." (4.0312(2)). So the logical constants can't take on the forms of what they represent, since they represent nothing. Hence there would seem not to be any way in which the rules of logical syntax, as so far described, would apply to the so-called manipulation of symbols. How, then, can Wittgenstein's claim, "If we know the logical syntax of any sign-language, then we have already been given all the propositions of logic" (6.124) be defended?

I think the answer is that Wittgenstein would want to say that although the rules of logical syntax with which we have been concerned so far are ontologically grounded by virtue of the Form-Signalizing Principle, there are other rules of logical syntax that are merely linguistically generated, stemming from our determination to use words and signs in accordance with agreed-on conventions. The signs for the logical constants, and the corresponding expressions in natural language, are cases in point. It is, for instance, a wholly arbitrary matter that we choose to use the sign "~" to mark the "boundary" (*NB* 26(4)) between any two propositions, one of which is the negation of the other. Likewise, there is something arbitrary in our use of "v" to show that one or other of any two propositions flanking it says something true. But once we have laid down these arbitrary conventions, Wittgenstein insists, we must abide by these new linguistically generated syntactical rules.

There is a sense, then, in which, as he puts it, tautologies such as "P v ~P" are "made so as to be true" (*NB* 55(14). But this does not mean that such tautologies owe their truth *solely* to these linguistically-generated rules, that is, solely to our arbitrary determination to use the truth-functional constants and other "special twiddles and manipulations" (*NB* 39(18)) in rule-governed ways. That would make the propositions of logic themselves arbitrary, which they are not. Rather, the truth-functional tautologies owe their truth both to those ontologically grounded syntactical rules that arise from the representing elements in the tautology, and to those linguistically generated syntactical rules that arise from human conventions for the nonrepresenting elements. *Together*, these rules ensure that a tautological proposition such as "P v ~P" is "is true for all the truth-possibilities of the elementary propositions." (4.46). Together, that is, they ensure that tautologies "admit *all* possible situations." (4.462).

The story I have just been telling is what I think Wittgenstein is getting at in 6.124 (here quoted in full):

> The propositions of logic describe the scaffolding of the world, or rather they represent it. They have no "subject-matter'. They presuppose that names have meaning and elementary propositions sense; and that is their connection with the world. It is clear that something about the world must be indicated by the fact that certain combinations of symbols—whose essence involves the possession of a determinate character—are tautologies. This contains the decisive point. We have said that some things are arbitrary in the symbols that we use and that some things are not. In logic it is only the latter that express: but that means that logic is not a field in which *we* express what we wish with the use of signs, but rather one in which the nature of the natural and inevitable signs speaks for itself. If we know the logical syntax of any sign-language, then we have already been given all the propositions of logic.

Whether my account is sound or not, one thing is certain: that, according to Wittgenstein, the propositions of logic—whatever may be the role of logical syntax in their generation—are not just reflections of human convention but also reflections of ontology, of how things *must* be in the world. At one point he asks, "How can logic—the all-embracing logic, which mirrors the world—use such peculiar crotchets and contrivances [e.g., "~", "v", "&", "⊃"]?" And he answers, "Only because they are all connected with one another in an infinitely fine network, the great mirror." (5.511). The fact that the crotchets and contrivances, twiddles and manipulations, are arbitrarily chosen doesn't make logic a mere human artifact (as conventionalists have sometimes thought of it): it merely enables us the better to mirror the modal features of the world.

Wittgenstein emphasizes the ontological foundations of logic in both his early works. In the *Notebooks*, he repeatedly talks about an internal connection between logic and the world. He speaks of "the logic of the world" (*NB* 14(9) and 6.22) and "the all-embracing world-mirroring logic" (*NB* 39(18)) and describes logic as "a condition of the world" (*NB* 77(7)). Likewise, in the *Tractatus*, he claims, "The fact that the propositions of logic are tautologies *shows* the formal–logical–properties of language and the world" (6.12).

In the *Notebooks*, Wittgenstein observes, "My work has extended from the foundations of logic to the nature of the world." (*NB* 79(17)). We can now see that the foundations of logic, in his account, are not wholly separable from the nature of the world. Rather, the foundations of logic are *provided* by the nature of the world. No words can better sum up his final view of the connection between logic and the nature or essence of the world than the eloquently brief words of the *Tractatus*: "Logic is not a body of doctrine, but a mirror-image of the world." (6.13).

Notes

1. Although, as I shall argue, Wittgenstein seems to have meant different things on different occasions by "*Satz*" (sometimes using it to mean "proposition", sometimes to mean "sentence" or "propositional sign") this does not give his translators the licence to substitute what they take to be his meaning for what he in fact says. So although it turns out that Wittgenstein all too often uses "*Satz*" when he should have used "*Satzzeichen*" ("propositional sign"), Pears and McGuinness properly translate "*Satz*" and "*Satzzeichen*" as "proposition" and "propositional sign", respectively, throughout.

2. An additional argument against always identifying a *Satz* with a sentence-token can be derived from consideration of 4.465 in which Wittgenstein claims: "The logical product of a tautology and a proposition says the same thing as the proposition. This product, therefore, is identical with the proposition." This would be obviously false if by "proposition" ("*Satz*") he here meant sentence-token. The sentence-token "(Pv~P).Q" is certainly not identical with the sentence-token "Q". On the other hand, these two sentence-tokens arguably do (in Wittgenstein's sense of the word) "say" the same thing.

3. As William Kneale and Martha Kneale [1964] observe: "Having made a distinction between sentences and propositions we can also see why it was unnecessary for Aristotle to exclude prayers, commands, etc., from logical consideration. The linguistic expressions of these are not statements . . . But we cannot formulate a prayer, command, etc., without expressing a proposition, and that proposition must be true or false." p.52.

4. Talk of an object, such as Moore himself, as a "constituent" of a proposition (as opposed to the possible state of affairs that the proposition represents) sounds strange to most modern ears. Yet it seemed natural enough to both Russell and Wittgenstein.

5. A propositional sign such as "This is a sentence" is not a counter-example. For the word "This", though it may refer to the propositional sign within which it occurs, is not itself that propositional sign. And obviously, any attempt to replace it with the propositional sign to which it refers would generate an incompletable series.

6. For a sympathetic treatment of Wittgenstein's handling of these issues, see James Griffin [1964], pp. 137–9.

7. Recall (from Chapter 4, note 18) that I follow Anscombe in translating "*Bedeutung*" as "reference". I think it unfortunate that Pears and McGuinness translate it as "meaning". Not only do they thereby leave one wondering exactly what difference there is between this and "sense" ("*Sinn*"); by virtue of the fact that most English readers suppose that there is *no* difference, many of Wittgenstein's claims are rendered susceptible to an interpretation that, in Anscombe's translation, they do not sustain.

8. I think that Mill's intent, when he says that proper names are not connotative, is best understood in the light of his claim, in the very next paragraph, that a proper name is "a word which answers the purpose of showing what thing it is we are talking about, but not of telling anything about it." I also think that the last

sentence needs to be qualified by inserting "essential" before "attribute". (I concede, however, that Mill would see neither need nor sense in accepting this amendment since, unlike Wittgenstein, he does not think that individuals have any of their properties essentially.)

9. As it stands, Kripke's definition is somewhat misleading: it suggests that if a term "t" is a rigid designator in any possible world then it is a rigid designator in every possible world; and it further suggests that if "t" rigidly designates an object x in any possible world, then x exists in every possible world. A more felicitous formulation, which would better capture Kripke's intent, would be: "A term 't' is a rigid designator of an object x if in the actual world 't' is used to designate x in every possible world in which x exists."

10. Unfortunately this point about the independence of semantic role from causal history has tended to be obscured as a result of the fact that Kripke also believes that certain causal stories about how the reference of a name is typically assigned in the first place, e.g., by "initial baptism", and then transmitted to other members of the linguistic community, probably happen to be true. His thesis of rigid designation is presented in the context of his so-called Causal Theory of Reference, and although, strictly speaking, it is independent of that theory, this fact is all too often overlooked.

11. For Kripke they include the variables and constraints of logic, and certain actuality-ascribing definite descriptions.

12. James Griffin ([1964], pp. 41–65) has argued this point so persuasively and at such length that I shall not urge it further.

13. Calling it the latter seems to me misleading. It suggests that Leibniz's Principle is a linguistic one, having to do only with substitutivity of expressions in sentences, rather than—as he intended it—as a metaphysical principle about the identity-conditions of any object whatever.

14. The example that follows hearkens back to the familiar one whereby Russell sought to show that the definite description "the author of Waverley" is an incomplete symbol that "does not stand simply for Scott, nor for anything else." Russell's argument [1918] is, "If it stood for Scott, 'Scott is the author of Waverley' would be the same proposition as 'Scott is Scott', which it is not, since George IV wished to know the truth of the one but did not wish to know the truth of the other." (p.245).

Oddly, Russell fails to note that since George IV might well have wished to know whether "Scott is Sir Walter" expressed a true proposition without wishing to know whether "Scott is Scott" did, it would follow by parity of reasoning that "Sir Walter" does not simply stand for Scott, nor for anything else. Yet he certainly would not want to draw this conclusion. For, as already noted, he thinks that both "Scott" and "Sir Walter" *can* be used "as" names, and holds that when they are so used, "Scott is Sir Walter" is a "pure tautology." Russell might well have welcomed the Wittgensteinian response that I offer in the next section since it would accommodate his sound intuition that, in these circumstances, "Scott is Sir Walter" is indeed every bit as tautologous as "Scott is Scott".

15. It is interesting to recall the passage in which Wittgenstein first introduced the saying/showing distinction and to see how it applies fairly straightforwardly to

the case of Problem I. Wittgenstein, it will be remembered, wrote: "In any ordinary proposition, e.g., 'Moore [is] good', this *shows* and does not say that 'Moore' is to the left of 'good'; and *here* what is shown can be *said* by another proposition. But this only applies to that *part* of what is shown which is arbitrary. The *logical* properties which it shows are not arbitrary, and that it has these cannot be said in any proposition." (*NB* 110).

Adapting this to the example in Problem I, and observing the sentence/proposition distinction a little more carefully, it becomes obvious that Wittgenstein might well say, "The ordinary sentence, (2) 'Scott is identical to Sir Walter', *shows* and does not say that 'Sir Walter' is another name for Scott; and *here* what is shown can be *said* by another sentence, [viz., (11) in the text]. But this applies only to that *part* of what is shown which is arbitrary [viz., that we have made an arbitrary determination to use 'Sir Walter' as another name for Scott]. The *logical* properties which [2] shows [e.g., the identity of an object with itself] are noncontingent and hence cannot be said in any [contingent] proposition."

16. Note that if George does *not* recognize "Scott" as the name of Scott, then, although he may well believe *that* (1) expresses a true (even a necessarily true) proposition, he will not—on the account being offered here—know *which* proposition it is that (1) expresses.

17. The same sort of solution can be given for the parallel paradox that is supposedly generated by George's assent to the sentence

(17) "Scott is the author of *Waverley* "

and nonassent to the sentence

(19) "Sir Walter is the author of *Waverley*".

Let us suppose that George recognizes "Scott" as a name of Scott. Then the Belief-Attribution Principle entitles us to attribute to him the belief that Scott is the author of *Waverley* . But, in the event that he does not also recognize "Sir Walter" as a name of Scott, nothing warrants us in concluding that he fails to believe that Sir Walter is the author of *Waverley* . By invoking the Belief-Expression Principle it is easy to explain his failure to assent to (19) consistently with his belief in the truth of the proposition that (19) expresses.

18. Note, however, that early in the *Notebooks*, Wittgenstein did speak of propositions too as having reference. Thus, "The completely analyzed proposition must image its reference." (*NB* 18 (11)), and "The reference of the proposition must be fixed, as confirming or contradicting it, through it *together with its method of presentation*." (*NB* 22(1)). But it is clear that by "the reference of a proposition" Wittgenstein did not mean, as did Frege, the truth-value of that proposition. Rather he means that which determines the truth-value of the proposition, by confirming or contradicting the proposition. And what determines this truth-value, of course, is the existence or nonexistence of a state of affairs, i.e., is some segment of reality. Thus the Tractarian parallel of *NB* 22 (1) is "[a proposition] must describe reality completely." (4.023(2)).

19. As Max Cresswell [1973] has observed, the principle seems not to have

been explicitly stated by Frege himself but rather to result from "the general tenor of his views on the analysis of language." (p. 75, note 97). Despite these problems of attribution and even of formulation, writers like Donald Davidson frequently refer to "Frege's Principle" as if all were clear on both counts.

20. There is a marked difference in this respect between his position in the *Notebooks* and his position in the *Tractatus*. In the former he speaks of the possible situation which a proposition represents as its *Bedeutung*, i.e., its reference. This already demarcates his view from Frege's since for Frege, the reference of a proposition is not a possible state of affairs but a truth-value. But in the *Tractatus*, he makes the difference between his view and Frege's even more evident by saying that the possible state of affairs which a proposition represents is the *sense*, not the reference, of that proposition.

21. Compare, "In a proposition a situation is, as it were, constructed by way of experiment." (4.031). And again, "One name stands for one thing, another for another thing, and they are combined with one another. In this way the whole group—like a *tableau vivant*—presents a state of affairs." (4.0311).

22. Compare, "If a sign is *possible*, then it is also capable of signifying." (5.473(2)).

23. Plausible examples of such unexpressed truths would be those (of natural science, logic, or mathematics) that no-one will discover before the universe reaches its ultimate "heat-death".

24. Note further that both formulations, though seemingly akin to Tarski's so-called "Semantic Theory of Truth", properly attribute truth to *propositions*, not, as Tarski does, to sentences. This, both Kneale and Mackie, argue, not only enables the Simple Theory to avoid the well-known paradoxes at least as well as does Tarski's but also enables us to avoid his conclusion that, by virtue of allowing for the construction of their own metalanguages, natural languages such as English are inconsistent. See, especially, William Kneale and Martha Kneale [1964], pp. 588–92.

25. Unfortunately the thesis is not always well understood. Many commentators write as if Wittgenstein's conception of the truth-conditions of propositions had application *only* to compound truth-functions of elementary propositions and as if, in his view, it is the *truth-values* of these elementary propositions that are the truth-conditions for compound ones. But both these views are mistaken. As to the first, in 4.463(1) Wittgenstein talks of truth-conditions for propositions in general: "The truth-conditions of a proposition determine the range that it leaves open to the facts." As to the second, it is clear that the truth-conditions for an elementary proposition p cannot without triviality be said to consist in the truth-value of p, but must consist rather in the *circumstance* or *state of affairs* whose existence or nonexistence determines the truth-value of p. Most, but not all, contemporary discussants of so-called truth-conditional semantics are correct on both points.

26. He might well have added that the *impossibility* of an individual case also shows something about the essence of the world. But this, I think, he would regard as obvious, for the reasons given in *Wittgenstein's Lectures: Cambridge 1930–1932*: "If you know how to use a word and understand it you must already know in what combinations it is *not* allowed." [emphasis added] (p. 120).

27. As for contradictions, Wittgenstein predictably holds that a contradiction shows "the impossibility of a situation." (5.525).

28. Though I am quoting from Anscombe's translation of the *Notebooks*, I have taken the liberty here, and also when quoting *NB* 26(12), of substituting Pears and McGuinness's "state of affairs" (their translation of Wittgenstein's "*Sachverhalt*") for her "situation" .

29. See 4.031(2): "Instead of, 'This proposition has such and such a sense', we can simply say, 'This proposition represents such and such a situation'."

30. This fact, it may be recalled, led me to argue in Chapter 3, section 13, that, contrary to Wittgenstein, completely analyzed (elementary) propositions *cannot* be independent of one another.

31. The class paradox, he thought, arose from the naive idea, fostered by ordinary language, that for every predicate there exists a class of things (in some cases the null class) that fall under that predicate. According to Russell, it was because Frege presupposed the soundness of this idea that he was led to provide faulty, because paradox-generating, foundations for arithmetic. His theory of types was supposed to repair those foundations.

32. Ever since Aristotle, philosophers have debated whether type-distinctions, or category-distinctions, are ontological or linguistic in character, some saying the one, some the other, and some being equivocal about the whole issue. If I understand Wittgenstein correctly, he would say that they are *both* but would add that we need only to attend to distinctions between kinds of symbols since these mirror distinctions between kinds of things.

33. If we do this we will understand that, "In a certain sense, we cannot make mistakes in logic." (*NB* 2(3), 5.473(3)).

34. My reconstruction of what Wittgenstein might say were he to offer a detailed explanation of what has gone wrong in the Liar Paradox obviously owes much to Kneale's diagnosis as given in "Russell's Paradox and Some Others". There Kneale says that it is a fundamental principle of semantics that "for propositions and predicates alike expression is logically prior to designation." ([1971] p. 335).

35. In both cases he may, I believe, plausibly be taken to be subscribing to what John Mackie calls "the principle of Metaphysical Common Sense", viz., that "*no state of affairs can involve its own presentation.*" ([1973] p. 248). Mackie suggests that this principle, when taken together with Kneale's "expression is prior to designation", suffices for the solution of *all* the paradoxes.

5

Worlds in Perspective

> In every possible world there is an order even if it is a complicated one.
> (WITTGENSTEIN, *Notebooks 1914–16*)

1. Introduction

Throughout the preceding four chapters, I've portrayed the early Wittgenstein as a de re possibilistic atomist operating within the framework of a possible worlds ontology. He is an *atomist* insofar as all the items in his ontology, linguistic as well as nonlinguistic, are taken to be combinatorial constructions out of simple objects (individuals, things), simple properties, and simple relations. He is a *possibilistic* atomist insofar as the elements of his atomistic ontology are taken to include merely possible individuals, properties, and relations along with actual ones. He is a *de re* possibilistic atomist insofar as he thinks of his metaphysically simple individuals as having de re (internal, essential) formal properties that determine the range of all their possible combinations in possible states of affairs and therewith, with the help of the notion of consistency, determine the range of all possible worlds. I have also portrayed him as someone who constructs his theories of language and logic along the same modal atomist lines.

If I am right about all this, Wittgenstein should secure an even more important place in the history of philosophical ideas than his repute as the founder of logical atomism, as more traditionally conceived, has already won him. He is the precursor of a number of the ideas that many contemporary modal theorists, working in the areas of metaphysics, philosophy of language, and philosophy of logic, think worthy of discussion. And, in all three areas, he is the pioneer of ideas that, even today, have been insufficiently explored.

Not only that: the scope and power of his account of modality put him into competition with many of these latter-day modal theorists. In this final chapter, therefore, I shall compare and contrast what he has to say about the metaphysical foundations of modal notions with what certain others—most notably Robert Merrihew Adams, David Armstrong, Rudolph Carnap, David Lewis, Nicholas Rescher, and Robert Stalnaker—have to say about these and related matters. In so doing I'll be able to bring to light several features of his theory that I haven't yet discussed. I'll also be able better to offer an overall assessment of the success and significance of his modal atomism.

171

I start with a question that confronts anyone who wishes to talk about a multi-plicity of possible worlds.

2. Which World is Actual?

According to David Armstrong (in his recent book *A Combinatorial Theory of Possibility*), the question gets one into serious trouble if one begins, as do Leibniz and Wittgenstein, with the presumption that there is an infinity of possible worlds only one of which is actual. Sharpening up an argument that, he says, originated with D. C. Williams and has been endorsed by David Lewis, he presents the following "proportional syllogism":

> (1) All but one of the infinity of worlds are merely possible. (hypothesis)
> (2) This is a world.

Therefore (very probably)

> (3) This world is merely possible.

Now, he argues, it is one of those bedrock propositions of Moorean commonsense that (3) is false. Hence, given the equally bedrock truth of (2), it follows (by modus tollens, he says, but in fact by antilogism) that (1) is false. In his words, "the conclusion (3) is absurd. It is obvious that this world is actual. So we have good reason to reject (1) as false." (p. 14). He takes his argument to be a knock-down refutation of the kind of possible worlds realism adopted by Leibniz and Wittgen-stein.

Certain contemporary theories of actuality, Armstrong suggests, can be seen as offering different responses to this argument. His own response is to deny that there are any worlds other than the actual one and to construe *talk* of merely possible worlds as an exercise in the construction of fiction in which we entertain the idea of other worlds as combinations, or recombinations, of the elements of our world. (More of this in due course.) Lewis's indexical theory of actuality, he suggests, can be seen as the response of someone who asserts that *every* possible world is actual relative to itself. And Adams's true-story theory (an example of what Lewis calls an "ersatz" theory) can be seen as a response that fits somewhere between: it accepts only one actual world but augments it with the inclusion of certain abstract entities, propositions, and tries to construe talk of other possible worlds as talk about sets of these actual but abstract entities. What Armstrong presumes is that his argument has shown the Leibniz/Wittgenstein view to be a lost cause.

But has it? That there is something radically wrong with proportional syllogism can be demonstrated by logical analogy. Consider a lottery in which millions of tickets are issued but only one of them will win the single grand prize that is offered. Then we might equally argue:

> (1)* All but one of the millions of tickets in the lottery are losers.
> (2)* This is one of the tickets in the lottery.

Therefore (very probably)

(3)* This ticket is a loser.

Suppose, however, that the ticket you are holding is in fact the winning ticket. Does this give you good reason for denying (1)*? Surely, the falsity of (3)*, taken together with the truth of (2)*, gives you no reason whatever to reject (1)*.

Again, consider Armstrong's own fictionalist account of possible worlds. Then, by proportional syllogism, we might argue:

(1)** All but one of the infinity of worlds that philosophers talk about are merely fictional (hence nonexistent).

(2)** This is one of the worlds that philosophers talk about.

Therefore (very probably)

(3)** This world is merely fictional (hence nonexistent).

Clearly, Armstrong would find (3)** as repugnant to commonsense as the original (3). Yet he certainly would not want to conclude from the falsity of (3)**, together with the undoubted truth of (2)**, that (1)** is false. For (1)** is an expression of his own fictionalist (nonexistence) theory of merely possible worlds.

This ad hominem against Armstrong should bring the point home. The argument from proportional syllogism, despite its distinguished sponsors, is a thoroughly bad one deserving to be banished forever from the conceptual armory of philosophers. We can preserve both our bedrock Moorean intuitions about the actuality of our own world and our intuitions about the possibility of infinitely many nonactual worlds without any implausibility (let alone contradiction) whatever.

The kind of realism about possible worlds that Leibniz and Wittgenstein share is as much a live option as is that of Lewis and needs to be taken as seriously as the rival theories of "ersatzers" like Adams and Stalnaker, nominalists like Carnap, conceptualists like Rescher, and fictionalists like Armstrong himself.

But in what does the actuality of the actual world consist?[1] Some account is needed. So, let's look first at the theories of Adams and Lewis, and then see whether we can determine with what theory Wittgenstein might plausibly be credited.

3. Adams's True-Story Theory of Actuality

Robert Merrihew Adams develops this theory in his paper "Theories of Actuality" [1974]. Adams, like Armstrong, is an actualist. He believes that only one world, the actual world, exists and that all the materials needed for the construction of other possible worlds are to be found in this one. But whereas Armstrong is a self-described "Naturalist" who believes that all these materials are concrete entities, capable in principle of treatment by the natural sciences, Adams is what Armstrong would describe as a "Non-Naturalist", that is, is someone who believes that allowance must also be made for the existence in the actual world of certain abstract entities, such as propositions (as distinct from sentences), as well.

Now according to Adams, each possible world, including the actual one, may be represented by what he calls a *world-story*, where a world-story is a maximally consistent set of propositions. How, then, does the actual world differ from all the other worlds, those that are merely possible? Adams's answer is appealingly straightforward: "we can say that the actual world differs from the other possible worlds in that all the members of its world-story (the set of all the propositions that are true in it) are true, whereas the stories of all the other possible worlds have false propositions among their members." (p. 204).

At first glance, this accords well with Wittgenstein's account of which world is actual. He writes: "If all true elementary propositions are listed, the world is completely described. A complete description of the world is given by listing all elementary propositions, and then listing which of them are true and which false." (4.26). Clearly, we may assume that by "the world" here, Wittgenstein means the actual world. Moreover, licensed by Wittgenstein's claim, "The truth or falsity of *every* proposition does make some alteration to the general construction of the world" (5.5262), we may omit the restriction (in 4.26) to elementary propositions. Finally, for Wittgenstein's talk of the truth of all the propositions in the world's complete description, we may substitute Adams's talk of the truth of all the propositions that are members of its world-story. We then have a revision of 4.26 that makes it look very much as though Wittgenstein would want to endorse Adams's true-story theory of actuality.

Yet appearances are deceptive. To be sure, Wittgenstein would want to endorse some *version* of a true-story account of actuality. But his version would be significantly different from Adams's. In order to see why, let's look a little closer at the details and the motivation of the true-story theory, as Adams develops it.

Adams calls himself a "soft actualist" and contrasts his position with that which he calls "hard actualism". Hard actualism is the position according to which there is only one world, the actual world, and all talk of other possible worlds is just a fiction that we indulge for heuristic reasons when thinking about modality. Armstrong, in Adams's terminology, is a hard actualist. Adams is not. That is to say, Adams does not—as does Armstrong—*deny* the existence of nonactual possible worlds. He is prepared—with Leibniz and Wittgenstein—to allow that there *are* nonactual possible worlds, but insists that "they are logically constructed out of the furniture of the actual world." (p. 203). He asserts their quasi-existence, but then soothes his actualist conscience by claiming, "if there are any true statements in which there are said to be nonactual possible worlds, they must be reducible to statements in which the only things there are said to be are things which there are in the actual world and which are not identical with nonactual possibles." (p. 206).

Two sorts of motivation play a role in Adams's theory. First, like Russell, he wants to put a "realistic bias" into the study of metaphysics by not admitting the existence of anything nonactual. Secondly, again like Russell, he wants his theory to satisfy the dictates of Occam's Razor by making do with as few explanatory entities as possible. And he tries to do this by effecting a theoretical "reduction" of the whole range of possibilist paraphernalia to a few supposedly uncontentious actualist ones.

Adams's ploy is to take, as his basic stock of *actualia*, the actual world and all its constituents, where the latter are taken to include actual objects, properties, relations, set-theoretical entities such as sets, and—not least—propositions (which he takes to be independently existing, nonlinguistic, nonmental abstract entities). Adams will allow, with possibilists, that the *actual* world is distinct from the propositions that are true in it. But he will not allow, as do possibilists, that *merely possible* worlds are distinct from the propositions that are, as he and they both want to say, true "in" these worlds. For, on his account, there really are no such worlds as distinct from their propositional representations.

This is where his reductionism comes into play. He invokes the notion of a world-story, where a world-story is a maximally consistent set of *propositions*. The actual world, then, is the unique world such that all the propositions that are members of its world-story are in fact true. Other possible worlds are such that at least some of the propositions that are members of their world-stories are false. But propositions are not true or false "in" these nonactual worlds in the same way as they are true or false "in" the actual world. To say that a proposition is true "in" a merely possible, non-actual, world is just to say that it is a member of the consistent set of propositions that are members of its world-story. To say that a proposition is false "in" a merely possible world is just to say that it is *not* a member of that set. World-stories, in short, *substitute* for possible worlds for every case other than that of the actual world. Membership in, or lack of membership in, a world-story play the roles of truth "in", or falsity "in", a world for every case other than that of the actual world. So we need not think of there being *worlds* in which actually false but possibly true propositions are true. We need only think of actually false but possibly true propositions being members of *consistent sets of propositions*, some of whose members are in fact false in the actual world. And since he has already admitted propositions, and sets thereof, as actual (albeit abstract) entities, Adams claims that he has thereby reduced merely possible worlds to logical constructions out of constituents of the actual one. He says: "The true-story theorist . . . regards a merely possible world as logically constructed out of the set of propositions that are true in it, and he sees the truth of a proposition *in* a possible world as basically a matter of relations of consistency among propositions, rather than of correspondence with an independent object." (p. 206).

Adams's theory is ingenious. But, as with so many reductionist theories, its ingenuity doesn't compensate for the problems it generates. Adams himself draws attention to some of the "formal problems and threats of paradox" that arise if we, in effect, drop Wittgenstein's restriction to elementary propositions and think, as Adams does, of a world-story as a consistent set composed of one member of *every* pair of mutually consistent contradictory propositions. But I'll ignore these formal problems, and argue instead that Adams's theory leads to two seriously counter-intuitive results. Since Wittgenstein's does not, his version of the true-story theory—I'll argue—is to be preferred to Adams's.

The first problem for Adams has to do with our de re beliefs about actual objects in counterfactual situations. Suppose we entertain the de re belief, of Ronald Reagan,

    (1) Ronald Reagan could have remained a film actor.

Now (1) is a proposition that possible worlds theorists, whether possibilists or actualists, will want to analyze, initially at least, as equivalent to

(2) There is a possible world in which Ronald Reagan exists and remains a film actor.

The appeal of (2), as an analysis of (1), lies in the fact that it gives expression to our de re belief that the very person, Ronald Reagan, who in fact was President of the U.S.A., might in other possible circumstances—or, more grandiosely, in other possible worlds—have stayed in the profession for which he was better equipped by aptitude and experience. That is to say, (2) expresses the content of a de re belief about Ronald Reagan and what he might have been now had the world been different from the way it is. Adams, however, thinks that (2) needs to be analyzed further as something like

(3) The proposition, that Ronald Reagan remained a film actor, is a member of some world-story not all of whose propositions are in fact true.

But does (3) express the content of our de re belief about Reagan in the way that (1) does? I think not. To be sure, if (1) is true, then (3) will be true also. But the converse does not hold. (3) does not give an analysis of what (1) or (2) *means*. If we believe (3) to be true, we entertain a de dicto belief about a proposition and we attribute the property of being a member of a certain set to that proposition. By way of contrast, if we believe (1) or (2) to be true, we have a de re belief about Ronald Reagan and we attribute to *him* the de re modal property of possibly remaining a film actor. So we certainly do not believe the same thing if we believe (1) or (2) to be true as we do if we believe (3) to be true. In offering (3) as a reductive analysis of (1), Adams is changing the object of belief.

On Wittgenstein's account, no such reductive analysis is offered or required. He is quite unabashed when speaking about the possible existence of nonactual circumstances, states of affairs, situations, and whole worlds, in ways that do not admit of an Adams-style reduction to representations of those worlds, that is, to world-stories. He thinks of propositions as being true or false *in* the various possible world that a god might create (5.123). Other possible worlds, for him, are the *truth-makers* of merely possible propositions. The truth-possibilities of elementary propositions, for Wittgenstein, *correspond* (4.28) to the possibilities of existence and nonexistence of states of affairs. They do not themselves, when taken in maximally consistent sets, *constitute* such possibilities. In short, for Wittgenstein, the truth of a proposition like (1) is a entirely a matter of whether or not the proposition

(4) Ronald Reagan is a film actor

is true *in* some possible world other that the actual one, where—as 5.123 makes clear—it could not be true in a world unless Ronald Reagan existed in that world. So the question whether (4) is true *in* some merely possible world, for Wittgenstein, is not a matter of whether (4) is a member of some consistent set of propositions, as Adams would have us believe. Rather, it is a matter of whether (4) corresponds to some possible state of affairs that exists in some merely possible world. Contrary to

Adams, that is, Wittgenstein would hold that the truth of (4) in a possible world *is* a matter of "correspondence with an independent object".

The second problem for Adams's reductive analysis has to do with the possible existence of alien objects, such as elementary particles, Sherlock Holmes and Pegasus, or what-have-you, that do not in fact exist. It is, as Ramsey put it, "an unusual view" that any imaginable world must contain all and only the objects of the real one. It is unusual because, as I have argued in Chapter 2, it is so seriously counter-intuitive that few would be tempted to adopt it were it not for Occamist-cum-Russellian scruples, scruples that would have us pare down our ontology to the very minimum.

But how is such paring down to be effected? Adams doesn't tell us. And it is hard to see how he could. Adams wants to be able to talk about only those things that "are in the actual world and are not identical with non-actual possibles." Yet we can readily envisage there having been more elementary particles than there are in the actual world. And these *are* identical with nonactual possibles, not with any actual propositions or proposition-parts.

By way of contrast, Wittgenstein's ontology, we have seen, is much more accommodating. It allows for the existence of object-enriched worlds and thereby allows for the full plenitude of possible non-actuals that intuition seems to require. If a god were to create a world in which the proposition

(5) Sherlock Homes sniffs cocaine

is true, then, as 5.123 and *NB* 98(2) both tell us, in that world he creates all the "constituents" of the proposition and hence all the objects whose names occur in the proposition, including Sherlock Holmes. Yet Sherlock Holmes, paradigmatically, is a nonactual possible.

Wittgenstein's account of the matter, then, has greater scope than does that of Adams. It enables him to say, with Adams, that the actual world is the world all of whose world-story members are just plain true, that is, is the world that is completely described by the totality of true propositions. Wittgenstein's theory, in short, does the principal job that Adams's theory is supposed to do. It singles out a unique world from among infinitely many possible worlds. But it does this job without the counterintuitive consequences that attend Adams's theory.

4. Lewis's Indexical Theory of Actuality

David Lewis, like Leibniz and Wittgenstein, is a realist about possible worlds: he thinks there are infinitely many of them in addition to the actual world. But his response to the question, Which of them is actual?, is to say that all of them are—or, more accurately, that all of them are actual relative to themselves.

Lewis's account rests in part on a *semantical* analysis of the term "actual". He claims that "actual" is an indexical term insofar as it functions in much the same way as do terms like "this", "we", and "our". Such terms are said to be indexical insofar as their referents are determined, on any given occasion of their use, by certain features of the context of use. According to Lewis, "the actual world" *means* the same as "this world", "our world", "the world in which we live". Thus, as a first step towards answering the question, Which world is actual?, Lewis would answer, "The actual world is the one *we* live in." He says, in *Counterfactuals* [1973]: "Our world is only one world among others. We call it alone actual not because it differs from all the rest but because it is the world we inhabit." (p. 184).

This much of Lewis's theory seems to accord well enough with many of the things that Wittgenstein says or would want to say. Wittgenstein, as I understand him, would certainly want to say, with Lewis, that there are many (perhaps infinitely many) possible worlds and that we live in just one of them. He, like Lewis, is a possibilist. True, he might want to quibble with the suggestion that the world we call "actual" differs from the rest only by virtue of being the one we inhabit, for, as we have just seen, he believes that the actual world is distinguished from all others also by virtue of being the one that is completely described by the totality of propositions that are true simpliciter. But he would certainly agree that the world we call "actual" may be identified by means of such indexical expressions as "this world" (*NB* 72(18)), "my world" (5.6), "our world" (6.1233), and "the world we live in" (*NB* 127).

Nevertheless, Wittgenstein would not subscribe to certain of the other theses that Lewis incorporates into his indexical theory. Lewis [1970] maintains the quite general thesis: "All such sentences as 'This is the actual world', 'I am actual', 'I actually exist', and the like are true on any possible occasion of utterance in any possible world." (p. 186). More elaborately, Lewis [1973] claims: "The inhabitants of other worlds may truly call their own worlds actual, if they mean by 'actual' what we do; for the meaning we give to 'actual' is such that it refers at any world *i* to that world *i* itself. 'Actual' is indexical, like 'I' or 'here', or 'now'; it depends for its reference on the circumstances of utterance, to wit the world where the utterance is located." (p. 184).

On the face of it, Lewis is saying (and has generally been taken to be saying) that every possible world is equally actual. But this, it turns out, is not his intent. In "Counterpart Theory and Quantified Modal Logic" [1968], he claims that the actual world is "unique". And in his more recent book, *On the Plurality of Worlds* [1986], he tells us, "actuality [is] a relative matter: every world is *actual at* itself, and thereby all worlds are on a par. This is *not* to say that all worlds are actual—there's no world at which that is true, any more than there's ever a time when all times are present." (p. 93). What his indexical theory tries to secure, then, is the idea that the actuality of the actual world, the world we live in, is in some sense *relative* as opposed to absolute.

Lewis himself does not explain exactly what the "absolute/relative" distinction amounts to. But Adams [1974], picking up on his terminology, explains Lewis's relativism as follows: "We can say that for every possible world, w, the proposition that w is actual is true in w and false in every other possible world. This . . . has the consequence that the property of actuality is world-relative. Each world is actual, but only in itself." (p. 201). Adams goes on to contrast this with what both he and Lewis call the absolutist point of view, thus: "Alternatively, we can say that there is a world, w, such that the proposition that w is actual is true in every possible world.

W is actual in every possible world, and no other world is actual in any possible world. Thus, w is, absolutely, the actual world." (p. 201).

Plainly, the sort of absolutism that Lewis is rejecting here is akin to that which I have described as "the God's-eye, absolutist point of view of S5". Consequently, we can expect that Wittgenstein would once more disagree with Lewis's position. He might well agree with Lewis's idea that certain other worlds are inhabited by individuals who don't inhabit ours. And he might agree that such inhabitants, if any, may use the term "actual world" to refer to the worlds they inhabit rather than to the world we inhabit, for what they use this or any other term to refer to, he would insist, is always "arbitrary" (3.322). But, unlike Lewis, he would want to say that if they call their own worlds actual, then unless they are using "actual" in a different way from us, they speak falsely. He would therefore want to reject Lewis's argument for relativism.

Lewis's argument for the relativity of actuality turns crucially on his supposition that the *meaning* of "actual", for the inhabitants of other worlds, should be the same as it is for us, where by "meaning" he seems to mean something like a Fregean sense (*Sinn*): something which can pick out different bearers in different possible worlds. But for Wittgenstein, only whole propositions have meanings or Fregean senses. Parts of propositions don't have *Sinn* but only *Bedeutung*, that is, reference.[2] Thus, for Wittgenstein, a phrase like "the actual world" functions as a rigid designator of its bearer: it uniquely individuates the world in which you and I live. Hence, if the inhabitants of other worlds use the expression "the actual world" with the only meaning it can have, namely, its reference, and use it with the same meaning as we do, they will speak truly only if they use it to *refer* to our world. But in that case, actuality is a property that just one world, our world, possesses. And it possesses that property absolutely, not just relative to its inhabitants.

Lewis elaborates his theory in still another way, going beyond the bare thesis contained in the first passage quoted. He holds that no object ever exists in more than one possible world. Nothing is a "trans-world" object. Rather, all objects are "world-bound". In cases where others would want to say that one and the same object, A, has a given property, F, in one world, say W_1, and lacks it in another world, W_2, Lewis says that A has F in W_1, and that some "counterpart" of A, say A^*, lacks F in W_2. As he puts it, "The counterpart relation is our substitute for identity between things in different worlds. Where some would say that you are in several worlds, in which you have somewhat different properties and somewhat different things happen to you, I prefer to say that you are in the actual world and no other, but you have counterparts in several other worlds." ([1968], p. 111). This feature of his theory is not strictly a consequence of his indexical analysis of "actual". But it fits nicely with it, since the indexical analysis makes different worlds actual relative to different inhabitants and does not allow any two worlds to be actual relative to the same inhabitants.

Once more, however, Wittgenstein would disagree. Consider, first, his claim in 2.012 that objects have "written in to them" the capacity to occur in different alternative possible states of affairs, situations, and worlds. His view is that one and the same object (not just some counterpart of that object) *is* able (indeed is necessarily able) to occur in different counterfactual situations.

Consider, second, his claim "Thus one proposition 'fa' shows that the object a occurs in its sense, two propositions 'fa' and 'ga' show that the same object is mentioned in both of them." (4.1211). Clearly, the two propositions "fa" and "ga" may be such that only one, let us say "fa", is true in the actual world W_1, whereas the other, "ga", is false in W_1. Nevertheless, since "ga" has sense, it is possibly true. Hence there must be a world, let us say W_2, which a god might create, in which "ga" is true. But, "ga" could be true in W_2 only if a existed in W_2 as well as in W_1. For a god could not create a world such as W_2 in which "ga" is true "without creating all its objects." (5.123). This is why Wittgenstein says that the *same* object, a, is mentioned in both propositions. The object referred to by "a" in "fa" isn't just a counterpart of the object referred to by "a" in "ga". Rather, the very same object is mentioned in both these propositions because it occurs in both the worlds—indeed in all the worlds—in which these propositions are true.

Consider, third, Wittgenstein's way of drawing the distinction between internal and external properties (and relations). It would break down if trans-world identity were ruled out in the way that Lewis thinks it is. For Wittgenstein, a property is internal to an object just when "it is unthinkable that its object should not possess it" (4.123): that is, just when the object possesses that property in every possible world in which the object exists. But if an object exists, as Lewis says it does, in only one possible world, then if it has property F in any world, it has F in every world in which it exists, and hence has F as an internal property. Wittgenstein would, therefore, have to reject Lewis's ontology on pain of making every possible property of an object an internal, essential property of that object. Again, for Wittgenstein, a property is an external property of an object just when there is some possible world W_1 in which the object exists and has that property, and there is some possible world W_2 in which the object exists without having that property. But if, as Lewis claims, an object can exist in only one possible world, it follows once more that if an object has a property in any world, it has that property in every world in which that object exists and hence that the object cannot have any of its properties externally. In short, Wittgenstein's way of drawing the distinction between essential and accidental properties commits him to the rejection of an ontology of world-bound individuals. Objects must be capable of preserving their identity across possible worlds. Mere Lewisian counterparts will not do.

Fourth, it is essential to Wittgenstein's theory of propositional language—in particular, of his Compositional Freedom Principle—that we should be able to arrange names of things "experimentally" in propositional combinations so as to picture different ways things could be but are not, that is, ways things are arranged in possible worlds other than our own: "In the proposition we—so to speak— arrange things *experimentally*, as they do *not* have to be in reality" (*NB* 13(2)). But it is a presupposition of our being able to do this both that we are able to *think* of one and the same object's occurring in different hypothetical situations in different worlds and that we are able to *refer* to this object by using one and the same name in all the different possible propositions that, as he puts it, are "correlated with [these] hypothetical situation[s]." (*NB* 38(5)). Not only can one and the same object occur in different possible worlds. One and the same object can be referred to, in the actual world, by use of one and the same name: "Identity of object I express by identity of name. . . . Difference of objects I express by difference in signs." (5.53). Wittgenstein, as we have seen, subscribes to Saul Kripke's "rigid designation" theory of names: a name of anything has as its referent in other possible worlds the very same thing that it has as its referent in the actual world. Not only, contrary to Lewis, does Wittgenstein, like Kripke, regard it as possible for one and the same object to occur in two or more worlds. He also, contrary to Lewis, uses identity of name to signal identity of object in this and any other possible world.

Now it seems to me that Wittgenstein's stance on the issues that divide him from his fellow possibilist-cum-realist, David Lewis, is much more in accord with our ordinary ways of thinking about these matters and to that extent is much more defensible than is Lewis's.

As against Lewis's relativist account of actuality, we do, I submit, think of our own world as having a unique status in the metaphysical scheme of things, such that if inhabitants of other possible worlds were to claim actuality for their worlds they would be wrong. If, in a possible (fictional) world that Sherlock Holmes inhabits, Holmes were to claim actuality for his world, we would reject his claim as false (fictional). For his world is a nonactual world and notwithstanding any of our egalitarian sympathies, no amount of pleading by him could alter our conviction that it is he and his surroundings, not we and ours, that are are merely possible objects.

As against Lewis's counterpart theory, we do, I believe, normally side with Wittgenstein and Kripke in thinking of objects as able to preserve their identity across worlds rather than as being world-bound. When, for instance, we think of Ronald Reagan as someone who might have remained a film actor, we think about a possible world in which Ronald Reagan himself—not some Lewisian counterpart of Reagan—never became president.

Not only do we think of Ronald Reagan in this way. We also use his *name* in the way that Wittgenstein claims. Wittgenstein claims that by identity of name he expresses identity of object. And so, I submit, do we. Consider the way we think about alternative states of affairs in the past. I doubt whether anyone who knows to whom the name "Ronald Reagan" refers in the actual world would fail to understand that we are referring to *that very same person* when we use the sentence "Ronald Reagan might have remained a film actor" to express the possibility of a state of affairs which we already know does not exist in the actual world. Or consider the way we think about alternative possibilities for the future, none of which is yet known to us. Once more, I doubt whether anyone who knows the actual referent of "Ronald Reagan", would fail to understand that we are referring to *him* if, say, we were to use sentences such as "Ronald Reagan dies in 1995", " . . . in 1996", " . . . in 1997", and so on, to express various possibilities as to his eventual demise. Yet, for Lewis, since the worlds in which these sentences are true are different worlds, and any inhabitant of one world is necessarily distinct from any inhabitant of another world, we must be referring to different persons in each case. Indeed, on Lewis's theory, since all but one of these sentences will be true only in some nonactual worlds, and of all the possible worlds in which Reagan or his counterparts exist, Reagan himself exists in only one, only one of these sentences can refer to the actual Ronald Reagan; and since we do not yet know (in 1992) which of these sentences is about Reagan himself (as opposed to one of his counterparts), we do not know to whom we are referring if we entertain the suppositions envisaged by the other sentences! Lewis's theory seems to make nonsense of our ordinary ways of speculating and speaking about how things might come to be, and how they might once have been, for actual objects. Surely, in all these cases, counterfactual and future-conditional alike, we use the name "Ronald Reagan", in the way Wittgenstein believes we do. We use it to refer to the actual Ronald Reagan, not—as Lewis believes—to some counterpart who is totally distinct from him insofar as he lives in another space and time. Wittgenstein's account, I conclude, preserves our intuitions about these matters. Lewis's does not.

5. Wittgenstein's Absolutist Theory of Actuality

By an "absolutist theory of actuality" I mean a theory which incorporates the following theses:

   (i) There is *only one* actual world.
   (ii) The actual world is completely described by (but is not identical with) the set of all propositions that are true simpliciter.
   (iii) The actual world is *our* world.
   (iv) If the inhabitants of other possible worlds ever *refer* to the actual world or objects that exist within it, they speak truly only if they refer to our world or to objects that exist within it.

Finally, and most importantly

   (v) The actual world possesses the property of actuality *absolutely,* in itself, not just relative to its inhabitants.

As I see it, there is compelling evidence that this is the theory to which the early Wittgenstein is committed. It also seems to me that it is the theory to which most of us are committed by our ordinary ways of thinking and talking.

However, it has seemed to some theorists that any absolutist theory is fatally flawed insofar as it commits one to a belief in the noncontingency of actuality.

Adams [1974], for instance, points out that absolutist theories (such as the one which he calls "the simple property theory of actuality") force us "to deny that the nonactual possible worlds are possibly actual." But, he continues, "that denial entails that there is no such thing as contingent actuality. We would have to conclude that the actual world, in all its infinite detail, is the only possible world that could have been actual. And we would be left to wonder in what sense the other possible worlds are possible, since they could not have been actual." (p. 201).

The force of the objection can, perhaps, be felt better if we turn from abstract arguments to concrete examples. Consider, then, the propositions

   (6) Ludwig Wittgenstein wrote the *Tractatus*

and

   (7) In the actual world Ludwig Wittgenstein wrote the *Tractatus.*

Proposition (6) is true but only contingently so. It is true because in the actual world Ludwig Wittgenstein did write the *Tractatus*. It is contingent because there are possible worlds in which Ludwig Wittgenstein did not write the *Tractatus* and perhaps never wrote anything at all. How, then, does (6) differ from (7)? Many of us, I suspect, are disposed to say, unreflectively, that they "amount to the same thing", that to assert the truth of (6) is somehow "equivalent" to asserting the truth of (7). Yet, if we subscribe to the absolutist theory of actuality, they do *not* amount to the same thing since (6), if true, is contingently true, whereas (7), if true, is noncontingently true (that is, (7), if true, is necessarily so).

Is the noncontingency of actuality-ascriptions a defect in the absolutist theory?

I think not. To be sure, if we maintain the theory, then we will have to alter our unreflective disposition to suppose that the truth of (6) is strictly equivalent to the truth of (7). And, more generally, we will have to abandon the supposition that the *truth* of a proposition, P, is equivalent to the *actual truth* of P. Yet on reflection, there turn out to be other theoretical considerations, of an even broader kind, that constrain us to accept these consequences and to re-educate our dispositions accordingly.

The fact is that we have many good and powerful reasons for holding that *any* modal ascription, if true, is necessarily so, where by "a modal ascription" I mean the ascription, to something, of a property such as being possible, being impossible, being necessary, being nonnecessary, being contingent, or being noncontingent. The system of modal logic, S5, provides us with a set of axioms and rules of inference—to which, as we have repeatedly seen, Wittgenstein implicitly subscribes—whereby to prove the noncontingency of such modal ascriptions. It enables us to prove, for instance, that if the proposition

(8) It is possible that Ludwig Wittgenstein wrote the *Tractatus*

is true, then it is necessarily so; that if the proposition

(9) It is not possible that Ludwig Wittgenstein has the property of being an event[3]

is true then it is necessarily so; and so on. But these modality ascriptions, on a Leibnizian-cum-Wittgensteinian view, are translatable into the possible-worlds idiom in such a way that (8) is equivalent to

(10) There is some possible world in which Ludwig Wittgenstein wrote the *Tractatus*

(9) is equivalent to

(11) There is no possible world in which Ludwig Wittgenstein has the property of being an event

and so on for each of the other afore-mentioned modal properties.

The question naturally arises, then, as to why we should not treat

(7) In the actual world Ludwig Wittgenstein wrote the *Tractatus*

as the possible-worlds translation of still another modal ascription, namely, the actuality-ascription

(12) Actually, Ludwig Wittgenstein wrote the *Tractatus*.

Admittedly, S5, as originally and standardly conceived, makes no provision for an actuality-ascribing operator that would rank alongside "M" or " $\diamond$ " (for possibility), "L" or "$\square$" (for necessity), "C" or "∇" (for contingency), and the like. But it is hard to see why such an operator—perhaps appropriating the letter "A"—should not be introduced along with these others so as to enable us to express further true theses— axioms and theorems—about actuality in an enriched S5.

6. The Logic of "Actually"

Now, as we saw in Chapter 2, section 11, just such a system, S5A, has been devised by John N. Crossley and Lloyd Humberstone [1977].[4] It has precisely the features that we are seeking. Among the more significant are the following:

(a) Its semantics singles out one possible world, W*, from all the others and designates it "the actual world".
(b) It provides for a modal operator "A", to be read as "Actually", and defines Aα (where α is any well-formed formula) as true if and only if α is true in the actual world, W*.
(c) It contains an axiom, AP $\supset$ $\square$AP, which ensures that any actuality ascription, if true, is necessarily true.
(d) It makes "actually" function (as the authors point out) as a Wittgensteinian name or Kripkean rigid designator.[5]
(e) Notwithstanding the fact that if P is contingent its truth-value will vary from world to world whereas that of AP will not, it has the consequence that AP and P always have the same truth-value in the *actual* world: that is, while AP $\supset$ P is not a theorem, A(AP $\supset$ P) is a theorem.

The last of these features, (e), helps us to understand our initial disposition, which seemed so troubling, to suppose that the truth of a proposition, P, is "equivalent" to the actual truth of P; to suppose, for instance, that the truth of

(6) Ludwig Wittgenstein wrote the *Tractatus*

is equivalent to the truth of

(12) Actually, Ludwig Wittgenstein wrote the *Tractatus*

which, as we have already seen, is equivalent to

(7) In the actual world Ludwig Wittgenstein wrote the *Tractatus*.

We can now see that the supposition conceals a confusion. In the actual world proposition (6) is *materially* equivalent to proposition (7). In the actual world both propositions have the same truth-value. But (6) is not *logically* equivalent to (7). These propositions do not have the same truth-value—are not materially equivalent—in *all* possible worlds. So even though (6) is plainly contingent, it does not follow that (7) is contingent. Two propositions, of differing modal status (with respect to contingency and noncontingency), can be materially equivalent (have the same truth-value) even although they cannot be logically equivalent (have the same truth-value in all possible worlds).

Feature (e), of S5A, also enables us to avoid another objection that threatens to impugn the absolutist account. We might be tempted to suppose that, even if (6) and (7) are not logically equivalent, (7) nevertheless logically implies (6). More generally, we might suppose that AP logically implies P. Yet if we were to hold this we really would be in trouble. On the one hand, we are committed by the S5A axiom, $AP \supset \Box AP$, to saying that any true actuality-ascription is necessarily true, and so are committed to saying that (7), if true, is necessarily true. On the other hand, we are committed by a thesis of the underlying system S5, namely, $\Box(P \supset Q) \supset \Box(\Box P \supset \Box Q)$, to saying that anything logically implied by a necessary truth is itself necessarily true. Hence, we are committed to saying that if (7) implies (6) and (7) is necessarily true, then so is (6). But (6) is clearly not necessarily true.

The solution, this time, lies in reminding ourselves of the distinction between material implication and logical implication. We may allow that (7) *materially* implies (2). But this does not mean that (7) *logically* implies (6). So even though (7), if true, is necessarily so, it does not follow that (6) is necessarily true. The formalism of S5A may help us to see this point more clearly. It contains $A(AP \supset P)$ as a thesis. But it does not contain $AP \supset P$ as a thesis.

There still remains the problem of the seeming counterintuitiveness, remarked on by Adams, of the view—to which our theory is committed—that the actual world is the only one that could have been actual, or, to put it less globally, that any actual state of affairs is the only one that could have been actual. Our intuitions certainly lead us to assert the truth of the proposition

> (13) A world in which it is not the case that Ludwig Wittgenstein wrote the *Tractatus* is a possible one (that is, is a world that could have existed).

Indeed its truth follows from the contingency of (6). And at first glance (13) may seem to be equivalent to

> (14) A world in which it is not the case that Ludwig Wittgenstein wrote the *Tractatus* could have been actual (that is, could have actually existed).

So it may seem that our intuitions lead us to say that (14) is true. Yet the absolutist theory denies that (14) is true. According to it, whatever is actual is necessarily actual. Likewise, whatever is not actual is necessarily not actual.

This problem, on the face of it, is more troubling than that posed by our disposition to suppose that the truth of P is equivalent to the actual truth of P (to suppose that $P = AP$). Unlike the latter, the present problem cannot be solved by invoking the distinction between material equivalence and logical equivalence, allowing that the former holds but denying that the latter does. For (13) and (14) are not even materially equivalent. Rather, according to our theory, (13), if true, is noncontingently true since it is of the form $\Diamond \sim(6)$; and (14), if false, is noncontingently false since it is of the form $\Diamond A \sim(6)$. Both (13) and (14) involve modal ascriptions (of possibility) and hence, even in basic S5 without an actuality operator, are noncontingent.

The problem is not intractable, however, since it yields to another distinction, one that goes hand in hand with the distinction between truth and actual truth. I mean, of course, the distinction between existence and actual existence.

Consider (13) and (14) again. What leads us to say that (13) is true is our conviction—surely a correct one—that a world or state of affairs in which it is not the case that Ludwig Wittgenstein wrote the *Tractatus* could have *existed*. But it does not follow from this that (14) is true, that is, that such a world or state of affairs could have *been actual*, that is, that such a world or state of affairs could have *actually existed*. Existence simpliciter, on our theory, is no more to be conflated with actual existence than is truth simpliciter with actual truth. To be sure, the properties of existence and actual existence, like the properties of truth and actual truth, are coextensive *in the actual world*. However, they are not coextensive in all possible worlds. Consider the state of affairs of Wittgenstein's having written *Hamlet* . Although this state of affairs does not exist in the actual world, we would surely want to say that it does exist in some nonactual possible world. But clearly it does not *actually* exist in some nonactual possible world. To suppose the contrary would be to suppose that actuality is a world-relative property that states of affairs can possess relative to the worlds in which they exist. It would be to revert to the already discredited relativist theory of actuality.

The distinction between existence and actual existence, then, enables us to safeguard the absolutist theory of actuality from some seemingly recalcitrant intuitions. And it provides us with a simple reply to Adams. He objects that the absolutist theory of actuality leaves us "to wonder in what sense the other possible worlds are possible, since they could not have been actual." We can now tell him just what that sense is. Clearly, there is no possible world in which a nonactual world is identical with the actual world. Hence, if a possible world is distinct from the actual world, it is necessarily distinct from it and could not have been identical with it.[6] Other possible worlds can exist without actually existing.

The distinction between existence and actual existence was sketched in section 11 of Chapter 2. There we saw that there are at least two ways of accommodating Wittgenstein's claim that there are possibilities of existence and non-existence beyond anything actual, within the expressive resources of already available logics. One, that of his fellow-possibilist David Lewis, involves the use of the letter "A" as an actuality predicate to be predicated of individuals and read as " . . . is actual". The other, that of Crossley and Humberstone, involves using the letter "A" as a propositional operator to be read as "Actually . . ." or as "In the actual world . . . ". It is the latter device that I shall employ in what follows.

By combining it with the standard device, in quantified logic, for asserting existence simpliciter, "$(\exists x)$", we obtain the concatenation of these two symbols, namely, "$A(\exists x)$", and employ this concatenation as a means of distinguishing actual existence from existence simpliciter. So equipped, we can read something of the form "$A(\exists x)\emptyset x$" as "In the actual world there exists an x which has property $\emptyset$", or more simply as "Actually there exists an x which has $\emptyset$."

Thus, in a quantified version of S5A (not presented by Crossley and Humberstone) one may distinguish between the two domains of quantification (the restricted and the unrestricted) in a way that is notationally different from Lewis's but does much the same job. The restricted domain, then, will be that in which "A($\exists$x)" ranges over only those objects which actually exist, that is, exist in the actual world, whereas the unrestricted domain is that in which "($\exists$x)" ranges over any objects whatever: objects that exist in the actual world and objects that exist merely possible worlds as well. To be sure, the reading that we are giving to the unrestricted existential quantifier is more liberal than that which it is ordinarily given. For the ordinary reading, as we have seen, treats "there exists" as tantamount to "there actually exists". But the advantages of our new reading are clear. We can then say, without any appearance of contradiction, something that is surely self-consistent, namely, that there exist possible worlds which are not actual.

Plainly, there is no contradiction between

(15) ($\exists$x) $\varnothing$x

and

(16) ~(A($\exists$x) $\varnothing$x)

Hence, we can perfectly well say without contradiction both that a possible world, W, exists

(17) ($\exists$x) Wx

and that that very same possible world does not actually exist

(18) ~(A($\exists$x) Wx)

A fortiori, we can say without contradiction both that a world, W, for example, a world in which it is not true that Ludwig Wittgenstein wrote the *Tractatus*, is such that it could have existed, as is asserted by

(19) $\Diamond$(($\exists$x)Wx)

and that that very same world could not have *actually* existed[7], as is asserted by

(20) ~$\Diamond$(A($\exists$x)Wx)

It follows that we can say, without contradiction, both that (13) is true and that (14) is false.

7. What Is the Status of Merely Possible Worlds?

In sections 3 to 6, we have considered the question, Which world is actual?, and some of the answers that have been given. And I've argued that Wittgenstein's answer is more philosophically satisfactory than those given by either Adams (as an actualist) or Lewis (as another realist).

But not all possible worlds theorists think an answer is required. Those who share Armstrong's conviction that there are no such things as merely possible worlds will reject the question itself as arising out of false presuppositions. They, like Armstrong, will attempt to reduce talk of the merely possible to talk of something actual. Such is the ploy of those who are nominalists or conceptualists about other possible worlds.

Possible worlds nominalists are disposed to say that talk of possible worlds, in general, is merely that: a fanciful way of talking. This way of talking, they are also likely to say, is misleading since it leads us into supposing that expressions like "possible world", "counterfactual situation", and their kin, stand for certain sorts of extralinguistic entity when in fact, properly understood, they are to be seen as having reference to sentences, sets of sentences, and the like. Rudolph Carnap is a good example of a possible worlds nominalist.

Possible worlds conceptualists, like nominalists, deny that the troublesome expressions have genuine metaphysical import. But, unlike nominalists, they hold that these expressions have reference to our ways of thinking or conceptualizing. Talk about possible worlds, they would say, is properly to be construed as being about a certain range of mental constructions or psychological concepts. Nicholas Rescher is a good example of a possible worlds conceptualist.

Possible worlds realists, by way of contrast with these others, take possible worlds to be metaphysical entities of some sort or other: entities, reference to which is philosophically indispensable to a proper account of modal notions; entities that are not reducible either to linguistic or to psychological ones; entities that, in some sense, really do exist (though not all of them actually exist). Leibniz and Lewis are possible worlds realists. And so, I've argued, is Wittgenstein, though his realism, as we've already seen, is very different from Lewis's.

In the next few sections, I take up the issue of the ontological status of other possible worlds, once more comparing and contrasting Wittgenstein's answers with those of his rivals.

8. Nominalism about Other Worlds: Historical Ironies

Contemporary-style theorizing about possible worlds, the kind that regards it as providing some sort of semantics for language and logic alike, is widely held to have begun with Rudolph Carnap who, in 1947, published his important work *Meaning and Necessity*. Yet Carnap really didn't believe in possible worlds at all. Certainly he didn't believe in non-actual ones. And he was even chary about speaking of the actual or real world. Carnap was a nominalist (though I'm not sure that he ever called himself that). For him, all discourse that purported to be about reality, discourse in what he called "the material mode", should if possible be replaced with discourse only about our *talk* about reality—discourse in what he called "the formal mode." Wittgenstein's easy-going reference to possible worlds, to reality, and to the nature of being, was not for Carnap. It smacked of metaphysics; and metaphysical statements, he held, are "devoid of cognitive content". (p. 868). Such talk, for him, had to be replaced by talk of state-descriptions and other linguistic, logical, or mathematical items.

The history of possible worlds theorizing, as it relates to Wittgenstein and Carnap, involves a threefold irony.

First, although Carnap himself openly acknowledged his indebtedness to Wittgenstein for the basic ideas that he presented in *Meaning and Necessity*, historians of the subject seem to have ignored Wittgenstein's seminal role entirely and to have given all the credit to Carnap. For instance, Jaakko Hintikka [1973]—one of those chiefly responsible, along with Kripke and others, for the elaboration of possible worlds semantics in the late 1950s and early 1960s—tells us, "Carnap was not the last Mohican of Fregean semantics, based on the extension-intension contrast, but rather the first and foremost herald of a new epoch of possible worlds semantics." (p. 374).[8] Yet the fact is that Carnap himself certainly did not think of himself as "first and foremost" in this field. Rather, as we shall see, he gives the credit to Wittgenstein.

Chief among the semantic concepts that Carnap employs in *Meaning and Necessity* are those of *state -descriptions*, of the *range* of a sentence, of the *interpretation* or meaning of a sentence, and of *L-truth*, *L-falsity*, and *L-implication*. And for each of these he somewhere or other acknowledges his indebtedness to Wittgenstein. Of state-descriptions, he says that they "represent Leibniz's possible worlds or Wittgenstein's possible states of affairs." (p. 9). Of the concept of the range of a sentence, he says [1942] that in 4.463(1) "Wittgenstein uses the concept of the range of a proposition for informal, intuitive explanations", and goes on to say that his own discussion "is an attempt to define the concept in an exact way." (p. 107). Regarding the concept of the interpretation of a sentence, he says [1947] that it is determined by its range together with the rules of designation for the predicates and individual constants since "to know the meaning of a sentence is to know in which of the possible cases it would be true and in which not, as Wittgenstein pointed out." (p. 10). Carnap, here, is alluding to and restating Wittgenstein's claim, in 4.024, "To understand a proposition means to know what is the case if it is true. (One can understand it, therefore, without knowing whether it is true.) It is understood by anyone who understands its constituents." Finally, of his L-concepts, Carnap [1943] tells us that in 4.463(3), "Wittgenstein shows that L-truth (tautology), L-falsity (contradiction) and L-implication are determined by the ranges" (p. 107). More generally, writing about the semantic method developed in *Meaning and Necessity*, Carnap says, "Some ideas of Wittgenstein's were the starting-point for the development of this method." (p. 9).

Carnap sets the historical record straight in another respect as well, when he reminds Donald Davidson that the motivation behind *Meaning and Necessity* was to provide a generalization of Wittgenstein's ideas, not, as Davidson had suggested, a semantics for quantified modal logic. Carnap [1963] writes:

> It is correct that the concept of L-truth plays a fundamental role in my semantics. But the introduction of this concept together with the concept of state-descriptions on which it is based, was not motivated by the aim of giving a semantical analysis of modal languages with variables. At the time of the Vienna Circle we had already developed both concepts by a generalization of Wittgenstein's concepts of tautology and truth-possibilities respectively. (p. 913)

Clearly, Carnap's indebtedness to Wittgenstein will need to be taken into account when the time comes for the writing of a definitive history of possible worlds semantics.

The second irony is that, whereas Wittgenstein's ideas were metaphysically robust enough to serve as the underpinnings of a number of the most fruitful ideas that are nowadays referred to as "possible worlds semantics", Carnap developed Wittgenstein's ideas along nominalist lines and thereby precluded himself from the discovery of these modern developments. As Hintikka [1973] puts it

> All that Carnap had to do was to take a good hard look at his state-descriptions and to ask: what are they supposed to be descriptions *of* in some realistic, down-to-earth sense? One natural answer is that they are descriptions of the different possible states of affairs or courses of events (in short, "possible worlds") in which the speaker of a language could possibly find himself and which he could in principle distinguish from each other. From this answer it is only a short step to the crucial idea that the rules for using the language will have to be shown—in principle—by the way a well-informed speaker would use it in these different circumstances according to the rules, i.e., by the extensions which the expressions of the language would have in those several "possible worlds". This is all we need to arrive at the basic ideas of possible worlds semantics. (p. 375)

Strangely, however, neither Carnap nor Hintikka seems to have noticed that the fundamental ideas that Carnap needed to formulate, in order to develop a full-fledged possible worlds semantics, had already been formulated by Wittgenstein. Why did Carnap turn his back on the firm foundations that Wittgenstein had laid, and try to build on his own less substantial one? Why did Carnap turn to nominalism rather than taking Wittgenstein's talk of possible states of affairs and possible worlds at face value? Hintikka does not give us an answer. But it can be extracted from some of Carnap's own remarks.

Carnap apparently thought that his nominalism was enjoined upon him by some of the things that Wittgenstein himself had said. Toward the end of the *Tractatus*, Wittgenstein said a number of things—particularly in 6.45, 6.522, 6.53, 6.54, and 7—to the effect that talk about the mystical and the metaphysical is an attempt to say what cannot be said; he even included his own Tractarian propositions among those which are "nonsensical". Curiously, the paradoxical nature of these apparently self-immolating Tractarian statements did not prompt Carnap and his friends in the Vienna Circle to enquire as to exactly what Wittgenstein meant by "the mystical", "the metaphysical", "what cannot be said", or "the nonsensical". So it seems to have escaped their attention that, by these terms, Wittgenstein merely meant whatever is not a contingently true or false proposition about the actual world, that is, about the world that the propositions of natural science try to describe. They took these remarks of Wittgenstein's, about the "nonsensical" character of all attempts to "say" anything metaphysical, quite literally because these remarks accorded so well with their own positivist predilections. Yet, in so doing, they were led to reject as strictly "meaningless" all the metaphysical claims that Wittgenstein had taken as the explanatory basis of his linguistic and logical doctrines. Carnap [1963] says that he and his fellow positivists were led to conclude, "The statement asserting the reality of the external world (realism) as well as its negation in various forms, e.g., solipsism and various forms of idealism, in the traditional controversy are *pseudo-statements*, i.e., devoid of cognitive meaning." (p. 868). They all, as he goes on to explain, "rejected the thesis of realism not as false but as being without cognitive meaning ('meaningless', as we usually said at that time, following Wittgenstein)."

Here, then, is our third, and perhaps greatest, irony. Not only did Carnap take the *Tractatus* to be an antimetaphysical tract, despite its robust metaphysical content. By following what he took to be its precepts, he debarred himself from a number of the insights that are possible only if we take Wittgenstein's talk of the actual world (reality) and other possible worlds seriously.[9] His rejection of ostensible talk about things (the material mode) in favor of talk about linguistic expressions (the formal mode) led him to reject Wittgenstein's talk about possible states of affairs and possible worlds in favor of talk about state-descriptions, that is, about sentences and sets of sentences. He was drawn instead to a form of nominalism with respect to possible worlds.

9. Problems for Carnap's Nominalism

In a number of respects, Carnap's nominalism resembles Adams's soft actualism, which it antedated by over a quarter of a century. In effect, Adams's world-story account is a rewrite of Carnap's state-description account. Instead of Carnap's talk of maximally consistent sets of sentences, Adams employs talk of maximally consistent sets of propositions. Otherwise there is little, of a formal nature, to distinguish the two accounts.

Both are actualists. Carnap's actualism, however, is not quite as "soft" as Adams's. Both Adams's propositions and Carnap's sentences are thought of, by their sponsors, as constituents of the actual world. But Adams's propositions are avowedly abstract entities, whereas Carnap's sentences are supposed to be much more commonplace, and much more respectable, concrete denizens of the actual world. So even though Carnap has to take recourse, in his account, to certain abstract entities such as sets, he seemingly doesn't have to rely on as many as Adams does.

By virtue of its actualist commitments, Carnap's theory is susceptible to the same sorts of objections as Adams's. For instance, our de re belief that Ronald Reagan could have remained a film actor is not a belief about the membership of the sentence "Ronald Reagan is a film actor" in a certain set of consistent sentences, but, as Wittgenstein would insist, is a belief about Reagan himself and the possibility of an independently existing state of affairs in which he might figure. Again, it seems to most of us that there are many respects in which the *world* could have been different from the way it was, is, or will be, and that these alternative ways the world could have been are in no way a function of the fact that language-using creatures regard certain sets of sentences as maximally consistent. Rather, these alternative ways are features of the world itself.

By virtue of his theory's being even "harder" than that of Adams, it is exposed to some new objections as well: objections to do with the supposed concreteness of sentences.

Consider the possibility that the world should have had a different evolutionary history such that no language-using creatures, and hence no sentences, ever emerged. The world, we feel, surely *could* have been different in this sort of way. Yet, according to the Carnapian account, such a world, if it had existed, would be one in which no alternative states of affairs could possibly exist. For it is a necessary condition of there being consistent sets of sentences that there be sentences. If, then, it is a necessary condition for a putative state of affairs to be possible that the sentence describing it be self-consistent and if there were no sentences, the state of affairs we are envisaging as possible would not be possible after all. In short, his nominalist theory goes against our conviction that many states of affairs and totalities thereof, other than those that actually exist, might well have existed even if there never had been humans or other sentient beings who uttered, or thought in terms of, sentences about them.

A second problem, inherent in Carnap's theory, emerges when we press for an account of what he considers a sentence. Plainly, it will not do, for any nominalist, to say that so-called possible worlds are reducible to maximally consistent sets of sentence-*types*. Since sentence-types are abstract entities, they are every bit as repugnant to the metaphysically squeamish as are propositions and possible worlds. To rely on them would be to abandon the supposed advantages of admitting into one's ontology only those entities which have physical existence in the actual world. It would be to abandon the kind of nominalist program to which Carnap was committed. But neither will it do to suppose that the physical instantiations of sentence-types, namely, sentence-*tokens*, will do the job. A sentence-token, after all, is taken to be made up of constituent vocables, inscriptions on paper, magnetic patterns on tape, or the like. And these, in turn, are taken to be made up of molecules, atoms, and subatomic particles in various spatiotemporal configurations. Yet it should be clear that there are not enough sentence-tokens to stand in a one-to-one relation to their own multiple constituents. Hence no state-description consisting of actual sentence-tokens could ever do justice even to the description of itself, let alone to the description of all the other events and states of affairs that constitute the actual world. Worse still, any description of the actual world, if it is to do justice to mathematics, must take account of the real numbers, stating for each that the number in question exists. Yet there is a nondenumerable infinity of real numbers and there are, at best, only countably many sentence-tokens. In short, there are not enough sentence-tokens to permit a full description of the actual world. Still less are there enough to permit full descriptions of the infinitely many other possible worlds for which Carnap, along with Wittgenstein, wants to allow.

Third, the Carnapian approach runs into difficulties over the interpretation of even such indisputable truths as those expressed by the modal theses, "$P \supset \Diamond P$" and "$\Box P \supset P$". For each thesis, someone like Wittgenstein can offer an interpretation that allows us to "see", quite straightforwardly, just why it expresses a necessary truth. As to "$P \supset \Diamond P$", a Wittgensteinian will read it as saying something like, "If a proposition, P, is true then there is some possible world in which P is true", where the logical connection between antecedent and consequent is established by the following facts: that (on a correspondence theory of truth) P can be true only if the state of affairs, S, whose existence it asserts does in fact exist; that if S exists then there also exists some totality of states of affairs (even if only a one-membered totality) of which S is a member; and that if a totality of states of affairs exists that "makes" P true, then there exists at least one possible world in which P is true. As to "$\Box P \supset P$", a Wittgensteinian will read it as saying something like, "If a proposition, P, is true in all possible worlds then it is true", where the logical connection between antecedent and consequent is established by the fact that whatever holds for all cases (worlds or whatnot) holds for any given one of these cases.

Consider, by way of contrast, the readings that someone of Carnap's persuasion would have to give. As to "$P \supset \Diamond P$", they will have to read it as saying something like, "If P is true, then P is a self-consistent sentence", where the notion of self-consistency is treated in a purely syntactical way, such that to say that P is a self-consistent sentence is just to say that its denial is not derivable as a theorem of some specified formal system. But there is an insuperable problem for this sort of interpretation. Our ordinary notion of self-consistency is a preformal one, capable of being instantiated, but hardly exhausted, by sentences whose denials are formally underivable. This follows, as David Lewis has pointed out, from a result of Kurt Godel. As Lewis [1973] puts it, "no falsehood of arithmetic is possibly true [self-consistent], but for any deductive system you care to specify either there are falsehoods among its theorems or there is some falsehood of arithmetic whose denial is not among its theorems." (p. 183).

As to "$\Box P \supset P$", Carnapians will have to read it as saying something like, "If P is a member of every state-description, that is, of every maximally consistent set of sentences, then P is true." The problem this time is to understand why such a claim should be true, let alone necessarily so. How is one supposed to get from the notion of consistency, syntactically construed, to the semantical notion of truth? A connection would be established were the antecedent modified to read, "If P is *true* in every state-description. . . . " But then the burden of explanation would fall in a different place. What could it mean for a proposition to be "true" in a state-description if we are forbidden to ask what state-descriptions describe? The connection becomes obvious if, contrary to Carnap, we allow that state-descriptions are descriptions of those ontological items that we call totalities of states of affairs, that is, possible worlds. But for someone, like Carnap, who is determined to "replace the ontological theses about the reality or irreality of certain entities . . . by proposals or decisions concerning the use of certain languages", such an explication is unavailable. It is surely much more illuminating to be able to say, with Wittgenstein, "Truth-possibilities of elementary propositions mean possibilities of existence and nonexistence of *states of affairs*." (4.3) [emphasis added], or again that necessarily true propositions are "true for all the possibilities of the elementary propositions" (4.46(2)), that is, that they are "true for every situation" (4.466(2)). Given Wittgenstein's account, it is immediately evident why "$\Box P \supset P$" is a *truth* of logic. Given Carnap's, it is not.

10. Conceptualism about Other Worlds

An interesting and sophisticated form of possible worlds conceptualism has been advanced by Nicholas Rescher in his book *A Theory of Possibility: A Constructivis-*

tic and Conceptualistic Account of Possible Individuals and Possible Worlds [1975].
I'll take it to be representative of the conceptualist viewpoint.

Rescher calls his theory "constructivistic" because he believes that "'merely
possible' individuals (and states of affairs and worlds) are *intellectual constructions
(entia rationis)* developed from a strictly actually-pertaining starting-point." (p. 2).
His constructivism has two main features: (i) It is a form of actualism insofar as
"The whole approach proceeds from the starting-point afforded by the actual world,
for it is the actual world that provides the machinery for the entire constructive
process. (The actual world furnishes the inventory of individuals and the taxonomy
of properties in whose terms the whole development proceeds.)" (p. 84). (ii) It
attempts to construct possible worlds out of an inventory of actual individuals and
properties by using "an already available logic" (p. 3). As he explains, "we presuppose a system of (non-modal) logic as given to serve as the guiding mechanism of
the construction." (p. 123).

Rescher also calls his theory "conceptualistic". By this he means that "we take
these [mere] possibilities to correspond to intellectual constructions, and thus to be
of the status of *entia rationis* produced by certain characteristically mental pro-
cesses." (p. 197).

I've already discussed actualism, which is feature (i) of Rescher's constructivism, in connection with Adams. And since many of the points raised before apply
mutatis mutandis to Rescher, I'll concentrate here on feature (ii): his insistence that
nonmodal logic is the "decisive guide" in our construction of possible worlds. That
dealt with, I'll turn to his arguments for their conceptualistic, mind-dependent
status.

11. Rescher's Chicken and Egg Problem

A problem for any sort of philosophical constructivism is where to start one's
constructions. In Rescher's case, the question is, Does one start from what he calls
the "chicken" of an already available "system of (non-modal) logic" (p. 123) or
from the "egg" of modal intuitions about possibilia in general and possible worlds in
particular?

Rescher's answer is that one should treat possible worlds "as *constructs* in
whose manufacture the machinery of an already *available* logic plays a decisive
role." (p. 3). In his view, "Necessary truths, from this standpoint, are not necessary
because they are 'true in all possible worlds'; *au contraire*, possible worlds are so—
i.e., are possible—because they do not conflict with truths that qualify as necessary
on independent grounds." (p. 5). In short, "our determination of what sorts of
putative worlds are indeed *possible* is decisively guided by the logical system with
which we began." (p. 124).

The primacy that Rescher is claiming for the "chicken" of logic does not lie in
the historical order in which logic and possible worlds semantics developed. It lies,
rather, in the explanatory order that he thinks we must adopt if we are to get a grip
on the concept of what a possible world is. He is claiming that the nonmodal logics

that we already have are both necessary and sufficient for the construction of possible worlds. They are necessary in the sense that nothing will count as possible, in the relevant sense, unless it complies with the formal criteria of consistency that these logics supply. They are sufficient for the construction of possible worlds in the sense that nothing will count as *impossible* (and therefore as excluded from the realm of possible worlds) unless it complies with the formal criteria of *inconsistency* that these logics supply.

An obvious objection to Rescher's constructivism is that he is too sanguine in his belief that the formal systems of logic currently "available" suffice to draw a definite boundary between the realm of the possible and that of the impossible. After all, but a moment's reflection is needed for us to realize that, before the development of (nonmodal) quantified logic, many statements whose necessary falsehood is demonstrable therein were undemonstrable as such by the coarser-grained criteria of truth-functional propositional logic. And how, without question begging, can it be thought that no finer-grained logics will one day emerge that will seem further to delimit the realm of the possible? We can allow that satisfaction of the formal criteria of currently available logics is a necessary condition of a proposition's being possibly true. But that is very different from the claim that these criteria are "decisive" in the sense of being sufficient as well, that is, that whatever does not conflict with available formal criteria is genuinely possible.

A more crucial objection derives from David Lewis's observation (already noted) about Godel's proof that no finite set of axioms suffices to establish a complete and consistent basis for arithmetic. Since there are necessary truths of arithmetic whose truth cannot be established by the formal criteria of any single finite consistent system (let alone any "available logic"), the impossibility of the denials of these truths will likewise be non-demonstrable. Even if we cannot produce actual *examples* of arithmetic falsehoods whose impossibility is nondemonstrable within available systems, we know from Godel that such falsehoods do exist.

Third, it is easy to cite actual examples, outside arithmetic, of impossibilities which certainly cannot be certified as such by means of the resources of any available logic. For all we know, these impossibilities may forever elude the formal proscriptions of any logical system whatever. As a case in point consider Wittgenstein's example (given in 6.3751) of the impossibility of two colors' being present simultaneously at the same place in the visual field. This state of affairs, Wittgenstein explicitly says, is "logically impossible". Yet it seems improbable that it will ever be decisively established as such by the machinery of formal logic. Even less tractable would seem to be those impossibilities that flow from the essential properties of things, or kinds of things: the impossibility of a speck in a visual field lacking color; of a tone lacking pitch; of an object of the sense of touch lacking some degree of hardness (all remarked on by Wittgenstein in 2.0131). Intuitively, most of us will want to say, with Wittgenstein, that in any possible world in which there exist specks in visual fields those specks will be colored; that in any possible world in which sounds occur those sounds will have some pitch or other; and so on. These are all examples of de re necessary truths: truths about the internal (essential) properties of things and kinds of things. Yet their necessity, and the impossibility of their denials, seems in some sense to follow from what Wittgenstein refers to as "the nature of all being" (*NB* 39(9)) rather than from anything purely formal. It seems, therefore, to fall well outside the ambit of Rescher's constructivist program.

What these observations suggest is that, if we are forced to choose—in the explanatory order of things, between the "egg" of modal intuitions about possible worlds and the "chicken" of formal logic, then we must say that in the beginning was the egg. For, to elaborate on a point already made, it is clear that formal logic cannot, in the way that possible worlds theory can, do justice to the phenomena that call for explanation, where these phenomena include the full range of necessities, de re as well as de dicto. This is not to deny that logic has an important role to play in what Rescher calls "the exfoliation of possibilia" (p. 125). But it is to deny that it has the complete say-so in their construction.

12. Problems about Mind-Dependency

Turning now to Rescher's conceptualism per se, let's examine his defence of the claim that possibilia are mind-dependent, that "they can be said to 'exist' in only a subsidiary or dependent sense—that is, only in so far as they are to be *conceived of* or *thought of* or *hypothesized* and the like." (p. 199).

When it is thus stated, Rescher's position seems unequivocal enough. However, like most forms of conceptualism, it is conceptually unstable. Under attack it tends to collapse into either a form of nominalism or a form of realism. Rescher virtually admits this. His position tends to be nominalistic, he tells us, "in that it finds nonexistent possibles to be rooted in the language-using capacity of minds." He continues:

> But it is also conceptualistic, in embracing possible as well as actual languages, stressing the need to consider not only actual language-utterances, but also what is potentially utterable by language users. Indeed this emphasis on what is possible— on the *discussible* rather than more narrowly upon the *discussed* - even endows our seemingly nominalistic position with a faintly realistic coloration. (p. 122)

It is far from clear, once the nominalist and realist tendencies in Rescher's position are taken away, that there remains anything genuinely conceptualistic in the original sense of "mind-dependent". In what follows I'll treat the nominalist residue as indefensible, by virtue of my earlier arguments against Carnap, and concentrate on showing that Rescher's conceptualism, if it is to be rendered at all plausible, is forced to take refuge in a realism of abstract unactualized possibilities.

When one first reads Rescher's assertion that unactualized possibilities exist "only in so far as they are to be *conceived of*", it is natural to take him to be subscribing to the bold claim that their *esse* is *concipi*. Yet it soon turns out that he is not saying that they exist only insofar as they *are* conceived of, but instead that they exist only insofar as they are *to be* conceived of, where the expression "are to be conceived of" means the same as "are *conceivable* ".

Why this move from an emphasis on what is actually conceived to what is possibly conceived? Rescher makes it in response to several objections: that possibilities need to be accorded an objective basis independent of any specific minds (p. 202); that it was surely possible, before there were any minds in the universe, that there should be minds (p. 206); that allowance has to be made for *unthought-of* possibilities (p. 213); and that, if possibility were mind-dependent, then events in the extramental world could not possibly be other than they actually are (p. 218).

There is another reason, too (unacknowledged by Rescher), which forces his move towards realism. As we saw in Chapter I, section 5, Wittgenstein wants to provide for the possibility of there being *infinitely* many nonactual combinations of states of affairs. And in this he is surely right. Indeed, it may plausibly be argued, as it is by David Lewis, that there is a nondenumerable infinity of possible states of affairs. But since there would seem to be only countably many actual conceivings of states of affairs, the number of possibilities, if infinite, must outstrip the number of psychological events (or states of affairs) of conception.

The main trouble with Rescher's retreat from "conceive" to "conceivability" is, of course, that it invites the charge of circularity. An explanation of the ontological status of unactualized possibilities that requires reference to unactualized possibilities of conception is no explanation at all. Rescher makes a brave attempt to evade this charge when he claims, "our position is not *circular* but *reductive*: its stance is that *all* possibilities are in the final analysis inherent in and derivative from mental possibility." (p. 218). Yet surely this gives the game away. For, in order to meet the previously considered objections, Rescher must allow that mental possibility (by which, it is clear, he means "the capacity of minds to conceive, hypothesize, project, etc.") ranges far beyond mental actuality (actual conceivings, hypothesizing, projecting, and so forth). However, if it is allowed that there is even *one* possible but nonactual state of affairs of conceiving, then, as we have already seen, it must also be allowed that there are many maximally consistent sets of states of affairs such that that nonactual state of affairs of conceiving is a member of each. But this is just to allow, what the realist insists on, that there are many nonactual possible worlds, the existence of each of which is independent of both languages and minds. Rescher's emphasis on the *discussible*, rather than the *discussed*, does not give his position only a "faintly realistic coloration". It gives his position a thoroughly saturated realistic hue.

13. Kinds of Realism Regarding Other Worlds

Wittgenstein, like Leibniz, is a realist with respect to the ontological status of merely possible worlds. Nowhere in the *Notebooks* or the *Tractatus* does he display any inclination to adopt a nominalist ploy or to speak in anything less than a robustly realistic way about possible worlds and possible states of affairs. And we know, on quite general grounds, that, like Frege, he was strenuously opposed to any threatened intrusion of psychologism (of which conceptualism, after all, is a form) into the philosophy of logic. I have already argued that he is to be located somewhere within the realist camp. But where?

Three theses seem to me comprise the core of possible worlds realism:[10]

   (i) Modal statements—about necessity, possibility (actualized or unactualized), and the like—are either true or false.
  (ii) Their truth or falsity is a function of the properties of independently existing objects, namely, possible worlds and their constituents (not of the conventions of human language or the functioning of human minds).
 (iii) Their possessing these truth-values is independent of our ability (or inability) to determine which truth-values they possess.

Thesis (i) rules out the view, advanced by Russell and the early Quine, that modal statements are strictly meaningless. Thesis (ii) rules out both nominalism and conceptualism. Thesis (iii) rules out any form of conceptualistic constructivism, and emphasizes the non-epistemic, metaphysical character of possible worlds realism.

Other theses, however, might also be added. Among those which have seemed plausible to some who think of themselves as realists, are the following:

  (iv) Other possible worlds may have concrete entities among their constituents.
   (v) Other possible worlds themselves are concrete entities.
  (vi) The constituents of other possible worlds, though not identical to any in the actual world, are sometimes sufficiently like them to be regarded as their "counterparts".
 (vii) The inhabitants (if any) of other possible worlds have just as much right as we do to claim actuality for themselves and their surroundings.

Now a distinction has sometimes been drawn between the so-called moderate realism of Robert Stalnaker [1976], who stops after the first three, and the more extreme realism of David Lewis, who endorses all seven theses. But since it would, I suggest, be a futile exercise to try to say precisely where the line of demarcation between moderation and extremity should be drawn, I'll use these two epithets only occasionally, and then with deliberate caution.

We have already examined theses (vi) and (vii), and (if my arguments are sound) have found them to be both seriously counterintuitive and inconsistent with Wittgenstein's position. It remains for us to examine each of the first five and try to determine Wittgenstein's commitments with respect to them. In the course of doing so, however, we shall also take a look at the views of Stalnaker and a further look at some of the views of Lewis. If I am right, Wittgenstein's position is to be located somewhere between the supposed moderation of the former and the alleged extremity of the latter.

(i) The Truth and Falsity of Modal Statements

By a "modal statement" I mean a statement, or putative statement, that asserts that something has a modal property or stands in a modal relation to something else. Two sorts of modal property-attribution need to be distinguished: First, there is the de dicto case in which a modal property is attributed to a "dictum", that is, to a statement or proposition, as when we say that a proposition is necessary, tautologous, impossible, contradictory, possible, contingent, or the like. Second, there is the de re case in which a modal property is attributed to an object, as when we say that an object has a certain property essentially, necessarily, internally, contingently, accidentally, externally, or the like. Furthermore, modal statements include any statement that asserts that a modal *relation* holds between two or more propositions, as when we say that one proposition implies, entails, is consistent with, is inconsistent with, is independent of another.

On this account, none of the following:

(21) Either the earth is round or it is not the case that the earth is round
(22) Socrates is self-identical
(23) If the Pope knows that there are 9 planets then there are 9 planets

is a modal statement. They may be tautological or necessarily true, but since they do not *say* that they have these or any other modal properties, they do not count as modal statements. On the other hand, each of the following

(24) Necessarily, either the earth is round or it is not the case that the earth is round
(25) Socrates is essentially self-identical
(26) The Pope's knowing that there are 9 planets entails that there are 9 planets

is a modal statement. They ascribe modal properties to propositions or objects (as in statements (24) and (25), respectively) or assert the presence of a modal relation between propositions (as in statement (26)).

Now it is clear that numerous modal statements occur in both the *Notebooks* and the *Tractatus*. To pick just three examples [with emphases added], "A speck in the visual field, though it *need not* be red, *must* have some color" (2.0131(2)); "States of affairs are *independent* of one another" (2.061); "The statement that a point in the visual field has two different colors at the same time is a *contradiction.*" (6.3751(3).

But does Wittgenstein regard statements like these as true or false? An argument could be mounted for saying that he does not. After all, he does say such things as the following: "Tautologies and contradictions lack sense" (4.461(3)); "the propositions of logic say nothing. (They are the analytic propositions)" (6.11); and "One cannot say of a tautology that it is true, for it is *made so as to be true*" (*NB* 55(4)).

We must proceed carefully here, however. In the first place, the objection fails since the tautologies, contradictions, propositions of logic and analytic propositions that he is talking about in the passages just cited turn out to be *non*modal statements belonging in the same category as (21), (22), and (23). So, even if statements like (21), (22), and (23) were taken, quite literally, to lack sense, say nothing or even lack a truth-value, it would not follow that the corresponding modal statements— (24), (25), and (26)—are neither true nor false. Second, and more importantly, we need to realize that although Wittgenstein is often tempted to say that only statements about what is contingent or accidental can really be "true or false", or count as "genuine propositions", he does not mean this in the sense that we usually associate with those words. For him, remember, tautologies and contradictions "lack sense" only in the sense of not having their truth-values determined by any contingent matters of fact. The propositions of logic "say nothing" only in the sense that, since they are true in all possible worlds, they say nothing *that would enable us to distinguish other possible worlds from the actual world.* For similar reasons, he says that the propositions of logic or the propositions of mathematics are "pseudo-propositions". But this is little more than a rhetorical device for reminding us how unlike contingent propositions they are. He says, in the first clause of *NB* 55(4), that one cannot "say" of a tautology that it is true. But in the second clause he succumbs to ordinary usage and finds himself "saying" it nonetheless. There can be little doubt, then, that Wittgenstein endorses thesis (i).

(ii) Truth-Values Determined by Independently Existing Objects

The evidence, this time, is quite straightforward and conclusive. In 4.46, Wittgenstein tells us that when a proposition is "true for all truth-possibilities of the elementary propositions" the proposition is a tautology and that when it is "false for all the truth-possibilities" it is a contradiction. Take these claims together with his explication of what he means by "truth-possibilities of elementary propositions", namely, "possibilities of existence and non-existence of states of affairs" (4.3), and recall that sets of possibilities of existence and nonexistence of states of affairs just *are* possible worlds. It then follows that the truth or falsity of tautologies and contradictions is a function of the agreement or disagreement of these propositions with possible worlds, or, to put it more simply, that possible worlds are their truth-makers.

In effect, then, (ii) is the principle behind the construction of Wittgenstein's truth-tables. He explains: "We can represent truth-possibilities by schemata of the following kind ('T' means 'true', 'F' means 'false'; the rows of 'T's' and 'F's' under the rows of elementary propositions symbolize their truth-possibilities in a way that can be easily understood)." (4.31). Thus it turns out (a) that a proposition or proposition-schema (5.101) is a tautology if it is true for all truth-possibilities of the elementary propositions, that is, if it is true for all possibilities of the existence and non-existence of the corresponding states of affairs, that is, if it is true in all possible worlds; (b) that a proposition or proposition-schema is a contradiction if it is false in all possible worlds; and (c) that a proposition or proposition-schema has sense, that is, is contingent, if it is true for some and false for other possible worlds.

(iii) Truth-Values Independent of Human Knowledge

A philosopher who subscribes to this thesis will want to deny anything like Rescher's conceptualism or Brouwer's mathematical intuitionism. Despite the fact that Wittgenstein, in his later thinking, seems to have flirted with the latter, I believe his early writing was wholly antithetical to it.

Consider once more his claim, "For n states of affairs, there are $[2^n]$ possibilities of existence and non-existence." (4.27(1)). In Chapter 2, I argued that this passage, when taken together with *NB* 14(4), *NB* 127(2), and 4.2211, shows that he believes it possible for there to be infinitely many possible combinations of states of affairs, that is, infinitely many possible worlds. Now it is unlikely that he thought the human mind capable of considering each of all these infinitely many possible worlds in order thereby to determine the modal status of any given statement. But even if he did think that human minds had such capacities it still would not follow that he thought that the modal status that a statement has is somehow dependent on our knowledge of it. There is no suggestion, in his early work, that being tautological and being contradictory are epistemological properties. On the contrary, he defines them, in 4.46, quite independently of any epistemological considerations, in terms of possibilistic truth-conditions in what we nowadays call a possible-worlds semantics.

So far, we have seen that Wittgenstein is committed to each of the core theses that I take to be definitive of modal realism. These three theses, however, are also endorsed by Stalnaker and constitute what he calls "moderate realism". Before proceeding further, to the examination of Wittgenstein's stance regarding (iv) and (v), let's take a look at some of the differences between Wittgenstein and Stalnaker regarding (i), (ii), and (iii).

14. Stalnaker's Moderate Realism

Robert Stalnaker, in his paper "Possible Worlds" [1976], coined the term "moderate realism" in order to mark off his position from what he called the "extreme realism" of David Lewis. His own position, it turns out, is remarkably similar to that of Robert Merrihew Adams. Indeed, Stalnaker devotes a good deal of his paper to arguing that, were Adams to adopt two further claims that he believes to be true, Adams's soft actualist account would become "equivalent" to his own possible worlds account with the sole difference that "one takes as primitive what the other defines." (p. 233).

The two further claims are

(I) Necessarily equivalent propositions are identical.

and

(C) For every set of propositions, there is a proposition which, necessarily, is true if and only if every member of the set is true.

The first of these is forced on Stalnaker by virtue of the fact that, whereas Adams reduces possible worlds to sets of propositions (Adams's primitives), Stalnaker tries to effect the reverse reduction of propositions to sets of possible worlds (Stalnaker's primitives). A consequence of Stalnaker's reduction, of course, is claim (I). For, if we refuse to distinguish between propositions and worlds, we thereby preclude ourselves from speaking of propositions as being true (or false) "in" worlds. And then, instead of saying that there can be two or more nonidentical necessarily true propositions that are true "in" the set of all possible worlds, we shall have to say that any two necessarily true propositions are *identical* with the set of all possible worlds, from which it follows—by virtue of the transitivity of identity— that any two necessarily true propositions are identical with one another. Stalnaker realizes that (I) has some "notoriously problematic consequences", but thinks they can be explained away and should be accepted in the interests of the theoretical economy that (I) brings about. (For instance, instead of saying that P implies Q if and only if the set of worlds in which P is true is included in the set of worlds in which Q is true, we can simply say that P is a subset of Q.)

The second claim, (C), Stalnaker points out, is "reasonable on almost any theory of propositions" since "if there are propositions at all then there are sets of them, and for any set of propositions, it is something determinately true or false that all the members of the set are true" (whether or not it is humanly possible to grasp them or even refer to such sets of propositions). (p. 232).

Not only does Stalnaker *call* himself a realist with respect to the status of non-actual possible worlds; his theory satisfies each of the core conditions—(i), (ii), and (iii)—for possible-worlds realism. He believes modal statements to be true or false, not just some form of metaphysical nonsense or strictly meaningless blather. He believes that their truth or falsity is a matter of whether possible worlds are as these modal statements, when analyzed, say they are. And, as his espousal of thesis (C) shows, he believes that their truth or falsity in no way depends upon our epistemic powers.

Yet Stalnaker is also an actualist. Indeed, like Adams, he is a soft actualist. Both he and Adams believe that to talk about nonactual possible worlds is to talk about certain kinds of abstract entities that exist in the actual world. Only, whereas Adams believes that other possible worlds are "logically constructed" out of those actually existing abstract entities which we call propositions, Stalnaker believes that other possible worlds don't need any constructing at all since they just "are", that is, are identical to, another kind of actually existing abstract entity, namely, those uninstantiated properties which he calls *ways things might have been*. Adams, he complains, is an "eliminative reductionist" since he tries to reduce statements about nonactual possible worlds to statements about sets of propositions. But nonactual possible worlds, by his own account, need no such reduction to allegedly more respectable entities. "Why," he asks, "cannot *ways things might have been* be elements of the actual world as they are?" (p. 230). *Ways things might have been* and *ways things are*, for him, are both properties that are elements of the actual world. They differ, principally, in so far as the properties of being *ways things might have been*, though capable of instantiation, are in fact uninstantiated, whereas the property of being *the way things are* happens to be instantiated.

By virtue of his claim that nonactual possible worlds are identical with *ways things might have been*, and hence are "respectable entities in their own right", Stalnaker apparently takes sides with Lewis against Adams. But it may be doubted whether Lewis would take much comfort from Stalnaker's verbal support. Lewis thinks of nonactual possible worlds as "ways things could have been", certainly, but takes these to be *instantiated* properties. The fact that Stalnaker accepts Lewis's characterization of nonactual possible worlds as "ways things might have been" certainly does not carry him further down the road to Lewis's extreme realism than thesis (iii). Rather, his claim that other worlds are abstract properties commits him to the rejection of (iv), that they have concrete entities among their constituents; of (v), that they themselves are concrete entities; and of (vi), that they may be inhabited by concrete counterparts of objects that exist in the actual world.

It might be thought, however, that Stalnaker would agree with (vii). For he does say that he agrees with the indexical analysis of the adjective "actual", an analysis that Lewis thinks entails (vii), the relativity of actuality. But although Stalnaker agrees with what he calls "the *semantical* thesis that the indexical analysis of 'actual' is correct", he disagrees with what he calls "the metaphysical thesis that the actuality of the actual world is nothing more than a relation between it and things existing in it." (p. 229). Stalnaker is making a point somewhat similar to one I made on Wittgenstein's behalf when I argued that one might well say, with Wittgenstein, that the actual world is the world that is picked out, in the actual world, by such indexical-loaded expressions as "this world", "our world", and "the world we live in", and yet at the same time insist on the *metaphysical* claim that the world so picked out is the actual world absolutely, not just relative to us. As Stalnaker expresses it, "the standpoint of the actual world *is* the absolute standpoint, and . . . it is part of the concept of actuality that this should be so. We can grant that fictional characters are as right, from their standpoint, to affirm their full-blooded reality as we are to affirm ours. But their point of view is fictional, and so what is right from it makes no difference as far as reality is concerned." (p. 229). To repeat, Stalnaker's "agreement" with Lewis is verbal only. Although he endorses the semantical construal of the indexical theory of actuality, he rejects the metaphysical construal that yields (vii).

15. Stalnaker on Propositions and Sets of Worlds

Stalnaker's identification of propositions with sets of worlds gives his theory a certain economy and elegance that it would otherwise lack. But it runs into difficulties on at least four counts.

First, it is counterintuitive. We think, and speak, of propositions as having truthmakers, as being true "in" certain states of affairs and worlds, false "in" others. We think of propositions, not worlds, as the objects of belief and seem not to have assigned any viable meaning to expressions like "Stalnaker believes such-and-such a set of possible worlds." In other words, we think and talk of propositions as being true or false—in the kind of way that Wittgenstein maintained—according to whether they "correspond" (4.28) to possibilities of existence and nonexistence of states of affairs. We can, without absurdity, pair off propositions with the sets of worlds in which they are true. But that is different from identifying them with those sets of worlds.

Secondly, it entails that there is only one necessarily true proposition (and, for that matter, only one necessarily false proposition). This is counterintuitive, since it conflicts with our ordinary disposition to say, for instance, that the proposition

(27) $2 \times 2 = 4$

is different from the proposition

(28) $3 + 4 = 7$

Surely, we want to say, they must be different since they are about different numbers and involve different arithmetical operations. Again, it is counterintuitive by virtue of the fact that it entails that if I believe any necessarily true proposition—of logic, say, or mathematics—then I believe all of them. Yet surely my knowledge of logic and mathematics doesn't come so easily. As for myself, I do know some truths of both domains, but I certainly don't know them all. Moreover, if knowing truths of mathematics is a matter of proving them, and Godel is right, I *can't* know them all since, as he proved, there are true but unprovable propositions in any mathematical or logical system rich enough to contain Peano's axioms for arithmetic. We can say, if we like, that all necessary truths are *equivalent*, indeed logically equivalent. But we invite needless paradox and self- inconsistency if we say, with Stalnaker, that all necessary truths are strictly *identical*.

Third, identifying propositions with sets of worlds has the consequence that the conjunction of a necessary truth with a contingent proposition is not just equivalent to that contingent proposition but identical to it. Consider, for instance, the conjunction (or "logical product", as Wittgenstein calls it) of the necessarily true proposition (27) and the contingent proposition

(29) Ronald Reagan was President.

Since the conjunction of (27) and (29) is true in exactly the same set of possible worlds as is (29) alone, the conjunction of (27) and (29) is logically equivalent to (29). Yet if, with Stalnaker, we choose to identify propositions with sets of worlds, then we must also say that the conjunction of (27) and (29) is *identical* with (29). But how can this be? Surely, the conjunction of (27) and (29) is a compound proposition with two propositional constituents, one of which is the necessary truth (27), whereas (29) is not a compound proposition and certainly does not have (27) as a conjunct.

Now I think Wittgenstein is not as clear as he might be about the distinction between propositional identity and propositional equivalence. On the one hand, of precisely the sort of case we have just been considering, he tells us, "The logical product of a tautology and a proposition says the same thing as the proposition. This product, therefore, is identical with the proposition." (4.465). We might accept the first claim, since the logical product of the two will indeed say the same contingent thing as—be true in the same states of affairs as—the genuine proposition. The two will be equivalent. But, if we distinguish strict identity from equivalence and take him to be talking about strict identity, we will want to reject the second claim. Again, and more generally, he tells us, "If *p* follows from *q* and *q* from *p*, then they are one and the same proposition." (5.141). In the case we have been considering, the product of (27) and (29) does follow from (29), and (29) does follow from the product of (27) and (29). So, once more, he is claiming that where P is equivalent to Q, P is the "same" proposition as Q.

On the other hand, there is a passage in the *Notebooks* that demonstrates his recognition of a distinction between strict identity and related notions. In *NB* 113(2) he asserts that there are many nonidentical necessary truths, of the kind that he calls logical propositions or tautologies: "*Logical propositions*, OF COURSE, all shew something different: all of them shew, *in the same way*, viz., by the fact that they are tautologies, but they are different."

It may be that the apparent discrepancy between this passage and those from the

Tractatus is a consequence of Wittgenstein's deliberate policy of not going into details in the later, more compressed work and that he had not really lost sight of the distinction at all. If this were the case, we might charitably suppose him to be saying, in the *Tractatus*, that equivalent propositions are identical, not *tout court*, but *identical in respect of* the worlds in which they are true, or something like that. However, it may be that he changed his mind or simply forgot his earlier insights. Be all that as it may, the fact remains that his earlier remarks reflect the sound intuitions that lead most of us, on reflection (if not before), to distinguish between different necessary truths. And this is something we can do only if we reject Stalnaker's identification of propositions with sets of worlds.

The fourth criticism that might be made of Stalnaker, in quite general terms and on general Wittgensteinian grounds, is that Stalnaker's move does not permit us to make some of the finer-grained discriminations between propositions that we can, and commonly do, make. We can and do distinguish between the compound proposition

(30) Stalnaker is now thinking of proposition (27), that is, $2 \times 2 = 4$

and the compound proposition

(31) Stalnaker is now thinking of proposition (28), that is, $3 + 4 = 7$.

The fact that (30) could be true whereas (31) is false, *shows* that they are different. And the fact that they have different simple propositions—(27) and (28)—as their constituents, explains why they are different. Likewise, the fact that (27) and (28) have different concepts as their constituents explains why they in turn are different. What makes the difference between two nonidentical equivalent propositions, ultimately, is the fine-grained structure (= the determinate "connection of its elements" (2.15)) of the propositions themselves. Stalnaker's account of propositions, and of propositional identity, is too coarse-grained to permit these distinctions. This is why Stalnaker cannot accommodate these facts or their explanations within his theory. But Wittgenstein can. For him, remember, identity of object is expressed by identity of sign. And, more pertinently, difference of object—whether the object is a compound proposition, a simple proposition, or a constituent concept in a simple proposition—is expressed by difference of sign (5.53). Hence, for him, (30) and (31) are not the same.

16. Stalnaker's Commitment to Actualism

Stalnaker tells us, "by 'possible world' we mean nothing more than 'way things might have been' . . . ." (p. 229). And, since *ways things might have been*, he further believes, are abstract properties that exist in the actual world, he concludes that we can talk about nonactual possible worlds within the general conceptual framework of actualism. Nonactual possible worlds are those *ways things might have been* which, though they exist in the actual world, are not instantiated in it.

But does this defence of actualism work? Once more, it is hard to see precisely how our intuitions about the existence of nonactual objects, such as "additional" elementary particles, and nonactual states of affairs such as Ronald Reagan's remaining a film actor, are to be accommodated. I've already argued that Adams's soft actualism founders in its attempts to address these issues. And, I'll now argue, Stalnaker's fares no better, for two main reasons.

In the first place, consider how, on Stalnaker's account, we are supposed to analyze the claim that Ronald Reagan might have remained a film actor. Since he tells us, "by 'possible world' we mean nothing more than '*way things might have been*'", we ought, presumably, to be able to substitute the latter expression for the former in all non-quotational occurrences. So let's try. From

(2) There is a possible world in which Ronald Reagan remains a film actor

we derive

(33) There is a *way things might have been* in which Ronald Reagan remains a film actor.

But this is strictly absurd. A *way things might have been*, remember, is a property. And how can the object that is Ronald Reagan, or the state of affairs of his remaining a film actor, be "in" a property? Of course, (33) might be read as nonabsurd: by construing the expression "*a way things might have been*" as referring to an *instantiation* of a possible-world property (that is, to a genuine possible world) rather than to a possible-world property tout court. But that will not do for Stalnaker. For, according to him, there is only one such instantiation, namely, that which we call the actual world, and in that world it is false that Ronald Reagan remains a film actor. There are no other instantiations of *ways the world might have been* for Reagan to feature in.

We might try to be still more accommodating by altering syntax a little and considering

(34) There is a *way things might have been* which includes Ronald Reagan's remaining a film actor

where "a *way things might have been*" is to be taken as denoting a *set* of uninstantiated properties and "Ronald Reagan's remaining a film actor" is taken as denoting the complex property of *being Ronald Reagan and remaining a film actor*. But this will not do either. For it will then follow that if we say, "Ronald Reagan might have remained a film actor", we are not talking about Ronald Reagan and something that might have happened to him but are talking about something else, the membership of one uninstantiated property in a set of uninstantiated properties. Probably Ronald Reagan could not care less whether the uninstantiated property of *being Ronald Reagan and remaining a film actor* is a member of a wider set of uninstantiated properties. But I venture to assert that he cared very much about the possibility that *he* would remain a film actor and fail in his attempt to become President.[11] Stalnaker's account, like Adams's, changes the subject of discourse.

A second problem has to do with the distinction between existence and instantiation. It is essential to Stalnaker's defence of actualism that properties can exist without being instantiated. In itself the distinction between existence and instantiation is relatively trouble-free. We need some such distinction in order to accommodate our intuition that it is possible for there to exist properties, such as that of *being the missing shade of blue* that Hume talked about, that are not instantiated in the actual world. But Stalnaker's use of the distinction raises questions that I think he might find difficult to answer. He wants to say that properties in general, the property of *being a way things might have been* among them, "exist" in the actual world while denying that some of them, the property of *being a way things might have been* in particular, are "instantiated" in the actual world. Why, one wants to know, does he not apply the same distinction to the case of nonactual possible objects? Why, for instance, will he not say that nonactual possible objects, such as "additional" elementary particles or Sherlock Holmes, also "exist" in the actual world without being instantiated in it? He does not want to say any such thing, of course. But it is difficult to see how he can avoid saying it except at the cost of retreat to a long-discredited account of what objects are. Thus the preceding questions become urgent once we ask the further question, What, on his account, is an object apart from its properties? If an object is just a structured collection of properties, as some would suggest,[12] then there would seem to be no good reason for Stalnaker to deny that the structured collection of properties that constitutes a nonactual possible object, such as Sherlock Holmes, "exists" in the actual world, even though that collection is not "instantiated" in the actual world. But if he were to allow that, then he would thereby be allowing that Sherlock Holmes also "exists" in the actual world even though he is not "instantiated" in the actual world. And that would not sound right. Stalnaker [1976] finds it comforting to be able to point out that, in his theory, abstract properties such as *ways things might have been* are "elements of the actual world". (p. 230). But it certainly would go against the grain for him to have to admit that, by the same token, the structured collection of abstract properties that (on the suggestion before us) is identical with Sherlock Holmes is also an element of the actual world. Yet it is difficult to see how he can avoid such a conclusion without adopting the rival theory that objects are somehow distinct from all their properties, that they are featureless substrata which somehow "support", "have", or "possess" properties. Stalnaker, in short, is faced with a dilemma. If he thinks of objects, in general, as structured collections of properties, and if properties, in general, are abstract objects that exist in the actual world even when not instantiated in it, then he should also allow for the existence in the actual world of those structured collections of properties that are identical with nonactual possible objects. If he does not think of objects in this way, then, at the very least, he owes us an account of what objects are that will enable him to avoid the conclusion that they are—as Locke would have put it, disparagingly—a "something I know not what" that "supports" properties.

The distinction between existence and instantiation, then, is made to bear a weight, in Stalnaker's theory, similar to that borne by the older distinction between subsistence and existence. Many philosophers, the early Russell among them, found it plausible to say that abstract entities such as properties and relations have a "mode of being" different from that of ordinary spatiotemporal things. Properties and relations, it was said, "subsist"; only spatiotemporal objects "exist". As Russell said in *The Problems of Philosophy* ,

We shall find it convenient only to speak of things *existing* when they are in time, that is to say, when we can point to some time *at* which they exist (not excluding the possibility of their existing at all times). Thus thoughts and feelings, minds and physical objects *exist*. But universals do not exist in this sense; we shall say that they *subsist* or *have being*, where "being" is opposed to "existence" as being timeless. (pp. 99–100)

Stalnaker changes the terminology (in a way that is likely to mislead), so that what the early Russell said "subsists", Stalnaker says "exists" and what Russell said "exists", Stalnaker says "is instantiated".[13] My objection to Stalnaker's actualist attempt to do away with nonactual possible objects might be couched in terms of the older terminology by saying that, unless he can give us an account according to which an object is not just a structured collection of properties, he must allow that nonactual possible objects "subsist" even if they don't "exist" in the actual world. But to allow that, of course, would be to abandon strict actualism for a terminological variant of possibilism.

17. Stalnaker and the Internal/External Distinction

A further unwelcome consequence of Stalnaker's position is that it entails the impossibility of anything's ever having any properties other than those it in fact has. That is to say, it entails that, in the previously defined senses of "essential" and "accidental", every property of an object is an essential property of that object and that no properties are accidental. To be sure, Stalnaker does not consciously embrace such a conclusion. Nevertheless, it is easy to show that he is committed to it.

Stalnaker claims that it is important to distinguish the property of being *the way things are* from the world (if any) that instantiates that property:

The way things are is a property or state of the world, not the world itself. The statement that the world is the way it is is true in a sense, but not when read as an identity statement (Compare: 'the way the world is is the world'). This is important, since if properties can exist uninstantiated, then *the way the world is* could exist even if a world that is that way did not. (p. 228)

The actual world, then, is to be identified not with the property, *the way things are*, but with the instantiation of that property. So we may infer

(35) The actual world = the instantiation of *the way things are*.

Stalnaker also asserts

(36) Other possible worlds = *ways things might have been*

while denying that there are any *instantiations* of such properties. His "other possible worlds", then, are what Lewis calls "ersatz worlds" since they are intended as substitutes, in Stalnaker's theory, for what more realist-minded theorists regard as genuine possible worlds, that is, for what Stalnaker would call "instantiations of *ways things might have been* ".

Now Stalnaker's avowed actualism entails

(37) Other possible worlds [ersatz worlds] exist *in* the actual world.

So we can immediately infer, from (37) and (35), that

(38) Other possible worlds [ersatz worlds] exist in the instantiation of *the way things are.*

And again, from (36) and (38), we infer that

(39) *Ways things might have been* exist in the instantiation of *the way things are.*

Not daunted by what is beginning to sound a bit like mumbo jumbo, we press on. Stalnaker claims that ersatz worlds are not in fact instantiated. But now we want to know what *possible* instantiation Stalnaker's ersatz worlds might have? What entities might possibly instantiate such properties as *ways things might have been* ? Clearly, these ersatz worlds cannot possibly be instantiated by (or in) the actual world (for presumably the actual world cannot instantiate the property of being any "other" world, distinct from itself). That is to say, it is surely true that

(40) *Ways things might have been* cannot be instantiated by (or in) the instantiation of *the way things are.*

But equally, since there are no entities "outside" the actual world—no non-ersatz possible worlds—for his ersatz worlds to be instantiated by, it is surely also true that

(41) *Ways things might have been* cannot be instantiated by (or in) the instantiations of *ways things might have been.*

But being instantiated by (or in) the actual world and being instantiated by (or in) some non-ersatz "other" world—the two possibilities encompassed by (40) and (41), respectively—plainly exhaust all the possible modes of instantiation for *ways things might have been.* And since *ways things might have been* cannot be instantiated in either case, our unwanted conclusions follow swiftly. We may think that Ronald Reagan could have turned down the Presidency and remained a film actor, that he could have instantiated the complex property of *being Ronald Reagan and remaining a film actor.* But we are wrong. No uninstantiated properties, no unactualized possibilities, can ever be instantiated by him, by you, by me, or by anyone or anything else. If a property is not in fact instantiated, then it is impossible for it to be instantiated. Every property is essential to the objects that instantiate it.

The preceding criticism is couched in the sort of language which Stalnaker uses. It may become clearer if stated in more colloquial terms. Given that by "*way things might have been*" he means "the property of *possibly being otherwise* ", the argument goes like this: Since the property of *possibly being otherwise* is not instantiated in the actual world, there is nothing in the actual world that *has* the property of *possibly being otherwise.* Since, in merely possible (nonactual) worlds there exist no objects that are possible instantiators of any properties whatever, there is nothing in a merely possible world that has the property of *possibly being otherwise.* Hence there is nothing in any possible world that has the property of *possibly being otherwise.*

Stalnaker's moderate realism, then, for all that it promises to take possible worlds talk seriously while avoiding the extremities of Lewis's position, runs into serious problems. And it does so, I have argued, mainly by virtue of both its reductionism (propositions being reduced to sets of worlds) and its actualism (the refusal to allow the existence of entities that do not exist in the actual world).

18. Extreme Realism and the Issue of Concreteness

Lewis's realism, it will be recalled, was characterized by his commitment to all of theses (i) to (vii), as enumerated in section 13. Now one of the things that philosophers like Stalnaker find "extreme" about this sort of realism is its readiness to embrace theses (iv) and (v): the beliefs that other possible worlds either contain concrete entities (thesis (iv)) or themselves are scattered concrete objects (thesis (v)). As Stalnaker [1976] puts it, "Even a philosopher who had no qualms about abstract entities like numbers, properties, states and kinds might balk at this proliferation of full-blooded universes which seem less real than our own only because we have never been there." (p. 228).

Lewis commits himself to both (iv) and (v) when, in *Counterfactuals*, he answers a hypothetical person who asks what sort of thing a possible world is by saying, "I can only ask him to admit that he knows what sort of thing our actual world is, and then explain that other worlds are more things of *that* sort, differing not in kind but only in what goes on at them." (p. 184). As he expands it, his claim that other worlds are of the same "sort" as the actual world turns out to involve saying that they, like it, contain concrete entities, such things as "I and all my surroundings". Thus, in rejecting the nominalist's attempt to identify possible worlds with sets of sentences, he argues, "given that the actual world does not differ in kind from the rest, it would lead to the conclusion that our actual world is a set of sentences. Since I cannot believe that I and all my surroundings are a set of sentences (though I have no argument that they are not), I cannot believe that other worlds are sets of sentences either." (p. 184). In short, other possible worlds, as well as the actual one, are sometimes inhabited by what he calls "concrete particulars", that is, by things like people, flames, buildings, and puddles. And these worlds themselves are concrete as well.

Lewis addresses the issue of concreteness more fully in *On The Plurality of Worlds*:

> I take it, at least, that donkeys and protons and puddles and stars are supposed to be paradigmatically concrete. I take it also that the division between abstract and concrete is meant to divide entities into fundamentally different kinds. If so, then it is out of the question that an abstract entity and a concrete entity should be exactly alike, perfect duplicates. According to my modal realism, the donkeys and protons and puddles and stars that are part of this world have perfect duplicates that are parts of other worlds. This suffices to settle, whatever exactly it might mean, that at least some possible individuals are concrete. And if so, then at least some possible worlds are at least partly "concrete". (p. 82)

As for whole worlds, he writes:

> And what of a whole world? Is it sufficiently donkey like, despite its size? And perhaps despite the fact that it consists mostly of empty space-time? I am inclined to say that . . . a world is concrete rather than abstract—more donkey-like than number-like. (p. 82 f)

Doubtless, the distinction between concreteness and abstractness isn't entirely clear. Lewis goes to some lengths to sort out what the difference might amount to and still finds it somewhat elusive. Nevertheless, we may agree with him that there is indeed a difference, and that it is paradigmatically exemplified by cases of donkeys, protons, puddles, and stars on the one hand, and numbers on the other hand. Construe theses (iv) and (v) in light of these paradigms. Are they defensible? And what would Wittgenstein want to say about them?

For a start, these two theses do seem to accord with our ordinary ways of thinking about alternative possible states of affairs. Think about a particular object: a donkey, a puddle, or a star. And, if you can, look at one of them. Now suppose that you had not looked at that particular object. Suppose, that is, that the world had been different in this respect, namely, that you had not looked at it after all. Would a world in which you had not looked at the donkey, puddle, or star be one in which the donkey, the puddle, or the star somehow lost its concreteness and became an abstract object? Surely, in entertaining any of these counterfactual possibilities, you are thinking of worlds whose objects are every bit as concrete as those of the actual world. The very same concrete donkey, puddle or whatnot that features in the actual world features also, *as a concrete object*, in our thinking about these other possible worlds. Thesis (iv), then, certainly has the support of our ordinary ways of thinking about unrealized possibilities.

And so does thesis (v). Think of the possibility that the world might have been populated by just one fewer proton, or other presumed elementary particle. Are you, in doing so, thinking of a world that somehow has lost all the concreteness of the actual world? Surely not. Rather, I suggest, you are thinking of a world in which there is just one fewer of the concrete objects that are constituents of the actual world, and all those that remain are just as concrete as they would be had the world not been depleted in this way.

But, it might be argued, if worlds are, as Wittgenstein and others so often think of them, totalities of objects-in-configuration, and we think of these totalities as maximally consistent sets of states of affairs, then, since sets are paradigmatically abstract objects, it will follow that worlds themselves are abstract objects, notwithstanding the fact that they may have ever so many concrete objects among their constituents. This argument, if we were to be persuaded by it, would drive a wedge between (iv) and (v), allowing us to accept (iv) while rejecting (v).

Now there is indeed a sense, and a common enough one at that, in which any totality whatever may be thought of as comprising a set, and therefore as being an abstract object. Hence, if we think of whole worlds in this way, we do indeed think of them as abstract, not concrete, objects.

But note, first, that in this sense, it is not just other, nonactual, possible worlds that must be counted as abstract objects. By set-theoretical criteria, the actual world, too, is an abstract object. Yet do we in fact think of the actual world as an abstract object? For most purposes, those having little to do with set-theoretical considerations, I suggest we do not. Rather, we most often think of the actual world as an enormous spatiotemporally widespread but nonetheless concrete object, having many concrete objects—donkeys, protons, puddles, stars, and the like—as parts.

Note, second, that the legitimacy of thinking about worlds as sets of states of affairs (and hence as abstract objects) does not in any way count against the legitimacy of thinking of worlds in this other (perhaps more natural) way, as concrete objects. Set-theory doesn't provide the only conceptual framework for thinking about totalities. The mereological theory of Leonard and Goodman [1940][14] provides another. When we conceive of totalities in accordance with mereological theory, we think of the totality which is the actual world itself as comprising a vast, though scattered concrete object. And there is no bar to our thinking of at least some other non-actual worlds in the same way.

It will not do, then, to try to dissipate the intuitive plausibility of (v) by insisting on the way of thinking that would have it that nonactual worlds are merely abstract objects. For, in whatever sense the actual world is to be thought of as the concrete mereological sum of all the objects that are its parts, so, too, may other possible worlds be thought of as the concrete mereological sums of the objects that are their parts. After all, as we have just seen, certain other worlds may differ from the actual world in having just one fewer concrete part. Thesis (v), then, seems as much in accord with our ordinary ways of thinking about worlds as does (iv).

Not only that. Both theses seem forced on us if we accept anything like the sort of essentialism which Wittgenstein espouses. This conclusion is obvious regarding (iv). After all, our paradigms of concrete objects—donkeys, protons, puddles, and stars—are *essentially* concrete objects. Nothing would count as a donkey, a proton, a puddle, or a star, if it were an abstract rather than a concrete object. But then, if we hold, with Wittgenstein, that an essential property is a property that an object cannot fail to have in any world in which the object exists, it follows that those donkeys, protons, puddles, stars, and the like that exist in other possible worlds are concrete objects in these other worlds as well as in our own.

On reflection, it is hard to see how anyone who is happy about possible worlds, about the trans-world identity of some of the objects in those worlds, and about the idea that a property is essential to an object just when it belongs to that object in every world in which the object exists can deny that concrete particulars can feature in possible worlds other than the actual one. Our possible-worlds theory wants to be able to accommodate such intuitions as that

(42) It is possibly but not actually true that Ronald Reagan remains a film actor.

And a natural way of doing so is to construe (21) as equivalent to

(43) There is a possible but nonactual world in which Ronald Reagan remains a film actor.

But it is surely arguable that Ronald Reagan (or, at the very least, his body) is *essentially* a concrete entity, located in space and time, and hence that he is a concrete entity in whatever world he inhabits. Hence, if (42) and (43) are true, we must be prepared to allow concrete particulars *among* the constituents of other possible worlds. And we must also allow that there are at least some other possible worlds, those in which concrete entities such as Reagan exist, that have their own space and time. Certainly, Wittgenstein would have to allow this. For Reagan is a spatial object. And a spatial object, Wittgenstein tells us, "must be situated in infinite space." (2.0131). That is to say, since being situated in space is an essential property of any spatial object, being situated in space is a property that Reagan, along with other spatial objects, has in every world in which he exists. And the same argument applies to the property of being situated in time: it, too, is essential to any object that has it.

The argument from essential properties, just advanced, does not show that whole worlds, as distinct from certain world-constituents, are concrete. But, taken in conjunction with the argument, previously advanced, that totalities of concrete objects may be thought of as mereological sums of these objects, and hence as themselves concrete objects, it does show that thesis (v)—as well as thesis (iv)—is forced on anyone who takes up the kind of realistic position about possible worlds that Wittgenstein adopts and combines it with the essentialist theses that Wittgenstein also adopts.

Wittgenstein, then, is a modal realist whose position falls somewhere between the so-called moderate realism of Stalnaker and the so-called extreme realism of David Lewis. He endorses theses (i) through (v), whereas Stalnaker goes only as far as (iii). Yet he would disagree with the further two theses, (vi) and (vii), which are the hallmark of Lewis's extremeness.

19. Armstrong's Combinatorialist Theory of Possibility

At the beginning of section 2 of this chapter we took a look at Armstrong's attempt (by means of a proportional syllogism) to refute Leibnizian-cum-Lewisian-cum-Wittgensteinian realism about merely possible worlds. His attempt failed. Nevertheless, he has offered other arguments for dispensing with talk of merely possible worlds. I want now to take a brief look at some of these with a view both to determining their adequacy and to highlighting still further features of Wittgenstein's rival position.

What makes Armstrong's theory of possibility—as developed initially in [1986], subsequently more fully in [1989]—particularly pertinent to our present interests is the fact that he thinks of it as a latter-day version of Logical Atomism, one that builds on the combinatorial atomism of Wittgenstein but that, he contends, "traces the very idea of possibility to the idea of the combinations—*all* the combinations—of given actual elements." ([1986], p. 37). If Armstrong is right,

Russell's rejection of modal notions was soundly motivated: modal notions can indeed be *reduced* to nonmodal, actualist ones.

Armstrong agrees with Wittgenstein on a number of scores. Like Wittgenstein, he thinks it plausible to posit a fixed ontology of simple individuals (objects), simple properties, and simple relations whose combinations determine the range of all possible states of affairs, and therewith the range of all those totalities of states of affairs that they both call possible worlds. Like Wittgenstein, he holds that these simples do not exist apart from their combinations in states of affairs from which they are "abstractions" (Armstrong) or "the end-products of analysis" (Wittgenstein). Like Wittgenstein, he thinks that all complexes constructed out of these simples are structured entities having what both (with somewhat different meanings) call "structural properties".[15] As plausible candidates for the role of simple individuals, Armstrong, again like Wittgenstein, suggests the occupied point-instants or material points of physics, while avowing ignorance as to what they will ultimately turn out to be. As to possible worlds, both agree that these are generated out of simple individuals, properties, and relations in a minimum of two stages: first, by combinations of these fixed elements so as to produce elementary states of affairs, merely possible as well as actual; and second, by combinations of possible states of affairs so as to produce whole worlds, merely possible as well as actual. Finally, both agree that there is a need to find what Armstrong calls "truth-makers" (ontological bases) for modal talk.

Yet the differences between the two combinatorial atomisms are great. I draw attention here to some of the more important.[16]

The main differences between them are threefold: (i) Unlike Wittgenstein, Armstrong believes in the actual existence of all the simple individuals, simple properties, and simple relations in his fixed ontology. He rejects the very idea of there being, in other possible worlds, individuals, properties, or relations that are genuinely "alien" to ours. This is a consequence of the fact that Armstrong is an avowed "actual-world chauvinist" who wants his theory to be accommodated within a *Naturalist* ontology, one making do with only those entities which exist in "the single world of space and time" ([1989], p. 30). (ii) Unlike Wittgenstein, Armstrong believes in the *unrestricted promiscuity* of his simple elements (simple objects, simple properties, and simple relations) as well as of the elementary states of affairs that their liaisons produce. Wittgenstein, we have seen, certainly does not grant this to his simple elements. Armstrong [1989], by way of contrast, allows for "all" combinations of the simple elements: "all simple properties and relations are compossible" (p. 49). He implicitly rejects Wittgenstein's claim that simple individuals have essential formal properties that in some cases preclude them from having other properties or from entering into certain combinatorial relations with other simple individuals. (iii) Most importantly, unlike Wittgenstein, Armstrong believes in *modal reductionism*. His theory purports to reduce modal notions in general to the extensionalist notion of "all" combinations of simple elements; he rejects the idea of there being irreducible modalities at the core of his ontology.

In what follows I'll argue that despite the evident kinship between Armstrong's atomism and Wittgenstein's, Armstrong's theory fails in each of the three main respects in which he departs from Wittgenstein.

20. Problems for Armstrong's Reductionism

(i) The Problem of Aliens

One of Armstrong's basic premises [1989] is, "all *mere* possibilities are (non-existent) recombinations of actual elements." (p. 54). Yet this, he admits, rules out the widely entertained supposition that there could have been both alien individuals (individuals that are neither identical with nor compounded out of actual individuals) and alien universals (properties or relations that are neither identical with nor compounded out of actually instantiated universals). Aliens of any sort plainly cannot be constructed combinatorially out of local residents. So, strictly speaking, on Armstrong's theory, they are *impossible*.

Armstrong is happy enough to accept this conclusion about alien universals. Our supposition that Hume's famous "missing shade of blue" is a possible alien property might be explained away, he suggests, by treating it as a compound, structured property combinatorially accessible from simple and actual propertied individuals. But no genuinely alien property is really possible. We may think it is. But this, he suggests, is only because we too readily confuse *doxastic possibility* with logical or metaphysical possibility. It may, he points out, be doxastically possible for Goldbach's conjecture—that every even number is the sum of two primes—to be false; yet, for all we know, it may in fact prove to be a necessary truth, one whose falsity is logically impossible. Alien universals, Armstrong would have us believe, are at best only doxastically possible, not really (logically) so.

Genuinely alien individuals, on the other hand, do seem to Armstrong to be really possible, not just doxastically so. Why, he asks, should there not have been an "additional" mouse in his study, a mouse that is neither identical with any actual mouse nor compounded of any actual particles? This, he admits, "seems to be a genuine possibility" (p. 58) despite the fact that it cannot be derived combinatorially.

The reason why Armstrong bites the bullet in the one case but not the other stems from the fact that he thinks that distinct universals each have their own distinct special natures or "quiddities" but that distinct individuals do not each have their own distinct special natures or "haecceities". Where, if there were alien universals, would their quiddities be found? For a Naturalist-Combinatorialist, he argues, they are not to be found anywhere. Hence alien universals are impossible. But individuals, he claims, are unlike universals in this regard. For a naturalist, like him, they do not have any distinct essences or haecceities but are "merely, barely, numerically different from each other." (p. 60). And so, he concludes, "we can form a *fully determinate* concept of an indefinite number of alien individuals 'by analogy'." (p. 60).

But how is this analogical concept formed? Obviously, and admittedly, not by purely combinatorial methods. Yet to say, as Armstrong does, that we can reach them "conceptually", by analogy, isn't good enough. For what can this mean other than that the existence of alien individuals falls within the bounds of conceivability, that is, within the bounds of what is doxastically possible? And since (on his own account) what is doxastically possible outstrips what is logically possible, their being doxastically possible is no guarantee of their real possibility. Since he claims that alien universals are "possible" only in the doxastic sense of that word, and being conceptually constructable seems to yield nothing more than doxastic possibility, it is puzzling that he should insist on discriminating between these two classes of aliens, admitting the one but excluding the other.

This is a complaint about internal consistency. And there is another. For it would seem that once he allows alien individuals to be conceptually constructed, then he is committed to allowing for a certain range of alien universals to be so constructed as well. For suppose that there are precisely n actual individuals and that there is an n-placed relation holding between them. Then, since we are supposing that no actual, instantiated relation has more than n places, and relations (being universals) are impossible (in the logical, though not the doxastic sense) if they are not actual, it must be logically impossible for any relation to have $n + 1$ places. But if, as Armstrong allows, it is logically (not just doxastically) possible for there to be $n + 1$ individuals, it must surely also be logically possible for there to be $n + 1$ relations between them. Expand your ontology in respect of individuals, and I do not comprehend how you can fail to expand it in respect of relations between them. (Nor would the quiddity of this posited $n + 1$ relation be, as it were, left behind. It seems, rather, that one can form just as "fully determinate" a concept of an indefinite number of alien relations as one can of an indefinite number of alien individuals.) It would be inconsistent, I am saying, to admit alien individuals and shut the door on alien relations between them.

More serious still, for Armstrong, is the fact that his admission of alien individuals as logically possible threatens the very foundations of his combinatorialism. That alien mice and alien particles are indeed logically, not just doxastically, possible is one of those Moorean common sense propositions (I called it "third-degree possibilism" in Chapter 2) that are "to be rejected at great intellectual peril." (p. 57). Now it is one of Armstrong's virtues that—like the possibilists, Lewis and Wittgenstein, but unlike his fellow-actualists, Adams and Stalnaker—he recognizes this as one of the desiderata that an account of logical possibility must accommodate. Yet on his account, alien individuals are *neither* identical with *nor* combinatorially constructable out of actual individuals. Hence his unadorned combinatorial theory of possibility falls short of delineating the boundaries of the logically possible.

Armstrong, to be sure, suggests that his recourse to the conceptual, analogical construction of alien individuals "is a minor and acceptable qualification." (p. 60). But this is mere hand-waving and does not allow him to avoid a serious dilemma. Combinatorialism, unadorned by conceptualism, does not go far enough. It renders impossible much (for instance, alien particles) that Armstrong recognizes as logically possible. So it will not do. Yet combinatorialism, when supplemented by conceptualism, yields too much. It yields an account of the doxastically possible and so renders possible much (such as, the falsity of Goldbach's conjecture) that Armstrong believes may turn out to be logically impossible. Adorned or unadorned, combinatorialism yields results that do not even achieve coextension with the notion of the logically possible.

(ii) Problems of Compossibility

Since Armstrong's theory purports to derive the very idea of possibility from that of *all* the combinations of actual elements, it is essential that there be no restrictions either on the combinations of simples or on the combinations of the elementary states of affairs that the combinations of simples yield. Yet, I shall argue, neither level of combination can be entirely unrestricted. Hence, if I am right, Armstrong's combinatorial explication of possibility once more fails to satisfy even the minimal adequacy-condition of yielding an extensional equivalence between combinatorialism and the notion of possibility.

Consider, first, combinations of elementary states of affairs. Any combination, according to Armstrong, must yield a possible world. "The simplest way to specify a possible world", he tells us, "would be to say that *any conjunction* of possible atomic states of affairs, including the unit conjunction, constitutes such a world." (p. 47). Like Wittgenstein, he therefore requires that elementary states of affairs are logically independent. But whereas the doctrine of independence can—as I argued in Chapter 3, section 12—be dispensed with in Wittgenstein's case without severe damage to his atomism, it cannot be dispensed with in Armstrong's case without destroying the very foundations of his combinatorialism.

Armstrong recognizes the threat. In a chapter entitled "Are there de re incompatibilities and necessities?" he points out that, in his account, it should be possible for an individual to instantiate any combination of universals, "provided only that the universals so combined are *wholly* distinct, having no common constituents." This, he explains, is because "if we do not have this promiscuous compatibility, then we get logical incompatibility of a sort not envisaged by the theory." (p. 77).

There is little difficulty, Armstrong shows, in dealing with cases of incompatible properties, such as *being red* and *being green*, provided we treat them, as Wittgenstein did, as complex, structured properties that do have common constituents. For then their incompatibility turns out to be a function, as Wittgenstein had argued, of such principles as that "particles that are in different places at the same time cannot be identical." (6.3751). Armstrong admits that both this, and the mereological principle "if x is a proper part of y then x cannot be identical to y", are *necessary* truths, thereby inviting the objection that he is illicitly invoking modal principles in order to put restrictions on promiscuity. But he answers that the necessity of these principles is *analytic*, being true "solely in virtue of the meanings of the terms in which it is stated." (p. 80). Such an appeal to a separate source of modal notions is puzzling since it once more suggests that mere combinatorialism will not suffice. But let this pass. He has greater difficulties to confront.

Arguably, the greatest threat to unmitigated combinatorial freedom at the level of elementary states of affairs is posed by the fact that some simple relations must surely be *asymmetrical*. Especially must this be so if, as a good Naturalist, Armstrong wants to hold that the actual world is a complex, or complex of complexes, of *spatiotemporally* related elements. Consider an example that Armstrong himself selects for discussion, the exclusion of b's occurring before a when a in fact occurs before b. And let's take it that a's occurring before b is an elementary state of affairs. Then, by the same token, b's occurring before a must also be an elementary state of affairs. The trouble then is that, as Armstrong allows, the two seem de re logically incompatible, that is, such that the exclusion of the one by the other is a logically necessity.

Armstrong's treatment of this example is both cursory and far-fetched. Arguing that there is no real logical incompatibility here, he writes, "Might not time be circular? . . . If the circularity or noncircularity of time is a contingent matter, then the proper independence of 'a is before b' and 'b is before a' is established." (p. 85).

That this is at best an evasion of the issue should be clear from the fact that, elsewhere, he insists on the dictum "To be is to be determinate." (p. 56). The trouble is, of course, that if this dictum is correct then the *occurring before* relation must also be *determinate*. Accordingly, let us suppose that a occurs just *one minute* before b (in a given inertial frame). Then no wild, and undefended, hypothesis about the circularity of time will enable him to avoid the conclusion that a's occurring one minute before b is genuinely incompatible with b's occurring one minute before a (unless, of course, he is prepared to embrace the still wilder, and manifestly false, supposition that time repeats itself every minute).

Nor, more generally, will any other stratagem suffice to rescue Armstrong from the unavoidable de re incompatibility of Rab with Rba where a, b, and R are all simple and R is asymmetrical. His only seeming recourse would be to provide plausible reasons for denying that simple relations are ever asymmetrical and for holding that all manifestly asymmetrical relations are both complex and reducible to simple ones that do not have this troublesome property. But what could these reasons be? Surely, the task of defining manifestly asymmetrical relations in terms of simple ones that are not asymmetrical is beyond anyone's competence, for purely logical reasons. Armstrong's doctrine of independence is as much a myth as is Wittgenstein's and for much the same reasons.

Armstrong also needs unrestricted freedom of combination at the level of his elements. Now it goes without saying that all simple individuals, *if* they are considered abstractly as "merely, barely, numerically different from one another", are compossible. But Armstrong insists also that likewise "*all simple properties and relations are compossible*." (p. 49). He needs all simple individuals, simple properties and simple relations to be compossible.

But how can they be? Let F be a simple property (monadic relation), R some simple dyadic relation, and S some simple triadic relation. Then F can, as it were, "combine" with one individual—say a—to produce simple state of affairs Fa; R with two simple individuals—say a and b—to produce simple state of affairs, Rab; and S with three—say a, b, and c—to produce simple Sabc. However, Armstrong adopts the obvious truth which he calls the *Principle of Instantial Invariance*: "for all numbers, n, if a relation is n-adic in one instantiation, then it is n-adic in all its instantiations." (p. 40). It follows that given the monadicity of F, F *cannot* combine with more than one individual; that given the dyadicity of R, R *cannot* combine with any number of simple individuals other than two; that given the triadicity of S, S cannot combine with any number of individuals other than three; and so on. More generally, if T is n-adic, T cannot combine to produce states of affairs with fewer or more individuals than the precise number n. For such states of affairs are simply *not* possible.

Note that this consequence of the *essential* -adicity of relations (broadly construed so as to include the monadic case) is implicitly recognized by Wittgenstein and poses no threat to his restricted combinatorialism. For just as he would insist that simple individuals have formal properties that make some of their combinations possible but others impossible, so also he would insist that the -adicity of a relation determines the range of its possible combinations. This, surely, is what he is getting at by means of his example of an *impossible* sign, namely, "Socrates is identical". Immediately after reminding us that whatever is logically possible is syntactically permissible in language, he explains, "The reason why 'Socrates is identical' means nothing is that there is no *property* [emphasis added] called 'identical'." (5.473). Identity (as distinct from self-identity), he is saying, has the wrong -adicity to be combined with just one individual to produce a possible state of affairs of the kind that can be pictured in language by a meaningful proposition (though we could, of course, he points out, have made an arbitrary determination to use the *word* "identical" in a different way, for instance, as a monadic predicate).

Now Armstrong, it must be acknowledged, builds into his theory a clause that, at first glance, seems to make it invulnerable to the -adicity problem. It is a clause that ensures that the unrestricted promiscuity which his simples are touted as enjoying is somewhat curtailed. Not all combinations of simples, it turns out, are permitted, but those only *which respect the form of atomic states of affairs* (pp. 47–48). Significantly, this important qualifying clause is omitted from the oft-repeated formulation of his theory as one in which *all* combinations are possible—perhaps because Armstrong thinks that it, too, is "a minor and acceptable qualification." Yet its inclusion is every bit as disastrous for his analysis of the concept of possibility as is his reluctant recognition of alien individuals. He claims that by means of the notion of *all the combinations*, "the notion of possibility is given an analysis, an analysis which uses the universal quantifier" (p. 47). Yet unrestricted combinations of the elements, we have seen, sometimes yields the impossible. As part of his analysis, therefore, he has to take recourse to the notion of respecting the form of states of affairs, a notion that he himself leaves unanalyzed and that (I'll now argue) smuggles in the notion of possibility through the back door.

(iii) The Problem of Circularity

The trouble with the notion of respecting the form of a state of affairs, as Armstrong employs it, is that it is irremediably modal. For what does he mean by "form"? Armstrong nowhere gives an account of this crucial notion. He rests content with examples: those that would be described by the atomic statements "Fa", "Rab" (with R dyadic), and "Sabc" (with S triadic). So far so good. But what, we need to know, would it be like for a combination of elements *not* to respect the form of a state of affairs? Presumably, it would be for the elements to combine in ways such as would be described by ill-formed—what Wittgenstein would call "nonsensical"—medleys of symbols: "Fab" (where F is monadic), "Ra" or "Rabc" (where R is dyadic), and so on. Such combinations—on anyone's account (not just Armstrong's)—would *not* respect the form, or forms, of atomic states of affairs. And the reason, of course, is not that these concatenations of symbols fail to respect some arbitrary syntactical convention for well-formed formulae (or anything like that), but rather that the corresponding combinations of elements yield *impossibilities*. Thus, when properly analyzed, the insertion of the qualifying phrase "which respects the form of states of affairs" has the effect of smuggling the notion of possibility back into the analyzans from which it was supposed to be absent. It means that the notion of possibility for elementary states of affairs, and the possible worlds that are their conjunctions, is being analyzed as "all the combinations which are *possible* for given, actual elements."

Armstrong, then, is faced with a fatal dilemma. If by "all combinations of given actual elements" he really does mean all combinations, then his theory is clearly false, since the -adicity problem shows that some combinations are not possible (either linguistically or metaphysically). But if, to avoid this, he adds the constraint of respecting form, his account becomes circular and his attempt at a reduction of modal concepts to nonmodal ones thereby fails.

Wittgenstein, remember, took pains to point out the modal nature of the notion of form. The form of an elementary state of affairs or of any elementary proposition that pictures it, he had said, is "the possibility of its structure", i.e., the possibility of determinate combinations for its elements. Wittgenstein also insisted, "the connection of the propositional components must be possible for the represented things." (*NB* 26(13)). But then, for him, no reduction of modalities is either needed or possible.

21. Wittgenstein's Modal Primitivism

What motivates many theorists to attempt some sort of modal reductionism are not only concerns about theoretical economy but also concerns about understanding. They profess not really to understand what modal notions, in general, mean or what are the boundaries of their application. They would allow that, given a firm grip on just one of them—the notion of necessity, for instance—the others would be within their grasp. But the problem is to secure that first firm hold. Their puzzlement is deep enough, they say, in the case of de dicto necessity—except, perhaps, to the extent that it can be explicated in terms of the notion of analyticity and this in turn in terms of the linguistic rules or conceptual schemes that humans impose on the world. It is deeper still, they claim, in the case of alleged de re necessities that are supposed to obtain in the world itself, independently of how we speak or think. What does it even *mean*, they ask, to suppose with Wittgenstein that objects in themselves have formal properties that are part of the natures of those objects and so de re necessary to them?

The question is a crucial one for Wittgenstein, or at least for the Wittgensteinian account of modality that I have mined from his early writings. In order now to answer it, I offer a simple geometrical model of the de re modal primitivism that lies at the base of his theory. I'll try to show how the rest of Wittgenstein's modal atomism can be erected on that base, and thereby try to secure for his theory an intelligibility and plausibility that many think it must lack.

The model is intended to explicate Wittgenstein's modal atomism minus the myth of independence (the myth that, he eventually saw, has to be abandoned in any case if his metaphysical theory is to hang together).

A Geometrical Model of Modal Atomism minus the Myth of Independence

The elements of our model are members of the set of all possible two-dimensional figures in pure geometry. There are, of course, *infinitely* many such figures in geometrical space. It will suffice to consider just a few instances of their physical instantiation:

$$A_1 \qquad\qquad B_1 \qquad\qquad C_1 \qquad\qquad D_1$$

The elements of our model (A_1, B_1, C_1, D_1 and all the others) go proxy for the possible simple objects of Wittgenstein's ontology.

Each of the figures is *simple* (2.02) in the sense that it has no proper parts that themselves are two-dimensional figures.

Each figure has a distinctive *form*, which is "part of the nature of the object." (2.0123). The form of a figure is *de re necessary* (*essential, internal*) to it in the sense that "it is unthinkable that its object should not possess it" (4.123). A_1, for instance, has the essential formal property of *being four-sided and equilateral*; B_1 has the essential formal property of *being three-sided and equilateral*; and so on. Moreover, if a figure lacks a given formal property, then that property is one which that figure cannot have (it is, so to speak, an essential nonproperty of the figure). For instance, the simple figure B_1 cannot have the formal property of *being four-sided and equilateral*. (Contrary to Armstrong, some simple objects and simple properties are *not* compossible.)

The essential formal properties of a figure determine the range of its *combinatorial possibilities* (its combinatorial potential), where the combinatorial potential of an figure is a function of whether or not it and some other figure or figures can "fit into one another like links of a chain" (2.03) with wholly coincident sides. In this sense, figures "contain the possibility of all situations." (2.014). The relationship between the form of a figure and the set of all its combinatorial possibilities is one of interdependence insofar as any change in its combinatorial possibilities must also determine a change in its form. This, perhaps, is why Wittgenstein claims, "The possibility of its occurring in states of affairs *is* [emphasis added] the form of an object." (2.0141).

As examples of the combinatorial potential of A_1, we have its ability to fit together with other figures in our model in the ways shown. It can combine with B_1 to produce the *possible elementary state of affairs* (elementary geometrical complex)

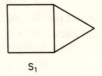

S_1

with D1 to produce possible state of affairs

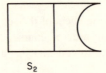

S_2

with B_1, C_1 and D_1 to produce possible state of affairs

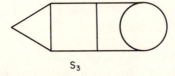

S_3

with D_1 and C_1 to produce possible state of affairs

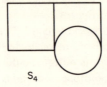

S_4

and so on. Likewise, C_1 and D_1 can combine to produce possible state of affairs

S_5

and so on. Plainly, many other combinations are possible for just these four simple figures, let alone for others of the infinitely many simple figures not here depicted.

The combinatorial potential of each simple figure, like its form, is *internal* to it: "Every one of these possibilities must be part of the nature of the object." (2.0123). Again, "In logic nothing is accidental: if a thing *can* occur in a state of affairs, the possibility of the state of affairs must be written into the thing itself." (2.012).

Not all properties of a simple figure, however, are internal to it. Some are merely *external* or *accidental* (2.01231). For instance, when A_1 is combined with B_1 in possible state of affairs S_1, A_1 comes to have the external relational property of *being combined with B* $_1$ and B_1 comes to have the external relational property of *being combined with A* $_1$.

Two or more simple figures may, as it were, be different tokens of the same type, that is, may share the *same form* (2.0233). Two simple figures of the same form will, of course, have precisely the *same range of combinatorial possibilities*. We may suppose, in fact, that there is a potentially infinite number of simple figures all having the same form as A_1, and likewise for B_1, C_1, and so on. Let A_2—A_n be figures having the same form as A_1. Then A_1—A_n may all be said to belong to the same *logical kind* (*NB* 70(9)).

Each of the figures in a given logical kind may be supposed to possess its own *haecceity*. For instance, A_1 has the essential properties of *being identical to A_1* and *being different from any other figure*. Likewise for A_2, and so on. The different haecceities of figures belonging to the A-kind make them different figures (figure-tokens), despite their sameness of form. ("If two objects have the same logical form, the only difference between them, apart from their external properties, is that they are different." (2.0233).)

Different figures of the same form may, of course, feature in different possible states of affairs (the elementary geometrical complexes of the model). We supposed previously that A_1 combines with B_1 to produce S_1. Were any other figure having the same form as A_1, say A_2, to combine in the same way with B_1, the possible state of affairs thereby produced would have the same determinate mode of combination, that is, the same *structure*, as S_1 but would not be identical to S_1. Mindful of Wittgenstein's admonition to use different names for different objects (5.53), we might refer to this state of affairs as S_{1*}. The states of affairs S_1 and S_{1*}, then, would be *nonidentical states of affairs having the same structure*.

The complex relational property possessed by a state of affairs by virtue of its structure may be called a *structural property* of that state of affairs. Having such and such a structural property, that is, having just such and such propertied parts standing in just such and such a relation, will be *internal* to that state of affairs (4.122–4.123): a state of affairs that lacked that structure would not be that very state of affairs.

Now the forms of simple figures not only determine what *can* combine with what but also what *cannot* combine with what. The forms of simple figures impose *limits* on their combinatorial freedom. Unrestricted promiscuity is not possible. Figures of kind A and figures of kind C, for instance, *cannot* "fit into one another" in the requisite way since the former have no round sides and latter no straight ones; their sides cannot be coincident. Putative elementary states of affairs (the elementary geometrical complexes of our model) involving the combination of these constituents would comprise *impossible situations* (5.525).

The determinate connection between the constituent figures in a state of affairs may be regarded as determining a *relation* between those simple figures—various dyadic relations in the cases of S_1, S_2, and S_5, a triadic relation in the case of S_4, and so on. The *-adicity problem* for elementary states of affairs is reflected in the fact that, where R is a dyadic relation defined over combinatorial structures of the same kind as S_1, that relation *cannot*, by Armstrong's Principle of Instantial Invariance (quoted earlier), hold for any complex figure having more than (or fewer than) two simple figures as its constituents. Once more, combinatorial freedom is restricted. Contrary to Armstrong, some simple figures and simple relations are *not* compossible.

Impossible situations can arise in other ways as well. For instance, if S_1 and S_2 are, as we have been supposing, *complete but distinct* states of affairs, then it is de re impossible for one and the same simple figure, say A_1, to combine with B_1 to produce S_1 and at the same time to combine with D_1 to produce S_2. This is in the same vein as Wittgenstein's claim "A particle cannot be in two places at the same time" (*NB* 81(10) and 6.3751).[17]

However, where two states of affairs are *wholly distinct*, as are S_1 and S_5 (since they have no constituents in common), then the existence of one *is* independent of the existence of the other and no incompatibility arises. "There is no possible way of making an inference from the existence of one situation to the existence of another, entirely different situation." (5.135).

Of the possible simple geometrical figures in our model and their immediate combinations in states of affairs, only some, we may plausibly suppose, are physically instantiated or actual. Those simple figures that are physically instantiated, such as A_1, B_1, C_1, and D_1, will count as *actual* objects; those that are not will count as nonactual, *alien* objects.

Consider some alien object whose simple formal properties, for example, *being an 237-sided figure*, are not possessed by any actual figure. Any such property will count as an *alien property*.

Those combinations of simple figures that are physically instantiated, for example, S_1 through S_5, will count as *existing states of affairs* ; those that are not, as *nonexisting states of affairs*.

Let n be the greatest number of simple figures combined with one another in any actually existing state of affairs. Consider some nonexisting but possible state of affairs in which n + 1 simple figures are combined with one another. Then the n + 1-adic relation in which its constituent figures stand to one another will count as an *alien relation*.

Any possible *totality* of possible combinations of simple figures, in our model, will count as a possible world (of geometrical figures). Of these possible totalities, just one will count as *the actual world* in logical (or geometrical) space. All the others will count as *merely possible worlds*.

The particular place that a possible simple figure occupies in geometrical space is a stand-in for Wittgenstein's concept of *logical place*, and the set of the possible combinations of these simple figures is a stand-in for Wittgenstein's concept of *logical space*. "Spatial and logical place agree in both being the possibility of an existence." (*NB* 27(11)). "In geometry and logic alike a place is a possibility: something can exist in it." (3.411). "A picture presents a possible situation in logical space." (2.202).

Comments on the Model

So much for the model. I think it helps to throw light on many aspects of Wittgenstein's de re possibilistic atomism and to show that what he says about his atoms and their possible combinations is both self-consistent and, in our geometrical interpretation, true.

But what is most illuminating about the model, I think, is that it gives the lie to those who would claim that they simply *cannot understand* what it means either to speak of simple objects as having certain essential properties or to speak of these properties as determining the combinatorial possibilities for those objects. I submit that, once philosophical prejudices are cast aside, most of us *can and do understand* these claims perfectly well.

Moreover, if we turn from pure geometry to applied and consider ordinary three-dimensional physical objects—pieces of plywood, for instance, as they might be manipulated by children learning to work with spatial concepts—it becomes *even more* intuitively obvious (a bedrock proposition of Moorean commonsense) that a piece of plywood having shape A is *essentially* square (it would not be that piece of plywood were it of some other shape), that it *can* combine in the requisite way with another piece of plywood having shape B but *cannot* combine with a piece having shape C, and so on.

Nor is it at all plausible to claim that these necessities, possibilities, and impossibilities are all functions merely of the ways in which we describe the objects. Describe them as you will, and it will not alter what can and what cannot (as a matter of geometrical-cum-logical space, as it were) be combined with what. These necessities, possibilities, and impossibilities are all de re; they are modalities that are grounded in the natures of the objects themselves.

De re modal primitivism of this sort, it is worth noting, should not be wholly repugnant to Naturalist Combinatorialists like Armstrong. Suppose one were to turn one's back (as he does) on possibilistic intuitions about aliens and as an "actual-world chauvinist" concern oneself only with local residents. Why shouldn't a Naturalist allow that, for all he or she knows, simple objects in the natural world—the ultimate simples of physics, for instance—may have their own essential properties in the manner envisaged in our Wittgensteinian model? Wittgenstein himself, it may be remembered, hints at something like this when (in *Philosophical Investigations*, 521) he invites us to compare "logically possible" with "chemically possible", where the latter is a function of the valencies or combinatorial possibilities for given elements and these in turn are a function of the internal natures of those elements. A metaphysics that renounces compossibility of simple properties, Armstrong observes [1989], is in this respect more Aristotelian than strictly Leibnizian. But given the difficulties confronting compossibility, this Aristotelian basis for what is otherwise a Leibnizian metaphysics, a basic ontology that allows for de re necessities, possibilities, and impossibilities, has much to commend it. Not only does it, as Armstrong admits, give us "the manifest image of properties and relations". It also seems more likely to be an inescapable feature of whatever story natural science will eventually tell about the basic elements of reality.[18]

Armstrong claims that his own Naturalistic Combinatorialism, by virtue of its (attempted) reduction of modal notions to nonmodal ones, "makes possibility epistemologically accessible." According to him, "The only Naturalistic alternative for a theory of possibility seems to be that modality is an irreducible feature of this world—a theory of de re compatibilities and incompatibilities." As for that, he argues, "the epistemology of this view is very obscure." (p. 102). But is it? If my argument three or four paragraphs back is sound, the notions of de re necessity, compatibility, and incompatibility are every bit as epistemologically accessible as are the pieces of a jigsaw puzzle.

Wittgenstein's metaphysical modal primitivism, as I have portrayed it, seems to me to satisfy our intuitional desiderata at least as well as, if not better than, any of its contemporary rivals. And, as we saw in the previous chapter, it also offers tenable foundations for a theory of language and logic.

Notes

1. As against someone who alleges that the question makes sense only against the background of the supposition that the actual world needs to be distinguished from other possible worlds, I would point out that the roughly parallel question (with epistemic overtones), "How can we be sure that we ourselves and the world we think we live in are not fictions?" poses similar problems of demarcation.

2. Recall that Pears and McGuinness translate "*Bedeutung*" as "meaning" thereby making it less than clear how the *Bedeutung* of an expression is supposed to differ from its *Sinn* (sense). Accordingly, I follow Anscombe who—in her translation of the *Notebooks*—translates "*Bedeutung*" as "reference".

3. As an example of an impossible situation, remember, Wittgenstein cites the putting of an event into a hole (*NB* 106(5)). Wittgenstein himself, however, could be put into a hole. Hence he is not possibly an event.

4. Crossley and Humberstone also develop a second "actuality-logic", S5AR, in which $\Box p \supset Ap$ is not a thesis. But the differences between these two systems in no way bears upon the issues we are discussing here.

5. Kripke has pointed out that a definite description can be made "rigid" if we take it to "denote, with respect to all possible worlds, the unique object that (*actually*) $\emptyset$'s . . ." [emphasis added]. See his [1977], p. 259.

6. This is a corollary of Kripke's famous proof of the noncontingency of statements asserting identity or nonidentity. He states it informally in the Introduction to [1980]: "Waiving fussy considerations deriving from the fact that x need not have necessary existence, it was clear from (x) $\Box$ (x = x) and Leibniz's law that identity is an 'internal' relation: (x) (y) (x = y $\supset \Box$ x = y). (What pairs (x,y) could be counter-examples? Not pairs of distinct objects, for then the antecedent is false: nor any pair of an object and itself, for then the consequent is true.) If 'a' and 'b' are rigid designators, it follows that 'a = b', if true, is a necessary truth. If 'a' and 'b' are *not* rigid designators, no such conclusion follows about the *statement* 'a = b' (though the *objects* designated by 'a' and 'b' will be necessarily identical)." (p. 3).

7. The distinction between the restricted and the unrestricted existential quantifiers could, of course, be marked, in logic and ordinary English alike, in other ways. Terence Parsons and Richard Routley seem to favor retaining "($\exists$x)" as an unrestricted quantifier to be read, not as "there exists . . ." but as "there are . . ." or even as "for some . . .", while introducing an existence predicate "E", or "E!", for cases where we want to attribute what I have called "actual existence" but what they

simply call "existence". By way of contrast, Alvin Plantinga seems to favour reading "(∃x)", as I have, as "there exists . . .", while using the term "obtains" where I would say "actually exists", and where Parsons and Routley would say "exists". No doubt there are still other ways in which we may choose to mark, either in symbols or in ordinary English, those occasions on which we want to speak about anything whatever (the unrestricted case) and those occasions on which we wish to speak only of those things that exist in the actual world (the restricted case). The particular way in which we mark the distinction is unimportant. That it be marked somehow is a matter, I submit, of considerable importance.

8. Although critical of his omissions, I am indebted to Hìntikka for the perspective he gives to the post-Wittgensteinian history of possible worlds semantics.

9. Admittedly, Wittgenstein had said that words like "object", "thing", and so on, do not express proper concepts but only pseudo-concepts, and that when they are used as if they were proper concept-words, "nonsensical propositions are the result." (4.1272). But this is a reflection of his doctrine that such formal concept-words can only be used to *show*, not to *say* something. It needs to be remembered that the showable, according to Wittgenstein, *can* be expressed. It can be expressed "in" language even though it can't be expressed "by" language (4.124). Our discussion of the saying/showing distinction in Chapter 4, section 3, shows that it does not warrant Carnap's positivist construal.

10. These three theses parallel those stipulated for mathematical realism by Penelope Maddy [1981], p. 495.

The parallel between mathematical realism and modal realism has been remarked upon, by Fabrizio Mondadori and Adam Morton [1976], thus:

> In the philosophy of mathematics the realist's gambit results in mathematical realism, sometimes called Platonism, the view that there is a domain of specifically mathematical objects such as numbers and sets, by reference to which mathematical statements acquire their truth-values. In the philosophy of modality it results in what we shall call *modal realism*, the doctrine that there are specifically modal objects: possible worlds, counterparts of actual objects, positions in logical space, or what have you, which are the specific subject matter of discourse, by reference to which modal sentences are true or false. (p. 238)

11. In similar vein, Kripke [1980] objects to Lewis's counter-part theory: "Probably . . Humphrey could not care less whether someone else, no matter how much resembling him, would have been victorious in another possible world." (p. 45, fn. 13).

12. John Mackie, for instance, suggests, "When we say that this cat, for example, has property X, whatever X may be, we can take the subject-term, 'this cat', as referring to the whole collection of properties, including X, and then to say that it has X will be to say that it has X as a constituent, as a member of the collection." See his [1976], p. 79.

13. The choice of terminology to mark this distinction varies, confusingly, from philosopher to philosopher. Thus whereas Stalnaker, as we have seen, claims that merely possible worlds, since they are identical with properties, "exist" but "are not instantiated", Alvin Plantinga says that his candidates for merely possible worlds,

namely, maximally consistent sets of states of affairs, "exist" but "do not obtain". Wittgenstein's terminology is different again. For him, states of affairs may "exist" or not exist; but simple objects only "subsist"!

14. This is the conception of worlds that features in Lewis's thinking. By way of explaining the notion of a mereological sum, I can not do better than quote from footnote 51 to page 69 of Lewis's [1986]: "The *mereological sum*, or *fusion*, of several things is the least inclusive thing that includes all of them as parts. It is composed of them and of nothing more; any part of it overlaps one or more of them; it is a proper part of anything else that has all of them as parts."

15. See Chapter 3, note 4, for a cautionary reminder about what Wittgenstein means by "structural property".

16. For others, see my [1989], pp. 15–41.

17. Wittgenstein, in *NB* 81(11), notes that the "cannot" here "looks more like a logical impossibility." He then adds: "If we ask why, for example, then straight away comes the thought: Well, we should call particles that were in different places different, and this in its turn all seems to follow from the structure of space and of particles." The last clause here shows that he thinks of the ultimate ground of logical impossibility as lying not in linguistic facts about what we would *call* what but deeper still in metaphysical facts about the structure of logical space.

18. At the latest count, there are something like twenty different kinds of fundamental particles of matter—all but three experimentally detectable—posited by the so-called Standard Model, each kind with its distinctive internal nature and consequent range of combinatorial possibilities. This number may be doubled if one takes into account the antimatter counterparts of each of these. And it may be still further increased if experimental evidence gives credence to the existence of the supersymmetric particles posited by Grand Unified Theories. See "The Ultimate Quest", *Time*, Vol. 135, No. 16, 16 April, 1990, p. 59.

Selected Bibliography

Adams R. M. (1979) "Primitive Thisness and Primitive Identity," *Journal of Philosophy* 76, pp. 5–26.

Adams R. M. (1974) "Theories of Actuality," *Nous* 8, pp. 211–231; reprinted in Loux (1979), pp. 190–209.

Anscombe G. E. M. (1959) *An Introduction to Wittgenstein's Tractatus* (London: Hutchinson University Library).

Aristotle *Posterior Analytics*, in *The Works of Aristotle*, Vol. 1, ed. Sir David Ross (Oxford: Clarendon Press, 1928).

Armstrong D. (1986) "The Nature of Possibility," *Canadian Journal of Philosophy* 16, 4, pp. 577–594.

Armstrong D. (1989) *A Combinatorial Theory of Possibility* (Cambridge: Cambridge University Press).

Black M. (1964) *A Companion to Wittgenstein's Tractatus* (Ithaca, N.Y.: Cornell University Press).

Bradley F. H. (1897) *Appearance and Reality*, 2nd edition (Oxford: Clarendon Press).

Bradley R. D. and Swartz N. (1979) *Possible Worlds: an Introduction to Logic and Its Philosophy* (Oxford: Basil Blackwell; and Indianapolis: Hackett Publishing Co.).

Bradley R. D. (1984) "Essentialism and the New Theory of Reference," *Dialogue* 33, pp. 59–77.

Bradley R. D. (1987) "Wittgenstein's Tractarian Essentialism," *Australasian Journal of Philosophy* 65, 1, pp. 43–55.

Bradley R. D. (1989) "Possibility and Combinatorialism: Wittgenstein versus Armstrong," *Canadian Journal of Philosophy* 19, 1, pp. 15–41.

Carnap R. (1942) *Introduction to Semantics and Formalization of Logic* (Cambridge, Mass.: Harvard University Press).

Carnap R. (1947) *Meaning and Necessity* (Chicago: University of Chicago Press).

Carnap R. (1963) in *The Philosophy of Rudolph Carnap*, ed. P. A. Schilpp (La Salle, Ill.: Open Court).

Copi I. M. and Beard R. W., eds.(1966) *Essays on Wittgenstein's Tractatus* (New York: Macmillan).

Cresswell M. (1973) *Logics and Languages* (London: Methuen and Co. Ltd.).

Crossley J. N. and Humberstone I. L. (1977) "The Logic of 'Actually'," *Reports on Mathematical Logic* 8, pp. 11–29.

Donnellan, K. (1974) "Speaking of Nothing," *Philosophical Review* 83, pp. 3–31.

Evans G. (1982) *Varieties of Reference*, ed. J.McDowell (Oxford: Clarendon Press).

Fogelin R. J. (1986) "Wittgenstein and Intuitionism," *American Philosophical Quarterly* 5, 4, pp. 267–274.

Frege G. (1892) "On Sense and Reference", in *Translations from the Philosophical Writings of Gottlob Frege*, eds. P. Geach and M. Black (Oxford: Basil Blackwell, 1966).

Goddard L. and Judge B. (1982) *The Metaphysics of Wittgenstein's Tractatus* (Bundoora, Victoria: *Australasian Journal of Philosophy*, monograph 1).

Goodman N. and Leonard H. S. (1940) "The Calculus of Individuals and Its Uses," *Journal of Symbolic Logic* 5, pp. 45–55.

Griffin J. (1964) *Wittgenstein's Logical Atomism* (Oxford: Clarendon Press).

Hertz H. (1956) *The Principles of Mechanics* (New York: Dover), originally published in 1894.

Hintikka J. (1963) "The Modes of Modality," *Acta Philosophica Fennica*. (Helsinki: Fasc. 16) pp. 65–81.

Hintikka J. (1973) "Carnap's Semantics in Retrospect," *Synthese* 25, pp. 372–397.

Hintikka M. B. and Hintikka J. (1987) *Investigating Wittgenstein* (Oxford: Basil Blackwell).

Kaplan D. (1975) "How to Russell a Frege-Church," *Journal of Philosophy* 72, pp. 716–729.

Kim J. (1979) "Causality, Identity, and Supervenience in the Mind-Body Problem," in *Midwest Studies in Philosophy* 4: *Studies in Metaphysics*, eds. Peter French, Theodore Uehling, and Howard Wettstein (Minneapolis: University of Minnesota Press).

Kneale W. (1972) "Propositions and Truth in Natural Languages," *Mind* 81, pp. 225–243.

Kneale W. and Kneale M. (1964) *The Development of Logic* (Oxford: Clarendon Press).

Kripke S. (1976) "A Puzzle about Belief," in *Meaning and Use*, ed. A. Margalit (Dordrecht, Holland: D. Reidel).

Kripke S. (1977) "Speaker's Reference and Semantic Reference," in *Midwest Studies in Philosophy* 2: *Epistemology*, eds. Peter French, Theodore Uehling, and Howard Wettstein (Morris, Minn.: University of Minnesota Press).

Kripke S. (1980) *Naming and Necessity* (Cambridge, Mass.: Harvard University Press).

Lee D., ed. (1980) *Wittgenstein's Lectures, Cambridge 1930–32* (Oxford: Basil Blackwell).

Lewis C. I. (1918) *A Survey of Symbolic Logic* (Berkeley: University of California Press).

Lewis D. K. (1968) "Counterpart Theory and Quantified Modal Logic," *Journal of Philosophy* 65, pp. 113–126; reprinted in Loux (1979), pp. 110–128.

Lewis D. K. (1970) "Anselm and Actuality," *Nous* 4, pp. 175–184.

Lewis D. K. (1973) *Counterfactuals* (Cambridge, Mass.: Harvard University Press).

Lewis D. K. (1986) *On the Plurality of Worlds* (Oxford: Basil Blackwell).

Leonard H. S. and Goodman N. (1940) "The Calculus of Individuals and Its Uses," *Journal of Symbolic Logic* 5, pp. 45–55.

Loux M. J., ed. (1979) *The Possible and the Actual* (Ithaca and London: Cornell University Press).

Lycan W. (1979) "The Trouble with Possible Worlds," in Loux (1979), pp. 274–316.

MacColl H. (1908) *Symbolic Logic and Its Applications*, (London).

Mace, C. A., ed. (1957) *British Philosophy Mid-Century* (London: Allen and Unwin).

Mackie J. (1972) "Metaphysical Commonsense," *British Journal for Philosophy of Science* 23, pp. 247–255.

Mackie J. (1976) *Problems from Locke* (Oxford: Clarendon Press).

Maddy P. (1981) "Sets and Numbers," *Nous* 15, 4, pp. 495–511.

Malcolm N. (1958) *Ludwig Wittgenstein: A Memoir* (London: Clarendon Press).

McGuinness B. F. (1956) "Pictures and Forms in Wittgenstein's *Tractatus* ," *Archivio di Filosofia*, reprinted in Copi and Beard (1966), pp. 137–156.

Mill J. S. (1843) *A System of Logic*, 8th edition (London: Longmans, Green and Co., 1965).

Mondadori F. and Morton A. (1976) "Modal Realism: The Poisoned Pawn," *Philosophical Review* 85, pp. 3–20; republished in Loux (1979), pp. 235–252.

Moore G. E. (1919) "External and Internal Relations," *Proceedings of the Aristotelian Society* n.s. 21, pp. 40–62; reprinted in *Philosophical Studies*, (London: Routledge Kegan Paul, 1951), pp. 276–309.

Moore G. E. (1968) "Reply to My Critics," published in *The Philosophy of G. E. Moore*, vol. 2, ed. P. A. Schilpp (La Salle: Open Court).

Nakhnikian G. and Salmon W. (1957) " 'Exists' as a Predicate'," *Philosophical Review* 66, pp. 535–542.

Parsons T. (1980) *Nonexistent Objects* (New Haven and London: Yale University Press).

Passmore J. (1968) *A Hundred Years of Philosophy*, 2nd edition (Harmondsworth: Penguin Books).

Plantinga A. (1974) *The Nature of Necessity* (Oxford: Clarendon Press).

Plochmann G. K. and Lawson J. B. (1962) *Terms in Their Propositional Contexts in Wittgenstein's Tractatus* (Carbondale, Ill.: Southern Illinois University Press).

Ramsey F. P. (1923) "Review of Tractatus," *Mind* 23, pp. 465–478; reprinted in Copi and Beard (1966), pp. 9–23.

Rescher N. (1975) *A Theory of Possibility: A Constructivistic and Conceptualistic Account of Possible Individuals and Possible Worlds* (Oxford: Basil Blackwell).

Rescher N. (1979) "Russell and Modal Logic," in *Bertrand Russell Memorial Volume*, ed. G. W. Robert (London: George Allen and Unwin).

Routley R. (1980) *Exploring Meinong's Jungle and Beyond* (Canberra: Australian National University).

Russell B. (1905) "On Denoting," *Mind* 14, pp. 479–493; reprinted in *Logic and Knowledge*, ed., R. C. Marsh, (London: George Allen and Unwin, 1956), pp. 41–56.

Russell B. (1912) *The Problems of Philosophy* (London: Oxford University Press).

Russell B. (1918) "The Philosophy of Logical Atomism," *The Monist* 28, pp. 495–527; 29, pp. 33–63; pp. 190–222; and pp. 344–380; reprinted in *Logic and Knowledge*, ed. R. C. Marsh, (London: George Allen and Unwin, 1956), pp. 177–281.

Russell B. (1919) *Introduction to Mathematical Philosophy* (London: George Allen and Unwin).

Salmon W. and Nakhnikian G. (1957) " 'Exists' as a Predicate'," *Philosophical Review* 66, pp. 535–542.

Stalnaker R. (1976) "Possible Worlds," *Nous* 10, pp. 65–75; reprinted in Loux (1979), pp. 225–234.

Stenius E. (1960) *Wittgenstein's Tractatus: A Critical Exposition of the Main Lines of Thought* (Oxford: Basil Blackwell).

Urmson, J. O. (1956) *Philosophical Analysis: Its Development between the Two World Wars* (Oxford: Clarendon Press).

Wittgenstein L. (1929) "Some Remarks on Logical Form," *Aristotelian Society Supplementary Volume* 9, pp. 162–171; reprinted in Copi and Beard (1966), pp. 31–37.

Wittgenstein L. (1960) *The Blue and Brown Books: Preliminary Studies for the Philosophical Investigations*, 2nd edition (New York: Harper & Row).

Wittgenstein L. (1961) *Tractatus Logico-Philosophicus*, trans. D. F. Pears and B. F. McGuinness (London: Routledge and Kegan Paul). The first German edition appeared in the journal *Annalen der Naturphilosophie*, 1921. The first English edition was published in the series *International Library of Psychology Philosophy and Scientific Method* (London: Routledge and Kegan Paul, 1922).

Wittgenstein L. (1975) *Philosophical Remarks*, ed. Rush Rhees (Chicago: University of Chicago Press; and Oxford: Basil Blackwell).

Wittgenstein L. (1961) *Notebooks 1914–1916*, eds. G. H. von Wright and G. E. M. Anscombe with English trans. by G. E. M. Anscombe (Oxford: Basil Blackwell).

Wittgenstein L. (1986) *Philosophical Investigations*, 2nd edition, trans. G. E. M. Anscombe (Oxford: Basil Blackwell).

Wright G. H. von (1982) *Wittgenstein* (Oxford: Basil Blackwell).

Index of Passages

233

Index